EGYPT, TRUNK OF THE TREE

VOL. II

EGYPT, TRUNK OF THE TREE

A MODERN SURVEY OF AN ANCIENT LAND

Vol. II : The Consequences

How Egypt Became the Trunk of the Tree

Simson Najovits

Algora Publishing

New York

ISBN: 0-87586-256-X (softcover)
ISBN: 0-87586-257-8 (hardcover)
ISBN: 0-87586-201-2 (ebook)

Library of Congress Cataloging-in-Publication Data

Najovits, Simson R.
 Egypt, trunk of the tree : a modern survey of an ancient land / by Simson R. Najovits.
   p. cm.
Includes bibliographical references and index.
 ISBN 0-87586-256-X (alk. paper) — ISBN 0-87586-257-8 (pbk. : alk. paper)
 1. Egypt—Religion—History. 2. Egypt—Civilization. I. Title.
 BL2441.N23 2003
 932—dc21
                    2003002755

Printed in the United States

TABLE of CONTENTS

TIMELINE

c. 4000–3100 BC: Predynastic Naqada Civilization

Totemism, animism, nature religion, female fertility and male ithyphallic figurines, divinized and demonized animals and plants, amulets, fetishes and magical beliefs and techniques.

c. 4000–3500 BC: An agro-sedentary society and corresponding religious values emerge.

c. 3500 BC: The fusion of indigenous Nile Valley, African, North African and West Asian ethnic types into the Egyptian Mediterranean type is probably almost completed.

c. 3300 BC: Harnessing of the Nile: irrigation canals and ditches. Probable Sumerian influence in technology, crafts, art and religion.

c. 3100: The invention of hieroglyphic writing, "the words of the gods."

Divine kingship among henotheistic gods probably exists in many towns and regions.

c. 3100- 2686 BC: Early Dynastic Period

c. 3100 BC: Legendary date for the unification of Upper (the south) and Lower Egypt (the north) into *Ta-Wy*, "The Two Lands" by a legendary (?) Upper Egyptian King – Menes, Narmer, or Aha — who defeats Lower Egypt and is the god Horus on earth.

A surplus agricultural economy, specialization in crafts, division of both parts of Egypt into *sepat*, regions, and major urban centers. A distinctive Egyptian culture emerges.

By at least 2950 BC: The invention of papyrus.

c. 2700: First elaborate mummification.

c. 2686–2181 BC: Old Kingdom

Early in this period, the Goddess Maat represents the divine order and harmony of the world, "truth," as it was instituted with creation, "the first time," *zep tepey*.

Memphis gradually becomes Egypt's capital and major city, taking-over from Abydos and Thinis.

c. 2660: Egypt invents cut stone. The building of the pyramids begins with Djoser's "Step Pyramid" and the three great and "true" pyramids in Giza are built within the next 150 years. These tomb-pyramids are a major aspect of Egypt's solar religion. Ninety-seven major pyramids going up to c. 1550 have been found.

From at least the 4th Dynasty (c. 2613–2494 BC): An elaborate polytheistic system is established with pantheons, enneads (nine gods and goddesses in animal-headed-human, human and animal forms) and chief gods and a theological system based on the immanence and diversity of the divinities in Nature and the divinity of the pharaoh who rules on earth and maintains prosperity. The maintenance of magic, including the widespread use of amulets and spells.

Several rival, and sometimes contradictory, creation myths are elaborated in Heliopolis, Hermopolis, Memphis and elsewhere. They all basically postulate that the universe emerged from a watery chaos with a primeval mound, the *benben*, and then either Atum, Re, Ptah or Amun-Re created the gods and mankind, with the goddess Maat maintaining divine order, truth and justice.

Re is firmly established as chief god in the solar religion and has amalgamated several gods into a single chief and sun god, Re-Horakthy, with the amalgamated gods, including Horus, becoming aspects of Re, but also with these amalgamated gods continuing to have independent existences.

    c. 2550: The conventional date for the first "wisdom texts" (*sebayt*), but they seem to have been written at later dates. These texts, notably that of Ptahhotep (c. 2414–2375 BC) are already an indication of the flirt that Egypt carried-on with ethics, with the notion of "doing the maat," doing the correct thing, but what is usually stressed in the wisdom texts is correct and expedient behavior in society rather than the "spiritual" ethics that we generally associate with the much later Hebrew and Christian Bible.

    c. 2494–2345: 5th Dynasty. An exceptional period of artistic creation and somewhat atypical to Egyptian art's fundamental trend of depicting people and things not as they are, but how they should ideally be. Egypt has surpassed Sumer in architecture and art, but not in technology.

    c. 2375–2125: The Pyramid Texts, the world's oldest body of elaborate religious and magical doctrines designed to ensure an afterlife for the pharaoh. Only the pharaoh has a soul (or rather souls) and a right to an afterlife.

    The rise of Osirisian resurrection and afterlife beliefs, merging chthonian and solar values, and the Osiris/Seth/Isis/Horus myth as the founding myth of the nation. The reigning pharaoh, already Horus when alive, becomes Osiris in the afterlife.

c. 2181–2055 BC: First Intermediate Period

A troubled period of disunity, decline in royal power and perhaps some religious pessimism.

c. 2055–1650 BC: Middle Kingdom

A time of renewal and expansion after the collapse of the Old Kingdom and the troubled First Intermediate Period, with many texts, like *The Protests of The Eloquent Peasant*, indicating a thirst for justice and other texts, like *The Admonitions of Ipuwur* and the *Dialogue of a Man with his Ba*, constituting warnings against a return to the calamity and spiritual crisis of the First Intermediate Period.

The Coffin Texts, now in generalized usage, indicate that the right of the individual to five souls and an afterlife have now been extended to everybody, but in practice the high cost of tomb construction and furnishing and mummification limit these rights to the notables and the rich. Osiris is now not only the pharaoh's savior god, but history's first savior god for everybody, offering resurrection and an afterlife to all — or, rather, all those who can afford it.

c. 1650–1550 BC: Second Intermediate Period

The West Asian Hyksos establish themselves in Egypt by immigration or war and establish the 15th and 16th Hyksos Dynasties.

c. 1550–1069 BC: New Kingdom

c. 1550 BC: The Hyksos are defeated and expelled by Ahmose, ruling from Thebes.

The New Kingdom is the apex of Egyptian political, imperial, economic, religious and artistic power carried-out under the aegis of the Theban god Amun who amalgamates all the gods as his aspects.

Thebes becomes Egypt's greatest city and its Karnak Temple becomes the biggest space ever built in the world for a religious purpose.

The *Book of the Dead* codifies all the existing beliefs in the afterlife and how to magically, technically (and more infrequently, ethically, and by fraud, if necessary) earn an afterlife, the right to "*wehem ankh*," repeating life, in the *Duat*.

c. 1504–1492 BC: Thutmose I, the first pharaoh to be buried in a rock-cut tomb of the Valley of Kings on the Theban West Bank, which will become an immense artistic and engineering achievement.

c. 1473–1458: Hatshepsut usurps the throne and is perhaps the first woman to become a powerful pharaoh rather than the supposed female pharaohs before her, who might have been regents rather than pharaohs.

c. 1458–1425: Thutmose III extends Egypt's control to the Euphrates River and deep into Nubia. Egypt is more and more a part of an Egyptian-West Asian Continuum.

c. 1352–1336 BC: Akhenaten (Amenhotep IV) invents the first monotheism with Aten (the sun-disc) solar monotheism.

A revolutionary period in art, known as Amarna Art, with a combination of naturalistic, realistic painting and sculpture and a perhaps a new — and to some, a grotesque — aesthetic system to indicate the divinity of the pharaoh, his family and associates.

c. 1323–1295 BC: Horemheb completes the elimination of solar monotheism and restores the strongest Amun-Re chief god polytheistic system, but Amunism includes a strong monotheising tendency.

c. 1279–1213 BC: Rameses II, one of Egypt's greatest builders and the longest reigning pharaoh.

Rameses II builds the Abu Simbel Temple in Nubia formally dedicated to Amun, Re and Ptah, but in fact largely dedicated to himself as a god.

c. 1274 BC: The Battle of Kadesh (on the Orontes River) results in a stalemate between Rameses II and the Hittites and consequential power sharing in the Levant.

During Rameses II's reign, *The Hymn to Amun* presents the triad of Amun, Re and Ptah, as an organic unity of all the gods with Re and Ptah as aspects of the supreme, creator, concealed Amun. This may have been a prefiguration of Christian multiform monotheism.

c. 1250 BC: The most probable time for the legendary (?) exodus of the Hebrews from Egypt.

c. 1209 BC: The first mention of Israel in history on Pharaoh Merenptah's stele, found in 1886 by William Matthew Flinders Petrie, the founder of modern scientific archaeology.

c. 1099–1069 BC: Rameses XI's reign culminates the general decline in royal and Egyptian power, which had been ongoing since the previous mid-century.

c. 1069–747 BC: Third Intermediate Period

This period is marked by rival pharaohs, some of them Libyan, ruling from different cities, frequently in competition with fundamentalist Amun-Re High Priests in Thebes.

c. 747–332 BC: Late Period

Political, religious and artistic decline and the rise of extreme zoolatry mark this period. It is opened with the Nubian (Kushite) conquest and then rule of Egypt until c. 656 BC.

> c. 716–702: Shabako claims that an Old Kingdom papyrus from the Ptah Temple in Memphis has been found and recopied. This papyrus, "copied" on the Shabako Stone declares that Ptah created the world with his heart (the mind for the Egyptians) and the tongue (the word). This doctrine may have influenced both the Hebrews and the Christians.

> c. 669–660 BC: The Assyrians conquer and vassal Egypt and sack the Karnak Temple in 663 BC.

> c. 605 BC: The Battle of Carchemish, on the Euphrates River, the Babylonian King Nebuchadnezzar II defeats Egypt and Babylonia emerges as the new super-power.

c. 525–404 BC: First Persian Period

The Persian Cambyses conquers and occupies Egypt. The core of "Egyptian" Egypt in religion, politics, art and social values is mocked by the Persians and undergoes a generalized decline.

> c. 440 BC: Herodotus visits Egypt and triggers an early phase of "Egyptomania" by describing Egypt's magnificent monuments, attributing to her a vast influence on the Greek religion and frequently misinterpreting Egyptian beliefs and customs.

From 5th Century BC: Plato and other Greek philosophers admire Egypt's achievements in many domains, but generally do not attribute any Egyptian influence on Greek philosophy.

c. 404–343 BC: Brief period of restored Egyptian independence.

> c. 360–343 BC: Nectanebo II is the last indigenous pharaoh of Egypt.

c. 343–332 BC: Second Persian Period

c. 332–32 BC: Ptolemaic Period

> c. 332 BC: The Macedonian Greeks, led by Alexander, conquer Egypt and gradually but deeply modify Egyptian beliefs. Alexandria is founded and gradually becomes the world's greatest center of science and philosophy. Greek rationalism and Egyptian magical thinking clash, but the Greek religion is frequently identified with the Egyptian religion. Greek becomes the official language of Egypt.

> c. 305–285 BC: An Egypto-Greek god, Serapis, is invented, merging Osiris, Apis the bull aspect of Ptah and several Greek gods including Zeus and Dionysos.

Early 3rd Century BC: Manetho, an Egyptian priest, writing in Greek, establishes a Kings' List spanning 30 Dynasties.

c. 30 BC–AD 395: The Roman Period

c. 32–30 BC Octavian (Augustus) attacks Egypt and becomes pharaoh.

The Romans continue the transformation of Egypt begun by the Greeks.

First Century AD: The cult of the Egyptian mother goddess Isis is popular throughout the Greco-Roman Mediterranean world.

The Instruction of the *Papyrus Insinger* (a wisdom text, perhaps written at the end of the Ptolemaic Period) mixes traditional Egyptian advice on expediency and correct behavior in society with austere, pessimistic Greek religious ideas on fate, fortune and destiny being decided by the gods rather than on the traditional Egyptian ideas of maat order and harmony.

From the Second Century: The rise of Christianity in Egypt.

From the Third Century: Christian Alexandria is a key player in the frequent Christological quarrels concerning the nature of Jesus.

394: The last inscription written in hieroglyphics.

395: The conventional date for the end of "Egyptian" Egypt with Egypt becoming a part of the East Roman Empire as a Christian nation.

Fifth Century: Egypt elaborates Monophysite Christianity — in which Jesus has only one nature, divine — and comes into conflict with most of the rest of Christianity.

535: The last Egyptian polytheistic temple (the Isis Temple in Philae) is closed down by the East Roman Emperor, Justinian I.

642: The Moslems conquer Egypt and gradually convert it into a Moslem country, with a Christian (Coptic) minority remaining.

Egyptomania and Egyptology

From the 15th Century: A largely "imaginary" Egypt arises in Europe among philosophers, theologians, esoterics and scientists and attributes vast religious, esoteric and scientific knowledge to the ancient Egyptians, including the existence of an original or concealed monotheism. Many of these views, including some very loony ones, persist in modern "Egyptomania."

1798–1801: Napoleon conquers and occupies Egypt. He is accompanied by a scientific and artistic team who catalogue, describe and sketch Egypt's monuments and discover the Rosetta Stone, written in hieroglyphics, demotic Egyptian, and Greek.

1822–1832: Jean François Champollion, using the Rosetta Stone, deciphers hieroglyphics, and opens the road to the rediscovery of a "realer" Egypt.

19th and 20th centuries: Western museums and the Cairo Museum constitute and catalogue vast collections of Egyptian art.

1885: The German Egyptologist Adolf Erman, in *Life In Ancient Egypt* and other books, makes the first scientific and realistic attempt to understand ancient Egypt and concludes that it was truly magnificent, but also that its religion was confused, contradictory and incoherent right from the start and became more so as its history unfolded.

1912: The American Egyptologist James Henry Breasted, in *The Development of Religion and Thought in Ancient Egypt* and other books, concludes that Egypt represented the earliest chapter in the moral development of man, followed by an analogous development later among the Hebrews.

1919: Heinrich Schäfer, in *Principles of Egyptian Art*, deciphers the codes of Egyptian art.

1939: Sigmund Freud, in *Moses and Monotheism*, declares that Moses' Hebrew monotheism was a version of Akhenaten's Atenism.

1939 to the present: Egyptologists and historians increasingly debate to what extent Hebrew monotheism used Egyptian Atenism and Amunism as counter models, models, or both, or was an independent invention.

1948: The Dutch Egyptologist Henri Frankfort, in *Ancient Egyptian Religion: An Interpretation*, concludes that the Egyptian religion was always thoroughly polytheistic, was concerned with divine order and maintenance of harmony rather than evil or ethics in the Biblical sense, and that its religion was a coherent system based on a multiplicity of approaches, multiple answers and meaningful inconsistency.

1955: The Senegalese scholar Cheikh Anta Diop, in *Nations Nègres et Culture*, declares that

Egypt was a black African civilization.

1950 to present: Most major Egyptian religious, political and societal texts are reliably translated (notably by R.O. Faulkner and Miriam Lichtheim); Egyptian history is dealt with scientifically by many historians (including Alan Gardiner and Nicolas Grimal); Egyptian art is decorticated by many art historians (including H.A. Groenewegen-Frankfort and W. Stevenson Smith); and together with the easy availability of ancient Egyptian sites, makes it increasingly possible and valid to carry out independent speculation on what Egypt was and wasn't.

Chapter 9. The Central Preoccupation of the Egyptian Religion: The Search for a Solution to the Scandal of Death

The Osirisian Revolution

Like many revolutions, the Osirisian revolution began in obscure ways. It is impossible to unravel many of its constitutive aspects and attribute them solely to Osirisian-type thinking. Nevertheless, Osirisian concepts lie at the center of gravity between what the Egyptians invented before and after the rise of Osiris.

Unsurprisingly, and even mundanely, the Egyptian goal was to live well, to have pleasure, *reschut*, long life, *ankh*, prosperity, *udja*, and good health, *seneb*. Magical appeasement and then the manipulation of the gods had been standard practice (for probably thousands of years before Egypt) to obtain these goals in this life. But before the Egyptians, what occurred in the afterlife remained a vague notion.

Death was scandalous to the Egyptians, perhaps more than to other peoples. The Egyptians developed an overriding obsession towards finding a solution to the problem of death, and this distinguished the Egyptian religion from all other religions for thousands of years. The goal became not only to live well but, because life was so good, to eternally and happily "repeat life," *wehem ankh*, after death. The Egyptian goal was endless life, the defeat of death.

Thus, one of the great peaks which mark the achievements and illusions of human history, which constitute the specific nature of man, occurred in Egypt. And this peak emblematically took the form of an accelerated search for a solution to the problem of death. As we shall see in this chapter, "repeating life," *wehem ankh*, was a highly complex system involving *aper*, being "equipped" — that is, material and magical architectural, artistic, ritualistic and bodily preparations; threats and supplications to the gods; a sprinkling of decent behavior and judgment (a kind of proto-morality); and a vast magical system of survival of the body and several souls in the afterlife.

The Egyptian approach to the problem of death and the afterlife was the most optimistic solution ever elaborated until their time. The end of life, death, was simply unacceptable. This reflected their optimistic nature, their love of the body and the joys it procured, *a contrario* to the Hindu solution to the problem of death which reflected a pessimistic nature and the rejection and destruction of the body. Death was intolerable for the Egyptians; it was desirable for the Hindus. Perhaps, above all, the Osirisian revolution represented the highest point of optimism and hope reached in the ancient world before the evolution (from the sixth century BC) of Zoroastrian/Hebrew/Christian resurrection/afterlife concepts.

Death posed such difficult problems for man that it took over 60,000 years or more, the interim between the Neanderthals and the Egyptians, to come up with radically new ideas and launch a new trajectory of wishful thinking and illusion which would eventually lead to the inventions of Paradise and Hell based on morality and the final judgment and final destiny of all mankind.

Egypt, probably largely independently and right from the start of the Early Dynastic Period (c. 3100–2686 BC), innovated, made major breakthroughs and may have exercised significant influence on other peoples in the search for a solution to the problem of death. What had somehow occurred in Egypt was a fabulous bringing to fruition of all of man's imaginative efforts and abstract reasoning concerning death. The Egyptians sketched out and invented a new type of afterlife aimed at permanently defeating death.

The origins of the notions of an afterlife, Paradise and Hell are enveloped in considerable obscurity. At least sixty thousand years ago, the Neanderthals imagined phenomena which did not necessarily exist or certainly did not exist. Perhaps based on their experience of dream life, they seem to have imagined the existence of an afterlife, invented ritual burial for entry into the afterlife, and possibly believed in the existence of the soul. Even if we can have no exact idea of what the afterlife meant for the Neanderthals, the decoration of some dead bodies and the inclusion of foods, goods, weapons and ornaments in their graves, clearly indicate that they believed that life somehow did not end with death, that an aspect of life, or a spirit, continued. The seeds of Paradise, the concepts of immortality or consolation, or a paradisiacal reward, for the first life, are already at least potentially contained in such a view. However, the Neanderthals and all other peoples at least until Egyptian times seem to have sought solutions to death which were not explicit.

It is difficult to establish any kind of a burial pattern before the Neolithic period (8000 BP). Relatively few clearly intentional Paleolithic tombs (probably less than 100 authentic burials) have been discovered throughout the world and finds of clearly voluntary collections of skulls and bones, although far more abundant, are also insufficient to draw definitive conclusions. It is only possible to conclude that cults of skulls and bones and intentional burials must have existed and that the burials with decorated bodies, ornaments and *gratuitous* objects seem to have been linked to religious beliefs and a hope in an afterlife. The criteria by which it was determined who was ritually buried remain in the domain of speculation.

If we have to speculate, it is not illogical to consider that at least in some periods before Neolithic times and afterwards, ritual — religious — burial and the afterlife may have been reserved for powerful politico-religious leaders, sorcerers and deified heroes, and men rather than women. This does not exclude that there could have been societies and periods in Paleolithic times, especially after the Upper Paleolithic Period (35,000 BP), when burial and an afterlife hope may have been shared by the many.

In any event, it seems that ritual burial was reserved for the few in Early Dynastic Egypt (c. 3100–2686 BC) and probably in Sumer. One must conclude that if the Egyptians eventually extended afterlife privileges from their kings to others, this meant that such privileges had not existed in a general way for some time previously. The immensity of the Egyptian invention of an afterlife accessible to all is therefore clear. Probably for the first time in history, salvation with the afterlife was accessible to all.

The existence of other places — original Paradise, an abode in the sky for the gods or for demonic gods in an Underworld — is evident in the (impossible to date) notions of deified and demonized humans in all religions with the exception of original Buddhism. Early Egyptian concepts placed some presumably immortal deities and demons in the sky and in the underworld, and the *Duat* afterlife is at least a partial extension of these concepts. However, they do not seem to have had the concept of the dead going to or returning to a place which was Paradise. The Egyptian system of *wehem ankh*, of happily "repeating life," was a hint of Paradise, but not Paradise.

For the Sumerians, the notion of Paradise was that of an original state before a great flood, a past golden age, and a "pure and bright" place, *Dilmun*. This Sumerian land, or city, resembling Paradise, was like the Hindu *Krita Yuga* or the Hebrew *Gan Eden*, Garden of Eden; it had nothing to do with a moral reward. Sumerian mythology also vaguely suggested the possibility of a Paradise of immortality with a specific location and with geographical access by magic, but it was a place where only a single person lived — Ziusudra (Utnapishtim) — and was not an afterlife moral reward.

In Animism, including African proto-animism, which could have influenced Egypt, venerated ancestors did not necessarily have a radiant, immortal existence in a specific heavenly or underground location, but they continued to have an invisible existence and played key roles in this life. In Egypt, like in earlier and later animism, the dead could haunt the living and make life miserable for them or be courted for favors and predictions.

In Sumer, death was seen as the cruel end to life. There was no notion of anything like an eternal soul and only a person's bloodless, breathless *etemmu*, his phantom, somehow continued to vegetate after death. The ghostly *etemmu* was in the dark, indifferent, meaningless, hapless *Kur* underworld, cut off from the gods and man, which had probably been invented well before 3000 BC. Like the later Hebrew *Sheol* underworld, neither magic, nor trickery, nor ethics could change this situation. Sumer's view of the afterlife was a kind of sinister epilogue to life, something which just happened and which led to an uncertain, dismal condition.

However, Sumerian religion and mythology affirmed that the goddess Inanna had returned from the realm of the dead and that Dumuzi was resurrected annually. As we have seen in Chapter 6, these and other related concepts could indicate that there might have been an initial impulsion from Sumer or Sumerian-influenced West Asians on Egypt's afterlife concepts. It is also significant that at the Ur Royal tombs from c. 2700 BC, the Sumerian kings were buried with incredible riches and hundreds of sacrificed servants and soldiers, indicating that some kind of hope in a positive afterlife must have existed at least among the elite. We have seen too how Sumer's greatest (semi) mythological hero, Gilgamesh, despite his enormous efforts and the use of great magic, could not gain immortality. The revolutionary difference between Sumer and Egypt was that the Sumerians dreamed of immortality and the Egyptians instituted it.

The Egyptian system of immortality through "repeating life" was certainly the most significant twist to the afterlife since its invention. Sixty-thousand years ago, as in Egyptian times, the hope, the wishful thinking and the assumption that led to the invention of the afterlife was that the dead were not dead, that something lived on. For the Egyptians, the starting point was that the body was a temple, both in this life and in the afterlife. From this, the Egyptians optimistically decreed that the body repeated life, lived on eternally in the afterlife, and was joined by several companion souls.

The entirety of this Egyptian process, involving radically new beliefs and techniques to win an afterlife while still in this life and just after death and new funerary and burial techniques aimed at maintaining a person alive in the afterlife, constituted a revolution, the Osirisian revolution. The raw elements of this revolution may have existed before 3100 BC and certainly almost immediately afterwards, when the pharaoh, after death, went to the "East" and to "lightland" in the sky. From the Fifth Dynasty (c. 2494–2345 BC), when the god Osiris began rising to prominence, Osirisian death and resurrection concepts became the central pillar of the Egyptian religion. Osirisian mythology and theology also surely indicated to what an extreme extent the Egyptians — probably more than any ancient people — were poetically and desperately searching for religious reassurance and answers concerning death.

Old and new notions were merged. Old notions about the continuation of life after death in an afterlife, the immortal existence of a soul or souls and the struggle between opposites, notably light and darkness, were gradually refined, expanded and transformed. The new notion of protecting the body in monumental tombs was invented around 3100 BC. Notions concerning the preservation of the body — keeping it from decay — received a big boost around 2700 BC with the invention of elaborate embalmment, mummification. From the mid-Fifth Dynasty (c. 2494–2345 BC), the invention of the myth of Osiris as the first god to die, become the first mummy, be resurrected and go to the afterlife became the savior-god model for the pharaohs, personifying hope in a life without death.

By the end of the Old Kingdom (c. 2181 BC), the Egyptian religious and societal system had gone far beyond the earlier Sumerian system, or any other system anywhere in the world. This was notably the case in the extension of soul and afterlife rights from the pharaoh to the entire population, in the search for a solution to the problem of death for everybody. Having souls and entering into the *Duat*, the afterlife, immortality, was now the birthright of not only the pharaoh, but of everybody. Imitating the savior Osiris could now do for humans what he had accomplished for himself and for the pharaoh. This achievement, as illusionary as it may have been, was astounding, especially for Old Kingdom Egypt, which although a time of almost touchingly naïve religious, political and technological certitude and of social cohesiveness, nevertheless had to overcome its massively inegalitarian societal system for any general progress to be possible.

At the end of the Old Kingdom, during the Sixth Dynasty (c. 2345–2181 BC), the Egyptians also invented a system of judgment linking morality and the afterlife — although it has to be considered a failure because it seems always to have operated in a magical and fraudulent way. By about the beginning of the Middle Kingdom (c. 2055 BC), the system of *wehem ankh*, "repeating life," was solidly linked to the notion of the personal savior god·Osiris and was fully operational. This notably included the building of solid, monumental tombs, the preservation of the body with mummification, elaborate magical rituals, forms of theoretical judgment — proto-Paradise-like reward and proto-Hell-like punishment — before entering the afterlife and the resurrection and survival of the body and its joining by several companion souls in the afterlife.

As we shall see in this chapter, the Osirisian Revolution also involved the failed attempt to expand the old notions of primeval cosmological and collective harmony of the goddess of order, truth and justice, Maat, and to link them to ethical behavior. The pharaohs from at least 3100 BC "lived by *maat*," "*ankh-em-maat*," which meant that they carried out the correct rituals and applied the correct laws to assure *maat*, natural harmony, for Egypt and its people. The Osirisian revolution implied *doing the maat* in the old way as well as new notions of individual decency — proto-morality — and a tenuous, symbolic moral judgment upon death. Over the centuries, the Osirisian system implied that all this was not only for the pharaohs, but for everybody.

More than a thousand years of effort, from about the beginning of the Early Dynastic Period (c. 3100 BC) to the beginning of the Middle Kingdom (c. 2055 BC), were required to invent the system of *wehem ankh*, "repeating life," and notably the tenuous, symbolic ethical link between doing the *maat* in this life and the afterlife. Perhaps even more than 1500 years were required for the elaboration of the entirety of the system, if the invention of massive, complicated rock-cut tombs and the more complex magic of the New Kingdom *Book of the Dead* are included in the process.

The Egyptians were actively fumbling around to find a satisfactory solution to the problem of death throughout this entire period. The very least that can be said is that they came up with more numerous and more elaborate answers than any of their contemporaries. Despite the confusion and contradictions, no clearer description of the afterlife had ever been given. A qualitative leap towards the notion of Paradise had been made, albeit in a muddled and frequently contradictory manner. They had made a start down the path to one more infantile illusion: that a good life existed in the invisible future after death and that gods provided it.

The Egyptians were certainly the first people in history to expend such great efforts to invent a clear resurrection/afterlife system and no people has equaled them yet. Of course, how they could possibly have believed in this sys-tem still defies the imagination. How could they possibly believe that once in the *Duat* afterlife, the mummified dead body would be resurrected as Osiris and that not only would several souls join up with the body, but the innards that had been extracted, placed in canopic jars and mummified, would also return into the body — not to mention the brain, which had been discarded — and that everything would be reconstituted and resume functioning as in life?

The explanation might lie in the fact that even today millions believe in the fairytales of the Persian/Christian/Moslem Final Resurrection of all bodies. But the paradox is that the Egyptians, who were basically a materialistic, pragmatic people, unwittingly were at the origin of the most incredible of fairytales. Seen in retrospect, their resurrection/afterlife system was sheer infantile poetry of the *Peter Pan* or *Pinocchio* type, the type of poetry which nobody believes and which nevertheless exercises an irresistible attraction.

The path opened in ancient Egypt today appears to most of mankind as having been a vast misapprehension or lie. Perhaps, the Sumerians and the Hebrews were more lucid and realistic than the Egyptians in the way they defined the body and the lack of a real afterlife. Perhaps, from the 14th century BC, the Hindus imagined a more incredibly complex system which mingled immediate pessimism and destruction with long range moral worth and desir-able extinction. But until the sixth century BC and the rise of the Zoroastrian Persian concepts that evil in this life would be authentically and definitively punished and good would be authentically and definitively rewarded in the afterlife, it was the Egyptian vision which represented the groundswell of human aspirations. The confused and fabulous afterlife, *wehem ankh*, repeating life, was the beginning of an answer — of "credible" fantasies — to many age-old ques-tions — a simple, radical, new concept.

The Egyptians no doubt over-reacted to the reality of death, but they also no doubt had understood better than any other people that death was an immense scandal. Despite their infantilism, the new twists to the concept of the afterlife constituted extraordinary and radical turning points in the history of mankind. As confused, complex and subtle as the Egyptian death notions were, they nevertheless represented new hopes and new possibilities. The Egyptians had succeeded in attenuating the terribleness of death.

THE INVENTION OF PROTECTIVE MONUMENTAL TOMBS AND UT, THE PRESERVATION OF THE BODY

The advent of agriculture in Mesopotamia, Egypt and elsewhere had gradually led to changes in burial customs. The dead were no longer buried nearby, but away from the living, in separate locations. In Egypt's case, these burials took place in the desert at the edge of the farmed lands along the Nile. Greater amounts of supplies, clothing, tools and weapons were included in the graves. Shallow graves gave way to elaborate, protective structures of mud-brick, first in Sumer and then in Egypt.

During the First Dynasty (c. 3100–2890 BC), before we can find any mention of Osiris, two major developments concerning the solution to the problem of death took place. They would become major aspects of the Osirisian system: the invention of monumental mastaba tombs and the invention of *ut*, mummification, the preservation of the body. This evolution was due to many factors and Osirisian influence is an inextricable part of the mix.

Around 3100 BC, monumental rectangular mud-brick superstructures were placed over the mud-brick encased pit tombs (which had already attained a considerable degree of monumentality, notably in Abydos and Sakkara) and the still earlier shallow graves in the desert. (This new structure is now called the *mastaba*, from the Arabic word for "bench"). It was at about this time that *kenes*, coffins and sarcophagi, also came into use in both Egypt and Sumer. In Egypt, the invention of the coffin seems to have had to do with providing a home for the *ka*, double soul, and helping to provide safe passage of the body into afterlife.

The monumental mastaba were built for increased protection against robbers and wild animals and to "equip" the dead pharaohs and notables and their *ka* and *ba* companion souls, that is, to provide them with a solid, well-furnished, eternal home. By the Fourth Dynasty (c. 2613–2494 BC), the mastaba, in addition to the substructure burial chambers at the far end of the structure, or deep under it, contained the *ka*-statue of the deceased (in a chamber now called the *serdab*), steles and inscriptions lauding the deceased's great achievements, and reliefs and paintings of daily life. One of the most important elements in the mastaba was the offering table, where *hetep*, offerings, to keep the dead alive were placed.

With the mastaba and coffins, it is obvious that great care and effort were exercised concerning the importance and dignity of the dead body and what happens to it. The mastaba were not only places where funerary services were organized, but they also eventually became chapels where commemorative rituals were carried out and *hetep*, offerings, continued to be made.

About 400 years later, around 2660 BC, seeking a gain in monumentality beyond that achieved by placing one mastaba upon another, the royal architect Imhotep invented an even sturdier and more eternal structure, the pyramid tomb, the so-called Step Pyramid at Sakkara for Pharaoh Djoser (c. 2667–2648 BC). The invention of monumental building with cut stone, the most eternal material available to man, was also made at this time, perhaps also by Imhotep.

The birth of the pyramid, descended from the elaborate mud-brick tombs and the mastaba and perhaps from the Sumerian platform temple structures, seems to have gone hand-in-hand with the invention of elaborate attempts at mummification of the early pharaohs. The placing of the mummified pharaoh in the pyramid tomb constituted a high point in the search for a solution to the problem of death.

However, there is no way of knowing whether the invention of mummification was in some way linked to the god Osiris or was superimposed onto Osirisian theology afterwards. Mummification as a system facilitating resurrection was a logical application of Osirisian theology, but there is of course no way of establishing whether it was invented concurrently with the Osirisian resurrection myth, as many Egyptian texts claim, or whether it emerged independently as a part of afterlife theology in general. The god of death and protector of tombs, Anubis, one of Egypt's oldest gods, was the legendary inventor of embalmment and mummification, which he supposedly first practiced on Osiris. Anubis was represented as a dog or a jackal, or a dog-headed human, and it is possible that in this dog role he was meant to discourage other dogs and jackals from preying on buried bodies.

In any case, both mummification and massive tombs were eventually justified by Osirisian concepts and became integral parts of the Osirisian revolution.

For the Egyptians, the preservation of the body, the prevention of decomposition, was the absolute first step in the process of survival after death, in gaining an afterlife in which the souls could survive because the body had been preserved. From very early in Egyptian civilization, the raw element of the preservation of the body after death existed.

So-called *natural* or *spontaneous* mummification, natural drying in the sand, must have been going on for thousands of years in Egypt's hot, dry, desert climate, when most bodies were wrapped in mats and placed in shallow graves in the desert rather than receiving formal, ritual burial. The most famous *natural* mummy is red-haired "Ginger," a body dating to c. 3400 BC that was found in the desert near Gebelein (*Aphroditopolis* in Greek, *Per-Hathor* in Egyptian), north of Esna, and is now in the British Museum.

Some Egyptologists have speculated that the invention of embalmment and mummification came from directly observing that bodies buried in the desert dried and remained well preserved. Certainly, *natural* mummification must have influenced the Egyptians, but both the first intentional and elaborate embalmment and mummification efforts from as early as 2700 BC and even earlier attempts at artificially preserving dead bodies must have required some kind of a theological conceptual thrust.

They therefore could have owed at least something to Osirisian concepts of preserving the body not merely to preserve the body, but for specific purposes — for resurrection in the afterlife where the deceased would resume his life, including breathing and eating. This notably implied that all the organs of the deceased and his capacity to use his limbs would be restored. Moreover, the body had to be preserved in an identifiable way so that the *ka*, the double, the soul, of the deceased would be able to recognize it and the *ba* roaming soul would be able to linkup with the deceased and his *ka*. Such a view makes the observation of desert burials insufficient in itself and favors a combination of what was learned from desert burials and the application of Osirisian or other afterlife concepts.

It seems probable that attempts to artificially preserve and protect the body, using techniques which later became parts of the mummification process, were practiced at very early dates. Barbara Adams (of the Petrie Museum in London) and Renée Friedman (of the University of California) report that between 1996 and 1999 they found more than 150 bodies in the Nekhen (Hierakonpolis) HK43 Predynastic necropolis, some of which were partially wrapped in several layers of linen and matting. They date pottery found near these bodies to at least 3600 BC. [1]

Evidence shows that primitive (and inefficient) mummification, using resin-soaked wrappings, was in practice from the Early Dynastic Period (c. 3100–2686 BC). This was still the main system in use during and after Imhotep's time in the Third Dynasty (c. 2686–2613 BC). A foot treated in this way — perhaps Pharaoh Djoser's foot — was found in the Step Pyramid.

The first known portrayal of a mummy is on a wooden tablet found in 1936 by W. B. Emery (1903–1971) in the Sakkara mastaba (3035) of Pharaoh Den's (c. 2950 BC) vizier, Hemaka. Evisceration, one of the central aspects of mummification, does not appear to have been invented before Pharaoh Snofru's time (c. 2613–2589 BC). Controversy surrounds what is sometimes considered the oldest complete mummy ever found, that of Merenra I (c. 2287–2278 BC), discovered in his Sakkara "Merenra shines in glory and beauty" pyramid by Gaston Maspero (1846–1916) in 1881. The eminent but controversial anatomist of Egyptian mummies, Grafton Elliot Smith (1871–1937), and others believe that this mummy probably dates to the Eighteenth Dynasty (c. 1550–1295 BC).

---

1. In www.hierakonpolis.org/main.html.

Perhaps, Imhotep was the genius who improved and structured some of the series of related concepts of the preservation of the body, mummification and massive stone solar tombs (the Step Pyramid) and linked these to Osirisian afterlife concepts and the system of souls. However, the likeliest probability is that many priests over at least a few hundred years gradually put together mummification techniques and their underlying afterlife concepts.

It is also clear that forms of intentional mummification took place even earlier, in distant civilizations: among the Amerindians of what is now Peru, Ecuador and Chile, from at least about 5000 BC. These were considerably less elaborate than the Egyptian; it seems that the preservation of a skeleton with skin was the goal of the Amerindians, rather than the Egyptian near-total preservation of the body and its organs and the integral resurrection of the body and its functions, soul and personality. It also seems certain that the Amerindians did not invent a soul/afterlife theology anywhere near the complexity of the Egyptian system.

After the techniques of *ut*, mummification, had been relatively perfected during the Middle Kingdom (from c. 2055 BC), Egyptian mummification was a complex technique which required 70 days and sometimes more to complete. The 70-day period became the preferred one because it corresponded to the cycle of the star Sirius, linked to Isis. Herodotus tells us that there were three categories of mummification — "the most perfect way," which resulted in a superb Osiris-like aspect; a "middle way," which was "less perfect than the first and cheaper"; and "a third manner" which was "the least costly" for "the poorer dead."[2]

The Egyptians called the mummy *sah*, a word linked to protection, but perhaps also to *sahu*, the superior, gleaming spiritual afterlife body and Osiris' star Orion. The term *mummy* came into use after the Arab conquest of Egypt in AD 642 and derives from a term of Persian and Arabic origin — *mummiya* — meaning bitumen, since mummification gave the body a blackened effect. *Mummiya* was also the term used from the 12th century for the substance obtained by grinding mummies into a medicinal powder. Tens of thousands of mummies were ground into powder and exported throughout the world for their supposed therapeutic qualities.

After the body was washed with *netjeryt*, natron salt crystals, in a *wabet*, a "place of purification," the actual process of *ut*, mummification, was carried out in the *per nefer*, "the house of beauty," by a team of specialist priests, headed by the *hery seshta*, "the overseer of mysteries," in the role of Anubis, the *imey-ut*, "the overseer of embalming or mummification," assisted by the *hetemw*, "the seal

---

2. Herodotus, *Books I-II*, 2.86.2, 2.87.1 and 2.88.1.

bearer of the god." Most of the gory work was done by the *wetyw*, "the bandag-ers." They removed the brain by draining it through the nostrils and then threw it away. All the innards were removed except the *ieb*, the heart, through an inci-sion on the lower left side of the stomach. As these operations took place, the *hery heb*, the lector priests, recited spells. During the New Kingdom (from c. 1550 BC), the genitals were also removed in memory of Osiris' castration by a fish.

The body and internal organs were then dried, sometimes for 40 days, using natron. The stomach, the liver, the lungs and the intestines were placed in so-called canopic jars, magically protected by Hapy, Imsety, Duamutef and Qebeh-senuef, the *mesu* Heru, the four sons of Haroeris, "Horus the Elder" and Isis. The body was then stuffed with linen, sawdust and plants and the skin was rubbed with honey, milk and aromatic ointments. The incision was then closed and a *wedjat*, the "eye of Horus" amulet, placed over it to ward off evil spirits and to guarantee that the deceased would fully recover all the functions of his body.

The intricate process of wrapping the body was then carried out. As much as 400 square yards or more of quality linen was employed. So-called "yester-day's linen," or used linen, was employed for the poor. Dozens of amulets were placed in special places between the layers of wrappings and especially a heart scarab made from green stone. *Tiet* Isis knots, Osiris *djed* stability pillars, *was* divine dominion scepters and images of gods and animals were also placed within the wrappings. A relief in the Hathor Denderah Temple lists 104 mummy amulets. The greatest protection and power was obtained by placing the great-est possible number of amulets in the mummy. In the New Kingdom, Spells 30A and B from *The Book of the Dead* were inscribed on the heart scarab to prevent the heart from testifying against the deceased when it was judged against Maat's *shut* feather of truth.

A mask representing the ideal likeness of the deceased was then fitted over the head. These masks were sometimes fabulous works of art. For the pharaohs and the rich, they were fashioned in gold, the never-fading color of the skin of the gods, the color of eternity. However, their pragmatic function was to enable the identification of the deceased by its *ka* and *ba* souls. The mummy was then placed in a *kenes*, in a rectangular or anthropoid coffin inscribed with magical spells (the Coffin Texts, notably from c. 2055 BC), or a series of coffins, like Rus-sian matrioshka dolls, and in turn the coffins were placed in an outer stone sar-cophagus. The goddesses Isis, Nephthys, Neith and Serqet vigilantly protected the coffin. All of these containers were placed in one or more shrines and all were identified with the sky goddess Nut. A *wedjat*, the eye of Horus, was painted on the exterior of the sarcophagus so that in addition to receiving protection, wel-fare and healing, the deceased could see outside. During the New Kingdom, vari-ous funerary texts with painted vignettes were placed next to the mummy. Of course, all this had more to do with magic than with beauty, but the beauty of this "equipment" was sometimes stunning.

Mummification and its related practices reached a qualitative and quantitative peak during the Roman Period (from c. 30 BC). By this time, many Greeks and Romans living in Egypt had adopted mummification and Osirisian concepts, while notably Grecizing and Romanizing the style and design of the sarcophagi.

The *sah*, the mummy, was now ready for a funeral service and burial, which as we shall soon see were extraordinarily elaborate ceremonies.

And so, the earliest elaborate attempts to preserve the body upon death — to thoroughly embalm and mummify — were in Egypt, before arising independently in many widely separated areas of the world, including China, the Pacific Torres Strait, the Canary Islands and today in the United States. Here too, Egypt's possible influence on other peoples is largely unverifiable, but it is not unreasonable to assume that it occurred, even if a link between Egypt and the earliest mummification efforts among the Amerindians is a loony notion.

OSIRISIAN CONCEPTS SPREAD, BUT THE AFTERLIFE REMAINS "VIRTUAL" FOR MOST

The role of the powerful *Uer-maa*, the "great seer" prophet-theologians of Onu (Heliopolis) seems to have been considerable in the Osirisian revolution, both conceptually and practically. It was a complicated, long and no doubt partially a haphazard process. Its opening gambit certainly concerned Re more than Osiris.

This occurred in the Fourth Dynasty (c. 2613–2494 BC) when the Heliopolitan theologians expanded the concept of divine kingship and linked it to the sun god Re. Pharaoh Radjedef's (c. 2566–2558 BC) praenomen throne name proclaimed that "Re is his support," but for the first time a *sa Ra*, son of Re, title was introduced as the pharaoh's birth name, his nomen. The pharaoh-god was now no longer only the living Horus, the incarnation of the god Horus; the pharaoh was also a god because he was the son of Re. This objectively limited his divine powers by making him dependent on Re. The Heliopolitan clergy then gradually ascribed creator and agricultural/Nile inundation functions to Re. An elaborate system ensuring an eternally positive afterlife in the sky among the circumpolar stars, or "the East," in "lightland," with Re was practiced in favor of the pharaoh. The system included pyramids as staircases for the dead pharaoh to ascend to the sky, funerary practices involving rituals, spells and amulets and techniques designed to facilitate entry into the afterlife and protection and well being once there.

However, at the same time, the inclusion of Osiris in the Heliopolitan Ennead of nine deities signified the inclusion of the Osirisian myth and the merger of Re solar theology with the chthonian aspects of Osirisian theology as practiced in places likes Busiris and Abydos. Both the pharaoh's link to Re and a rise in Osirisian cult and funeral practices for the pharaohs are clearly attested in the first Pyramid Texts, those of Pharaoh Unas (c. 2375–2345 BC). Osiris and Osirisian concepts had become fundamental for the pharaohs; the pharaohs gradually became Osirises upon death. Pyramid Texts Utterance 309 in Unas' "Pyramid which is beautiful of places" in Sakkara states: "Unas is gods' steward, behind the mansion of Re...Unas unseals his (Re's) decrees...Unas does what Unas is told (by Re)." However, in Utterance 217, Unas does not forget Osiris: "Osiris, Isis, go proclaim...This Unas comes, a spirit indestructible..."[3]

About 25 years later, Teti (c. 2345–2323 BC) is even far more explicit in Utterance 337, in his "Pyramid which is enduring of places" in Sakkara: "Heaven shouts, earth trembles, In dread of you, Osiris, at your coming!" This clearly indicates the growing importance Osiris has assumed for the pharaohs — Osiris is no longer just the god of Dead in the *Duat* nether world; he is now also linked to the pharaoh as a god in the sky.

In another 25 years, Pepy I (c. 2321–2287 BC), in Utterance 442, in his "Established and beautiful pyramid" in Sakkara, indicates: "Lo, Osiris has come as Orion... 'Good one'... 'Heir'... Sky conceived you (the King) and Orion...You shall rise with Orion in the eastern sky, You shall set with Orion in the western sky..." The meaning here is that at death, the pharaoh is transformed into the star Orion (Sah), into Osiris.[4]

The mummified, pyramid-entombed pharaoh was now Osiris upon death. The pharaoh's afterlife goal was still to merge in the sky, in "lightland," with the sun god Re, but the dead pharaoh was now also Osiris in the sky after being Horus while alive. Almost all of the Early Dynastic pharaohs had been identified with the falcon god Horus, but now the ruling pharaoh was simultaneously the son of Re, the incarnation of the Horus, who was the son of Osiris and Isis, and who had been joined to the earlier Horus falcon, and Osiris when dead. This development may have even begun during the Fourth Dynasty (c. 2613–2494 BC).

Nevertheless, even while the importance of Osiris was on the rise, the fervor of the Fifth Dynasty (c. 2494–2345 BC) pharaohs was massively centered on Re, as clearly indicated by their Re nomen birth names and the construction of sun temples, with names like "Pleasure of Re" and "Horizon of Re," by six out of

---

3. Lichtheim, Miriam, *Ancient Egyptian Literature, Volume I*, pp. 39 and 31.
4. *Ibid.*, Ut. 337, p. 40 and Ut. 442, p. 45.

nine of them. However, the fact that the last Fifth Dynasty Pharaoh, Unas, did not have a Re birth name and did not build a solar temple could perhaps be interpreted at least as an indication of a vast and complicated tendency centered on the rise of Osiris and its particular afterlife implications.

Osiris was not a threat to Re's functions as chief and royal god, but he gradually appropriated most of Re's afterlife functions and became the chief god of the world of the dead. Osiris, originally associated with agricultural fertility — the spring budding of grain, and the annual flooding of the Nile (the annual resurrection of the Nile), before being consecrated as the resurrected king/god by the Osiris/Seth/Horus/Isis myth, also recuperated these functions from Re.

Osiris carried out a vast process of monopolizing most of the attributes of the other gods linked to death. He "demoted" the chief death god Anubis, the "lord of the sacred land" (the cemeteries) who was associated with Cynopolis (near Hardai) and Abdu (Abydos). Anubis became the *imey-ut*, "the overseer of embalming or mummification," but Osiris oversaw these functions, as well as Anubis's function of tomb protection. Khentimentiu, the dog, or dog-headed, "Commander and Foremost of the Westerners" (god of the dead), whose temple in Abydos had been a key cult center since at least the First Dynasty (c. 3100–2890 BC), was assimilated and virtually replaced by Osiris by the Sixth Dynasty (c. 2345–2181 BC), even if the Khentimentiu Temple was not replaced by the Osiris Temple before the Twelfth Dynasty (c. 1985–1795 BC). Osiris also became associated with "he who is upon the sand" (in the *Duat* nether world), the falcon or falcon-headed crafts, fertility and mummified death god Seker of Memphis. The wolf or dog-headed opener of the way to the afterlife, the god Wepwawet, linked to Zawty (Lykopolis), and Sobek, the crocodile-headed god of the waters and fertility, linked to Fayum, also frequently came to be considered as aspects of Osiris, despite their continued independent existences. Osiris also eventually absorbed the Memphis Ptah-Apis bull, for upon the death of each successive Apis bull the dead Apis in the afterlife became Osorapis, a combination of Osiris and Apis. In the Late Period (from c. 747 BC), he was also an element in the Ptah-Seker-Osiris death combination.

Osiris' rise to prominence concerned not only the pharaohs but also the priests and notables. The founder of the Fifth Dynasty, Userkaf (c. 2494–2487 BC), also may have been the *Uer-maa*, the "great seer" of the Heliopolis Temple, but this Dynasty saw the emergence of a new trend among the high priests, nomarchs and top civil servants. Now, they did not necessarily emanate from trusted circles of the pharaoh's family; they started forming their own hereditary castes, and won increasingly autonomous power. The Heliopolitan clergy became so powerful that it may even have named some of the pharaohs of the Fifth Dynasty. This new power of the Heliopolitan high priests seems to have been axiomatically accompanied by pressure to obtain afterlife privileges for themselves.

Under the probable impetus of successive high priests, the pharaohs were being obliged to grant afterlife privileges to the high priests and nomarchs, to also allow them to also become Osirises upon death. This obviously implied an increase in Osiris' power. The rise of the *maat* code, interpreted not just as a system of primeval order but also as both a theoretical moral code and its consequential system of entry into the afterlife, from at least about 2300 BC, constituted a further reinforcement of the Osirisian revolution. Nevertheless, the quantitative limitations — the relativity — of that revolution and its afterlife consequences must be emphasized; it frequently has been estimated that no more than 5000 people during the entire Fourth and Fifth Dynasties received mummification and solid tombs upon death.

During the Sixth Dynasty (c. 2345–2181 BC), the movement towards the increase in the powers of the priests and the notables — both locally and nationally — and the decrease in the pharaohs' central authority was accentuated. It culminated in the virtual collapse of the pharaohs' omnipotence and in the collapse of the Old Kingdom around 2181 BC.

It seems that one of the main reasons for the collapse of the Old Kingdom was the immense economic burden on the entire population generated by religious obligations to the dead. Perhaps the pharaohs and the small elite used more resources on extravagantly preparing for death and providing *hetep* for the dead than they used for their everyday needs. There is good reason to suppose that the Egyptians believed that their economic system was capable of divinely generating limitless resources. In fact, embalmment, mummification, funerary rituals, elaborate pyramid and mastaba tombs and their funerary texts, art work and fittings, and the cult practices and *hetep* and *aut* offerings which continued after the pharaoh's death, and the huge number of priests and craftsmen required to carry out these obligations, may have run the economy into the ground. Overspending in Egypt's second economy, the economy of the dead, provoked the collapse of the first economy, the economy of the living, and provoked the collapse of the Old Kingdom, leading to widespread poverty and even famine.

The period of extreme religious, political and economic dislocation which this collapse initiated led to the advent of numerous minor pharaohs, would-be pharaohs and rival dynasties of the First Intermediary Period (c. 2181–2055 BC). Egypt was apparently split into several kingdoms, or groups of nomes; or, at the very least, the pharaohs who claimed power over the entirety of *Ta-Wy*, the Two Lands, were not in fact able to exercise such power. Presumably, not only did local kinglets crop up but greater feudal power redounded to the nomarchs as a result.

This period of reduced pharaonic power seems to have naturally culminated towards the end of the Sixth Dynasty with a rise in the importance of the local gods of the local nomarchs and a rise in the importance of Osiris. Before 2200 BC, during the last decades before the Old Kingdom collapsed, the *ka* double soul, the *ba* roaming soul and the *akh* transfigured soul, which at first only the gods and the pharaoh-gods possessed and which played indispensable roles in the afterlife, were granted to everybody. This was followed by the extension of afterlife privileges beyond the pharaoh and his family to the priests and notables. Another major aspect of the Osirisian revolution was thus achieved.

The next step in the Osirisian revolution, probably also achieved by the end of the Old Kingdom, was a virtual democratization of the afterlife, making it available to everybody, theoretically, including the lowest classes. The general demand for an afterlife must have been enormous. The heavy taxation imposed on the people to pay for the offerings needed to keep the royal and elite dead *alive in the afterlife* must have led them to reason that they too deserved a positive afterlife. This was logical enough — if the magic of the afterlife was not limited to the pharaoh-god, but could be extended even to non-members of his family, then surely it could be applicable to everybody.

The people's need for certitude of the afterlife also must have been accentuated by the period of dislocation and economic and political uncertainty opened by the collapse of the Old Kingdom and the anarchy occasioned by the absence of a central power during the First Intermediate Period.

By the opening of the First Intermediate Period, Osiris was the clear King of the Dead, the major savior god, for all Egyptians, for the entirety of the population. From this period, the savior god Osiris was intimately bound to the concepts of the Egyptian afterlife in the *Duat* Underworld and had become the ordinary man's connection to the gods. Osiris was also the central god in mankind's probable first attempt to link ethics and the afterlife with the establishment of a judgment in the "Hall of Two Maat," the "Hall of Two Truths." Despite Re's power, when it came to death and the afterlife, Osiris was now supreme. Despite continued respect for Re, immense fervor for Osiris can be seen in art and the Coffin Texts of this period.

At least from the beginning of the Middle Kingdom (c. 2055–1650 BC), it was an honor and an advantage to be buried in Osiris' city, Abydos. Several Middle Kingdom pharaohs built cenotaphs in Abydos and notables and ordinary people erected cenotaphs and steles. During the New Kingdom (c. 1550–1069 BC), pharaohs like Sety I and Rameses II built fabulous cenotaph temples in Abydos. The simulated pilgrimage of the mummified deceased to a holy Osiris site, like Abydos, was an essential funerary rite and even a prerequisite to winning an afterlife.

From perhaps as early as the Sixth Dynasty (c. 2345–2181 BC) and certainly from the beginning of the Twelfth Dynasty (c. 2055 BC), re-enactments of Osiris' good life, his treacherous murder by Seth, Isis' and Nephthys' quest and Osiris' mummification, funeral and resurrection were performed. These re-enactments were fervently celebrated and became one of the most popular annual Egyptian holidays and pilgrimages in the Abydos temple, in Denderah, Edfu, Busiris, Memphis, Philae and elsewhere. They took place during the agricultural sowing period from the 13th to 30th day of the *Choiak* fourth month of *akhet*, the inundation season. From the late fourth century BC, a recitation of the moving and loving *Lamentations of Isis and Nephthys* was added to the ceremony on the 25th day of *Choiak*. This was, of course, an ideal time for such ritual ceremonies in order to encourage the vegetation god Osiris to favor the growth of the sown seeds, mirroring his resurrection and spring renewal.

These re-enactments were fabulously elaborate at the Osiris Temple in Abydos. They involved hundreds of priests and priestesses in the roles of the gods and goddesses, 34 papyrus boats carrying the gods, an elaborate chest with a sculpture of Osiris inside, 365 ornamental lamps, incense, and dozens of amulets. The old fetish/amulet known as the *djed* column, which had become associated with Osiris' backbone, played a key role in the ceremonies.

The *djed* was associated with prehistoric tree worship as the trunk of a tree and perhaps with the grain harvest. It seems to have been first linked to Seker, an earth/fertility god and later the Memphite mummified death god, then to the crafts and creation god Ptah; finally it was linked to Osiris' spinal column and stability, strength and permanency. Tree worship was particularly strong in early Egypt. The raising, draping and anointing of a tree stump in many ritual variants is common to many societies with totemistic and shamanistic religious influences. In Egypt, this type of tree ritual seems to have been used in ceremonies in Memphis right from the beginning of the Old Kingdom (c. 2686 BC), as the ceremony of the raising of a *djed* pillar, dedicated to Ptah-Seker-Osiris was a key element in the pharaoh's *heb sed*, jubilee, ritual.

In its Osirisian variant, a huge sculpture of a *djed* was hoisted upright with ropes and stood there like a great tree symbolizing Osiris' spinal column, resurrection, the afterlife and endlessness. The *djed* was one of Egypt's main ritual emblems and *djed* figurines in faience were among the most popular personal amulets for use both in life and on mummies.

Given the *djed*'s attributes, it is easy enough to understand why it was so popular, but its very aspect also had (and continues to have!) considerable emotional impact. The *djed* seems to mysteriously project austere, elegant massiveness, strength, eternity and stability, just as a healthy tree or spinal column does and just as a massive stone column projects something which time least alters. It seems to eminently combine the qualities which amulets, in Egypt or elsewhere, must possess — protection and welfare and healing, *meket* and *wedja*.

Aside from the hoisting of the *djed* and the regal ceremonies of the boats, the Osiris re-enactments involved a bigger, and perhaps even biggest, part of secret ceremonies and rites in the inner temple of Abydos. These ceremonies were apparently centered on the cycles of the seasons and resurrection. It is also possible, but unverifiable, that secret Osirisian ceremonies took place in the out-of-bounds room that Sety I (c. 1294–1279 BC) built in his cenotaph temple or in the nearby Osireion Temple (or cenotaph) which Sety, or Merenptah (c. 1213– 1203 BC), may have built.

The Greeks called the Osirisian ceremonies "mysteries" and might have based their own mysteries in Eleusis, Delphi, Delos and elsewhere on these Osirisian reenactments, which in turn may have contributed to the invention of Greek theater and to so-called secret teachings.

Nevertheless, despite all this fervor and the fact that the right for everybody to have souls and an afterlife was clearly in effect, in practice the afterlife remained only virtual for most people. By the end of the Old Kingdom (c. 2181), being *aper*, "equipped," for the afterlife and maintaining oneself there with all its implications involved such high costs that it was reserved for the rich: probably not more than several hundred people per year. There was a profusion of magnificent tombs for the nobles, but tombs for the commoners remained elementary and makeshift. The wages in kind paid to craftsmen and peasants were usually just sufficient for subsistence; they could in no way cover the immense costs involved in the afterlife process. For the vast majority, there was no mummification; and burial continued to be in shallow graves at the edge of the western desert, with no tombs, but usually with some afterlife provisions. The crucial problem — how to muster the immense resources required to make the afterlife a credible reality — was never totally solved.

It was not until after the opening of the New Kingdom (c. 1550 BC) that the aspiration for an afterlife (thanks to the savior Osiris) and doing what was required to obtain it thoroughly infused all classes of Egyptian society. The emphasis on the afterlife was even more central than in previous periods, as illustrated by the great profusion of new funerary texts and funerary art. This development was certainly facilitated by the gradual improvement in mummification methods and a decrease in costs for the simplest categories of mummification. The desire for an afterlife seems to have been so ardent that even without lower costs it probably would have been widespread. Nevertheless, the quantitative limitations — the relativity — of this phenomenon must be emphasized once again: even if only a tiny percentage of tombs have so far been found, this number nevertheless indicates that all the requirements for an afterlife — mummification, elaborate funerary services and "equipment," funerary texts, *ka*-statues, *ush-abti*, tombs, goods and offerings — always remained the privilege of a minority.

The progressive rise of Egypt's most powerful and most amalgamating chief god, Amun, in Thebes, after about 2000 BC, not only did not affect Osiris' popularity, but gradually increased it as Thebes incorporated Heliopolitan theology. Osiris suffered a single setback in his status — a major eclipse in his worship during the brief reign of Egypt's proto-monotheistic pharaoh Akhenaten (c. 1352–1336 BC). For most of that time, the sun disk, the Aten, was imposed as the sole god and official policy eliminated Osiris' role as King of the Dead and the afterlife in favor of the intercessor role of Akhenaten himself. Osiris' role and the merger of Re solar and Osirisian afterlife concepts resumed after the Atenist interlude.

From then on to the end of Egyptian history, the beloved Osiris played a key role. It can be supposed that fervor for Osiris was immense. In any case, the Greek writers who visited Egypt, and notably Herodotus around 440 BC and Plutarch in the early first century AD, independently reported it in those times to be awesome and almost hysterical. The Greek occupiers of Egypt (from 332 BC) built shrines linked to Osiris in all 42 nomes of Egypt. During the Greek Ptolemaic Period, it is said there were 158 shrines to Osiris in Egypt. By this time Osiris had more than 200 titles and names, beginning of course with *Wennefer*, the completed, perpetually, eternally or continuously good or perfect being. In fact, if not in theology, Osiris was the most popular god in Egypt even if his wife Isis and their child Horus constantly increased their popularity.

HISTORY'S FIRST SAVIOR GOD

The concept that the afterlife was for everybody and not just for the politico-religious leader, the pharaoh-god, and then his entourage, was a huge innovation for Egypt and for the history of humanity.

If the afterlife is accessible to everybody, it is only a short step away to conclude that there is a savior behind this marvelous event. And with Osiris, the extraordinary notion of a personal savior was indeed inaugurated in the history of religion. Osiris evolved from being the identity of eternal life for the pharaohs, who in any case were gods and entitled to immortality, into a savior for all Egyptians, a provider of eternal life. All Egyptians could become the god Osiris upon death, just like the pharaohs. A personal savior who could fix things up and defeat death had been invented.

For the first time in history, with Osiris a god not only had effects on the collectivity and through the collectivity on the individual, he had a direct savior role for the individual who could implore his benevolence and take advantage of what he represented. In Osiris' case, this meant the afterlife, salvation through the afterlife.

This key role was accentuated by the benevolence of Osiris' character. As the good and just god, the *Wennefer*, he was the god who taught the people agriculture, taught them to be good and who wanted them to do the *maat* in more than just its meaning of primeval order.

Until the rise of Osiris, relations between the Egyptians and their gods were basically relations of rigid subservience. With Osiris, relations between a god and man became partially warm and affectionate. It was the afterlife promise he represented and these qualities of warmth that made Osiris the world's first savior god.

Osiris was the wild card of hope for the royalty and the notables, but also for the ordinary people in a rough-and-tumble world. Osiris was hope, just as the later Jesus represented immeasurable hope.

However, it must be emphasized that the Egyptian religious system based on materialistic acts and on magic did not collapse with the advent of the savior *Wennefer* Osiris — it was merely dented. The correct performance of magical mummification and funerary rituals, the building of a solid, well-provisioned tomb, magical funerary texts, and curses and threats to prevent desecration of the tomb remained as vital as Osiris' benevolence and affection. These material and magical acts remained far more important in obtaining a positive afterlife than what today we would qualify as personal morality. And, of course, the gods alongside Osiris, from the pharaoh-god up to Re, still demanded servility.

Nevertheless, with Osiris, we are indeed in the presence of a total national and personal savior god, a pre-eschatology and an attempt to link ethics, or at least orderly and decent behavior, and the afterlife. Salvation from death is being offered and we are also near to the key Christian concept of the physical healing power of the savior Jesus in this life.

However, we are obviously still far from the moral aspects of the Christian monotheistic savior notions, where love and salvation are for the good people, the moral people, provided through an afterlife Paradise. The Persian and Christian moral notions provided total salvation and bliss for the righteous in the next life. For the Egyptians and Osiris, love and forgiveness for sinners were irrelevant; for the Christians, they are fundamental. We are also nowhere near the Christian concept that the savior Jesus sacrificed himself and died to redeem all people, including so-called non-Jewish *goyim* or "pagans," that is, everybody.

The Osiris savior god concept was surely one of the prime examples of infantilism in the history of religion, only surpassed by the saviors who followed him. It is in no way facetious to note that even with the Egyptian population levels of the time — perhaps, as we have seen, about a million-and-a-half people in the Old Kingdom — it was an act of fundamental dishonesty and trickery to inculcate the idea that a god was able to personally attend to the needs of so many people and that everybody upon death could become Osiris. But it was also obviously a stroke of genius because the concept of the personal savior was not only gullibly believed in Egypt, but also took hold in Judaism, Christianity and Islam. It was also developed independently at later dates and in other forms in Hinduism and Buddhism. Obviously, the concept of the personal savior became a basic worldwide belief, largely through autonomous development; but the role of Egyptian influence may have been considerable.

The invention of the savior god defied any kind of common sense. The idea of such a personal savior (even assisted by an immense administrative staff!) was quite simply ludicrous and impossible. It is no exaggeration to say that even if unaccountable millions sincerely believed, and still sincerely believe today, in a personal savior god, this concept was, and still is, a key method of political and sociological control to keep people in line and prevent them from trying to be free. Once again, and starting in Egypt, human yearning and need were so great that totally unverifiable and outrageously crude magic won the day.

THE MERGER OF RE SOLAR AND OSIRIS CHTHONIAN THEOLOGIES

The Old Kingdom Heliopolitan theologians had succeeded in pulling off a masterful coup. They had not only gained an afterlife for themselves, but they had enormously increased their own power and wealth. Furthermore, in merging Egypt's two main myths, the Busiris and Abydos Osirisian death/resurrection/afterlife myth and the Heliopolitan Re solar cult/pharaonic afterlife myth, they had resolved the divine and theological rivalry of Osiris and Re. This solved one of Egypt's thorniest theological problems and perhaps some of its political rivalries between regions. The Heliopolitan theologians had imposed Re as the royal god and chief god of the nation and Osiris as the chief god of the land of the dead. What had perhaps begun as a power struggle between the powerful Heliopolitan theologians and the pharaohs eventually resulted in encouraging — probably unwittingly — the extension of the concept of the afterlife to all and in conciliating the sky and chthonian contradictions of Egyptian religion.

The harmonization of the Re solar afterlife beliefs designed for the pharaoh-gods and the new Osirisian *Duat* underworld, chthonian, afterlife rights which had been won by all the people was surely one of the most difficult problems which the Heliopolitan priests had to face. Moreover, when everybody became an Osiris upon death, and not just the pharaoh-god, theological contortions were required to organize a superior place for the dead pharaoh. The solution to these problems led to a subtle and paradoxical turning point in Egyptian theology.

Heroes, in prehistory as now, always received special afterlife treatment. In the case of Egypt's heroes — the pharaoh-gods — they variously went to the sky, to "the East," to a celestial "Field of Reeds," to an "imperishable star," to the sun, to "lightland," to Re. However, for tens of thousands of years, belief in an afterlife and its access in general were through burial; they were chthonian, something of the earth and the underworld.

With the advent of the Neolithic Age, the earth was being mastered by agriculture and technology and was becoming somewhat less of a mystery. It was perhaps in this context that the Egyptians saw the afterlife for their heroes, especially their king-gods, as being linked to the sky, the heavens, the sun and the stars, which were unknown and unconquered.

As we have seen, the Egyptian approach to reality was descriptive — they described what and who they saw, or rather what they believed they were seeing. We know from the first Pyramid Texts (from c. 2375 BC) and from even earlier tomb inscriptions that the Egyptians believed that the circumpolar stars, *Ikhemu Seku* ("The Imperishable Stars") were "eternal" since they never seemed to move, they never disappeared from view. Therefore, the *Duat*, the afterlife, for the pharaohs was first of all in these "eternal" stars and even as a star itself. But with the rise of Re solar worship, the Egyptians also observed that Re, the sun, crossed the sky and then disappeared beneath the horizon in the west, something which led them to conclude that the *Duat* was in the western underground. Gradually, the afterlife came to be seen as being in the west, a west in the underground or in the sky.

Egyptian Heliopolitan Re sun cult theologians apparently accentuated both primitive *seba*, star, and sun worship, and the look upwards to the heavens for a solution to the mysteries experienced by man on earth. Osiris had major sky characteristics as the "imperishable" star Sah, Orion, and in the Pyramid Texts, the dead pharaoh became Osiris in the sky, but Osiris' original and basic attributes were rooted in chthonian/agricultural beliefs in the earth and the underworld. These chthonian beliefs were incorporated into Heliopolitan theology and coalesced with the concept that Re nightly disappeared into the underworld.

This turning point in Egypt was accompanied by great theological confusion. The pyramids are clearly a tomb design which was an outcome of sky/ sun worship. The first pyramid at Sakkara, the Step Pyramid, built around 2660 BC, was most probably a staircase to the sky, a celestial staircase to the "imperishable, eternal" circumpolar stars, just as the earlier Sumerian platform temples and the later *ziggurats* reached to the sky. As clearly indicated in the Pyramid Texts, the pyramids were also linked to sky/sun/soul/afterlife concepts for the pharaoh. These two crucial concepts, sky and pharaoh, had to be adapted with the rise of the chthonian Osirisian cult when soul privileges were gradually extended to everybody and the *Duat* afterlife was essentially located for ordinary people in the underworld.

The Egyptian solar worship concept of an afterlife based on the simple observation that the sun always sets and rises, dies and is reborn, and the Osirisian agricultural afterlife concept based on the simple observation that spring agricultural rebirth and the inundation of the Nile always follow winter death, were complementary rather than contradictory. However, theological acrobatics had to be employed to conciliate the contradiction between the star/sun worship version of the afterlife in the sky, invented for the pharaoh-god, and the chthonian/agricultural version in the underworld of the earth, which was eventually applicable to everybody.

And now there were two ways of looking at this key question — a further major contradiction: the sun was omnipotent and yet now no longer entirely omnipotent when it came to the afterlife. This merger of Re Heliopolitan solar cult and afterlife theology with Osirisian chthonian/agricultural afterlife theology put a theoretical end to these contradictions, but in practice produced a confused result.

This confusion was particularly evident during the Middle Kingdom (beginning c. 2055 BC), when the magical afterlife spells of the Coffin Texts replaced the magical utterances of the Pyramid Texts. There were now several contradictory afterlife possibilities and combinations — in the east in the sky, in "lightland," as a star, as Orion, in a wonderful *Aaru*, "The Field of Reeds" which was sometimes in the sky and sometimes in the underworld, in the *Duat*, in the west, the *Amenta*, the *Khert-Netjer*, the divine place below in an underworld agricultural land of plenty, in the tomb with all one's earthly possessions and near the tomb. Immortality involved the body and some of its several souls living with the gods in the sky and some of these souls roaming about, including for temporary visits to the living.

The Middle Kingdom notables, with their newly gained afterlife privileges, clearly sought to imitate the afterlife procedures of the pharaohs which had been applicable only to them and some of their "great royal wives" as described in the Pyramid Texts. Many of the 1185 spells in the Coffin Texts (according to R.O. Faulkner's recension) describe a magical ascension to the sky and a joining with Re, as previously described in the Pyramid Texts, but also visits to the living. Spell 118 says: "I may go up into the Night bark and that I may go down into the Day bark, that I may judge in the crew of Re." Spell 149 says: "Becoming a human falcon...I have demanded a shape as a human falcon that I may walk as a man and go forth from hence, no god having hindered me. I am a human falcon who walks as a man and who is not opposed."

However, the notables who used these spells also sought to please and be identified with Osiris, simultaneously as the "imperishable" star Sah (that is, the Orion constellation), but also as the King of the Dead in the netherworld afterlife and this without impinging on Re's prerogatives. Spell 399 says: "Orion and the Great Bear are ready." Spell 695 says: "Burial in the West as a blessed...in order that he may go down to his possessions...stand in the presence of Osiris...my seat is his desert, the western desert is my horizon." Spell 330 puts great hope in Osiris: "I live and I die, I am Osiris. I have gone in and out by means of you, I have grown fat through you, I flourish through you." Spell 1130/1031 mingles hopes in Re and Osiris: "I shall shine and be seen every day as a dignitary of the All-Lord (Re) having given satisfaction to the Weary-hearted (Osiris). I shall sail rightly in my bark, I am lord of eternity in the crossing of the sky...As for any person who knows this spell, he will be like Re in the eastern sky, like Osiris in the netherworld."

And just as the pharaohs in the Pyramid Texts had simultaneously identified with the gods, threatened them and even sometimes pretended to be stronger than them, the notables in the Coffin Texts used the same stratagems. Spell 75 says: "I have come into being from the flesh of the self-created god, I am merged in the god, I have become he...I am stronger and more raging than all the Enneads." Spell 764 even appropriates the pharaoh's *henmemet*, the sun folk, the personal guards and attendants of the king in his resurrection process in the sky: "Ho N (the name of the deceased)! The watchers of the gods shall attend on you, those who are in their primeval state shall fear you, those who are in their towns shall dread you...the multitudinous sun-folk who are in the god's castle shall rejoice at you...for you are the great god...you shall mount up to Re in the sky and the gods who are in it will obey you for the power of the Foremost of the Westerners (Osiris) has been given to you."[5]

Despite this confused and amalgamated situation, in practice the Re solar cult afterlife principles continued to be applied to the pharaohs, even if they also became Osirises, and the Osirisian underworld concepts (together with fantasies about becoming like the dead pharaoh-god in the sky) increasingly provided an afterlife for the notables and rich commoners.

---

5. Faulkner, R.O., *The Ancient Egyptian Coffin Texts, Volume* I, pp.110, 127, *Volume II*, pp. 41-42, 260, Volume I, p. 254, Lichtheim, Miriam, *Ancient Egyptian Literature, Volume* I, pp. 132-133, Faulkner, R.O., *The Ancient Egyptian Coffin Texts*, Volume I, p. 72 and *Volume II*, pp. 294-295.

The dead pharaoh-god survived during the day cruising around the stars in the sky identified with Re in the *Mandet* solar bark — "the bark of millions of years" propelled by *heka*, magic — and then during the night descended into the underworld *Duat* in the *Meseket* bark with Osiris — as the *ba* night-sun aspect of Re — at the helm. The solar boat re-emerged at daybreak with Re and the pharaoh at the helm.

As for the ordinary dead — or at least those able to afford the pre-requisite "equipment" for the afterlife — they were Osirises, and basically lived in the underworld, although several of their souls, notably the *ba*, lived with the gods in the skies and also roamed about, both for visits to their resurrected bodies and for temporary outings to the world of the living.

The ideal situation for ordinary people seems to have been spending the day near one's tomb in the underworld *Duat*, with occasional visits to the living and sometimes even spending the night with Osiris, as Orion, or cruising in the *Meseket* bark identified with Osiris as the night sun aspect of Re.

This last and important option was possible because the Heliopolitan theologians, never lacking in inventiveness, had decreed that Osiris was the *ba* aspect of Re, the night sun of Re, and that the Heliopolitan sacred animal, the *benu* heron, previously assimilated with Re, was an aspect of Osiris. Furthermore, the *ba* of Re status had considerable importance for Osiris since he had now gained the solar attributes which all Egyptian gods needed if they were to embark on a major national career. Osiris was now simultaneously the chthonian King of the *Duat* Underworld, the star Orion and the night sun of Re.

Such views particularly prospered during the New Kingdom (c. 1550-1069 BC). In fact, it was probably not before the Third Intermediary Period (c. 1069–747 BC) that it is possible to speak about a synthesis between solar and Osirisian afterlife beliefs in which the body of common beliefs was greater than differences. This incredibly confused solution, with its variable afterlife systems and the survival of companion souls, did not stop the Egyptians, whatever their social class, from increasingly believing in the afterlife; indeed, in typical Egyptian fashion, they even added further possibilities and complications. This was notably true in the New Kingdom with the addition of numerous new funerary texts.

In the Late Period (beginning c. 747 BC), still another twist was added with many women seeking to become assimilated with the love and mother goddess Hathor upon death rather than with Osiris, perhaps because Hathor had become virtually identified with the warm, consoling Mother Goddess *par excellence* Isis, or perhaps because some Egyptian women were engaged in a prefiguration of a feminist movement.

A PRE-ESCHATOLOGY OFFERS AN AFTERLIFE FOR ALL WHO COULD AFFORD IT

The merger of Re and Osirisian theologies provided a theological foundation for the apex of the Osirisian revolution, for a pre-eschatology, or primitive eschatology which opened the road to the problem of a final destiny for man as raised by the later monotheistic eschatologies. The Egyptians were unable to go further than a pre-eschatology because they did not envisage that there might be a meaning and a linear development to something called history involving a final destiny for the world and mankind. The problem of altering this destiny was therefore irrelevant to them.

The Egyptians did not perceive the need for radical change, for convincing solutions to the problems of suffering and evil, for a final moral corrective and reward. Evil and suffering were not sufficient causes to provoke a change either in this basically pleasant world or in the destiny of mankind. The Egyptians sought to maintain the existing order of the world, not to change it, as did the later monotheisms.

For the Egyptians, the permanent, unchangeable, pre-ordained *maat* universal order founded by the gods functioned perfectly — on the condition that the pharaoh and his priests daily performed the correct magical rituals and applied the correct laws to prevent *izfeh*, disorder, chaos. If these conditions were met, the gods, the cosmos, the seasonal cycles, the earth, Egypt and the people and their relationship with the gods and between themselves were all part of a positive harmony and natural justice.

The later Persians, Hebrews, Christians and Moslems (and the Hindus, using their own system of reincarnation and *nirvana* based on moral worth) strongly felt that harmony based on absolute justice was not of this world. Eschatology — a final resurrection, a final judgment and final rewards and punishments — was the invention of the Persians in the sixth century BC and quickly spread. However, it does not seem to have played any significant role in Persian-occupied Egypt from 525 BC. It did not really take hold in Egypt until the massive Christian conversion of the Egyptians during the third century AD and then the massive conversion to Islam beginning in the mid-seventh century AD.

For the Egyptians, eternal life in the *Duat* afterlife was *wehem ankh*, repeating life; it was not an improvement; it was primarily a natural due which could be had if the correct magic and correct material techniques were used. Nevertheless, the idea that decent behavior in society was part of the natural harmony constituted the beginnings of a moral reward. The Osirisian revolution was an immense revolution for its time and its pre-eschatology certainly contributed to the gradual elaboration of eschatology with more elaborate salvation doctrines and systems of ethical, rather than magical, judgment after death and Paradise and Hell.

The Osirisian revolution constituted the crowning achievement in the Egyptian polytheistic system. Resurrection and the afterlife, a savior god and the possibility of a link between decency and religion had perfected the Egyptian religion into the most complex religious system ever invented until then. Its repercussions were enormous.

In economic terms, it constituted a second economy which was frequently as productive, or even more productive, than the everyday economy. In technology, it provided sanctification for agriculture, irrigation and the crafts. In art and architecture, it sparked unprecedented prolificacy. In political terms, it constituted one of the key frameworks and structures of society.

Perhaps the only thing that the astute Heliopolitan theologians never deigned to explain about their composite, subtle and paradoxical system was how all this mumbo jumbo of different types of afterlives and several separately surviving souls could possibly work, could possibly make any sense to anybody.

And yet, the Heliopolitan theologians were not only clearly right in assuming that all Egyptians (or almost all of them) would spontaneously believe their theology, this theology survived and was fanatically believed for three thousand years right into the opening centuries of our era. Other poetical, erroneous solutions — even if they were more spiritual and more moral — then came into vogue, like the Hebrew and the Christian soul/afterlife solutions.

In Egypt, the search for a solution to the central problem of death had been found — or, at least, it had been proposed and believed. And, it applied to everyone. However, the great divide between the royal religion and the people's religion extended into the afterlife. Given Egypt's stiff hierarchical society, it would be too good to be true to expect equality in the afterlife. In practice, the solution to the problem of death had been found only for those who could afford to be *aper*, "equipped" for survival in the afterlife. That required mummification, a solid tomb, fine clothing, furnishings, paintings, *ka*-statues and magical funerary texts. Being "equipped" in this way was not easily attainable for most commoners. Moreover, if a commoner was somehow able to afford this "equipment," that still did not mean an idyllic existence in the other world; the life one found in the *Duat* more or less corresponded to the rank one had held in life. It was not unusual for ordinary people to have to do farm work in the *Duat* because, while alive, they had not had the resources to pay craftsmen to sculpt *ushabtis* to do the work for them. The great divide represented by the need to be "equipped," including full or partial mummification, tombs, salvation doctrines and the numerous souls of a person, was gradually but never fully and coherently bridged.

Nevertheless, the very existence of an afterlife for everybody, and not just for the pharaoh, seems, from the Middle Kingdom (c. 2055–1650 BC), to have favored an improvement in social justice for all in this life. However, this improvement did not affect the rigid hierarchical nature of society or the belief that fulfilling one's assigned role in society according to one's position in the hierarchy and that magic, rather than morality, were the keys to winning an afterlife.

Despite all this, the important point is that a pre-eschatology had been invented. The coupling of the concept of living in the right way, the decent way, of the Osiris afterlife/salvation system with the *maat* primeval order was prodigiously new and audacious. A judgment based not only on *maat* as living according to the pre-ordained system of universal order, but also on *maat* moral obligations in this life for earning an afterlife was created, even if it was not respected and was perverted by magic.

As we shall soon see, the judgment in "The Hall of Two Truths" was a huge fake, but it may have well given ideas to other peoples — almost probably, to the Hebrews in their linking of ethics and God and perhaps to the Persians in inventing the Final Judgment. The Egyptians were the first people to sketch out the caveat that one faces the consequences in the next life if decency, or moral obligations, in this life are not respected. A crude answer to a fundamental question, the problem of evil and unjustified suffering in the world, was put on the agenda of mankind.

THE FIRST PEOPLE TO FLIRT WITH A LINK BETWEEN RELIGION, THE AFTERLIFE AND ETHICS

The flirtation with the notions that moral conduct might be a key factor in winning a satisfying afterlife and that wrongdoing would be sanctioned by a judgment involving a horrible "second death" brought Egypt to the brink of a major breakthrough in the history of mankind. Egypt almost invented Paradise as a moral reward, by almost solving the problem of sanctioning evil and suffering in this world.

Egypt attempted to meet this challenge, and failed. They took the preliminary steps in this direction, but somehow did not manage to construct a genuine link between morality and the afterlife.

The afterlife now no longer just happened, it was no longer just a matter of burial with provisions of goods, weapons and food for the hereafter and the organization of a funeral service. It was no longer an utterly indifferent, neutral and even dismal place, virtually incorporeal and cut off from other humans and the gods like the Sumerian *Kur*. Entry into the *Duat* afterlife and an eternally positive stay there could be carefully prepared and won well in advance of actual death. The *Duat*, and its magnificent *Aaru* Field of the Reeds and Lake of Flowers, was a place of true eternity, of the everlasting continuation of the life one had had on earth. The name for eternity was *shenu*, the same name as the royal cartouche of divine identity, which was round and without end.

Because the Egyptians were more preoccupied with death, with what happens after death to the body and its souls, and with the material well-being of the dead than any people before them (or after them), it was logical that they came so close to inventing the notion of Paradise as a place of physical contentment. It was just as logical that with their central animistic, magical outlook they did not fully implement the one further step — authentic moral judgment involving authentic moral recompense or punishment — which would have transformed their notion of the afterlife into a morally earned spiritual Paradise.

The astonishing thing is that they did invent the necessary moral system and recompense by gradually re-interpreting the meaning and role of goddess Maat. The Old Kingdom (c. 2686–2181 BC) *ankh-em-maat*, "living by *maat*," gradually came to mean not only respecting the primeval order, but doing the decent thing, the ethical thing in this life. The invention of a confession and a judgment in the "Hall of Two Maat" and the proclamation of a reward of immortality, of eternally and happily repeating life, *wehem ankh*, and a sanction for wrong behavior, dying a second time, *mit em nem*, theoretically set the stage for a comprehensive moral system.

It is not astonishing, given the Egyptian mentality, that they preferred *heka*, magic, and even blatant trickery, to the radical concept of morality to obtain an afterlife. They paid only lip service to the *maat* as an ethical concept because they pragmatically believed that *heka* was more efficient than an ethical interpretation of *maat*. The ancient Egyptian basically believed that no matter what kind of life he had led he could buy his way into the afterlife with the purchase of mummification, solid tombs, statues, *ushabti*, amulets and spells.

The very origin of the *maat* concept and the goddess Maat as the primeval personifications of magical cosmic, universal order was a barrier to establishing an independent ethical system. In fact, the usual translation of *ankh-em-maat* as "living by truth," doing the ethical thing, and the translation of "The Hall of Two Maat" as "Two Truths" frequently might be better translated using the term "order," for "Maat," rather than "truth." Especially for the pharaoh, the governor of the *maat*, *ankh-em-maat* probably originally meant that he had to respect the divine code of laws and rituals favoring universal harmony under the threat of causing the opposite of order, *maat*, that is disorder, *izfeh*. *Ankh-em-maat* meant living in conformity to the gods and to nature, which were the same things. Seen this way, *ankh-em-maat* always had more to do with living decently according to society's needs and within the pre-ordained universal and natural order than living ethically, "living in truth," as we understand this term today. However, in its most evolved forms, *maat* nevertheless represented highly decent and charitable behavior in society and at its maximum, an attempt at doing the ethical thing.

Many Egyptologists, and notably Cyril Aldred (1914–1991), in *Akhenaten: King of Egypt*, have correctly pointed out that it is "an over-simplification" to translate *ankh-em-maat* as somebody living by "truth" or morality. In his earlier *Akhenaten: Pharaoh of Egypt*, Aldred said, "...more has been read into this phrase than the words warrant. By *Maet* was meant the established order of things as they had existed at the creation of the world and not some abstract principle of verity"... that is, "the proper cosmic order at the time of its establishment by the Creator...by the gods [who] had first ruled Egypt after creating it perfect..."[6]

Translating *ankh-em-maat* solely as "living by truth" was a mistake that William Matthew Flinders Petrie (1853–1942), James Henry Breasted (1865– 1935), John A. Wilson (1899–1976) and a host of other eminent Egyptologists made with disconcerting consistency. Miriam Lichtheim (b. 1914), arguably the finest Egyptian translator, leaned in the right direction by systematically rendering *ankh-em-maat* as "lives by Maat" and indicating that it meant "divine order" before meaning "justice" and "rightness." Lichtheim also took into account that *maat* implied "the affirmation of moral worth."[7]

Both Nicolas Grimal (b. 1948) and Erik Hornung (b. 1933) adopted the wider view of *maat*, which takes into account both its origin and its evolution. Grimal noted that Maat "is not so much a goddess as an abstract entity...enabling [the universe] to conform to its true nature." For Grimal, "the basis of Egyptian morality was a respect for universal equilibrium, personified by the goddess Maat, against whom human conduct always had to be measured." Hornung sees "The concept of *maat*" in "its complexity" as "the order, the just measure of things, that underlies the world; it is the perfect state of things toward which one should strive and which is in harmony with the creator god's intentions....Maat symbolizes the partnership of god and man..." Aldred also saw a "partnership" in the *maat* concept: "Only continuous worship of the mysterious powers could keep the universe in an equilibrium favorable to the survival of

---

6. Aldred, Cyril, *Akhenaten, King of Egypt*, p. 111 and *Akhenaten, Pharaoh of Egypt – a new study*, p. 28.

7. Lichtheim, Miriam, *Ancient Egyptian Literature, Volume I*, pp. 4, 239, 245 and *Volume II*, p. 7.

man and his institutions. It was the constant affirmation of the pharaoh, the divine king who presided over the destiny of Egypt and its people, that he had restored the harmony (*maet*) of an ideal world as it had been established at the First Time, but which could easily be jangled out of tune by human neglect or wrongdoing."[8]

It was perhaps the incisive Henri Frankfort (1897–1954) who best summarized the various meanings and mysteries of *maat* (as with so many other Egyptian concepts): "...it [*maat*] is a concept belonging as much to cosmology as to ethics. It is justice as the divine order of society, but it is also the divine order of nature as established at the time of creation...We must sometimes translate 'order', sometimes 'truth', sometimes 'justice'; and the opposite of Maat requires a similar variety of renderings...The laws of nature, the laws of society, and the divine commands all belong to the one category of what is right."[9]

Maat was one of the oldest Egyptian goddesses and supposedly the daughter of the sun god Re and the wife of the Moon and Wisdom God Thoth. She clearly originated as the goddess of the truth of what constitutes the primeval universal order, rather than of truth in an ethical sense. She was the divine order that had been created at *zep tepey*, "the first time" or "first occasion," the time of creation. She ordained the correct movement of the stars across the sky and the change of seasons, as well as "correct" behavior. It was this concept of universal order, natural justice and "wisdom" which Maat first embodied before moral justice and ethical considerations were gradually added to her attributes. The ethical aspects of her attributes never became more important than the magical view of the universe that she represented.

Despite her probable origins in the usually animal-headed gods and goddesses of the Predynastic Period (before c. 3100 BC), she was most often portrayed in human form with an ostrich feather, the *shut*, in her hair, sometimes with an ostrich feather instead of a head and sometimes just as a feather or a pedestal. The oldest pictogram of Maat is a pedestal-throne representing rigor and rectitude — in other words, rigorous respect of the natural laws so that the gods can play their roles and *izfeh*, disorder, is prevented. The pedestal is also sometimes interpreted as depicting the primeval mound, the *benben*, from which the gods and creation arose.

Whatever interpretation one makes of the pedestal pictogram and its personification of a situation of perfection, Maat was an abstract reality rather than

---

8. Grimal, Nicolas, *A History of Ancient Egypt*, pp. 47 and 153, Hornung, Erik, *Conceptions of God in Ancient Egypt, The One and the Many*, pp. 213 and 25 and Aldred, Cyril, *Egyptian Art*, p. 11.

9. Frankfort, Henri, *Ancient Egyptian Religion, An Interpretation*, p. 54.

stricto sensu a nature goddess. She was the only Egyptian divinity truly created on the basis of an idea, of an abstract principle, and together with Hu, god of creative utterance, Sia, god of perception, and Heka, god of magic, she represents one of few deities in the Egyptian pantheon who are not directly personifications of elements in physical nature.

Even in the early part of the Old Kingdom (c. 2686–2181 BC) when the *maat* was still essentially the theological concept of natural order, there were also interpretations of *maat* which were clearly moral. This was especially true for the "Wisdom Texts," the *sebayt*, the "instructions" from a father to his son," even if these texts always basically remained a guide on how to live expediently and successfully in Egypt's hierarchical society, as well as how to live decently.

The oldest surviving *sebayt* dates to about 2550 BC (*The Instruction of Prince Hardjedef*) and the most famous is *The Instruction of Ptahhotep*. The exact date for the composition of *The Instruction of Ptahhotep* is uncertain. Ptahhotep was described as a vizier in Pharaoh Djedkare Izezi's time (c. 2414–2375 BC) and the text is preserved on three papyri and a wooden tablet, the best copy being the Prisse Papyrus dating from the Middle Kingdom (c. 2055–1650 BC and now in the Paris Bibliothèque Nationale). While it is doubtful that the text actually dates to Pharaoh Djedkare's reign, there are reasons to believe that the original version can be dated to the Sixth Dynasty (c. 2345–2181 BC), before being rewritten in the Middle Kingdom when concern about the obligation to live correctly in society in order to win an afterlife reflected the anchoring of afterlife rights for everybody.

Despite an emphasis on pragmatic, expedient and even servile behavior in a hierarchical society, *The Instruction of Ptahhotep* clearly dealt with moral values. It indicated that acting justly, morally, charitably, with the heart, and equitably, in government, in justice and in individual life had permanent results. Ptahhotep proclaimed: "Justice is great and its appropriateness is lasting. It has not been disturbed since the time of him who made it, (whereas) there is punishment for him who passes over its laws...Wrongdoing has never brought its undertaking into port."[10]

The Instruction for King Merikare (advice of a king governing from Herakleopolis to his son, during the First Intermediate Period, Ninth/Tenth Dynasties, c. 2160–2025 BC, inscribed on the Leningrad Papyrus, dating from the middle to the end of the Eighteenth Dynasty, perhaps from about 1300 to 1295 BC) went further than *The Instruction of Ptahhotep*. Decent behavior, at least if really human, *remet*, Egyptians and not "wretched Asiatics" were concerned, was more important than animal sacrifice in obtaining eternal life "like a god": "The council [the

---

10. Wilson, John in *Ancient Near Eastern Texts Relating to the Old Testament*, p. 412.

afterlife court Hall of Two Truths] which judges the deficient, knowest that they are not lenient on that day of judging the miserable...More acceptable is the character of one upright of heart than the ox of the evildoer." And this was said perhaps 1600 years before the Hebrew prophet Jeremiah (c. 650–570 BC) proclaimed the superiority of morality and love of God over animal sacrifice and ritual! In *The Instruction For King Merikare*, decent behavior in itself is positive: "A good demeanor is a man's heaven...Be not evil...Do justice whilst thou endurest upon earth."[11]

The Eighteenth Dynasty (c. 1550–1295) *Instruction of Ani* gives abundant advice on expedient and servile behavior, but it is also a model of decent, moral behavior: "Double the food which thou givest to thy mother and carry her as she carried (thee)...Thou shouldst not eat bread when another is waiting and thou dost not stretch forth thy hand to the food for him."[12]

Certainly the authors of Wisdom Texts had moral concerns which over the centuries progressively constituted a more moral interpretation of the *maat*. Unquestionably, they went beyond the concept of decent behavior as required for living in society, but they nevertheless always also remained manuals of correct behavior, of practical, and servile, self-interest. Phrases of this kind abound in the Wisdom Texts — Ptahhotep: "If thou art one of those sitting at the table of one greater than thee...let they face be cast down until he addresses thee..." Amennemope (c. 1186–1069 BC): "Do not eat bread before a noble." Amenemhet (c. 1985–1955): "Hold thyself apart from those subordinate to [thee]..." Ani: "Be on guard against a woman from abroad who is not known in her [own] town." "The horse slips into its harness, Obedient it goes outdoors, The dog obeys the word, And walks behind its master..." etc.[13]

It also seems wrong to believe that the Wisdom Texts at any time discarded the interpretation of *maat* as respect for primeval order, as doing what was conventionally right for the universe and for society. It seems impossible to interpret the Wisdom Texts as proof that moral principles were fundamentally more important than the primeval order and magic. The Wisdom Texts and their moral preoccupations seem to be exceptions to an overriding atmosphere of generalized lip service to *maat* as a moral principle.

This can be abundantly seen, not only from the previous Pyramid and Coffin Texts, but also especially from the New Kingdom (c. 1550–1069 BC) *Book of the Dead*. Egypt did not have a central body of writings like the Hebrew and

---

11. *Ibid.*, pp. 415 and 417.

12. *Ibid.*, pp. 420 and 421.

13. *Ibid.*, pp. 412, 424, 418 and 420 and Lichtheim, Miriam, *Ancient Egyptian Literature, Volume II*, p. 144.

Christian Bibles (the *Tanakh* and *New Testament*), the Hindu *Vedas* and *Mahabharata*, the Zoroastrian *Avesta* or the Moslem *Koran*, but if one ancient Egyptian book has to be chosen as being central to their beliefs and rituals, it would be *The Book of the Dead.*

The Book of the Dead (a more precise translation is *The Book of Coming Forth by Day*) probably first appeared in papyrus form, with colored illustrations, known as vignettes, after 1550 BC. However, more than half of the 200 magical spells in *The Book of the Dead* first appeared in the magical utterances of the Pyramid Texts (from c. 2375) and in Coffin Texts (from c. 2345 BC). The early Pyramid Texts versions were repeated in the Coffin Texts, frequently with dashes of even greater fantasy and more extravagant laudations for the gods in the magical efforts to obtain an afterlife.

The Book of the Dead fully assumes the heritage of the Pyramid and Coffin Texts. It is perhaps the supreme illustration of the consistent and incredible Egyptian effort to magically, rather than morally or spiritually, defeat death. In contradistinction to the central texts of all other religions, *The Book of the Dead* was not basically a book of ethics or spirituality. It was unquestionably a book of magic, of mind-boggling, absurd, hocus-pocus spells, incantations and threats. Despite its poetic flights, the bottom line of *The Book of the Dead*, just like the previous Pyramid and Coffin Texts and the later funerary texts, staggeringly exemplified a type of religion which was not only based on magic and materialistic techniques, but saw no harm in using trickery and lies to obtain the essential: not dying a second time, staying alive and flourishing in the *Duat* and coming out for visits. *The Book of the Dead* carried the hocus-pocus notions of the past, rather than morality, to one of its apexes in the history of man.

The basic goal of *The Book of the Dead* was to outline the magical incantations, spells, prayers, rituals, threats, trickery and techniques for use during the negative confession and judgment in the Hall of Two Truths Court, in the journey fraught with obstacles, dangers and terrible demons to the *Duat* "Other Land," for not dying a second time and prosperous survival in the *Duat* and for enabling one's *ba* soul to make journeys to the land of the living. *The Book of the Dead* combined all the key tendencies of Egyptian afterlife beliefs — star cult, solar cult and Osirisian afterlife theology, mummification, funerary preparations and *heka* spells and amulets. The end of E.A. Wallis Budge's translation of *The Book of the Dead* composed for the Eighteenth Dynasty (c. 1550– 1069 BC) *sesh*, scribe Ani, clearly sums it all up: "Make thou for me a seat for those who are in the Underworld...and who are among those who [endure] for millions of millions of years...Mayest thou grant unto the *ka* of Osiris Ani [the power] to go into and come forth from the underworld; and suffer him not to be driven back at the gates of the *Tuat*."[14]

The Book of the Dead was specially written and painted with vignettes for each individual who could afford to have a personal copy made and inscribed with his name. Its very presence in the tomb magically ensured protection and prosperity in the *Duat*. Above all, *The Book of the Dead* was bought from the priests with one's name already inscribed as being *maat-kheru*, "true of voice," that is having in advance successfully passed the test of judgment in "The Hall of Two Truths" Court. Spell 30B states: "I [Thoth] have judged the heart of the deceased...His deeds are righteous in the great balance...The vindicated Osiris N [the deceased] is straightforward, he has no sin, there is no accusation against him before us, Ammit shall not be permitted to have power over him."

Magic and counter-magic also played fundamental roles in the precautions of *The Book of the Dead* to ensure a safe passage to the *Duat*. Spell 24, "for bringing magic to N," "...collected magic in every place where it was..." Spell 23, "for the opening of the mouth," warned: "As for any magic spell or any words which may be uttered against me, the gods will rise up against it, even the entire Ennead."[15]

Sincere suffering over whether their behavior was moral seems to have been exceptional. There was very little of the obsessive concern with morality, suffering, sin and guilt which we find so frequently among the later Hebrews, Greek Orphics, Zoroastrians and especially Christians.

The judgment in "The Hall of Two Truths" at the entry into the *Duat* after-life was presided by Osiris, King of the Dead, assisted by Maat, Horus, Thoth, Anubis, Isis and Nephthys and 42 assessor god-demons — apparently, 42 for the 42 nomes and 42 misdeeds.

When presenting himself in the Hall, a dead Egyptian did not humbly confess his sins and ask for pardon. According to the *Book of the Dead*, he recited the fundamental Egyptian moral statement, known as the "negative confession" (Spell 125). Even the most naïve person, let alone the goddess Maat of truth, could not possibly believe this "confession." The deceased assured the gods and demons that he had "not done evil," that he had not acted wickedly against the gods, the king, or men, nor committed murder nor theft, nor "added to the weight of the balance," nor "taken milk from the mouth of children" and that he "given bread to the hungry, water to the thirsty." But he also made such extravagant claims as "I have not spied [eavesdropped]"... "I have not sulked"... "I have not raised my voice"... "I have not told lies"... "I have not caused tears"... "I have not quenched a needed fire"... "I have come to you without sin, without guilt, without evil, Without a witness against me." Moreover, the deceased never "committed adultery," nor "defiled myself [masturbation]," nor "copulated with

---

14. Budge, Wallis, E.A., *The Egyptian Book of the Dead*, pp. 367-368.

15. Faulkner, R.O., *The Ancient Egyptian Book of the Dead*, pp. 28, 52 and 51-52.

a boy." This strange mixture indicating that neither evil nor venial acts had been committed included a pretentious, "I live on *maat* [order, truth], I feed on *maat*," and an even more pretentious, "I am pure, I am pure, I am pure, I am pure!"[16]

Christian sinners and would-be sinners, anxious to beat their chests with *mea culpae* and mortify themselves, would have been deeply disappointed by this lack of spiritual suffering and a tearful-from-the-heart confession. R.O. Faulkner (1894–1982), in his translation of *The Book of the Dead*, quite rightly noted that although "long known by the self-contradictory title of 'The Negative Confession,' (it) is better named 'The Declaration of Innocence'."[17]

The *ieb*, the heart of the dead, which the Egyptians believed was the center of the life force, of thought, knowledge, courage, love and sadness, was then weighed against the order and truth of Maat's feather, the *shut*, by the jackal-headed embalmment and tomb protector god Anubis or the falcon god Horus. The ibis or baboon-headed Thoth, moon god of wisdom and writing and the *sesh*, the scribe, of Re, noted the result of the weighing. The deceased was then declared *maat-kheru*, "true of voice." The benevolent Horus then led the deceased to Osiris, to the dog-headed Wepwawet, the god-guide of the dead, opener of the way, and to Isis and Nephthys, protectresses of the dead and of course to the goddess Maat.

During the New Kingdom (from c. 1550 BC), the deceased took the major supplementary precaution of using a heart scarab amulet which silenced any possible admission of misdeeds. The heart scarab, using Spells 30A and 30B from *The Book of the Dead*, cast a spell on the heart to prevent it from telling unpleasant truths: "O my heart which I had from my mother...do not rise up against me as a witness in the presence of the Lord of Things; do not speak against me concerning what I have done, do not bring up anything against me...do not be opposed to me in the tribunal, do not be hostile to me in the presence of the Keeper of the Balance...do not make my name stink to the Entourage who make men..."[18]

The Egyptians did not imagine a Hell; they did not invent a system of permanent suffering after death. But they did elaborate a pretty good theoretical surrogate version, a pretty ferocious precursor.

Their system did not constitute an authentic Hell with a specific location where the damned would eternally suffer, burn or rot for his sins; it was still mercifully far away from later inventions like the butchery of the Hindu-Bud-

---

16. *Ibid.*, pp. 29-34 and Lichtheim, Miriam, *Ancient Egyptian Literature, Volume II*, pp. 124-132.

17. Faulkner, R.O., *The Ancient Egyptian Book of the Dead*, p. 29.

18. *Ibid.*, pp. 27 and 55.

dhist Hell, the torments of the Zoroastrian temporary Hell or the eternal fires of the Christian Hell.

The deceased who failed the judgment test in "The Hall of Two Truths" was damned to dying a second time, *mit em nem*, to extinction, no afterlife, eternal death. However, this horrific penalty for those whose *ieb*, whose heart, whose being, did not weigh up to the goddess Maat's *shut* ostrich feather of truth on the other side of the judgment scales remained theoretical rather than real — in practice, the "second death," death for eternity, could be easily avoided.

"The eater of the dead," the monster Am-Mut — a composite female monster-demon, lion, hippopotamus and crocodile — devoured the deceased's heart; the deceased had to eat his own excrement and was burned, and boiled; the demon baboon Babi ripped the person apart and the Shezmu, the god of the wine press, sometimes in human form, sometimes lion-headed, sometimes as a falcon, drew out all his blood.

However, it was the benefits of the *Duat* "Other Land" which were emphasized and not Am-mut. A positive outcome of the judgment was virtually ensured. Truth and ethical behavior and horrific punishments were indeed implied, but they were not applied; only the reward of the afterlife was applied. It was easy to use numerous amulets and magical spells, to just give the appearance of having respected *maat* decent behavior, or morality, easy to fake it all, fool the judges and warp the judgment in the "Hall of Two Truths."

And the Am-mut concept could not have had much dissuasive value even if it was clearly there as an indication of what happens to those who do not toe the line. There is probably not a single reference in ancient, classical Egyptian art and papyri to Am-Mut actually eating anybody, while of course the number of people who later roasted in the Christian Hell were (and are) legion. John Baines and Jaromir Màlek in the *Atlas of Ancient Egypt* report the existence of an image from the Roman Period (from 30 BC) in which Am-mut is actually in the process of devouring somebody who failed the test of truth and was not declared *maat-kheru*, "true of voice."[19] However, one example is very thin evidence and above all coming from the period of the Roman occupation of Egypt, from a period of decadence in classical Egyptian religion and art, it is likely that it had more to do with Roman feelings and Roman influence and interpretations of the Am-mut concept than a purely Egyptian belief.

And so there seems no way of escaping the fact that the judgment of the dead in "The Hall of Two Truths" was neither based on morality nor even decent behavior, but was basically deceptive and formalistic. The genuine application of the moral implications of the *maat* necessarily implied the rejection of magic.

---

19. Baines, John and Malek, Jaromir, *Atlas of Ancient Egypt*, p. 218.

More precisely, it implied the rejection of a hocus-pocus, manipulative type of magic in favor of a far more subtle, more cunning type of magic which would automatically reward moral behavior and compensate for suffering with pie in the sky. The Egyptian mentality — *especially* the Egyptian mentality — and the mentality of the entire ancient world was too rooted in mythology and primary magic to make such a leap possible. There was nothing which could vie with the primitive notions of laws derived from nature.

The intimate structure of Egyptian cosmology was so sacred and permanent, the magical system for its appeasement and manipulation so deeply anchored and socio-political roles and privileges so hierarchical that it was probably never possible for the Egyptians to make an about-face in favor of generalized concepts of good and evil. The Sumerians were even more reticent in this domain — contrary to the Egyptian *maat* code, the Sumerians did not even have formal law codes until about 2100 BC, when *Lugal* (King) Ur-Nammu of Sumer and Akkad (c. 2113–2096 BC) and then his son, *Lugal* Shulgi, established regulations which implied some kind of morality, but in no way linked morality and an afterlife.

We shall soon see how the search for a clear and lofty link between religion and ethics eventually catalyzed far more energy and motivation among other peoples, more religiously and philosophically modern peoples who came up with freer, franker, more sincere answers which replied to a thirst for justice. It was such an about-face in favor of concepts of good and evil which the later monotheistic Hebrews — with great difficulties and numerous relapses — would push to the forefront for the first time and which was followed by the lofty ethical ideals of the Zoroastrian Persian, the Buddhists and the Christians and the rationality, ethics and science of the Greeks.

The Egyptians, like the Sumerians, strongly believed that disorder, misfortune and illness were the result of wrong behavior in relation to the gods and the order and harmony of the world which the gods had created and could be corrected by magic, appeasement and manipulations to provoke the intervention of the gods. Sin in the sense of immoral behavior and divine justice sanctioning such sin were largely later Semitic concepts which neither the Sumerians nor the Egyptians could easily grasp. For the Egyptians, misfortune, either individually or as a nation, had nothing to do with ethics as the later Hebrews believed.

For the Egyptian, the cosmos and nature imposed their laws and being *just* meant observing these laws and honoring and adoring the gods who made them. Basically, the right order, the order which had to be maintained, was the permanent, natural, primeval order and not a moral order fabricated by humans. The right order was contained in nature and was visible to all with its positive and negative aspects — with the earth which gave food and poisons — with its situations of inferiority and domination — with animals who were prey and animals who were majestic — with the gods who assured a daily victory over the threat of chaos. A space existed for right, or correct, human behavior, but it was a space more linked to rules for harmonious life in society than to lofty ethical ideals. Wrong behavior was to be feared because it put the system out of kilter. The Egyptians had struck a deal with their gods — sacrifices, worship and respect of the *maat* primeval natural order in exchange for *ankh, udja, seneb* — life, prosperity, health — first for the pharaoh and then for everybody. There was no apparent reason to add morality to this deal.

The Egyptians believed that they effectively lived in accordance with true *maat* harmony; they were at peace with themselves — *Em hetep*, in peace! For the Hebrews, there was no such peace of mind; the deal — the *berit*, the covenant — with Yahweh had right from the outset implied the need for individual moral behavior, which was perhaps even stronger than the need for worship and appeasement animal sacrifices as main aspects of religion.

Unlike the later monotheisms, the Egyptians did not consider that the destiny of the world and mankind had to be altered and that a final goal had to be fixed. They were unable to fully perceive that solely basing the afterlife on a moral judgment did indeed provide a possible solution to the problem of evil and the final destiny of mankind and the world.

However, unlike the Sumerians and like the Hebrews, the Egyptians gradually glimpsed the relation that could be established between everyday life ethics and the afterlife and cosmological concepts. Frequently, wrong behavior for the Egyptians included what later civilizations considered as evil or immoral behavior. However, the Egyptians never fully grasped the deep eschatological significance which could be drawn from this relationship and almost always saw it as somewhat gratuitous compared to the power of magic. The Egyptian leaders and people always remained more obsessively focused on *heka*, magic, rather than on moral substance. The *modus operandi* of materialistic techniques, of correctly performing magical rituals linked to the application of the *maat* in its primeval meaning, is what counted most. When the talk and hype about morality were over, salvation and immortality could be won by materialistic rituals and funeral preparations in this life and the use of magic and fraud in the afterlife.

The Egyptian attitude was obviously sufficient to make the extraordinary leap towards preparing and favoring material immortality by magic, new techniques, arduous efforts and considerable expense over a period of more than 2500 years.

But all this was still not enough to take the next step — the invention of Paradise as we understand the term today. The invention of Paradise required a composite attitude that was simpler, subtler, and entailed more lying, was more devious, more infantile and less immediately materialistic. It seems that only an ethical or pseudo-ethical approach was sufficient to make the invention of Paradise possible. One can surmise that in this as in most other domains, a double process had to come into play — a sincere ethical attempt to explain and compensate for suffering and deprivation in this life, laced with a good dose of wishful thinking and a devious attempt to find an adequate system to control human behavior. And this was what the Zoroastrian Persians, the Hebrews, the Christians and the Moslems accomplished with their Heaven-Hell-general resurrection-final judgment and rewards system.

The notion of a morally earned Paradise superior to life on earth was just too enormously abstract for the highly materialistic Egyptians. Moreover, they were perhaps sufficiently satisfied with their lives to desire an eternal continuation of their lifestyle, a repeating of this life, *wehem ankh*, rather than a radical improvement.

The notion of finality, of radiant rewards and horrific punishments for ethical reasons had to come into play to make the notion of Paradise possible. It was not enough to be pleased with life, wanting to see it "repeated" forever after death. A need had to exist to favor orderly behavior despite difficult, or even terrible or hopeless, conditions in this life in the hope of obtaining a final, a permanent reward for these constraints in the afterlife. The need for a pseudo-ethical system of control providing a fabulous consolation or terrible punishment in the future had to exist. Living conditions in Egypt seem to have been acceptable enough so that a more radical system of controlling and consoling people — the promise, the reward, of Paradise or the threat of Hell — was unnecessary. Perhaps the existing methods of politico-religious control to prevent unrest and revolt, to accept the unacceptable aspects of this life, were sufficient. Perhaps, the guarantee of an afterlife involving the survival of the body and its souls was enough sop and the sop of Heaven, of pie in the sky, was superfluous.

Nevertheless, in the midst of all the prodigious effort and expense involved in the material preparations and magic connected to the afterlife, the ancient Egyptians were not insensitive to the problem of ethics. They struggled with the problem of ethics and were even on the verge of understanding what was at stake. The need for a link between ethics and religion, between moral principles and an eternal second life or an eternal second death, based on the notions of reward and punishment, seems to have been clearly felt.

As we have seen over and over again, while the *maat* precepts, *ankh-em-maat*, "living by *maat*," primarily meant respecting the primeval order of the universe and of society, at least from the time of the Wisdom Texts (c. 2550 BC), they could also be understood as living decently, as "doing the ethical thing." As such, it put the ethical justification for a Paradise into the hands of the Egyptians. It even put the link between everyday life, ethics and religion into their hands, since much in the *maat* was an implicit moral code for this life and not just a criterion for universal and societal order and entry into the afterlife. The ethical aspects of the *maat* in the negative confession in "The Hall of Two Truths" constituted a moral system, or rather it would have constituted such a system if was not assumed that the afterlife assessors could be tricked by claiming innocence of all wrongdoing and that magic and fraud were the omnipotent passport to the afterlife.

The flirtation with morality as constituted by the confession and judgment in "The Hall of Two Truths" simply showed that for the Egyptians *wehem ankh*, repeating life, the afterlife, was too important to be left to morality. Wholeheartedly doing the *maat*, wholeheartedly confessing sins and seeking repentance or wholeheartedly seeking a spiritual rather than a material existence in the *Duat* were unnecessary; magic, trickery and paying lip service to the *maat* code in this life and especially upon entry into the afterlife were sufficient.

And yet the mere formalistic judgment in "The Hall of Two Truths" and its tenuous link to the *maat* in the sense of doing the ethical thing were indeed prefigurations of authentic moral concerns. Especially after the opening of the New Kingdom (c. 1550 BC), when the basic reliance on magic was overridingly clear, the mere existence in Egypt of this tenuous link between morality and the afterlife represented an extraordinary claim and challenge. In the New Kingdom and afterwards, the magical guide book tendency of the funerary texts was accentuated with a profusion of books like *The Book of Gates*, *The Book of Caverns*, the *Amduat*, *The Book of That Which Is in the Nether World*, *The Book of the Night*, the *Writing of the Hidden Chamber*, etc. The main concern of these texts, like earlier Pyramid Texts, Coffin Texts, *Book of Two Ways* and *The Book of the Dead*, was if anything even more magically centered on protecting the deceased and safely leading him into the *Duat* afterlife. Nevertheless, the ethical aspects of the *maat* code survived and even grew in importance over the centuries and constituted the beginnings of an adequate body of regulations for reasonable, cooperative, charitable and even fraternal life in society, as well as a theoretical basis for ethical judgment in the afterlife. It was these notions and concerns that were amplified by other peoples — the Zoroastrian Persians, the Hebrews, the Christians and the Moslems — into the Heaven-Hell-general resurrection-final judgment and rewards system.

The Egyptians always stubbornly stayed on the brink. They never went the extra mile along an already traced road, that is, the genuine application of the principles of morality in the new *maat*, the genuine expansion of the old *maat* beyond its definition as a permanent, primeval, natural order and personified natural forces.

The hard fact seems to be that over more than 2000 years, from the Old Kingdom Pyramid Texts (from c. 2375 BC) to the Ptolemaic Period (c. 332–32 BC) *Book of Breathings*, which in the Roman Period (30 BC–AD 395) replaced *The Book of the Dead* as the main afterlife text, magical funerary texts provide the consistent illustration that even if decent behavior and charity were stressed, as in the Wisdom Texts, Paradise strictly based on moral principles, was not invented at any time in Egypt. Nevertheless, the concept of doing the *maat* in this life and the theoretical judgment on its criteria in the afterlife never ceased to exist. *Maat* marked the timid beginning of a new type of ethical religious caveat — do not perform evil and immoral acts if you want an afterlife; play the game of life according to the rules or face the consequences.

The Egyptians did not apply this caveat, but they set the stage for this infantile but attractive scheme. The paradox is that despite its overriding insistence on magic, Egypt opened the way to this type of thinking, or illusion.

An immense revolution, or perhaps more correctly a pre-revolution, had occurred. The Egyptian confrontation with ethics — the moral aspects of *maat* and "The Hall of Two Truths" judgment — vigorously contributed to opening a new road in ethics that eventually established morality as the touchstone of everyday life. Eventually, religion became not just a matter of the accomplishment of rituals, worship and offerings, but also a matter of ethics, moral worth and obligations. Eventually, elaborate ethical codes, without religion and based on the sole value of their implicit worth, were elaborated. The Hebrews linked ethics and religion in this life. The Persians transformed religion into a matter of rewarding individual ethical behavior and punishing individual evil behavior. Many Greek philosopher-scientists, from about the sixth century BC, abandoned the search for a link between ethics and religion and sought a solution to the problem of ethics independently of religion, to establish ethics as an independent value in itself. The Christians transformed the Hebrew *tsadaquah* principle of righteousness into an absolute of love, forgiveness and afterlife reward that became humanity's unsurpassable and impossible ideal. The rise of the democratic ideal, from the 18th century, led to ethics without religion.

The Egyptians never came near to any of these concepts, but the prodigious originality and daring of the Egyptian *maat* and Judgment should not be underestimated, even if these attempts failed. They posed some of the most fundamental problems faced by man — What is correct behavior? What is ethics? Is there a reward or a punishment?

GETTING TO THE *DUAT* AFTERLIFE AND PROSPERING THERE

It clearly behooved all Egyptians to expend great material, magical and ritualistic efforts in this life to earn the possibility of immortality, to continue their
lives, repeat their lives — *wehem ankh* — in the *Duat* "Other Land" and to avoid
being damned to a "second death" — *mit em nem*. If these efforts were correctly
accomplished, if one were correctly "equipped," the door to the *Duat* was open
and one could survive there unharmed, prospering, hobnobbing with the gods
and going out for visits. *The Book of the Dead* Spell 17 states: "...going in and coming
out of the realm of the dead, having benefit in the beautiful West [the land of the
dead], being in the suite of Osiris, resting at the food-table of *Wennefer* [Osiris],
going out into the day, taking any shape in which he desires to be, playing at
draughts [a board game known as *senet*], sitting in a booth, and going forth as a
living soul by the Osiris N [the name of the deceased] after he had died." Spell 110
adds: "...my magic is powerful in it...plowing therein, reaping and eating therein,
drinking therein, copulating therein, and doing everything that used to be done
on earth by N." And Spell 175 adds that the duration of this situation will be "for
millions on millions of years, a lifetime of millions of years," that is *heh*, infinity.[20]

As we have seen, the sheer cost of this "equipping" operation clearly
excluded the vast majority of the population. Of course, the pharaoh-gods had
none of these worries. Their monumental *mer*, pyramids, were near-perfect magical vectors for entry into eternity where they joined Re in "lightland" and became
Osiris.

The tomb, for a pharaoh or anybody else, and whether it was a mastaba, a
pyramid, rock-cut or a simple structure for commoners, had to obey a whole
series of magical requirements and had be solid and well protected. It had to be
protected from looters (who were sometimes the pharaohs and the priests themselves) and from people vengefully seeking to defigure the mask of the dead so
that his *ka* spirit/statue would not be able recognize him, thus causing a second
death. Incursions by robbers and evil spirits were prevented by an engraving on
the door of the tomb, showing the tomb protector god Anubis in the form of a
black dog above bound captives.

In addition to the "negative confession" and the heart scarab amulet which
silenced any possible admission of misdeeds, getting to the *Duat* often also
involved threats. This is very evident concerning the pharaohs in the Pyramid
Texts — for instance, Utterance 477 states: "Sharpen your knife, O
Thoth...remove the heads and cut out the hearts of those who would oppose

---

20. Faulkner, R.O., *The Ancient Egyptian Book of the Dead*, pp. 44, 103-104 and 175.

themselves to me when I come to you, Osiris." But threats were also a valid means for the notables, as we can see from the Coffin Texts and *The Book of the Dead* — for instance *Book of the Dead* Spell 20: "O Thoth...may you entrap the enemies of N in the presence of the tribunals of every god and every goddess."[21]

Staying alive in the afterlife through magical protection was a key preoccupation. From the New Kingdom (c. 1550), this task was guaranteed by placing a copy of *The Book of the Dead* in the tomb, as had previously been done with the Pyramid Texts and the Coffin Texts. These texts were sometimes distorted so as not to affect the dead, but only demons and intruders. Images of savage animals — snakes, scorpions, lions — were placed as protective forces near the mummies. These images were believed to be real animals and they were cut in two or painted with knives in them in order to render them harmless for the dead they were protecting. (This is reminiscent of the tactics used 17,000 years ago in Magdalenian art, which some prehistorians consider to have been a hunting magic religion.)

The *ka*-statue of the future deceased, his double and guardian soul, was placed in a separate chamber of the tomb and *hetep*, food and drink offerings, were made to it and to the *ba*. An essential aspect of the tomb was the so-called false door on which an image of the deceased was sculpted, seated behind an offering table, and where the living nourished the dead with daily food, drink and incense offerings, with special offerings being made on festival days and on the anniversary of the death. The central importance of the offering table for *hetep* in all Egyptian tombs from the earliest times to the end of its history indicates how vital was this concept of nourishing the *ka* and the *ba*.

Paintings and reliefs depicting the first life now became the real framework of "repeating life" and had the power to preserve this second, youthful, eternal life. Paintings of food could also magically become real food and were used when offerings to the *ka* and the *ba* were insufficient or absent. For the richest, beautifully decorated magical funerary texts, dozens of amulets and an immense amount of furniture, jewelry, utensils, fine clothing, tools, weapons and the usual goods of daily life were deposited in the tomb.

From the Middle Kingdom (beginning c. 2055 BC), statuettes known as *ushabti*, ("answerers"), were placed in the tomb. When persuaded with the correct magical incantations, the *ushabtis* did all the menial and farm work in the *Duat* in replacement of the rich dead "Westerner." Spell 6 in the New Kingdom *Book of the Dead* provides the magical formula which made this possible: "O *shabti*, allotted to me, if I be summoned or if I be detailed to do any work which has to

---

21. Faulkner, R.O., *The Ancient Egyptian Pyramid Texts*, p. 165 and Faulkner, R.O., *The Ancient Egyptian Book of the Dead*, p. 50.

be done in the realm of the dead...you shall detail yourself for me on every occasion of making arable the fields, of flooding the banks or of conveying sand...'Here am I,' you shall say."[22]

At first, a single *ushabti* was placed in the tomb to "answer" the call to do any necessary work, but by the New Kingdom (beginning c. 1550 BC), the pharaohs and rich notables were buried with a *ushabti* for every single day of the year (365) plus 36 overseers to make sure that the work was done. Of course, the average person and the poor could not afford to have a full set of *ushabtis* sculpted and were buried with only a few rudimentary figurines.

Magnificent *wia*, solar boats, were placed in special pits next to the pyramid tombs. These "Barks of the Gods" enabled the deceased pharaoh-god to travel across the watery sky to join Re in eternal afterlife, in the sun, in "lightland." The bark found in 1954 in excellent condition next to Pharaoh Khufu's Pyramid (c. 2580 BC) weighs more than 40 tons and is 141 feet long. It has been elegantly restored and is now on view in a small museum next to the pyramid. Smaller boats, or scale model boats, were often placed in the tombs of notables.

Later, in the New Kingdom, from the time of Pharaoh Thutmose I (c. 1504–1492 BC), the awesomely massive, solid rock-cut tombs, deeply concealed into the rock for fear of robbers, in the Thebes Valley of Kings and Valley of the Queens, constituted a radical architectural change, but of course, the goal was the same — to magically ensure an afterlife and to be *aper*, "equipped" in the tomb with all scenes and goods of this life for one's new life in the *Duat*. Scenes and spells from various funerary texts and scenes depicting the great deeds of the deceased, as well as scenes of the deceased hobnobbing with the gods, covered the walls. The private tombs of the notables in western Thebes depicted these same scenes on a less heroic scale. Some of the craftsmen's tombs in nearby Deir el-Medina indicate truly laudable efforts to be properly "equipped" for the afterlife. As privileged a category of the population as these craftsmen were, they were nevertheless economically and socially commoners and their efforts to be "equipped" must have implied immense sacrifices, including working on most of their days off.

After the 70 days required for mummification, the deceased was considered to be in a state enabling him to live eternally as a youth. An elaborate funeral service was then held. The mummy was taken across the Nile in a funeral boat amid the priests and the family of the deceased. It was met by *muu* dancers and harpists. Animals were ritually slaughtered and incantations recited by specialist *sem* funeral priests draped with leopard skins, while professional women wailers, the *kites*, shouted lamentations. A pilgrimage to the Osiris Temple in Abydos was

---

22. *Ibid.*, p. 36.

simulated. The fundamental ceremony of the "Opening of the Mouth" was carried out on the mummy and statue of the deceased by the son and heir and a *sem* priest. This was the ceremony which Horus had mythologically carried out on his father, Osiris. The mouth and other parts of the body of the dead person were touched and magically opened with a curved-bladed flint instrument (the *ur-heka* or *pesesh-kef*) and spells were performed so that the dead person's senses should be magically revived and notably allow him to continue breathing and eating in the afterlife. The Egyptians' favorite piece of meat, the *khepesh*, the foreleg of an ox, was sliced off as a food offering for the deceased. Then the mummy was placed in a coffin, or several coffins one within another. By about the Twelfth Dynasty (c. 1985–1795 BC), coffins were frequently in anthropoid form and elaborately decorated with Osirisian themes. A stone sarcophagus container, inscribed with magical Coffin Texts, further protected the coffins. The coffins and sarcophagus, together with all the furnishings, and notably the *ka-*statue and the *ushabti* statuettes, were then placed in the tomb and food offerings were spread out in front of the false door of the tomb.

At the beginning of the First Intermediate Period (c. 2181–2055 BC), judgment in "The Hall of Two Truths" was established with the negative confession, the weighing of the heart and the quasi-automatic declaring of the deceased *ma'at keru*, "true of voice."

The adventurous journey to the *Duat* of "the Westerner," that is the living dead, then began. The Egyptians made the geography of this journey clearer. By indicating what magic had to be used to overcome the terrible, demonic obstacles on the way — obstacles which, if not defeated, resulted in a second and definitive death — they made the trip safer. The origin of the concept that a journey was required to enter the afterlife is lost in the night of time (and is still symbolized in our dreams today), but the Egyptians were certainly among the first, or were the first, to explicitly indicate how to get to the afterlife.

Once in the *Duat*, the utterances, spells, incantations, threats and directives first of the Pyramid Texts, then the Coffin Texts and then *The Book of the Dead* and other funerary texts provided an afterlife travel guide for both a pleasant journey and a pleasant stay. *The Book of the Dead* described the obstacles and danger zones and how to skirt them: the evil monsters, crocodiles and serpents and terrifying gatekeepers, ferrymen and enemies and how to threaten, tame or defeat them. It gave the techniques, spells and rituals of how to avoid dying a second time, how not to be burned or boiled, how not to rot, how not to allow one's heart to be taken away or get one's head separated from one's body. It revealed the secrets to ensure that the *ba* and *ka* souls were joined to the body. It indicated how to breathe, eat, drink and walk. It warned that the dead should not eat excrements or drink urine. It provided the spells of how to transform into animals and gods, how to identify with Osiris and even how to hitch a ride on Re's solar boat. It provided the magic that enabled the *ba* and *akh* souls of the deceased to leave the underworld to pay temporary visits to the living.

The power, peace and joy in the *Duat* promised in *The Book of the Dead* were the central, cherished doctrines of the Egyptian religion. Spell 122: "To me belongs everything, and the whole of it has been given to me. I have gone in as a falcon, I have come out as a phoenix...and I enter in peace into the Beautiful West (the land of the dead)." Spell 119: "...I have spoken to you, Osiris; I have the rank of a god, I say what comes to pass..." Spell 180: "I rest in the Netherworld, I have power in the darkness, I go in and out of it...Praise to you who are at peace; give praise joyfully."[23]

The *Duat* "Other Land," in *Khert-Netjer* (the divine place below), in *Amenta* (the "West"), where the sun sets, was vast, containing twelve sections and numerous sub-divisions. It was frequently seen as the upside down version of the earth with the sky and the sun on the bottom. In most versions of the underworld, there was a place of great peace, beauty, abundance and play — the *Aaru* Fields, the Field of Reeds, or the Fields of Peace, or the *sekhet-hetep*, the Fields of Offerings — with farmlands irrigated from the subterranean Nile's waters. Here the resurrected dead ate delicacies, drank cool drinks, made love and played the *senet* board game.

Countless funerary texts and art and architecture indicate that there can hardly be any doubt that this magically obtained system of material resurrection and eternal afterlife for the body and its souls was firmly believed by the Egyptians...and yet there was a spark of something else, a spark of something loftier. Several spells in *The Book of the Dead* put matters on a plane which was moral and not strictly magical: Spell 175 assures Thoth that the deceased before him is "not among those who have done hidden damage" and pleads with him to do something about the gods who "have done hidden damage...made war...done wrong...done slaughter...reduced what was great to what is little..." Spell 185 simply proclaims: "My heart comes to you bearing Truth, my heart has no falseness."[24]

Above all, countless autobiographical inscriptions on tomb walls and funerary steles clearly show how much importance the deceased attached to proving that he had behaved decently according to Egyptian norms. The deceased sought to show that he amply deserved a happy afterlife because he had been respectful of the gods and the pharaoh, just and charitable with his fellow Egyptians, and — because that was what was expected of him — ferocious with

---

23. *Ibid.*, pp. 113, 119 and 177.
24. *Ibid.*, pp. 175 and 185.

"vile" foreigners. While most of these inscriptions must be seen as conventional, ritual statements, as statements that had to be made, rather than truth, it would be excessively cynical to doubt the sincerity of some of them. It would even be more cynical to doubt that decent behavior, at least in relationship to Egyptian norms, was prized and seen as a challenge by some.

Take, for instance, the Stele of the Treasurer Tjetji (c. 2060 BC, found in his Theban tomb and now in the British Museum): "I was one loved by his lord [the pharaoh], praised by him every day...The treasure was in my hand...being the best of every good thing brought to the majesty of my lord from Upper Egypt, from Lower Egypt...and what was brought...by the chiefs who rule the Red land [the deserts on both sides of the Nile], owing to the fear of him throughout the hill countries...I did not follow after evil for which men are hated. I am one who loves what is good...I did not take anything wrongfully...I am wealthy, I am great...because of his great love for me — Horus *Wahankh*, King of Upper and Lower Egypt, Son of Re, Intef who lives like Re forever — until he went in peace to his horizon [the afterlife]...May he cross the firmament, traverse the sky...To the place where Osiris dwells..."

The Stele of the butler Merer of Edfu (c. 2120 BC?) (now in the Krakow National Museum) expresses a similar preoccupation with being seen as a good person, worthy of the favor of the gods: "Never did I hand over a person to a potentate, so that my name might be good with all men. I never lied against any person...I nourished my brothers and sisters. I buried the dead and nourished the living..."[25]

Quotations of this type can be listed *ad infinitum*.

A CONVOLUTED SYSTEM OF SEVERAL SOULS AND THEIR SURVIVAL AFTER DEATH

The Egyptian concept of the soul — or more precisely, souls, since each individual had several companion souls with different functions — was primarily a matter of the afterlife and not this life. The souls, while not being of the same nature as the body, were just as material and representable. They were also just as destructible as the body if the correct magical and material procedures were not respected. Parts of these concepts seem to go all the way back to Neanderthal times and also to the beginnings of animism and shamanism. Other aspects of the Egyptian soul system were radical new inventions.

Complex notions of the several souls and their immortality, prefiguring the survival of the body with its souls in a paradisiacal physical and spiritual after-

---

25. Lichtheim, Miriam, *Ancient Egyptian Literature, Volume I*, pp. 91-93 and 87.

life, in Egypt or elsewhere, cannot be dated with any accuracy. It is clear that the pharaohs — their bodies and several spiritual entities, or souls — enjoyed immortal survival and union with the divine as far back as can be traced in the Early Dynastic Period (from c. 3100 BC). From the First Intermediate Period (c. 2181 BC), the body and souls of everybody were involved in simultaneous existence in the *Duat* nether world, below the western *ahket*, horizon, where the sun disappeared, in the sky near the gods for some of one's souls and on the earth with visits to the living.

The entirety of the system was never coherent and even became less so after the possession of souls and the right to an afterlife, to becoming an Osiris upon death, became the prerogatives not only of the pharaoh-god but of all. At the same time, the system taken as an entirety was extraordinarily subtle, even if of course it appears totally unconvincing, today.

The Egyptian soul system was intimately linked to the numbers five and nine. Five united souls in the afterlife constituted a unified person. These were the *ka* double soul, the *ba* roaming soul, the *akh* transfigured soul, the *ren* name soul, and the *khabit* shadow soul. A system of nine was constituted by the material body, *khat*, plus the five souls and three higher soul functions — the *khu*, the spiritual, intelligent entity, the *sahu*, the superior, gleaming spiritual body, and the *sekhem*, immortal power and knowledge. All five souls were linked, were interdependent, and in order to exist were dependent on the preservation, the survival after death, of the *khat*, the physical body (hieroglyphically represented as a leaping fish). The nucleus of the *khat* was the heart, the *ieb*, and also had to be preserved from decay. The *ieb* (hieroglyphically represented as a jug with handles) was believed to be the center of a person's life, being, intelligence, understanding and feeling. The Egyptians used this word *ieb* as the verb "to think" and as the noun for "heart." For the Egyptians, the heart was therefore also the mind.

Together, after death, the souls and the body became a physical and spiritual Osiris who repeated life, *wehem ankh* — ate, played and made love in the *Duat* afterlife as it had previously done on earth, on the condition that enough *ushabti* statuettes had been buried with the person to do the work.

The most important soul seems to have been the *ka*. It was hieroglyphically represented as two upraised arms, bent at the elbows, with palms facing outwards, a posture which has become a distinctive attitude of religious devotion and esotericism. Considerable debate still continues concerning the exact meaning of the *ka* — spirit, vital force, self, personality, etc. However, it seems to me that the likeliest definition was made as early as 1878 by Gaston Maspero (1846–1916), who defined it as "the double" of the person.

Versions of the *ka* double soul are common to countless societies in history. The *ka* was the Egyptian expression of the age-old concept that there is another being inside man, a voice, an ally, a soul, which has a separate and more perfect existence than the ordinary self. This double, this replica of the personality, this spirit which emerged during dreams and at death, may well be the oldest definition of the soul. It may also have been linked to the origin of the afterlife in Neanderthal times.

The Neanderthals and the Cro-Magnons may have associated souls, spirits, with a dreamland and a foretaste of the afterlife as we know the shamanists did and still do. In any case, the Egyptian *ka* was linked to these notions. The Egyptian practice — especially during the Late Period (after c. 747 BC) — of spending a night in temples and Houses of Life to provoke premonitory dreams strongly resembles shamanistic controlled or drug-induced dreaming, dream-time. The *ka* also bore a marked resemblance to the shamanistic guardian and ally soul notions.

During the life of a person on earth, the *ka* was present as a kind of independent double, as a kind of dream spirit, a more real personality, the *summum* of the positive attributes of a person. It was also divine vital, creative energy. When an Egyptian died, it was said that he had "gone to his *ka*." He therefore met his double, companion soul, ally, and became a *ka*. A dead Egyptian was called a *ka*.

Fourteen *kas* flowed through the blood of the gods Horus and Re and were transmitted to the pharaoh. At the end of the Old Kingdom (c. 2181 BC), when it was decided that the entirety of the Egyptian people had the right to possess a *ka*, the pharaoh transmitted a single *ka* to the individual person. The *ka* became the grain of the divine in man.

It is possible to establish a rough relationship between the concept of the *ka* and the Sumerian *me*. Both primarily concerned the gods before being extended to humans. Both implied a divine force of life which created all the material aspects of existence and the notion of being. However, the comparison has to stop here; above all, because the *me* was not a soul like the *ka* — the Sumerians did not postulate the existence of any soul-like entity in their religious system — but also because there were more than 100 *me* and many of them were negative or trivial.

The *ka* was resurrected with the dead body as the double, the companion soul, the ally and guardian. It was housed in the *ka*-statue placed in the tomb and theoretically resembled the deceased, but was usually an idealized version of the person. Upon death, the *ka* recognized its *khat*, as a *sah*, a mummified body. After death, the *ka* received food and liquid *hetep*, offerings (also called *kaw*) — meat, bread, cakes, vegetables, beer and wine. Just as the body had to be embalmed and mummified in order to survive, the *ka* had to be fed in order to survive.

The *ba* soul, hieroglyphically represented as a free flying human-headed bird (sometimes also with human arms), emerged only after death. It was one of the Egyptian souls which resembled animistic concepts, notably the idea that the soul could wander freely, incarnate itself in any matter and torment the living. The Egyptian word for the ram, an animal linked to great creative virility, was *ba*. It is therefore no surprise that the *ba* was seen as the most powerful part of a person, but the *ba* was also the most intangible, changing part of a person. The *ba* eternally roamed about at will. It lived with the gods, but also talked to its body and visited the living. With the help of magical spells, the *ba* could transform itself into any form.

Like the *ka*, it was vital that the *ba* recognizes its *khat* in its mummified *sah* body, in the afterlife. Like the *ka*, the *ba* consumed the *hetep*, offerings, which the living made, and also required sexual intercourse. The *ba* was also a kind of a mobile soul of the gods and could become one or more of his aspects, as Osiris was the *ba* night sun aspect of Re or the Apis was the earthly bull aspect of Ptah.

The freewheeling, roaming aspect of the Egyptian *ba* soul which lives with the gods seems to be closest to what came to be considered as the soul among the later monotheistic religions. However, the monotheistic and Egyptian soul systems differed fundamentally, even if the Hebrews, like the Egyptians, for most of their early history saw it as incapable of existence without the body. For the monotheists, and especially the Christians, the soul evolved into an immaterial and indestructible entity, contrary to the material, destructible body (and of course, contrary to the material, representable aspects of the *ba* and its need to be materially fed and enjoy sex). Moreover, for the monotheists, there could only be one soul just as there was only one god. It was perhaps because of these essential differences that the Egyptians, when they massively converted to Christianity in the third century AD, did not use the word *ba* or any other of the Egyptian soul words to designate the Christian soul, but rather the Greek word *psykhé*.

The *akh* (hieroglyphically represented as an ibis) was a glorious transfigured spirit which coalesced in the afterlife. When the *ka* and the *ba* and the other souls of the deceased linked up in the *Duat* afterlife, the person became an *akh*, the transfigured, immortal form in which he would live forever. Failure to overcome the obstacles connected to this linking up in the *akh* resulted in the person being damned to dying a second time, to *mit em nem*, being eternally dead, just as one was damned to a "second death" if one failed the judgment test in "The Hall Of Two Truths." The *akh*, like the *ba*, could also transform and was also a ghost who could torment the living, usually for not having provided offerings for the dead.

The *akh* and the *ankh* (hieroglyphically represented as a "T" with a superimposed oval) were not formally linked, but just as the *ankh* was life, the divine breath of life, the *akh* in the afterlife was the divine spirit form and force. The *akh* — *ax* — and the *ankh* — *anx* — were not only phonetically similar, but clearly had a common etymological derivation. *Ankh* as a verb meant living and was used to describe living on earth and also living in the afterlife.

Intimately linked to this notion of the *akh* as a glorious transfigured spirit was the *khu*, the spiritual, intelligent entity which was the result of transfiguration. The recitation of the correct spells enabled the *khu* to live with the *khus* of the gods. Still two other entities came into play here, the *sahu*, the new, superior, gleaming spiritual body, and the *sekhem*, which represented immortal power, energy, knowledge and the image of the dead. In some ways, the *sekhem* was analogical to the *ka* of the gods which lived in the idols of the gods. The pure *sekhem* lived with the *khus* of the gods.

The shadow, the *khabit* (hieroglyphically represented as a half circle and a stem surmounted by another half circle) occupied a key place in the Egyptian soul system. It also could separate from the body and go where it liked, although it usually stayed near its *khu*. It also nibbled on the offerings made by the living.

The mystery of the shadow, the very intriguing existence of a shadow, was "solved" by the Egyptians who decreed that the shadow is alive, like the person who cast it; somebody without a shadow is without real existence. The *khabit*/shadow was therefore naturally one of the companion souls of a person and had to be protected from injury. One of the 42 assessors in "The Hall of Two Truths" afterlife court was the "swallower of shades," a demon who could destroy the *khabit*/shadow soul. To remain alive in the afterlife necessitated the continued existence of the shadow and the deceased went in and out of the *Duat* afterlife together with his "shade."

Colloquial language and popular superstition echo this Egyptian notion that the shadow is real and an intimate part of one's being. A radiologist "shadow gazer" looks inside... being afraid of one's deep capacities, of the quality of one's soul, is being "afraid of one's shadow"... "putting a shadow" on somebody is getting a detective to accumulate knowledge concerning somebody... and, as the American radio program in the 1950's proclaimed: "the Shadow knows." Much as "touching wood" is a memory in language of ancient tree worship, the notion that the shadow is alive and strange hearkens back to primitive beliefs.

The shadow is also an excellent example of how mythological thinking works — all living things cast living shadows and so vampires who exist, but who are not alive, have no reflected images and no shadows.

As we have seen, a person's name, the *ren* (wavy lines surmounted by an oval and preceding a seated figure with an upraised knee and a raised arm to the mouth), was a major soul. It signified the very essence of a person's identity and was particularly primordial for the pharaoh. It was owned by the person and always had meaning, but it too lived with the *khus* of the gods. Without a name, one was sure to be damned and be subjected to a second and final death. It was for this reason that Egyptian mothers immediately gave a name to their newborn child. This established the child's identity and soul and constituted a wish to the gods for a good life. (It seems that the same type of logic is involved in the Christian practice of baptizing the newborn baby, bestowing a divine character, since if a baby dies without being baptized it goes to Limbo.)

The inclusion of the *ren*, the name, in the Egyptian soul system, like the inclusion of the *khabit*/shadow soul, was the reflection of both deep understanding and primitive fear — a person who does not know his real name due to accidental causes or adoption, or who does not know the real name, the identity, of his biological parents, is a person who will be subjected to great difficulties in life.

An amuletic bead called the *sweret* was used to protect the *ren*. The recitation and the writing on amulets and funerary texts of a person's name, his *ren* soul name, were among the elements which kept the dead alive as they battled the obstacles in the *Duat*. Knowing the names of the demons in the "The Hall of Two Truths" afterlife court and in the *Duat* — who tried to conceal their *ren* names — enabled a dead person to tame them and get past their snares.

Many texts show that knowledge of a person, a god or a demon was in his *ren*: *Book of the Dead*, Spell 125: "I know you and I know your names" (*I know you because I know your name*). In the Papyrus Turin, when Seth ties to fool Horus by not revealing his true name, Horus replies: "Tell me your name, that there may be recited (*sdi*) for you. Reciting is done for a man by his name, oh god greater than his appearance!"[26] And as we shall soon see, Isis gained many of her great magical powers by extorting Re's real, concealed *ren* from him.

The task of servicing the dead and their souls, of keeping them alive, of the after-sale servicing, so to speak, was immense. It eventually led to the establishment of a kind of bank transfer system for those who could afford it: the revenues from a plot of land or craftsmen's products were given to a priest, who then handled the servicing of the dead and its souls with food and lustrations.

The fact that the *ka*, the *ba* and the *akh* could be contacted for favors also led to an immense and frequently corrupt commerce. These souls could be contacted through the means of written notes, usually inscribed on the bowls used for offerings. During the Late Period (from c. 747 BC), mummified animals were also used as intermediaries and this led to the large-scale raising, sacrificing and mummifying of animals and to the fabrication of fake mummified animals.

Many civilizations invented simpler, more straightforward and more credible systems of the soul and its links to the afterlife than the survival-after-death

26. Faulkner, R.O., *The Ancient Egyptian Book of the Dead*, p. 32 and Borghouts, J. F., *Ancient Egyptian Magical Texts*, pp. 74-75.

obsessed Egyptians, but no civilization ever invented a more subtly complex system, if we want to use a charitable term, or a more convoluted, incredible system, if we want to use a realistic term.

In the final analysis, no society ever untangled the links between the soul and the afterlife. The mechanical link between the idea of the soul — which might be a credible notion on its own as some kind of subtly material aspect of the body — to the incredible idea of the afterlife has always resisted separation.

In the final analysis, the choice could be between more or less poetry, more or less of a charming fairytale, since all the soul/afterlife systems ever invented not only linked soul and afterlife, but were based on either materialistic magic or mental and emotional magic or on their combinations. The use of a purely emotional type of magic was especially marked concerning the Christian soul/ afterlife system, but of course it gradually underwent the most tortured attempts at rationalization by theologians and philosophers. The Egyptian soul system was so to speak naturally convoluted; it needed no additional element, except its spontaneous magic, good old Egyptian *heka*, to function powerfully. And, of course, its link to the afterlife was unquestioned.

DID THE COLLAPSE OF THE OLD KINGDOM LEAD TO DOUBTS IN THE AFTERLIFE SYSTEM?

A number of texts, and notably *The Admonitions of Ipuwer*, *The Dispute Between A Man and His Ba* and some *Harper's Songs*, have frequently been cited to illustrate a so-called spiritual crisis — a generalized questioning of the afterlife system — resulting from the troubled period following the collapse of the Old Kingdom (c. 2181 BC) and the succeeding First Intermediate Period (c. 2181–2055 BC).

There can be no doubt that these were times of great political and economic distress, but it is less certain that this distress extended into widespread religious doubt in these periods and during the opening period of the Middle Kingdom (from c. 2055 BC).

The controversial text known as *The Admonitions of Ipuwer* (Papyrus Leiden 344, now in the Rijksmuseum), supposedly composed during the peaceful Twelfth Dynasty (c. 1985–1795 BC) but relating events which supposedly occurred in the troubled First Intermediate Period, is frequently cited to illustrate the calamity and spiritual crisis which befell Egypt at this time. Whatever interpretation one makes of this text, it seems certain that Ipuwer, using the example of these troubled times, is basically and implicitly making a traditional plea for order.

If we accept that Ipuwer is more or less relating the pessimistic climate of the First Intermediate Period, rather than exaggerating for the purposes of his demonstration in favor of traditional order, then we are indeed in the presence of a situation in which everything has been turned topsy-turvy, in which "The man of character walks in mourning on account of the state of the land...Crime is everywhere, there is no man of yesterday...Lo, Hapy inundates and none plow for him...Every town says, 'let us expel our rulers.'...The robber owns riches, the noble is a thief...Foreign bowmen have come into Egypt...All is ruin!...Lo, the hot-tempered says: 'If I knew where god is I would serve him...Khnum groans in weariness...See, those who owned robes are in rags, He who did not weave for himself owns fine linen..."[27]

Does all this mean that there was vast spiritual crisis in Egypt at the time? Does it mean that the type of positive, hopeful autobiographies cited above and all traditional belief had fallen by the wayside? There is room for doubt. That "despairing pessimism," [28] as A. H. Gardiner (1879–1963) put it, existed in such circumstances is not surprising, but that the religious order of Egypt was fundamentally and massively questioned seems doubtful. The odds are that Ipuwer sought to make people fear disorder.

Nevertheless, what is indeed surprising is that doubts about the realness of repeating life, *wehem ankh*, did sometimes exist, even if they were extremely rare. If some oddballs in ancient Egypt were atheists, we will never know since it was, of course, impossible to profess atheism in any ancient society — but the expression of doubts concerning some aspects of religion seems to have been possible.

One of the most famous of these doubts was eloquently expressed in the *Harper's Song from the Tomb of King Intef* (presumably Intef I and not the two other Intefs referred to on Tjetji's stele). Harpers' songs were first composed and sung with harp accompaniment in the Middle Kingdom (from c. 2055 BC). They were songs glorifying death, the afterlife and the tomb and were sung at funerals and inscribed on the walls of tombs, but all these rules were broken by the unknown author of the *Harper's Song from the Tomb of King Intef* (c. 2100 BC, on the c. 1300 BC New Kingdom Papyrus Harris 500, now in the British Museum and on a carving from Paatenemheb's c. 1200 BC Sakkara tomb, now in the Leiden Rijksmuseum Museum).

The *Harper's Song for Intef* proclaims: "Prosperous is he, this good prince, Even though good fortune may suffer harm!...The gods (the pharaohs) who lived formerly rest in their pyramids, The beatified dead (the notables) also...And they who built houses (tombs) — their places are not. See what has been made of

---

27. Lichtheim, Miriam, *Ancient Egyptian Literature, Volume I*, pp. 149-163.
28. Gardiner, Alan, *Egypt of the Pharaohs*, p. 110.

them!...Their walls are broken apart, and their places are not — As though they had never been! There is none who comes back from (over) there, That he may tell their state...That he may still our hearts, Until we (too) may travel to the place where they have gone. Let thy desire flourish, In order to let thy heart forget the beatifications (becoming the *akh* transfigured spirit upon death) for thee. Follow thy desire, as long as thou shall live...Fulfill thy needs upon earth...wailing saves not the heart of a man from the underworld. Make holiday, and weary not therein!...Behold, there is no one who departs who comes back again!"[29]

It is obvious that this amazing text undermines the very foundations of the Egyptian religion, even if it was an exception. We know that it created a stir because there are records of several other Harpers' Songs which refute its ideas. However, the fact that it was not suppressed, and was even reproduced in other tombs and on papyri, does seem to indicate that not everybody was gullible about the existence of a radiant afterlife. At the very least, there were some who did not believe — even if they only hinted at what they did not believe, even if they did not dare say too loudly what they really believed and feared.

We meet with the same kind of skepticism in the Twelfth Dynasty (c. 1985–1795 BC) story known as *The Dispute Between A Man and his Ba* (the roaming soul) (the Berlin Papyrus 3024, now in the Berlin Ägyptisches Museum). Clearly, this man has lost much of his faith in the system and people here on earth. However, he still clings to the hope of resurrection and the afterlife and wants immediate death.

The man moans: "My *ba* will not converse with me...My *ba*, too ignorant to still pain in life, Leads me toward death before I come to it! Sweeten the West [the afterlife] for me! ...Tread on the evil, put down my misery! ...What my *ba* said to me: Are you not a man? ...What do you gain by complaining about life...? ...If you lead me [the *ba*] toward death in this manner, you will not find a place on which to rest in the West...If you think of burial, it is heartbreak...Those who built...excellent tombs...when the builders have become gods [gone into the afterlife], their offering stones are desolate..." The man bewails his loneliness and generalized greed and wrongdoing. For him, "Death is before me today like a sick man's recovery, Like the fragrance of myrrh..." The man's *ba* says that he will abandon him if he talks this way and that he must await the appointed time for death: "...when it is wished that you attain the West, that your body joins the earth, I shall alight after you have become weary, and then shall we dwell together!"[30] The *ba*'s threat of abandonment was the worst thing which could happen to the man — without a *ba* soul there could be no afterlife. For the weary

---

29. Wilson, John in *Ancient Near Eastern Texts Relating to the Old Testament*, p. 467.
30. Lichtheim, Miriam, *Ancient Egyptian Literature, Volume I*, pp. 163-169.

man in this story, the afterlife was even more of a central religious hope than it was for all Egyptians; it was his only hope for redemption from an unlivable life on earth.

In fact, what we have in this story is a very unorthodox approach both by the weary man and especially his *ba* that should know better. The man has implicitly put into question the *maat* order of the world, the concept that the world is being run in an orderly, correct and harmonious manner by the gods and the pharaoh. Surprisingly, as in the earlier *Harper's Song for Intef*, the value of building tombs and doubts concerning the happiness and justice which supposedly awaited everybody in the afterlife were questioned. And it was the *ba* soul who expressed these doubts and proclaimed that it would be wiser to wait as long as possible before embarking on the difficult "voyage" to the afterlife and living in uncertain conditions there.

The French Egyptologist Claire Lalouette (b. 19??) thinks that *The Dispute Between A Man and his Ba* was a "lingering echo" of the "social revolution" and "moral crisis" which had occurred two to four hundred years earlier during the First Intermediary Period. Her analysis is that "the individual who until then had lived in a coherent framework, in a hierarchical and well-balanced society, was suddenly left to himself, his traditional values being flouted... "[31]

This observation is certainly pertinent in explaining the background to the text, to the dislocation which followed the collapse of the glorious Old Kingdom, as expressed in *The Dispute Between A Man and his Ba*, as well as in *The Admonitions of Ipuwer*, but I wonder if it sufficiently takes into account how rare religious doubt or the contestation of the hierarchical order was in Egypt during any period. Perhaps, Lalouette and other Egyptologists, notably Gardiner, using a few texts written by exceptional people, simply went too far in an attempt to add a spiritual crisis to the political and economic crisis of the First Intermediary Period.

To begin with, the crisis engendered by the collapse of the Old Kingdom had ended at least two hundred years before *The Dispute Between A Man and his Ba* was composed. And the papyrus we have of *The Admonitions of Ipuwer* dates to the Nineteenth Dynasty (c. 1295–1186 BC) and can be interpreted as traditional praise of the concept that order is always a fundamental value, at least as surely as it can be interpreted as a report of what really happened in the First Intermediate Period. Moreover, great care has to be taken in distinguishing between the doubts of a few of the elite, the notables, and the situation of ordinary Egyptians. Ordinary Egyptians had just won fabulous victories — the right to possess souls

---

31. Lalouette, Claire, *Textes Sacrés et Textes Profanes de l'Ancienne Egypte, I, Des Pharaons et des hommes*, pp. 334-335, Note 110.

and the right to an afterlife, which they must have considered as immense hopeful developments despite the disastrous economic and social situation.

In any case, I stick to my interpretation — only a very few experienced the fundamental issue of religious doubt in ancient Egypt. The texts of the First Intermediary Period and immediately afterwards almost exclusively continued to express standard Egyptian beliefs. Doubt of any kind, and especially religious doubt, was never an Egyptian trait.

The doubts of the few could not have mattered much; the priestly machine for fabricating complex resurrection and afterlife theology was unstoppable and hope for an afterlife was unquenchable. The process rolled along, whatever the problems or contradictions encountered.

THE AFTERMATH TO EGYPT'S SYSTEM OF SALVATION, THE TREATMENT OF THE DEAD BODY AND THE AFTERLIFE

The possible influence on other peoples of Egypt's resurrection/afterlife system is largely unverifiable. The universal yearning for such systems and the question of the content of the afterlife, or its non-existence, and the related question of how to treat the body after death and its consequences are obviously so fundamental that all peoples everywhere have devoted considerable attention and resources to them. The great variety of solutions adopted leans towards a conclusion of a series of independent developments. It is, of course, impossible to either assume any kind of linear development or to reject its possibility; nevertheless, it is not unreasonable to assume that the foundation upon which the other eschatologies, except the Hindu, built their systems had something to do with the timid beginnings of the new system of values which had been made in Egypt.

It took about 1400 years before Egypt's complex and seemingly credible solution to the problem of death, attained by the Middle Kingdom (c. 2055 BC), was radicalized by new pie-in-the-sky concepts of the afterlife in the sixth century BC by the Persians. At that time the Zoroastrians invented, or brought to a flowering, a new system that despite some startling contradictions incontestably provided a more credible, and above all more moral, answer to the problem of death. Needless to add, it was just as infantile as the Egyptian answer, but its magic and wishful thinking were far better sublimated and it ended the Egyptian-type static vision of man's place and destiny in the universe. The Zoroastrian Persians invented Heaven and Hell. The Zoroastrian Persians proposed a new ethical destiny for the individual and mankind — an authentic eschatology.

The Persian Zoroastrians reasoned that there must be a final reward for the good, for doing the will of the good and wise sole god Ahura Mazdah. The Zoroastrians decreed that there would be a general resurrection of all the dead, the final defeat of evil by the Savior Saoshyant, and a world restored to its primordial state of perfect goodness. The Zoroastrian reward was *Pardes*, Paradise, *Wahisht*, Heaven, and eternal bliss after the final judgment and resurrection. And this time, and even before the final judgment and resurrection, there was no cheating. For the Zoroastrians, magic and lying could not replace moral behavior; the Persian judge of the dead, Rashnu, meted out impartial justice "to the highest and the lowest." Logically enough, the Zoroastrians reasoned that there had to be a sanction for evil. This sanction was *Dojangah*, "the Abode of the Lie," *Dozakh*, Hell.

Of all the monotheistic eschatologies that would be developed over the next 1300 years, the Persian, despite some terrifying aspects, remained the most optimistic, merciful and charitable. In the *Avesta*, it was decreed that the entirety of humanity that had ever lived, including the evil (after being punished and cleansed) would be saved. There would be a final redemption, ultimate justice, a *Frasokereti* (a "refreshing") during which everybody in Heaven and Hell would be resurrected and liquid metal poured over them as a judgment. The evil would suffer terribly, but the pure would experience the molten metal as a shower of "warm milk." Everybody — the pure and the redeemed sinners — would then live eternally in a new world where only truth and goodness existed. There was no Egyptian-type eternal, damned, "second death" status in Persian eschatology; punishment of the evil was temporary — they would return from Hell and be redeemed — and evil would definitely be defeated.

A surprising contradiction existed in the *logical* Zoroastrian system, as it did in the other monotheistic systems: if there was to be a resurrection of bodies, should they not preserve the body, as the Egyptians did, rather than let it decompose or destroy it? The Zoroastrians (like the African Dogons, perhaps at least 1500 years later) adopted one of the most radical methods ever devised for treating the dead body. This method was active exposure — placing the body in conditions facilitating its obliteration by birds, animals and the climate. Clearly, and so unlike the Egyptians, the Zoroastrians postulated a conflict between the material and the spiritual, between the body and the soul. Their strict dualistic view downgraded the body in this life and decreed that the dead body was impure. The Zoroastrians sought to avoid contaminating what they saw as the basic natural elements, earth, water and especially fire. These natural elements could therefore not be used for inhumation.

The Hebrews, despite their proximity to death-obsessed Egypt, either lucidly refused, or failed, to find a satisfactory pie-in-the-sky solution to the problem of death until they came under Persian influence, and even then it was a solution which was contested by other Jews.

The old Hebrew concept of *Sheol* was as hopeless and indifferent as the Sumerian *Kur* and the Hebrews, like the Sumerians, believed that nothing a man could do during his lifetime through deeds or magic could change this. The Hebrew burial method — in caves or in graves protected by a mere shroud — reflected the beliefs that man had been made "of the dust of the ground," was dust ("for dust thou art") and returned there ("and unto dust shalt thou return"). For the Hebrews, "...the breath of life," the "living soul" which "man became" belonged to God.[32] There was therefore no need to permanently preserve the body, even if there seems to have been great respect for the dead body and especially a focus on burying the entirety of the body.

Between the sixth and first centuries BC, the Judeans gradually, but only partially, adopted the Persian conceptual and moral modification of the final judgment and afterlife. For the prophet Deutero-Isaiah (c. 6th century BC), the "Days of the Messiah" would produce universal peace, prosperity and fraternity, in which "nation shall not lift up sword against nation, neither shall they learn war any more." For the Judeans, *Shamayim*, Heaven, the abode of God, would be on earth. The "Days of the Messiah" would precede the *Olam ha-ba*, the world to come, in Heaven, for the righteous. However, the Judeans continued to believe that suffering was the result of sin and, contrary to Zoroastrianism, sinners were not redeemed but, as in later Christianity, suffered eternal damnation.

The Judeans coupled their eschatology with the extraordinary concept that suffering brought a person closer to God. Deutero-Isaiah preached that it was good to be the suffering "servant" of God in the interval before the advent of the "Days of the Messiah" and the Final Judgment. Deutero-Isaiah's waiting tactic was perhaps one of the most extraordinary inventions and illusions ever concocted — suffering was a good thing, a sign that a person was righteous and a mighty instrument of individual knowledge and development. There was enough truth in this concept to render it operational not only for illuminati and masochists, but for great masses of ordinary people.

It is a pity that the Egyptians were never terribly interested in theological developments in Israel (or in any other society, for that matter) because it would have no doubt been both interesting and hilarious to know their reaction, the reaction of a people so fundamentally unconcerned by spiritual guilt and suffering.

During the sixth century BC, with the prophets Ezekiel and Zechariah, Judaism also gradually acknowledged a Persian-type future resurrection and an

---

32. Genesis 2:7, 3:19 and 2:7.

eternal afterlife — an evolution which culminated with mystics like Daniel (c. 165 BC) and the Maccabee warriors (c. 175 BC–AD 135). However, Judaism never ceased to emphasize individual and collective judgment in this life and no immediate afterlife Heaven or Hell just after death; and Judea's priestly caste, the Sadducees, continued to hold to the traditional view of no afterlife. Arguments continue in Judaism right into our time about what is exactly redeemed in the final resurrection — the body and the soul, or just the soul. The Hellenized Jewish Alexandrian philosopher Philo (c. 20 BC–AD 50) postulated that only the soul is immortal. The Reform Movement (which groups a majority of practicing Jews in the United States) also postulates the immortality of the soul, but the inexistence of a final judgment and resurrection.

The Hebrews connected their emphasis on this life and ethics to individual and national well-being, but they seem to have unwittingly pioneered the secular system that eventually led to ethical behavior being considered as a value in itself, a value unconnected to a possible afterlife.

And so the Hebrews, like the Sumerians, were either more lucid or less imaginative than the Egyptians. The differences between Hebrew and Egyptian thinking on the afterlife and on how to treat the dead body and their consequences were obviously immense, but as unproven as it may be, it is difficult to avoid considering that the Hebrew approach evolved from a rejection of Egyptian practices.

After the Zoroastrian revolution and the weak Hebrew response to it, the historical role of considerably amplifying the entire afterlife system fell into the hands of the Christians and the Moslems, especially concerning Hell for the Christians and Heaven for the Moslems.

The early Christians seem to have built on Egyptian magical afterlife concepts, Persian and Hebrew eschatolgies, and the frequent Greek philosophical view that ethics was a value in itself. The early Christians were obviously fundamentally opposed to the core meaning of the traditional Egyptian view of hierarchical privileges beginning with the gods, going all the way down into the lowest classes of society and extending into the magically earned afterlife. They were also dissatisfied with the Hebrew answer in the Old Testament *Book of Job* that rendered man incapable of understanding God's ways in meting out punishment and justice and God's way of using evil.

Jesus, or the early Church fathers, had postulated the most radical philosophy of love, total forgiveness and meekness which history had ever seen and cast it into an ethic which was a supreme religious value in itself; but its connection to an afterlife reward for moral behavior was its ambiguous point. For Jesus, not only ethics — works — but faith, belief in God the Father and God's free gift of grace were the justifications for the reward of eternal life. Augustine (AD 354–

430) and some of the fathers of the Early Church even went further by reducing the entire debate to needless speculation, given that faithful and good behavior were predestined and necessarily rewarded. Jesus' unique and lofty ethics were bent into a rigid system which depended not only on belief in God but on membership in the Church; the impossibility of earning Paradise for any person, including newborn children, who had not been baptized in the Church; policies of no salvation outside the Church; and forced conversions.

For the Christians, dreadful apocalyptic events would occur before the defeat of Satan and evil. Then, as John said in the *Book of Revelation*, "a new heaven and a new earth" would be created, "there shall be no night" in Heaven for those accorded everlasting life and the sinners would languish in Hell suffering everlasting punishment. The Christians also adopted the Hebrew concept of *creative suffering*, purification through suffering, while awaiting the "new heaven and new earth" and even amplified it into a scorn for the body, seeking suffering, including physical mortification, in order to come closer to the Son and the Father.

The Christian "new Heaven and new earth" was the radical eschatological answer to the problem of unsanctioned evil and suffering and unrewarded morality in the world, the absolute blissful answer; but whether it was faith, works or predestination which provided the access to Paradise remained a mystery. The Christian Hell and later Purgatory were also absolute answers — they were such terrible places that they have never ceased to raise questions among Christians about how a moral, wise God could plan such a destiny even for the evil and especially for unbaptized children.

The Christian solution to the problem of death was grandiose, but the compatibility of a good, omnipotent God and the idea that he chose who would go to Paradise, Hell or Purgatory was never solved by Christian theologians. The best of a bad lot of answers was made by Immanuel Kant (1724–1804). Kant proclaimed in a secular, but culturally Christian, manner that a God and an afterlife must exist because, clearly, morality is not rewarded in this life, so it must be rewarded in the next life due to the self-evident nature of the law of morality. Kant transformed Jesus' ethics of mutual respect into a secular touchstone and reduced religion's role to morality, but his eschatological answer, lacking as it did any element of active faith, was of course unacceptable to Christians, whatever their denomination.

Of all the eschatologies, the Moslem *Yaum al-Qiyama* final judgment, *Ba'th nushur* resurrection and *Janna al-na'im*, Heaven, "the gardens of delight" perhaps went furthest in its detailed promises. It was perhaps the most fabulous example of the material benefits to be gained in the afterlife by true believers and military servants of Allah. It resembled, in an amplified form, the promises of the good life in the Egyptian afterlife *Duat Aaru* Field of the Reeds. Indescribable bliss in the

Jannat al-na'im, including 72 beautiful, sexually exciting virgin *huris* and *khamr*, alcoholic beverages, which were prohibited for the living, were promised for believers. There are even suggestions in the Koran that believers might see Allah. All of this was attenuated by one of the most sublime religious concepts ever invented — intentionality. The Central Asian Moslem theologian El Bokhari (810–870) stated that one of Mohammed's most fundamental *h'adith*, traditional sayings, was: "Actions will only be judged by their intentions."[33] Nevertheless, over the centuries, the promise of extraordinary rewards led to a debate among Moslems over whether these promises were metaphorical or concrete and whether they discouraged people from believing in God as a value in itself. On the other hand, a huge pot of fiery tar in *Jahannam*, Hell, was the destiny of sinners, and especially *kafirs*, unbelievers.

While all this evolution was going on, only a single people, the Hindus, were developing an afterlife system which had nothing to do with the solutions sketched out in Egypt. From about 1400 BC, the Hindus had gone their own original way in seeking solutions to the problems of evil, suffering, the afterlife and the final destiny of mankind and the world. And, as usual, they came up with the most complicated, the most metaphysical, the most enigmatic and the most pessimistic answers. The Hindus surpassed the Egyptians in the complexity of their theology concerning what happens after death and how it fits into the cosmos.

The Hindu and the Egyptian way of thinking were extravagantly and diametrically opposed. Operating with both their own type of magic and a hyperbolic metaphysical quest, the Hindus anchored a system of incineration of the dead body and successive reincarnations and a final goal of extinction (*nirvana*), both based on moral merit.

The Hindus reacted to the tragedy and suffering of life — terms which would have been incomprehensible to the Egyptians — by postulating the elimination of all desire, the illusion (*maya*) of knowledge and material possessions and an end to *samsara*, the cycles of birth, death and rebirth with the final goal of Nirvana. The extinction of the individual self and identity — *Nirvana* — came after an indefinite number of afterlives, or rather reincarnations, in human, animal or plant form in which only a kind of soul was identical to that of previous lives. A kind of Hindu Heaven, *Svarga*, was postulated, but it was barely human, it was more for the gods than for humans. As for Hell, *Naraka*, it was a temporary place of great torment, but subordinate to both the concepts of *karma*, rebirth in

---

33. El Bokhari, *L'Authentique Tradition Musulmane* (translation by G.H. Bousquet), Fasquelle Editeurs, Paris, 1964, p. 35.

various forms within a rigid caste system according to merit in past lives, and to the final goal of *Nirvana*.

Hindu cosmology proposed a circular system of mind-boggling complexity. This involved a system of four *Yugas* (ages), from the *Krita Yuga* Golden Age to the Kali *Yuga* Dark Age. Together, the *Yugas* formed a *Mahayuga* (4,320,000 years in human time). After a *Kalpa* (2000 *Mahayugas*, 8,640,000,000 years in human time and 24 hours for Brahma, the creation and Chief God), the universe is destroyed and recreated. These Big Bangs and Big Crunches go on for a *Para* (a century in Brahma's time) and then everything ceases to exist, including Brahma, although some versions of this system claim that Brahma can choose to begin a new *Para*.

Of course, even had they been aware of it, the entirety of the Hindu system and the reasons for establishing it could not have influenced the optimistic Egyptians; in fact, it would have probably horrified them.

To begin with, the Egyptian radical and materialistic solution of preserving the body after death through mummification and the equally radical, but anti-materialistic, Hindu solution of destroying the body through cremation were diametrically opposed to each other. For the Egyptians, it seemed obvious that there could be no afterlife without the preservation of the body and its use as a "home" by the several souls. The optimistic Egyptians were intent on keeping the body alive after death, on continuing bodily joys. The pessimistic Hindus saw no need to drag the source of all trouble — the body — into future lives and *a fortiori* into *Nirvana*. For the Hindus, as for the Zoroastrians, perhaps in relation to their common Aryan origins, the destruction, the cremation, of the unimportant and even impure body was a prerequisite to further evolution. The blurring of individual identity in the cycle of rebirths within other bodies and the final extinction of the self in *Nirvana* would have also been particularly distasteful to the Egyptians, who placed such great emphasis on the deep identity of an individual, on his name, the *ren*, as a person's key soul.

None of the leaps made by the Hindus, the Hebrews, the Persians and the Christians were even vaguely possible in ancient Egypt. The austerity and pessimism, and especially the strange way of challenging the reality of death, of the Hindu system and its daughter, Buddhism, were diametrically opposed to the Egyptian method of perceiving human experience. The Persian, Hebrew and Christian eschatolgies and their emphasis on suffering and purification were beyond the grasp of the ancient Egyptians. The Egyptians wanted to feel comfortable, ritually pure and primevally innocent; the Hindus were fed up with life and sought hope in extinction; the Persians wanted to feel morally pure and the Hebrews, and especially the Christians, wanted to feel uncomfortable and guilty as well as morally pure. The ancient Egyptians probably could only have felt fairly comfortable with the Moslem definition of Heaven and its bodily pleasures. This could have been a factor in their later rejection of Christianity and adoption of the Moslem religion with only minority opposition.

Needless to say, the ancient Greek and modern Western view of ethics as a value in itself, detached from both primeval conceptions of divine cosmological order and disorder and a supposed afterlife, would not have been taken seriously by the ancient Egyptians.

CHAPTER 10. POLYTHEISM, THEOCRACY AND POLITICO-RELIGIOUS RIVALRY AND THE ADVENT OF MONOTHEISING CHIEF GODS

THE BIRTH OF MONOTHEISING CHIEF GODS

With the exception of the brief period of Atenist proto-monotheism, invented by Akhenaten (c. 1352–1336 BC), the basic thrust, the basic polytheistic philosophy, of the Egyptian religion remained the same for more than 3000 years, even if it was laced with great complexity, frequent changes, syncretism, mono-theising tendencies, utter confusion and contradiction. The ultimate stage in this confusion was the co-existence of the powerful Chief God Amun-Re and an equally powerful polytheistic system from at least the beginning of the New Kingdom in c. 1550 BC. At one and the same time, no Egyptian god (or any god anywhere before the Hebrew Yahweh) had ever concentrated so much soleness and power in his hands and the polytheistic system was never so exuberantly multiple. Even Henri Frankfort (1879–1954), the staunchest supporter of the theory of "multiple approaches and answers" rather than confusion and contradiction in the Egyptian theological system, admitted that Amun-Re was a "syncretic" god and "the closest approach to the worship of a supreme and universal god known within the scope of Egyptian polytheism."[34]

The failure of the attempt to solve this confusion by the introduction of Aten proto- monotheism in the mid-14th century BC and the restoration of the

---

34. Frankfort, Henri, *Ancient Egyptian Religion, An Interpretation*, p. 22.

system of a powerful chief god within a powerful polytheistic framework were completely in the Egyptian character.

Egyptian polytheism persisted basically because the Egyptians could never abandon the concept of many gods animistically, immanently personifying the entirety of the elements of the Universe. Unity within multiplicity always appears as an afterthought and was never more fundamental than diversity. This remained true whatever the powers of a chief god, and however close theologically (but usually not ethically) to forms of unity and pre-monotheism as the concepts these gods represented might be. Moreover, as real as the monotheising tendencies of a Re, a Ptah or an Amun-Re might be, the polytheistic framework in which they operated always remained the stronger of the two elements. Even when unity was strongly proclaimed, as with Amun-Re, it was never a simple unity; it was always unity composed of diversity, of totalizing, of *heh*, of millions. Moreover, the motive of Amun-Re's unity was heavily tinged with the Theban clergy's political desire to make him appear as the most powerful of all the gods.

Paradoxically, it was this confusion (or richness) which largely contributed to making Egypt, and not Sumer, the trunk of the tree of the history of religion, or at least the forerunner, and perhaps the instigator, of so many later mainstream religious concepts.

Gradual religious evolution and transformation in Sumer produced a less extravagant system than in Egypt. Confusion, or richness, engendered a frenzy for religious experimentation in Egypt. It led Egypt to explore and adopt many concepts that were not necessarily strictly polytheistic, while maintaining Egypt's basic polytheistic thrust and framework. This was notably the case for the chief gods, who incorporated monotheising tendencies and who for a long time were more powerful in Egypt than in any of the other polytheistic countries.

Although Amun-Re indisputably carried chief god theology to its apotheosis in Egyptian history, he was preceded by several other powerful chief gods, notably Horus, Re and Ptah, and also Osiris to the extent that Osiris was the chief god of the land of the dead. All these gods and their theologies constituted building blocks which eventually led to the Amun-Re chief god theology, followed by the proto-monotheistic Atenist revolution. It culminated in the Nineteenth Dynasty (c. 1295–1186 BC) with the strongest monotheising Amun-Re chief god theology within polytheism that the world had ever seen.

As we have seen, the falcon god Horus was Egypt's first chief god, from at least the time of the unification of the Two Lands, Upper and Lower Egypt (c. 3100 BC). However, Horus was basically a henotheistic and then a divine kingship and chief god, who assimilated many gods but was also eventually assimilated himself by Re. Horus was also subjected to a *de facto* and awkward amalgamation of two distinctly different series of Horuses — the falcon, Horus the Elder (Haroeris), and the Osirisian Horus the Younger (Harseisis) series of gods. All this gave Horus the basic nature of multiple forms, in contrast to the totalizing chief gods who followed him.

The Re solar theology of Heliopolis seems to have been the first to postulate monotheising chief gods (from about the middle of the Fourth Dynasty, c. 2566 BC). The accentuation of this tendency directly led to the totalizing Amun-Re chief god theology of Thebes in the New Kingdom (c. 1550– 1069 BC). In turn, this led Egypt into an unwitting pioneering (but aborted) role in forms of Aten monolatry and proto-monotheism. It also led to the later primitive plural monotheistic organic triad — Amun/Re/Ptah — within the polytheistic system.

The practice of reducing many gods to a few gods or to a single god, or rather of amalgamating the attributes of many gods in a single god, was naturally a part of chief god theology. In this manner, a limited number of very powerful gods co-existed and sometimes, as in the case of Amun-Re, were paradoxically nearly omnipotent alongside the other gods and goddesses who were not eliminated.

The amalgamation of gods into duos, triads and enneads and the transformation of the gods who had been amalgamated into aspects of a powerful chief god — the idea that the plural could become a collective singular, that two, three or more gods could be reduced to one — was widespread in ancient chief god theology and was particularly anchored in the Egyptian system. There are dissenting voices, but for me, Egypt ambiguously but surely went further down the road in developing these pre-monotheistic concepts than any other society.

In addition to this type of theological perception, or reasoning, or leaning, towards monotheism, the origins of the chief gods also seem to owe at least as much to politico-economic needs and theocratic clerical rivalry. In Egypt, as in other ancient polytheistic societies, there was frequent theological and politico-economic-military warfare inspired by the powerful theocratic clergies of the leading nomes and cities.

The clergies of Hierakonpolis and Edfu (Horus), Ombos and Avaris (Seth), Heliopolis (Re), Abydos and Busiris (Osiris), Memphis (Ptah), Hermopolis (Thoth), Thebes (Amun), Akhetaten/El Amarna (Aten) and Elephantine and Esna (Khnum) vied for prominence or total power at various epochs. Politics and economics played roles at least as important as theology in these battles. All of these cities sought to magnify the powers of their local, henotheistic god, to impose their henotheistic god as the chief god of a powerful local or regional triad, and to assimilate as many other gods as possible as aspects of their own chief god. Many of them invented their own ennead of gods, theology, and creation myth, and claimed that these were the oldest in Egypt. In a final stage, each sought to impose their chief god as the royal and chief god of all Egypt.

This system of the rise of local henotheistic gods to regional and national domination was a constant practice, but there were exceptions. One notable case was the creator god Khnum, who was a god of national importance before he became chief god of Elephantine and Esna and who was also included in two forms in the Abydos ennead. It also must be noted that numerous nome or local henotheistic gods consistently preserved domination in their zones despite the existence of the powerful, national chief gods.

The dominant chief god frequently mirrored on the religious level the absolute political power of the pharaoh and/or the central power of the nome nomarchs or the high priests of a leading temple. A strong totalitarian, theocratic state was a natural terrain for the rise of powerful chief gods. This was especially true before ethics and the divine were structurally, if not entirely effectively, bound up together, as occurred in later Israel.

The predominant chief god never eliminated the gods and functions he had assimilated, but rather these assimilated gods remained powerful as manifestations, or aspects, or the *ba* (soul) of the overall composite being of the predominant chief god. These assimilated gods, these gods who had become *ba* aspects of a chief god, were therefore overshadowed rather than totally absorbed. There was some overlap in functions, but the assimilated gods continued to be worshipped individually in their own right and they maintained some of their own prerogatives and attributes.

The composite form became the main identity of the chief god — or perhaps new identity is a better term — but his original separate identity also survived. Thus Ptah-Seker or Amun-Re were new gods, combining all the previous attributes of both gods concerned, but this never meant that textual and iconographic religious references to each god as such were abandoned.

At the same time, the considerable and apparently paradoxical extension of chief gods represented one of the key developments related to Egypt's evolution as the most complete polytheistic and theocratic system invented until its time. Egyptian chief god theology may well have been the vital and final polytheistic stage in the foundation of early Hebrew henotheism that decreed that Yahweh was the most powerful of all the gods. It may have also had some influence on Ahura Mazdah henotheism in Persia.

However, with the sole exception of the monotheistic Aten for a brief period in the 14th century BC, Egyptian chief gods, whatever their omnipotence, were never anti-polytheistic. These monotheising, or totalizing gods, rather completed and consolidated polytheism, giving it immense religious, theological and political flexibility.

THE CHIEF GOD ROLE OF THE SKY AND SUN GOD, RE

The earliest Egyptian god who clearly incorporated all of the characteristics of the chief god was the sun god Re. According to the New Kingdom *Litany of Re*, he eventually had more than 75 titles and names, on his own and due to his assimilation of other gods and their functions. Re's gradual acquisition of the functions, powers and appearances of other gods was typically of the chief god type within a polytheistic system. His accumulation of powers and subjugation of other gods as his aspects suggest changing religious and politico-economic needs. Re assimilated other gods for a much longer period than the previous and older chief and royally incarnated sky god, the falcon Horus. He also remained at the top of the heap of gods much longer than Horus did, even when this position became more theoretical than real.

Re's (*Ra*, the sun, in Egyptian) origin seems to be situated in early Egyptian *seba*, star, worship as the sun itself. This type of totemistic and animistic worship possibly went right back to the outset of the Egyptian Naqada II (c. 3500 BC) proto-agricultural religion, before any West Asian influence. In the First Dynasty (c. 3100–2890 BC), the pivotal aspect of sun worship in the Egyptian outlook was already apparent with a sun cult.

A specific worship of Re as a sun god can be dated to the Second Dynasty with, for the first time, a pharaoh adopting a Re name — Raneb (c. 2865 BC), meaning "Re is lord," or "lord of Re."

During the Third Dynasty (c. 2686–2613 BC), Re moved further to the forefront. This rise was surely in conjunction with the building of the first pyramid, the Step Pyramid, by Pharaoh Djoser (c. 2667–2648 BC) and its role as entry point for the pharaoh to an afterlife in the sky, in the sun, in "lightland." Re was now on the verge of taking over from the predominance of Horus (and also to a lesser extent, Seth) in the previous dynasties.

A further development of the sun cult can also be traced to Djoser, who probably built the first Sun Temple in Heliopolis. The central element in this temple seems to have been the *benben* stone, representing the original primeval mound on which the first rays of the rising sun were believed to have fallen. Just as the sperm of Atum, who had created the gods and man, was said to be contained within the *benben*, it was now Re's sperm as Re-Atum.

As we have seen, it was during the Fourth Dynasty (c. 2613–2494 BC) that the powerful theologians of Heliopolis might have twisted Pharaoh Radjedef's (c. 2566–2558 BC) arm so that he chose *sa Ra*, son of Re, as his fifth royal name, his nomen, his birth name, in addition to his praenomen throne name — "Re is his support." Radjedef and succeeding pharaoh-gods were no longer only the living the incarnation of the god Horus, they were also the god-sons of Re, the Chief God of the Heliopolis temple. The pharaoh was an incarnation of Re on earth, the *sa* Ra "son of Re," and his second *shenu*-cartouche contained a statement glorifying Re. Radjedef's successor and half-brother, Pharaoh Khephren (*Ra'kha'ef*, ruled c. 2558–2532 BC), the builder of one of three great pyramids at Giza, consistently used his status as *sa* Ra as a divine justification of his status and power.

With this Fourth Dynasty takeover of Re from Horus as official state god, Re's preeminence, Heliopolis' solar cult religion and its role as Egypt's main temple were affirmed. Re was now the uncontested royal and chief god. The concept of divine kingship linked to Re was solidly anchored, and the pharaoh's powers as a god were objectively limited by making him dependent on Re. Simultaneously, the Heliopolis theologians set up an elaborate system in favor of the pharaoh ensuring him an eternally positive afterlife in the sky, in "lightland," with Re. They also ascribed creator and agricultural/Nile inundation functions to Re. As we have also seen, these Fourth Dynasty changes had theological roots, but also seem to have been part of a vast political scheme to increase the powers and privileges of the Heliopolitan clergy as custodians of the Re cult.

Re assimilated the attributes of the Heliopolitan Ennead's traditional chief god, the primordial self-created creator god Atum, and pushed Atum into a virtual secondary status. Re also became the primeval young scarab, or scarab-headed, god Khepri, who pushed the sun across the sky as the scarab pushed a dung ball across the earth from east to west, from morning to evening. The *kheper*, the scarab, buried the dung ball in the evening as the sun is buried when it disappears below the western *akhet*, horizon. The eggs in the dung ball hatched, the larvae ate the dung for food and then one morning, a young scarab emerged as the new rising sun, as Khepri. The scarab glyph — *hpr* — "to become," *hpw* — early morning — and *hprw, kheperu* — "forms, transformations — were all linked to Khepri, who was "he who is coming into being."

Re's Khepri functions were particularly important since the solar-linked scarab, as a symbol of becoming and resurrection and as a cosmogonic and creative sexual force was one of the most basic Egyptian beliefs. The scarab was one of the most popular amulets in Egypt. Pharaohs frequently used scarabs as name seals and also inscribed important declarations on large stone scarabs and, as we know, the heart scarab also played a key role concerning entry into the afterlife.

Re was the undisputed head of the Heliopolitan Ennead and Chief God of the Heliopolis Temple. Re, as the strong midday sun and as both Kepri, the young, rising sun, and Atum, the old, setting sun, constituted a virtual assimilation of key sun functions of Horus. Horus, as Horemakhet, now appeared in Re's Khepri form of the sun on the eastern *akhet*, horizon, at sunrise. This combined sun and royal god, Re and Horus, Re-Horakthe, the sun, the sun of the two *akhet*, horizons, morning and evening — the sun throughout the day — became the light and the breath of the world. Re was now the lord of "lightland" in the sky, appearing in various solar phases as Horakthe, Khepri and Atum.

In fact, rather than combining, Horus was merged with Re, even if Re's assimilation of Horus' sun and royal patron functions resembled an association, a unification of the two main solar powers more than a brutal assimilation. His assimilation of most of the forms of Horus the Elder, as Re-Horakthe, was one of the principal aspects of his chief god status and of his role in divine kingship. But, in typical Egyptian fashion, both the various forms of the falcon Horus the Elder (Haroeris) and Horus the Younger (Harseisis), the son of Osiris and Isis, continued to coexist with the various forms of Re. Re was Horus and Horus was Re, but a multitude of national and local forms of Horus continued to exist.

Pharaoh Userkap (c. 2494–2487 BC) opened the Fifth Dynasty (c. 2494–2345 BC) by accentuating the reverence for Re by building a Re sun temple at Abusir, north of Memphis. All of the other Fifth Dynasty pharaohs, except the last two, followed his lead by building Re sun temples in addition to monumental personal pyramids. "Pleasure of Re," "Field of Re" and "Horizon of Re" were some of the names of these sun temples.

Re's power as a chief god grew steadily throughout the Fifth Dynasty, despite the rise in importance of Osiris for the pharaohs at least from Unas' time (c. 2375–2345 BC). Re had now achieved super chief god status, especially in Heliopolis, but also everywhere in Egypt. Re's powers were such that the attributes of all the other gods were secondary with Re seemingly assuming near total power in the sky and on the earth. Atum, the tired, old evening aspect of the setting sun, was also Re, but above all, it was now Re as Re-Atum, who as the *benu* bird was perched on the primeval mound, on the *benben*, was self-created, or self-existent, like Atum. It was now Re who had emerged on the *benben* mound from Nun, the primeval chaotic waters, and the *benu* bird became an aspect of Re, his *ba* soul. Re, or Re-Atum, was now the creator-godhead of the solar cycle and of the nine animal and human-headed gods and goddesses of the Heliopolis Ennead, Egypt's first and most important ennead. The entirety of the universe was expressed together in the Heliopolis Ennead led by Re.

Re was the "All-God," the governor of the entire universe, who every day majestically sailed across the sky and into the *Duat* nether world afterlife and then emerged after always defeating the enormous serpent Apophis, the chaos factor, the force pushing the orderly primeval universe into disorder. A choir of sun worshipping baboons and dancing, joyful animals saluted Re every morning.

A fervent cult to Re was also celebrated in his bull form, as Re-Mnevis, especially in Heliopolis. Re was incarnated in the Mnevis bull, "the mighty bull of Re," a bull carefully selected by the priests because he was magically black with only clump-like figures on his body and tail. Upon death, the Mnevis was mummified and sent to the afterlife. The Mnevis aspect of Re was so revered that even during brief interlude of Aten solar proto-monotheism, Pharaoh Akhenaten (c. 1352–1336 BC) did not dare to totally abolish the Mnevis cult as he had abolished the cults of all the other gods. Paradoxically, Re's accumulation of powers and amalgamation of gods reached an apex during Akhenaten's reign as the sole god, the sun disk Aten, was described as being Re. In fact, Re was no longer really or fully Re; the Aten was a distinct god.

Re's physical appearance, attributes, powers and roles changed frequently. His association with so many other gods, his assimilation of their powers and his composite forms involving other gods and animal attributes were so numerous that they led to an exceedingly complex and often difficult situation to follow. Most frequently, Re was represented as a falcon-headed human with a sun disk headdress encircled by a uraeus and he usually held an *ankh*, the amulet symbolizing the life force. This was notably his form as Re-Horakhte, Re and Horus, the sun in the two horizons. His link to trees, pillars and obelisks suggest very old forms of solar worship and protection from disorder, illness and evil lost in the night of prehistoric times. His falcon, or hawk, animal-headed form was linked to his assimilation of Horus, but might also have a Heliopolitan local, emblem/totemistic, and henotheistic, predynastic origin. His scarab form was linked to his assimilation of Khepri, but could have also had its own Re origins. His ram-headed form was linked to the night sun Osiris and to Atum. His black — but sometimes sun-red — Mnevis bull form clearly represented virility and strength, as well as still another link to the sun. His link to lions represented savage, warrior qualities.

Despite Re's power in the sky and on the earth, the key problem of power in the god Osiris' *Duat*, afterlife, nether land remained to be solved. At least since the end of the Fifth Dynasty, in Pharaoh Unas' time (c. 2375–2345 BC), Osiris and Osirisian concepts had become fundamental for the pharaohs, with the pharaohs gradually assuming the status of Osirises upon death. Just as he was Horus, the son of Re, during his lifetime, the pharaoh became Osiris in the afterlife. Even if the pharaoh also continued to be the companion of Re in "lightland," Re's afterlife functions had been considerably reduced in favor of Osiris. The inventive Heliopolitan clergy had the answer to this thorny problem of divine omnipotence as well — they decreed that Osiris was the night sun of Re and the *ba* soul of Re, thus creating another double sun deity and theoretically keeping Re's power intact. Re was now all the various forms of the sun, the day and the so-called night suns, and when he emerged from the *Duat* Underworld in the morning he was saluted as the resurrected god by Osiris' wife Isis and Seth's wife Nephthys.

In fact, Osiris was the King of the land of the dead, the *Duat*, Chief God of the Dead, and he became more and more so as afterlife privileges were extended to the entire Egyptian population. And yet in typical Egyptian fashion, Osiris fully existed but he was also an aspect of Re. Re, combined with other gods, was Chief God, the self-existent creator/sun/incarnated-in-the-Pharaoh god, ruler of the sky, the world and the *Duat* "Other Land" underworld. As we have seen, the Fifth and Sixth (c. 2345–2181 BC) Dynasties saw a further decrease in Re's powers when Osiris re-appropriated from Re the agricultural and Nile inundation functions which had originally been his.

RE GETS OLD AND TIRED, ALMOST DESTROYS HUMANITY

The growing popularity of Osiris, his awesome power to bestow an afterlife on all Egyptians and his re-appropriation of some of Re's key functions, as the Old Kingdom collapsed and the First Intermediate Period (c. 2181 BC) opened, was to some extent mirrored in the episode related in the Middle Kingdom (c. 2055–1650 BC) *Destruction of Mankind* myth contained in *The Book of the Divine Cow*. Re's importance had now effectively declined and he was gradually being seen as the old man of the gods, respected and powerful, but weakened, much as is analogically related in *The Destruction of Mankind*. *The Book of the Divine Cow* and its destruction of mankind myth was inscribed on the walls of several New Kingdom (c. 1550–1069 BC) rock-cut tombs in the Valley of Kings, including those of Tutankhamun, Sety I and Rameses II.

At some point, presumably after Re had reached his Old Kingdom apex and after he "had grown old, his bones being silver, his flesh gold, his hair true lapis lazuli" he is said to have put down a rebellion by mankind plotting against him. In fact (if we can speak about facts), the old age of Re obviously should correspond to the mythical period, before 3100 BC and before the pharaoh-gods, when the gods, and notably Re, successively and directly ruled the earth.

"Summon to me my Eye," shouted Re. This divinely powerful sun-eye — a *uraeus* cobra and a lioness — belonged to Re, but was separate from him. The gods and goddesses, and especially Nun, the personification of the primordial waters, begged Re to "stay on your throne! Great is fear of you when your Eye is on those who scheme against you."

So Re sent his Eye in the form of the goddess Hathor as a lioness (or in another version, the goddess Sakhmet) to slaughter all the rebels who were now fleeing in the desert. After Hathor had angrily and exuberantly slaughtered a considerable number of rebels ("it was balm to my heart"), Re changed his mind about destroying mankind in its entirety.

He had seven thousand jars of *henket*, beer, made, mixed them with red ochre to appear as blood and poured them over the place where Hathor intended to finish her plan "to slay mankind." Hathor liked the bloody appearance of this liquid, drank and drank of it, and got too drunk to do anything but sleep it off; and so she did not slaughter what remained of mankind. Re welcomed "in peace" the "gracious" Hathor, pleased that he had saved mankind.[35] However, by this time Re had become disappointed in mankind and retired to a behind-the-scenes role in the sky, leaving the government of the universe to the other gods.

This myth bears a startling resemblance to the earlier Sumerian myth in which the gods send a flood to destroy mankind because man made too much noise, thus preventing the gods from sleeping, with the powerful water god Enki finally deciding that Ziusudra (Utnapishtim in Akkadian) and his family would be saved. There is, of course, also a resemblance to the Sumerian and Egyptian myths in the later Hebrew myth in which mankind, except for Noah and his family and a pair of each animal and plant, is destroyed by a flood because of wicked behavior. And yet, these three great Middle Eastern destruction myths reveal the specific core character of each people and their specific relation to the gods or god: the Sumerians believed that man had been made to work for the gods and that everything in the universe was designed for the comfort of the gods, whose existence and desires needed no explanation; the Egyptians believed that the worst fault was to rebel against the primeval order of Maat and the gods; and the Hebrews believed that the greatest sin was immoral behavior, breaking the ethical covenant that Yahweh had made with man.

Another myth illustrating Re's lassitude and weakened capacity in relation to the stratagems of other divinities, despite his immense chief god status, is *The God and his Unknown Name of Power* (also called *The Outwitting of Re by Isis*), composed during the Nineteenth Dynasty (c. 1295–1186 BC), but presumably relating events which should also have occurred after Re had reached his Old Kingdom apex. This myth describes Isis as a "clever woman" with "a heart...craftier than a million men...choicer than a million gods," but who nevertheless ardently desired to know the real name, the *ren* soul name, of Re so that she could possess ultimate magical power.

Re was old and decrepit and saliva frequently drooled from his mouth. Isis gathered some of this saliva and transformed it into a sacred snake ready to

---

35. Quotations from Lichtheim, Miriam, *Ancient Egyptian Literature, Volume II*, pp. 197-199.

attack. She placed the snake along the path where Re took his daily walk through *Ta-Wy*, the Two Lands. The snake bit Re and he lay dying.

He cried out for help to the gods of his great Heliopolis Ennead, but was too weakened by the poisonous snakebite to explain what had happened to him. Re gathered his divine children around him and finally explained that he been bitten by something which he did not know, who was not among the beings he had created. "I am a noble, the son of a noble...who came into being as a god...My father thought out my name [the hidden name]. I am abounding in names and abounding in forms. My forms exist as every god...My father and my mother told me my name, [but] it was hidden in my body before I was born, in order that the power of a male or female magician might not be made to play against me."

The divine children of Re, including the crafty Isis, wept as they listened to this story. Isis, with her great magical powers, vowed to defeat the child of Re who had dared to attack him. Isis told Re "tell me thy name" so that she could use magic. Re recited a litany of his deeds — creation, sexual pleasures, the Nile, etc. — and his names — Khepri, Re, Atum. Of course, with these well-known names, the snake's poison remained in his body. Isis replied: Thy name is not really among those which thou hast told me. If thou tellest it to me, the poison will come forth, for a person whose [real] name is pronounced [recited in a healing spell] lives." Finally, Re whispered his real soul name, his *ren*, in the ear of Isis, getting her to promise that she would transmit it to her son Horus and that he would keep it secret. A jubilant Isis, "the Great, the mistress of the gods, who knows Re [by] his own name," recited a spell and chased the poison out of Re's body.[36] Isis now knew the name, which made her among the greatest of those who were *weret-hekau*, "great of magic" and the spell she used on Re became a standard spell to conjure the bites of scorpions and snakes.

It is interesting to note that *The Outwitting of Re by Isis* bears a considerable resemblance to a Sumerian tale. Just as Isis desired ultimate magical power in the form of Re's true *ren* name, Inanna desired ultimate magical power in the form of the *me*, which only the all-powerful Sumerian water god Enki (a "King of the gods" who had an equivalent status to Re) kept in his *Abzu* underwater palace in Eridu. Inanna seduced Enki, got him drunk and tricked him into giving her the *me*, which she took to her city of Uruk, transforming Uruk into a greater city than Eridu.

---

36. Wilson, John in *Ancient Near Eastern Texts Relating to the Old Testament*, pp. 12-14.

AMUN TAKES OVER, BUT RE ROLLS ALONG

Considerably weakened as Re was, he continued to roll along. During the Middle Kingdom (c. 2055–1650 BC), he was associated with the ram-headed cre-ator-potter god as Khnum-Re, the crocodile or crocodile-headed god of the waters and fertility as Sobek-Re, and the falcon-headed warrior god Montu as Montu-Re. In these cases, Sobek added a headdress with a sun disk and two feathers, Khnum added a sun disk, a uraeus and two feathers and Montu, a sun disk and uraeus headdress. During the New Kingdom (from c. 1550 BC), Re's form as a cat holding a knife and killing the giant, evil snake Apophis, became highly popular.

One can also say that Re had become a *nice old guy*, compared to the bluster-ing, arrogant, susceptible and power hungry Re of the Old Kingdom (c. 2686–2181 BC). This Re was fully the Re who created man, or at least the Egyptian man, *remet*, from his tears, *rimi*. He was the Re of the Middle Kingdom Coffin Texts, when there was a great thirst for social justice. He was the Re who claimed that he had created the same conditions for "the poor man" and "the great man," that he had "forbade them to do wrong," but "their hearts dis-obeyed."[37]

At about the same time as the nice old man Re was declining in favor of Osiris and being out-witted by Isis, he faced and, quite naturally, lost, his biggest challenge with Amun, Egypt's most syncretic, amalgamating, totalizing, mono-theising and universal god.

AMUNISM: THE APOTHEOSIS OF EGYPT'S CHIEF GOD MONOTHEISING TENDENCY

As we have seen in Chapter 4, Pharaoh Amenemhat ("Amun is at the head") I (c. 1985-1955 BC) and the Theban clergy decided that Amun was Amun-Re. It was this *new old* god, Amun-Re, who during the New Kingdom (c. 1550–1069 BC) became the greatest chief god in Egyptian history. The Re solar theology of Heliopolis was now also the theology of Thebes, but under the direction of the new composite Chief God, Amun-Re and a new theological system — Amunism.

Rivalry between Amun, an air god, with humble beginnings in Hermopolis as the god who protected people who had died of suffocation, and Re, the sun god, head of the mighty Heliopolitan Ennead, had been theoretically overcome with this fusion of Amun and Re into Amun-Re in the Theban Ennead. In their

---

37. Faulkner, R.O., *The Ancient Egyptian Coffin Texts*, Vol. III, pp. 167-168.

royal titulary, the pharaohs frequently combined Amun and Re names. The title *nesu netjeru*, "King of the Gods," was applied to this duo/unity and the incumbent pharaoh was considered incarnated as his son. The pharaoh was now *sa Amun-Ra*, rather than *sa Ra*.

Of course, it was Amun of Thebes and not Re of Heliopolis who held the top position in this duo. Once again, the Egyptian theologians resorted to a system which decreed that two gods were really a unity, while in fact favoring one of them. Amun-Re was more Amun than Re. It was Amun's usual depiction in human form or with a ram's head which prevailed and not Re's usual hawk-headed depiction or a combination of the usual Re and Amun forms. The old and tired Re had been virtually assimilated by Amun with the Theban Amun clergy considering that Re was an avatar of Amun and that all the gods were aspects of Amun-Re. Amun then began a career which, while it would have been impossible without Re and Heliopolitan solar theology, created the new system of Amunism which carried him much further down the road of chief god theology and monotheising tendencies than Re.

In addition to the basic Egyptian practice of amalgamating gods, Amun-Re was the perfect example of another basic Egyptian theological principle — whenever a local god achieved national importance or was seen as incarnating universal principles, the tendency was to "solarize" him, to assimilate him with Re and solar functions. Throughout Egypt's religious history, only a sun god could become a chief god. This had been the case with Horus and even with Osiris, who was dubbed "night sun," and it reached its apex with Amun who as Amun-Re was a solar god, but a solar god who had absorbed Re rather than being absorbed by Re.

Re's gluttony as a chief god, or the gluttony of the Re Heliopolitan clergy, had been immense for more than a thousand years, but it had its limits and drawbacks. Contrary to Amun-Re, with whom all the gods without exception became his *ba*, his aspects, the huge number of gods Re assimilated were probably difficult for even contradiction-loving Egypt to coherently digest. With Re, hundreds of other gods, and especially Osiris, had continued to have powerful individual existences; this could have contributed to the blurring of his image and his eventual weakening, even if he was never entirely dethroned. With Amun, while the existence of all the other gods and their individual identities were never challenged, their powers had been considerably reduced. With Amun, it was Re — and all the other gods — who were virtually swallowed up.

The theological evolution in Thebes that raised Amun to this immense chief god status and the political expediency of the Theban pharaohs to amalgamate Re as an aspect of Amun and thus reconcile the gods of Upper and Lower Egypt certainly played roles in Amun's growing importance. However, above all,

Amun's popularity throughout Egypt seems to have had much to do with the fact that he had been Pharaoh Ahmose's (c. 1550–1525) royal god.

From his base in Thebes, Ahmose finally succeeded in driving out from Egypt the hated Asian *Heka-khasut*, the Hyksos, who favored the god Seth, and in reestablishing Egyptian sovereignty over the entirety of *Ta-Wy*, the Two Lands. With this event, ending the Hyksos 15th and 16th Dynasties of the Second Intermediate Period (c. 1650–1550 BC), Ahmose ushered in the New Kingdom (c. 1550–1069 BC). He also quite naturally consolidated the rule of Amun-Re as Egypt's undisputed royal and main national god. Amun had made victory possible and quite naturally received the greatest reward possible.

With Ahmose I, Egypt embarked on an imperialistic policy aimed at establishing an empire in Nubia and in the West Asian *Retjenu*. By this time, Egypt had also become a much less closed country; it was already much less of an island unto itself and far more open to foreign influences, especially in the field of technology. However, despite the fact that Egypt's feeling of superiority had been thoroughly shaken by a century of foreign Hyksos rule, it remained extraordinarily arrogant and was still largely motivated by a feeling of religious superiority over all other humans. Now the necessity of defending Egypt by an aggressive offensive policy linked up with this somewhat shaken feeling of religious superiority. Egypt wanted to propagate a universal religion throughout its empire, but such a universal religion could only be its own religion led by Amun-Re.

Amun-Re was now on a road which not only led to his becoming the most powerful chief god in Egypt's history, but also on a road which led him to be lauded by the Egyptians as the universal god *par excellence*. And in fact, with the sole, brief exception of Aten in the mid-14th century BC, for whom even more comprehensive universality was claimed, Amun-Re was the most universal god ever invented until the sixth century BC version of the universal Yahweh.

Egypt had become the world's greatest imperial power, controlling vassal states in Syria and Canaan and forcing prudent respect from Babylonia, Assyria and the Anatolian Hittites. Egypt's political domination in this vast area — stretching in Nubia down to Napata and northeast to the banks of the Euphrates at Carchemish in the Asian *Retjenu* — achieved by Pharaoh Thutmose III (c. 1479–1425 BC), played a key role in Amun-Re's national and universal success.

The consolidation of Egypt's empire led to a new policy of universalism, but it was an imperialistic universalism, a universalism in which Egypt naturally dominated politically, economically and religiously. Egypt maintained fortresses but also built many temples and steles dedicated to the Egyptian gods throughout their conquered lands. Egypt was then truly the center of the world — the greatest political power, the most modern, most prosperous, most artistic society in the world, with its vanguard religion. Egypt's phantasm for at least 1500 years had been just that — that it was the center of the world — and this had finally become no longer a pretentious phantasm, but reality. Egypt had won the battle for control of the Levant and it would maintain a clear domination for much of the next 200 years.

It was Thutmose III, one of Egypt's greatest pharaohs, who anchored Amun-Re's supremacy and universality and his new role as what James Henry Breasted (1865–1935) has called "the world-god."[38] Thutmose III, a child when his father Thutmose II died in c. 1479 BC, had been unable to reign because his aunt Hatshepsut (c. 1473–1458 BC) had usurped power with the help of the Theban Amun-Re clergy, but in c. 1458 BC, the Amun-Re clergy switched its allegiance to Thutmose III (perhaps with the banishment or the death of Hatshepsut). Perhaps, this role of the clergy was at the origin of Thutmose III's immense reverence for Amun-Re, but in any case, the reverence was indeed boundless and Amun-Re rewarded Thutmose and the Egyptian people in just as boundless — or rather *borderless* — manner.

Egypt and its gods — and especially its greatest god, Amun-Re, "the King of the gods" — were now everywhere. An inscription by Thutmose III on a wall of the Amun-Re Karnak Temple states: "He [Amun-Re] ordained that all the foreign countries come, bowed down, because of the power of My Majesty..." Thutmose III's so-called "Poetical Stele," erected in the Karnak Temple (and now in the Cairo Museum) states: "For I [Amun-Re] bestowed on you the earth, its length and breadth...I have come to let you tread on Djahi's [Canaan] chiefs...on those of Asia...on eastern lands...on western lands...on lowlanders...on islanders...on Tjehenu [Libya]...on Nubians..." And indeed, Thutmose III gave all the credit for his victories to Amun-Re: "I have not done anything...against which contradiction might be uttered. I have done this for my father Amun...because he knoweth heaven and he knoweth earth, he seeth the whole earth hourly."[39]

As long as Egypt remained a powerful nation, all the pharaohs, and especially those of the New Kingdom, who succeeded Thutmose III, with the exception of Akhenaten, sought to follow this foreign policy of domination with Amun-Re in the role of imperial god. After the Akhenaten/Atenist interlude, great temples to Amun-Re continued to be built outside Egypt, notably at several locations in Nubia, and especially Abu Simbel (Rameses II, c. 1279–1213 BC);

---

38. Breasted, James Henry, *A History of Egypt, From The Earliest Times To The Persian Conquest*, p. 301.

39. Lalouette, Claire, *Textes Sacrés et Textes Profanes de l'Ancienne Egypte, I, Des Pharaons et des hommes*, p. 37, Lichtheim, Miriam, *Ancient Egyptian Literature, Volume II*, pp. 36-37 and Breasted, James Henry, *A History of Egypt, From The Earliest Times To The Persian Conquest*, p. 267.

and according to Rameses III (c. 1184–1153 BC), he built a magnificent Amun-Re temple in Beth Shan, in the Canaanite Jordan Valley, although archaeological evidence suggests that an Egyptian temple existed there earlier.

There can be no doubt that this universal political domination was also euphemistically universal religious unity, but in fact was religious domination. Thutmose's Stele states: "I [Amun-Re] let them see your majesty as lord of light, so that you shone before them in my likeness...I let them see your majesty as your Two Brothers [Horus and Seth]..."[40] Thutmose III as the pharaoh/god of Egypt and the Egyptian Empire clearly strove to have Egypt's gods, led by Amun-Re, dethrone or amalgamate the gods of the conquered lands. Egypt's gods now officially ruled wherever Egypt's pharaohs' military victories took them.

In Egypt, Waset (Thebes), the City of Amun, and *Ipet-isut*, "the most select of places" (the Karnak Temple) and its sister temple *Ipet-resyt*, "the southern place" (the Luxor Temple), became the greatest temple complex in Egypt. Thutmose III enlarged Karnak by building Pylon VI, the court preceding it and the central court and festival temple behind it. Amun-Re was directly worshipped in these fabulous temples, as well as in Memphis, Heliopolis, Hermopolis, Fayum, Tanis, Amada in Nubia and elsewhere. Even where he was not directly worshipped, Amun-Re was the great, supreme, unique chief state and royal god.

Amunism, Amun-Re theology, was the furthest the Egyptians went towards such an immense concentration of theocratic power and theological unity in the hands of a single god. Amun-Re was the epitome of Egypt's bent towards monotheising tendencies without rejecting polytheism. However, the theory of a monotheistic Amun-Re can be easily dismissed. Amun was no more of a monotheistic, or even near-monotheistic, god than Re. He remained an immanent, rather than a transcendent, god and part of an overwhelming polytheistic system in which diversity was the fundamental element. However, it is an entirely different matter concerning monotheising tendencies; the monotheising tendencies expressed through Amun-Re were real and they were real even when some pharaohs obviously sought to downplay them.

In addition to the usual assimilation of numerous other gods in a dynamic leaning towards omnipotence (but never fully achieving it), Amun-Re was dubbed with even more than the usual number of superlative, totalizing titles. As we have seen in Chapter 4, the Eighteenth Dynasty (c. 1550–1295 BC) *Hymn to the Sun (Amun-Re)* states: Amun is "UNIQUE"; he is the "chief of all gods"; the "father of the gods"; "father of the fathers of all gods"; "upon whose mouth the gods came into being"; "From whose eyes mankind came forth"; whose "name is hidden"; "the SOLE ONE WHO MADE [ALL] THAT IS"; "The SOLITARY

---

40. Lichtheim, Miriam, *Ancient Egyptian Literature, Volume II*, p. 37.

ONE, WITHOUT HIS PEER"; "The gods are bowing down to thy majesty."[41] Although many others gods are named with reverence in this hymn, the role of Amun as the supreme creator and supreme god who acts for the good of all is clear. He is the *nb-tm*, the *nib-tem*, the lord of all. All the enneads and cosmogonies were merely aspects of Amun. The royal state god and head of the Theban Ennead, Amun-Re, was everything. He had created all the other gods to serve as his emanations, his manifestations, his *ba*'s; and the other gods rejoiced in this situation. Everything, the entirety of diversity — *heh*, "the millions" — was a manifestation of Amun.

In Pharaoh Amenhotep III's time (c. 1390–1352 BC), and according to the Stele of the twin brothers Suti and Hor, "Overseers of the Works of Amun" (now in the British Museum), Amun-Re, was referred to as the direct amalgamation of no fewer than seven gods who had been directly reduced to a unity — Amun, Re, Horakhte (who in the Re-Horakthe form contained Re, Horus, Khepri and Atum), Aten and Khnum. Amun-Re was now self-created, the "Creator uncreated. Sole one, unique one, who traverses eternity."[42] Thus Amun was virtually pre-existent to creation, as Ptah had been (or would later become, depending on what date is ascribed to the plenitude of Ptah/Memphite theology).

The clear meaning of all this was that although Amun-Re was the greatest god and all the other gods were created by him, were aspects and manifestations of him and were dependent on him, it in no way even vaguely impinged on the individual existence and greatness of all the other gods.

Either the monotheising highpoint for Amun-Re or what Erik Hornung (b. 1933) has called the "complementary...one and the many," or perhaps both the monotheising and the "complementary...one and the many" highpoints,[43] was probably reached in early 13th century BC Thebes with the Leiden Papyrus I 350 *Hymn to Amun* (now in the Leiden Museum). Composed during Rameses II's time (c. 1279–1213 BC), this *Hymn to Amun* brought both the leaning towards omnipotence and the monotheising euphoria for Amun-Re to a boil with the invention of an organic triad. The *Hymn to Amun* decreed that "No god came into being before him [Amun]" and that "All gods are three: Amun, Re and Ptah, and there is no second to them. Hidden is his name as Amon, he is Re in face, and his body is Ptah." As John Wilson (1899–1976) has pointed out: "The text does not say: 'There is no fourth to them.' This is a statement of trinity, the three chief gods of Egypt subsumed into one of them, Amon."[44] Clearly, the concept of organic

---

41. Wilson, John in *Ancient Near Eastern Texts Relating to the Old Testament*, pp. 365-367.

42. Lichtheim, Miriam, *Ancient Egyptian Literature, Volume II*, p. 87.

43. See *Egypt, Trunk of the Tree*, Volume I, pp. 130-133.

44. Wilson, John in *Ancient Near Eastern Texts Relating to the Old Testament*, pp. 368-369.

unity within plurality got an extraordinary boost with this formulation. Theologically, in a crude form it came strikingly close to the later Christian form of plural Trinitarian monotheism.

However, given the context in which this triad was invented, it is impossible to make the leap from a monotheising leaning to any idea of virtual monotheism within polytheism or to an abandonment of a basic theology of diversity and immanence. *The Hymn to Amun* not only mentions many other gods and goddess (and even if it states that these divinities were created by the self-created Amun and are aspects of Amun), in typical contradictory Egyptian fashion it continues to respect their individual identities. There is also not the slightest move towards the most basic of all monotheistic tenets — transcendence. Amun and all the other gods remain eminently immanent in nature.

There is also no way of excluding the possibility that part of the intention of the Amun/Re/Ptah triad may well have been to foreclose any conceivable return to monotheism. It was conceived only about 70 years after the abortive Akhenaten/Atenist primitive monotheism experiment and one of its goals may have been to elaborate the most powerful possible chief god theology within polytheism, so as to make a return to monotheism unnecessary.

There are other very serious historical ambiguities concerning not only a so-called virtual monotheistic role for Amun-Re, but even for as big a leap towards unity and away from diversity as some Egyptologists tend to assume. Even if the monotheising tendency of the new triad was obvious, at least as compared to the usual central reality of polytheism, as many New Kingdom texts and inscriptions stressing diversity can be found as those stressing unity over diversity as regards Amun-Re. Moreover, political motives of a paradoxical sort may also have been present in linking the gods of Egypt's three greatest cities — Amun of Thebes, Re of Heliopolis and Ptah of Memphis. Even if this linkage had clearly taken place in favor of Amun, it gave renewed importance to Egypt's two other great cities, and especially to Memphis, and their gods. All this could have constituted one more attempt to limit the power of the Theban Amun clergy.

Although the organic Amun/Re/Ptah was created during Rameses II's reign, it did not stop this pharaoh from apparently entertaining considerable doubts about an exclusive All-God role for Amun-Re and for the Theban clergy's ambitions. One of Rameses II's main politico-religious goals was clearly to attenuate the preeminence of Amun and the power of the Theban Amun-Re clergy. This was a tendency expressed by many of his predecessors ever since Thutmose IV (c. 1400–1390 BC). Rameses II does not seem to have been convinced that the unity and all-powerful aspects of Amun-Re should be stressed in a way which could relegate the older chief gods like Re and Ptah to secondary roles. He strongly advanced a restoration in the worship of Re in his individual form and of Ptah and even of Seth as his father Sety I (1294–1279 BC) had done. He even seemed to believe that Amun's role should not impinge too far on his own role as a god almost equal to the "great gods," as the Abu Simbel and other temples clearly indicate.

Rameses II moved his capital from Thebes to Pi-Rameses in the Delta. He named one of his sons, Khaemwaset, Grand Commander of the Artificers of the Ptah Memphis Temple and another, Meryatum, Great Seer of the Re Heliopolitan Temple. He named a trusted ally, Nebunenef, who had formerly been a high priest of Osiris and then Hathor, as First Prophet of the Thebes Amun-Re clergy. In the famous *Bulletin* and *Poem* and other inscriptions describing his so-called victory at Kadesh in c. 1274 BC, superlative references to other gods than Amun, and notably Re, Horakhte, Seth, Atum, Sakhmet and Montu, abound and the names of his army divisions were Re, Ptah and Seth in addition to Amun.

On a strictly theological level, it also cannot be stressed enough how the complicated system of aspects rendered the Amun/Re/Ptah triad non-monotheistic. Amun had become Re and Ptah, but the triad also *de facto* incorporated numerous other gods. Dozens of other gods, as aspects of Amun, were all just beneath the surface of "All gods are three" and Amun the " Sole One, Unique One." Amun himself had a particularly powerful and individualistic aspect in the form of the ithyphallic procreation and fertility god Min. Of course, numerous aspects also came into play with Ptah, who had notably assimilated Seker, the crafts and death god and Tatenen, the god of the bowels of the earth and, of course, Re's aspects were practically uncountable. Moreover, the Amun/ Re/Ptah triad, like all the triads before it, did not eliminate the dozens of other triads, including the other triads in which Amun, Re or Ptah participated. Neither did it eliminate the existence and identities of the numerous other major gods nor the numerous strictly local gods.

The Amun-Re chief god context also obviously excluded almost all of the virtually consubstantial ethical and proto-democratic aspects of Judeo-Christian monotheism. It was also a context in which idolatry, zoolatry and magic were at the very heart of the system and in which Amun-Re himself was represented in numerous human and animal composite forms as well as in ithyphallic forms — all things which were abominations for authentic monotheism.

Nevertheless, there are striking similarities in the Amun/Re/Ptah triad to the Hebrew concept of Yahweh. Amun's attempt at omnipotence and his concealed nature can legitimately be seen as forerunners of what Yahweh would become. Amun's various unitary titles are linguistically, but not semantically, close to the later intransigent Hebrew *Shema* unity credo — "Hear, O Israel: The Lord our God is one Lord." However, in the same Book of Deuteronomy, Yahweh is described as "...God of gods, and Lord of lords, a great God..."[45] which is obviously close to Amun's titles and confusedly indicates a leftover from polytheism in the Hebrew religion.

There are even more striking similarities between the Amun/Re/Ptah triad and the Christian Trinity. The Amun/Re/Ptah triad was the first attempt to combine three divinities or divine powers into a thoroughly organic unity, as Christian plural monotheism later did. Using very different elements, but resulting in a similar set up, Christian Trinitarian theology as postulated in the first few centuries of Christianity by Paul and the Fathers of the Early Church decreed that the omnipotent Father was incarnated as the savior/son Jesus, who had two natures, divine and human, who was crucified, resurrected and then went to Heaven at the right hand of the father and that the Holy Spirit (Ghost) which is the spirit, the breath of the Father, was permanently with the Son...and that Father/Son and Holy Spirit are a single unit.

This Christian Trinity is less complicated than the Amun/Re/Ptah triad, but it is surely almost as artificially unitary and almost as difficult to understand. The lack of common sense credibility in the Amun/Re/Ptah triad did not bother the Egyptians, but the Christian Trinitarian concept also encountered few fundamental doubts, except for the Arians, who originated in Egypt, from the early Fourth to the late Fifth centuries, who believed that the Son was not divine.

It is obvious that even if much in Christianity's founding Biblical texts (but not its succeeding actions) were obviously the apex of what monotheism considered as the highest values — such as morality, love, fraternity and spirituality — theologically, Christian monotheism is not authentic unitary, exclusive monotheism.

In the final analysis, the context, the theology and the language of Amunism after the Akhenaten/Atenist experiment was a strange, contradictory mixture of polytheism, chief god theology and monotheising tendencies. Amun-Re was "UNIQUE," but the other gods existed and some of them were also *unique*. There was unity, but this in no way affected basic diversity, "the millions," *heh*. It was typical of the particularly strong status of Amun-Re as a chief god, the leftovers of the Atenist experiment and the fact that Egypt was never able to accede to the stage of authentic, full-blown monotheism. This situation was Egypt's fundamental religious reality.

Despite all the ambiguity about Amun's uniqueness, the definition of Amun in the above-mentioned Cairo *Hymn to the Sun* as the "UNIQUE...chief of all gods...The SOLITARY ONE, WITHOUT HIS PEER" probably comes closest to what he really was — the most unique in the category of so-called unique gods. Quite simply, the term "unique" and other superlative unitary terms could desig-

---

45. Deuteronomy 6:4 and 10:17.

nate any of the top gods, that is the so-called "great gods." Amun-Re was the *ntr.aA*, the "great god," *par excellence*, but simultaneously and in the same New Kingdom period, this did not stop either Re or Osiris in *The Book of the Dead* from being the "Lord of All," Osiris on the Amenmose Stele from also being "Lord of Eternity, king of gods," or Ptah on the Neferabu Stele from being "The One God among the Ennead" and in the Harris Papyrus from being "father of the gods" and "father of the fathers."[46]

Nevertheless, even before the Atenist monotheistic experiment, it was Amun-Re and his already strong universalist, monotheising chief god theology within polytheism together with its supporting Theban politico-economic sys-tem which had been one of the vital stages leading towards Atenist monotheism. And after Atenism, the restored Amunism, Amun-Re chief god solar theology (despite its being a vital component of the polytheistic system) and its context may well have been a key influence in the development of Hebrew Yahweh henotheism and then authentic monotheism.

However, if the Amun clergy was able to accept monotheising, or totaliz-ing, tendencies, at no point in its history was it able to accept anything even vaguely resembling real monotheism. It was perfectly logical that the Amun clergy used Amun-Re as the instrument to put an end to the Aten proto-mono-theistic experiment. They revolted against an evolution to which they had made a significant contribution and re-imposed their totalizing chief god in the tradi-tional polytheistic framework and from about the Twentieth Dynasty (c. 1186–1069 BC), skidded into religious totalitarianism, fundamentalism and fanaticism.

And yet as contradictory as all the above is, with the exception of the Atenist primitive monotheistic experiment, Amun-Re theology was the apothe-osis of Egypt's chief god monotheising tendency, capable of attributing immense powers to a chief god and capable of amalgamating diversity into unity, but never able to reject diversity and the immanence and existence of the many gods. Amun was "the one who made himself into millions,"[47] but the "millions" was the basis of Egyptian theology.

---

46. Faulkner, R.O., *The Ancient Egyptian Book of the Dead*, Spell 17, p. 44, Spell 1B, p. 35, etc., Lichtheim, Miriam, *Ancient Egyptian Literature, Volume II*, p. 109 and p. 81, etc. and Breasted, James Henry, *Ancient Records of Egypt*, Vol. 4, 308, p. 162 and 351, p. 177.

47. See p. 101 and *Egypt, Trunk of the Tree*, Volume I, p. 133.

CONFUSION BETWEEN MONOTHEISING TENDENCIES, MONOTHEISM AND THE CHIEF GODS

Great confusion persists concerning Egypt's chief gods and monotheising tendencies. Notably, there is the frequently repeated view that the strong Egyptian chief god system was in fact already a form of monotheism. Some Egyptologists have used the undoubtedly strong monotheising chief gods, especially Amun, to speculate that the Egyptian system was at least a latent monotheism. There are also views that even some of the earlier gods, like Horus, Re, Osiris and Ptah were virtually monotheistic in that with them many gods had been reduced to a few gods or to a single god. Many 19th century and early 20th century Egyptologists and historians went further and outlined complicated theories about a so-called Egyptian monotheism which persist right into our time. Some of these Egyptologists postulated that the pantheon of gods had always been a single deity and that its division into various aspects or gods was merely a matter of external organization so that ordinary people could better understand religion.

If one has no pro monotheistic ax to grind, all the theological and linguistic questions concerning a supposed Egyptian monotheism can be explained reasonably, and explained while according monotheising tendencies in Egypt their rightful place.

All of the views of an Egyptian monotheism are in one way or another linked to the lingering influence of what I call, in Chapter 14, the Egyptian hocus-pocus view in Europe, that is, an imaginary Egypt. This hocus-pocus view began with the Italian philosopher Marsile Ficin (1433-1499) who wanted to merge theology, and especially Christian revelation, magic, and science. Ficin translated the Greek *Corpus Hermetica* into Latin, and together with other esoterics believed that *Hermetica* was based on ancient Egyptian esotericism and theological wisdom, which was both the first source, the *prisca theologica*, of all religion and knowledge and a pre-figuration of Christianity. What ensued were frequently extraordinary and wild attempts to bridge the religious gap between Egypt and Israel (and thus to Christianity) by imagining an original and secret monotheism in ancient Egypt which had been transmitted to Israel.

The intellectual thrill of discovering that a *prisca theologica* supposedly existed must have been overwhelming. In any case, scientists like Nicholaus Copernicus (1473-1543), Giordano Bruno (1548?-1600) and Isaac Newton (1643-1747), fell into the trap of this original, great wisdom in ancient Egypt. Beginning in the 17th century, the Freemasons, fervently seeking a reference, a source, which was earlier than either Christianity or Judaism, adopted the Egyptian option. British and German scholars, often linked to the Freemasons, continued the hocus-pocus by postulating variants of the idea of a secret Egyptian monotheism. British Christian scholars, notably John Spencer (1630–1693), Ralph Cudworth (1617–1688) and William Warburton (1698–1779) were the inventors of this Egyptian monotheistic movement. This wave of religious admiration for Egypt — in fact, for an imaginary Egyptian philosophical and religious role — reached a curious high point with the German writer Friedrich Schiller (1759–1805).

The basic idea was that Moses' so-called divinely ordained monotheism originated with the Egyptians and was an esoteric or invisible aspect of the Egyptian religion that had been maintained as secret knowledge because ordinary people could only understand polytheism. Secret deism and pantheism were also seen in the Egyptian and Mosaic religions.

Spencer firmly rejected the Egyptian system, and notably idolatry, but believed that the Egyptians were at the origin of everything in human knowledge and religion and knew the truth, but kept it secret. Moses, for Spencer, was an Egyptianized Jew who had adapted or inverted Egyptian teachings into Hebrew ritual laws so that an Egyptianized Hebrew people could understand them. Moses had also included a secret system in his laws, just as the Egyptians had done.

Cudworth, in his *True Intellectual System of the Universe*, believed that there was a hidden primitive monotheism in Egypt that had postulated a first god, a supreme, invisible, concealed god who had given birth to the other deities. For Cudworth, *Hermetica* reflected the beliefs of the Egyptians and the Egyptian religion, expressed as a deistic *Hen kai pan*, "one and all," and Moses was taught this system by the Egyptians.

Warburton, a Protestant bishop, accentuated the notion of an Egyptian divinely inspired secret monotheistic doctrine behind necessary official polytheism and then degeneracy into idolatry and animal worship. According to Warburton, Moses the Hebrew had learned this secret monotheism from the Egyptians and revealed it to his entire people. But somehow, for Warburton, the original and secret Egyptian pantheistic/monotheistic god was not the same deity as the Judeo-Christian monotheistic god.

Schiller, who was probably influenced by the Freemasons, imagined in *The Legation of Moses* that polytheism was a perversion, that the Egyptians with their great wisdom had discovered monotheism which was basically pantheism and deism, but concealed it as their most important secret because only the initiated could understand it; and that Moses was initiated by the Egyptians and revealed the secret, supreme Egyptian god to the Hebrews and gave him a name, but revealed only those aspects of him and his outer meaning which he thought they could handle — which was quite little.

All of these people, with the exception of Schiller, seem to have been driven by an obsessive and overriding desire — usually linked to viewing the Egyptian religion through a Christian prism — to read forms of monotheism into Egypt's polytheism. Without underestimating a sincere religious quest on the part of Cudworth and others, the context of a conscious or unconscious hidden agenda; of Christian arrogance ("the people of God") and Church insistence on ortho-doxy must be taken into account in evaluating their views. During their time, polytheism was often seen as some kind of a blemish; first-hand knowledge of Egyptian religious texts was impossible; and knowledge in general about Egypt was relatively slim and not subject to strict historical and scientific method. Moreover, despite the rationalist Enlightenment and the advance of science, these scholars were also victims of the Egyptian hocus-pocus aspect to Europe and its incredibly imaginary Egypt.

It is nearly impossible today to understand how all these eminent scholars assimilated the Egyptian religion with forms of monotheism. Even in their time, no amount of academic hair-splitting or loony views about latent monotheism, concealed monotheism, virtual monotheism or real monotheism should have changed the obvious fact that the garment of Egyptian religion was plainly a deep expression and representation of outer and inner diversity, of polytheism. What they should have seen, had they been able to overcome their prejudices, was that there were monotheising tendencies within Egyptian polytheism that may have contributed to a process of evolution which eventually led to monothe-istic revolution.

The simple fact that the Egyptian polytheistic religion had to be seen for its own qualities and weaknesses and not in function of a supposed superiority and ultimate truth of the Christian historical and worldview just could not be accepted. It is still refused by many today. Many 17th and 18th century scholars and ecclesiastics could not accept the very idea that there could be many gods and goddesses, conveniently forgetting that Christian monotheism itself was multiform. They could not even imagine the possibility that there had been a gradual evolution from polytheism to monotheism involving monotheising ten-dencies and abortive attempts at monotheism. The maximum they could swal-low was that there was an Egyptian esoteric monotheism, or latent monotheism, which had numerous faults, but that it obligatorily fitted into a divine schema in which it could be qualified as a primitive prefiguration of Hebrew monotheism and of the final truth of Christian monotheism.

Of course, it was legitimate for scholars to ask the historical question whether monotheism had brought greater benefits to mankind than polytheism. Without taking into account whether one is a believer or an atheist, it certainly seems possible to conclude that monotheism is the subtler system of the two, or at least that it was historically the system which better facilitated ethical, democratic and economic progress. However, these early scholars, Freemasons and many later Egyptologists were right in the wrong way. At best, they imagined a universal pantheism and deism, which Egypt either invented or articulated. At worst, they not only wanted to see the superiority and ultimate truth of monotheism over polytheism rather than a series of historical developments, but they frequently molded the facts to fit their desires. Somewhere down the line, it was unbearable to them that monotheism did not come first, that a fabulously elaborate religion like Egyptian polytheism preceded monotheism and especially Christian monotheism.

In the late 19th century, through the study of the Egyptian texts themselves, it became increasingly impossible to demonstrate the views about the existence of an Egyptian monotheism (except for the brief 15-year period of Akhenaten/Atenist proto-monotheism in the mid-14th century BC). The views of the hocus-pocus link from Ficin to Warburton to Schiller and the Freemasons could now easily be seen as defying plain old common sense. In succeeding years and into our time, not a single Egyptian text has ever been found which could even vaguely indicate that there was a secret doctrine of monotheism, although many Egyptian texts have been found which point to what can easily be interpreted as monotheising tendencies.

Another persistent theory about forms of monotheism in ancient Egypt, bandied about for more than 150 years, is the concept that the hieroglyph *ntr* (*netjer*) unquestionably means *the god* and is a singular, thus indicating some kind of monotheism. As we shall now see, it can be argued that the term *ntr*, the god, is among the least weighty of the arguments used to prove the existence of monotheism in Egypt. Nevertheless, this concept has somehow powerfully survived into our time among maverick groups.

Netjer is the term for the divine used in the oldest Egyptian texts, but its origin and meaning are unclear.

The *netjer* banner hieroglyph seems to have evolved from prehistoric totemistic/henotheistic banners. Originally, the emblem (plant or animal) of a local totem was probably inscribed on the banners used for clan identity. Divinization of totems, systematized polytheism, pictograms, ideograms and hieroglyphs followed and a single, uninscribed banner in conjunction with the hieroglyph identifying a god was used to designate a specific deity and three or more banners to designate a pantheon of gods. There is also the possibility that the term *netjer* originated as the designation of the dead king in relation to ancestor worship. In any case, the best guess seems to be that *netjer* evolved into signifying a specific divinity, and the plural *netjeru*, many divinities.

The reasoning which assimilates the term *netjer* with monotheism clearly, and surprisingly, fails to adequately take into account the existence of several hieroglyph-ideogram singular and plural forms for *netjer* from at least the Early Dynastic Period (from c. 3100 BC). In addition to *p' ntr* for the god, these glyphs included the plural for gods, *ntr.w* (*netjeru*), the singular for goddess, *ntr.t* (*netjret*), the plural for goddesses, *ntr.wt*, the dual forms, *ntr.wj* and *ntr.tj* for couples of gods like Horus or Seth or couples of goddesses like Isis and Nephthys and the term *ntr nfr* (*netjer nefer*), the "perfect god," for the ruling pharaoh.

Moreover, there was not a unique glyph for *netjer*, indicating that there was perhaps not a unique origin or a single meaning for this term. A single banner-like figure, a falcon on a pedestal on top of a pole or a seated, bearded figure with upraised knees were the most usual representations of the singular *netjer*, but at least 20 other glyphs were also used for specific gods and goddesses. The glyphs for the plural of gods or goddesses were obviously also numerous: three or more banners, or a banner followed by the male determinative glyph of a seated, bearded figure with upraised knees and three slim vertical lines indicating the plural; this figure plus three lines; three falcons; a star and three lines; a banner preceding the female determinative glyph of a seated woman with a long wig and upraised knees; nine banners for a "company of the gods" (an ennead), 18 banners for two cycles (or enneads) of the gods and 27 banners for three "companies" (used this way, all the gods were included)...

The origin and the meaning of the Sumerian term for the gods, *dingir*, poses a similar type of problem to the Egyptian *netjer*. The ideogram for *dingir* was a star, which seemingly indicated something or somebody which was in the sky and which had a superior nature to man. *Dingir* (and then *ilu* in Akkadian), like *netjer*, came to mean "the god," but its meaning is just as unclear as the Egyptian term.

This type of problem is particularly acute with the Semitic terms *El* and *Elohim*, due to the Jewish stance that they both signify the same, sole god. For the early Canaanites and then the Hebrews, it seems that the general term for divine entities, specific gods, was *El* and the term for many gods was *Elohim*.

In Canaanite nature religion times and totemistic influences, and right into the Canaanite Late Bronze (14th century BC) and Early Iron Ages (after 1200 BC), the bull-horned, long-bearded father god *El* was the Canaanite Chief God. But *El* almost certainly began as a general term for a divinity, since there were different *El* deities in many Canaanite city-states — *El Elyon, El-Olam, El-Ro, El-Bethel, Eloah*, etc. Together, these tutelary, emblematic totemistic city gods were *Elohim*, the term for several deities, much as the later son of *El*, the Canaanite lord and rain, fertility, agricultural and dying/resurrecting god *Baal*, and the gods associated with him, were the *Baalim* ("lords").

Together with origins in the West Semitic family of gods named *Ya, Yau, Yah, Yahu, Yawe, Yam, Yarikh, Ybrdmy* etc., and perhaps with the Akkadian moon, wisdom, fertility and cowherder god of Ur, Sin (the Sumerian Nanna), the Hebrew Yahweh (*Yhwh*) was also an *El* in an early stage (*El-Shaddai*, the almighty) and a *baal*, a lord. Yahweh then went through a henotheistic stage when he was frequently referred to as Yahweh-*Elohim*, as a chief god of the *elohim*.

Whatever interpretation is made concerning the differences in approach in the Yahwist (J-source) and *Elohist* (E-source) sections of the Old Testament, it seems clear that the pre-Mosaic sections of the earliest parts of the *Torah* refer to at least memories of several gods, to *Elohim* and *baalim*. It is just as clear that Yahweh assimilated and consolidated in his person the powers and characteristics of many gods, notably many *Els* and many *Yas*. In some Hebrew heterodoxies, Yahweh even sometimes inherited El's wife, Asherah, in her mother goddess, tree goddess and pole/pillar (like the Egyptian *djed*) forms. Polytheistic temptations were far from extinct among the Hebrews when all this occurred — and they would continue for centuries — but the totalizing phase for Yahweh had been terminated and *Elohim* seems to have gradually become an accepted term for the plural majesty of the "true" god Yahweh. However, *Elohim* somehow continued to represent a reminiscence of a polytheistic notion. It was occasionally used when somebody like Abraham was dealing with non-Hebrews or an apparently non-Hebrew like Job referred to God. The use of the term *Elohim* as an acceptable, sole name of God persisted into the sixth century BC among staunch, uncompromising monotheists like Deutero-Isaiah and Jeremiah.

Totemism, nature religion, polytheism and henotheism are obvious in these Canaanite and Hebrew evolutions. The logic was strictly the same as for the Egyptian terms *netjer* and *netjeru*. Despite tortured explanations by monotheists, these hypotheses seem reasonable for both the Egyptian *netjer/netjeru* terms and the Canaanite /Hebrew *El/Elohim* terms.

Reasonable probability suggests that the term *netjer* was never used in anything but a basically polytheistic context. Monotheism, near-monotheism, or even early Yahweh or early Ahura Mazdah type proto-monotheisms is not evident in the use of the term *netjer*, the god. The best guess remains that *netjer* refers to the specific god who is being worshipped in a specific place without any contestation whatsoever of the other gods.

Despite some ambiguity when the specific name of a god is not used with the *netjer* glyph, *netjer* does not seem to have ever been a proper noun; it does not seem to have ever designated a sole god and only that sole god; it seems to have always meant *the* god, any of the gods (the *netjer* Re, or the *netjer* Ptah, or the *netjer* Amun, or the *netjret* Isis, etc., or even an obscure local god), rather than only a sole, identifiable god. Any god could be named in his titulary as "the great god," or even "the greatest god." When Isis is called "the mother of god," this in no way implied anything else but that she was the mother of Horus and the personification of the pharaoh-god's throne. Even when Isis became "mother of all gods," during the New Kingdom (c. 1550–1069 BC), this did not eliminate other mother goddesses. A priest was the servant of a specific god, of the god Re, or *the* god Horus or *the* goddess Hathor, etc.; a temple was the house of a specific god, of the god Osiris, or *the* goddess Isis, etc.

When naming any god, including the most powerful chief (or monotheising) of them like Re or Amun, or the most minor god, or the ruling pharaoh, the Egyptian language used the same term *netjer*; and when referring to gods in general, they employed the term *netjeru*. There was some ambiguity or leeway in expressing the meaning of combined ideograms which contained the term *netjer* — for instance, the most appropriate translation of *Khert-Netjer* (the nether world) seems to be "the divine place below," while the most appropriate translation of *netjeru Ta-Mery* seems to be "Lords of the beloved cultivated land [Egypt]."

The single, apparent, but probably not real, exception to these general rules is the *sebayt* (the Instructions), the Wisdom Texts. These texts usually name several gods, sometimes using the plural form for gods, *netjeru*, but frequently refer to the singular for god, *netjer* — *p'ntr*, the god — to indicate divine will, rewards and punishments. Among some Egyptologists, this has been interpreted as evidence of monotheism and of a two-tier system in which monotheism was the true, more or less concealed, Egyptian doctrine and polytheism was its outer garment for the use of ordinary people.

Such arguments simply ignore that the authors of the Wisdom Texts seem to be referring to the *netjer* in a general way, to the god, whether Re, Osiris, Ptah or Amun, etc. and that nowhere can we find any clear indication that they believed in the existence of a sole god. Furthermore, the overall thrust of the Wisdom Texts, like all other Egyptian texts, was clearly polytheistic and situated within the usual Egyptian cosmological and politico-religious order. At best (and even this is uncertain), it is perhaps possible to speak about a monotheising tendency, side by side with polytheism, in the Wisdom Texts.

It was Henri Frankfort, in *Ancient Egyptian Religion*, in 1948, who best clarified the *netjer*/polytheism/monotheism debate concerning the Wisdom Texts. In his typically succinct style and based on his thesis that the Egyptians had a "multiplicity of approaches" and "multiple answers" and several different and contradictory manners to address complex religious questions, Frankfort stated: "The original [in the Wisdom Texts] uses *netjer*, which may mean 'a god,' 'the god,' or 'God.' 'A god' is too vague and 'the god' too definite; the exact meaning of *netjer* is 'the god with whom you have to reckon in the circumstances.' Egyptologists generally translate it 'God,' and that rightly, since the relation of the Egyptian to the god with whom he had to reckon at a given moment was, temporarily, almost exclusive of all others."[48] In other words, *netjer* meant the god who was actually being addressed at a particular moment and this could be applied to any god.

Among early Egyptologists, E.A. Wallis Budge (1857–1934) was one of the strongest supporters of the existence of an old, or possibly an original, monotheism in ancient Egypt. He was perhaps one of the major victims of the hocus-pocus, imaginary Egypt. Budge particularly devoted considerable efforts to attempted explanations concerning the evident anomaly of *netjer* and *netjeru* in relation to monotheistic theology.

Budge would have loved to be able to credibly demonstrate the existence of monotheism in ancient Egypt. He basically believed that there was a *netjer*, "One God, who was self-existent, immortal, invisible, eternal, omniscient, almighty and inscrutable; the maker of heaven, earth, and the Other World...Side by side with this Being...[there was] a class of beings who were called *neteru*...i.e. 'gods'...the equivalents of the Archangels and the Orders of Angels which we find in other systems of religion."

Budge clearly believed that forms of polytheism and monotheism coexisted from early dates in ancient Egypt, "...for the evidence of the pyramid texts shows that already in the Fifth Dynasty (which he situated "about BC c. 3333"!) monotheism and polytheism were flourishing side by side." He believed that the Egyptian priests had converted this monotheism into polytheism for easier consumption by the masses.

In his huge introduction to the *Book of the Dead* (more than 150 pages), which reflects the 19th century debate on Egypt and monotheism, Budge frankly admitted, although it did not help his demonstration, that the meaning of the hieroglyph *netjer* had been "lost." But, "Whatever it may mean," wrote Budge, it clearly "should be reserved to express the name of the Creator of the Universe, and that *neteru*, usually rendered 'gods' should be translated by some other word, but what that word should be is almost impossible to say." For Budge, the Egyptians had "conceived the existence of an unknown, inscrutable, eternal and infinite God, who was One — whatever the word One may mean..."[49]

So, who was this supreme power, this mysterious, sole *netjer*, whose power and characteristics were different from all the other gods, the *netjeru*, who were not really gods? Despite millions of words and more than 50 books, Budge never really told us. It was not Horus, it was not Re; they were *netjeru*. He seems to suggest that it might be Atum, in his primeval role as the great self-created creator

---

48. Frankfort, Henri, *Ancient Egyptian Religion, An Interpretation*, p. 67.
49. Budge, E.A. Wallis, *Osiris & The Egyptian Resurrection, Volume I*, pp. 348, 352, 353 and Budge, Wallis, E.A., *The Egyptian Book of the Dead*, pp. xciii, xxxii, xxxiii, xci and c.

god. However, Budge only unconvincingly explains why Atum was consistently described in the same way as one of any old *netjeru* in the oldest inscriptions and papyri. If the *netjer* was the real, sole Egyptian God, hidden or not, would we not find at least some inkling of this situation in the abundant Egyptian religious texts? The fact is that we not only do not find such an inkling but, as we have seen, the term *netjer* was consistently used to describe any individual god and was used this way for hundreds of gods and goddesses over thousands of years.

Budge today comes in for virulent criticism about his overwhelming and consistent prejudice to impose monotheism on Egyptian polytheism and other views, notably frequent errors of interpretation, translation and dating (he generally employed a grid which made Egyptian civilization more than a thousand years older than it possibly can be). All these criticisms are justified; much of Budge's work is quite simply out of date, much of it is discordant and motley and some of it is marked by Eurocentric prejudice. However, the very fashionable trend to totally dismiss Budge (and other pioneer Egyptologists like Erman) cannot dismiss that his work cannot be ignored in any study of Egypt, both for the vastness of the subjects he tried to analyze and the role he played in bringing to the fore the problems which were later more credibly analyzed.

And Budge was far from being alone among early Egyptologists in holding such views about an Egyptian monotheism; he was merely one of the most stubborn supporters, along with the German Egyptologist Emile Brugsch (1845–1930). Numerous Egyptologists towards the end of the 19th century expressed variants of the view that the Egyptian religion was somehow monotheistic or latently monotheistic. Both due to their own studies and to the lingering influence of Renaissance *Hermetica*, the theory that the Egyptian religion had begun as a monotheism before degenerating into polytheism became highly popular among Egyptologists in Britain, France and Germany.

Several leading French Egyptologists, including Emmanuel de Rougé (1811–1872), Jacques Joseph Champollion-Figeac (1778–1867) and Auguste Mariette (1821–1881), expressed variants of the view that the Egyptian religion originated as a monotheism and that this monotheism was never eliminated even if the Egyptian religion was externally expressed as a polytheism. Gaston Maspero (1846–1916) began by believing that Egyptian monotheism was a development from polytheism, before adamantly concluding that the Egyptian religion was exactly what its texts described it as, a polytheism. Other French Egyptologists, notably the Abbé Etienne Drioton (1889–1961), in the late 1940s, revived the concept of a monotheism in ancient Egypt going back to at least the Old Kingdom (c. 2686–2181 BC).

Many other Egyptologists simply misconstrued monotheising tendencies like chief god theology and the amalgamation of many gods into a single god with the characteristics of authentic monotheism. This was especially the astounding case of a religious person like Siegfried Morenz (1914–1970), who believed that the Egyptian theologians always postulated a monotheism within outer polytheism.

One of the most unusual views about so-called Egyptian monotheism was held by the Senegalese historian Cheikh Anta Diop (1923–1986). Combining 19th century views on an original Egyptian monotheism, Biblical tales, and Afrocentrism, he postulated that "Moses lived at the time of Tell el Amarna when Amenophis IV (Akhnaton, circa 1400) was trying to revive the early monotheism which had by then been discredited by sacerdotal ostentation and the corruptness of the priests...Moses was probably influenced by this reform. From that time on, he championed monotheism among the Jews. Monotheism, with all its abstraction, already existed in Egypt, which borrowed it from the Meroitic Sudan, the Ethiopia of the Ancients."[50]

As to the latest debate concerning a possible Egyptian monotheism or premonotheism as contained in Ptah/Memphite theology on the Shabako Stone, which began in the early 20th century (and continues), here too the conclusion must be that it constituted a monotheising tendency and not monotheism. As we have seen and shall continue to see, this probably late eighth century BC theology strongly remained part of Egypt's multiple approach to the gods, despite its monotheising unifying aspects and Judeo-Christian-like abstract notion of creation from the heart (mind) and the tongue (word) of Ptah.

Erik Hornung (b. 1933), in *Einfülrung in die Ägyptologie* in 1967 (a book meant more as a compilation of Egyptological resources than as a vehicle for profound statements) summed up the monotheism/polytheism debate among Egyptologists: "...attempts were carried out to depreciate Egyptian polytheism under the pretext that it was 'specious' and to show the existence of an 'anonymous divine' assimilable to monotheism. If the veneration of a unique divinity can effectively exist, the multiplicity of the divine image remains very present in the consciousness of the Egyptian. Only the belief of Akhenaten, rediscovered by modern science as an ancient religious founder, can possibly be qualified as 'monotheism.' In the future, it might be more fruitful to talk about complementary concepts in a polyvalent logic in which the singular 'god' and its plural, such as they appear in the Egyptian texts, do not mutually exclude each other."

In *Conceptions of the Gods In Ancient Egypt: The One and the Many*, Hornung convincingly demonstrated that "...before Akhenaten the placing of one god in a privileged position never threatened the existence of the rest of the gods. The

---

50. Diop, Cheikh Anta, *The African Origin of Civilization, Myth or Reality*, p. 6.

one and the many had been treated as complementary statements that were not mutually exclusive."

Hornung's basic position is that "...the opposition monotheism/polytheism does not seem to provide the key, because it is too narrowly formulated." "[F]or them [the Egyptians] the nature of a god becomes accessible through a 'multiplicity of approaches'; only when these are taken together can the whole be comprehended...For the Egyptians the world emerges from the one, because the non-existent is one...the creator god differentiates not only the world but also himself...From the one emerges...the diversity of the 'millions' of created forms. God divided, creation is division...The divided elements are interdependent, but remain divided so long as they are existent...By becoming existent, the divine loses the absolute, exclusive unity of the beginning of things...So far it has not been possible to prove in any example, even in the instruction texts, that an Egyptian meant by 'god' either the Only — without there being any other god — or the One and the Highest of the gods. Contrary to what is continually asserted in imprecise terms, the Egyptian concept of god never included monotheistic notions within its terminology; even henotheistic or pantheistic notions cannot be certainly identified in the use of the word 'god'...monotheism may have been impossible in Egyptian logic...monotheism does not arise within polytheism by way of a slow accumulation of 'monotheistic tendencies,' but requires a complete transformation of thought patterns."[51]

And so for Hornung, the Egyptians had two interdependent, simultaneous approaches to their gods: the approach to the one, to a god, any god, as a unique being while he was being worshipped...and the approach to the many, to the many gods in their pantheon as representatives of the multiple aspects of the universe. This represents a diametrical swing of the pendulum compared, as we have seen, to some 17th and 18th century scholars and writers and some early Egyptologists who went overboard in attributing monotheistic characteristics to the Egyptian religion.

Hornung's proposal of situating the Egyptian religion within this framework of complementary, interdependent concepts — "the one and the many" — went a long way toward clearing the deck for a better evaluation of the Egyptian religion. Hornung and Frankfort provided powerful conceptual tools that virtually end the debate concerning the existence of an Egyptian monotheism outside of Atenism. The views of Egyptologists like Budge, Brugsch, de Rougé, Mariette and Drioton seem to have been definitively discredited. However, Hornung and

---

51. Hornung, Erik, *La Grande Histoire de l'Egyptologie (Einführung in die Ägyptologie)*, pp. 86-87, *Conceptions of God in Ancient Egypt, The One and the Many*, pp. 249, 252-253, 60 and 243.

Frankfort in no way ended the debate concerning the role of Egyptian monotheising tendencies in the evolution towards monotheism.

I think that Hornung is fundamentally wrong in refusing the existence of monotheising tendencies in Egypt and in doubting that there were henotheistic stages in Egypt. Even if he does not recognize it as such, Hornung's description of the Egyptian approach to "the one" is obviously a monotheising tendency. In Egypt, as in many other societies, the Predynastic local gods and Early Dynastic nome gods which preceded organized polytheism and then at times and in many localities coexisted with it seem to have constituted a henotheistic phase. I fully share Hornung's view that only a conceptual revolution — as occurred with Akhenaten's Atenism — could have given birth to monotheism. However, it seems impossible to dismiss the possibility, and perhaps the plausibility, that a combination of factors led to the invention of monotheism both in Egypt and in Israel. A clear link between Egyptian monotheising tendencies and Hebrew monotheism can only be supposed and not proven, but it seems impossible to deny that the Atenist monotheistic conceptual revolution was nourished by stages of henotheism and monotheising tendencies.

Perhaps, chief god theology is the key to the matter. Perhaps, it is this term that is best adapted to the post-henotheistic, polytheistic and monotheising attributes of gods like Amun and Ptah, and even to gods like Re and Horus. In chief god theology, the existence of many gods was not only acknowledged, as in henotheism, but they were actively worshipped alongside the chief god even if they had a far lesser status, something which was compatible with polytheism. However, as Egyptian history progressed, the status of the chief gods was no longer situated within some kind of an unlimited polytheism. The chief gods with the combined powers of the gods they had amalgamated gained the premises of unitary status and constituted a monotheising tendency. The chief gods, culminating in Amun and Ptah, clearly represented monotheising tendencies even if the nature of these tendencies was frequently confused, clearly within a polytheistic framework and even if much more than chief god theology was required to threaten polytheism. It would take much more than the premises of abstract reasoning as contained in Ptah/Memphite theology before the basic Egyptian multiple approach could be undermined.

The barriers to monotheism in Egypt were indeed almost insurmountable. Egypt was steeped in polytheism, in hundreds of gods, local, national and universal gods who always maintained their singularity. Egypt was steeped in immanence in nature, and not transcendence. Egypt was steeped in the principle of the multiple nature of universality — the *hch*, the millions of aspects in universality, even when they were somehow amalgamated in the functions of a single chief god. Not even the most extensive forms of monotheising chief god theology, such as in Amun-Re theology, could change the reality that polytheism is essentially an immanent, magical, ritual, animistic, material, multiple and pragmatic approach to the sacred — attributes which are opposed to monotheism.

In such a context, monotheising tendencies could not change the fact that the fundamental gap with monotheism could not be bridged because monotheism was based on the exclusivity of a single concept and transcendence. And yet, monotheising tendencies in Egypt as a concept among many concepts within a basically polytheistic system were real. The reality that several theological tendencies, including monotheising tendencies, were at work at various times in the more than 3000 years of Egyptian religious history is not irreconcilable with the fundamental and overwhelming polytheistic thrust of Egyptian religion.

Monotheising tendencies are not monotheism, but the coexistence and frequent tension between polytheism and monotheising tendencies in Egypt was real. We have seen and shall continue to see that Egypt seems to have been the trunk of the tree from which monotheism grew, even if there is no direct proof of this.

MONOTHEISING TENDENCIES AND THE GAP WITH THE THEOLOGY, ETHICS AND ESCHATOLOGY OF MONOTHEISM

As long as the tension between monotheising tendencies and polytheism was contained within chief god theology, it was creative and even gave coherency to the theocratic, totalitarian political system. As long as a monotheising tendency did not cross certain limits, as occurred with the Aten proto-monotheistic experiment, it in fact preserved the basic values of polytheism that were the popular bedrock of Egyptian custom and belief. In theocratic, polytheistic India, Babylonia and Canaan, this was also undoubtedly true, while in the theocratic Israel of Moses and the Judges and right until the sixth century BC, it led to a bitter struggle between polytheism and monotheism.

Egypt's monotheising tendency, engendered from henotheism and chief god theology, largely contributed to bringing Egypt to the frontiers of monotheism around 1350 BC with Pharaoh Akhenaten's proto-monotheism (even if the frontier with authentic monotheism was not really crossed, if we accept the standard comprehensive definition of monotheism). Moreover, the Egyptian Amun-Re chief god monotheising tendency and the Atenist proto-monotheistic experiment, together with the Babylonian Marduk chief god monotheising tendency, may well have been the main external influences which, between about the 13th and 6th centuries BC, led to the emergence of Yahweh henotheism and then to authentic, exclusive monotheism in Israel.

Chief god theology seems to have been stronger in Early Dynastic Egypt (c. 3100–2686 BC), especially with Horus and then Re, than in Sumer with either the earth god Enlil or the water god Enki. Even the later Akkadian moon and wisdom god Sin's (the Sumerian Nanna) chief god attributes were far from matching the powers Egyptians attributed to their chief gods, but Sin did have some typically monotheistic theological powers. It was probably not before the 18th century BC that the successor Sumerian state of Babylonia began experimenting with a chief god concept as strong as that invented in Egypt. Marduk became chief god in "Babylon, the center of the world" and was eventually revered to the exclusion, although not the denial, of the other gods.

In the Egyptian New Kingdom (c. 1550–1069 BC), the Chief God Amun-Re was even stronger than the Babylonian Chief God Marduk. It was within this context that the overflow limit leading into proto-monotheism was reached and then overstepped by Akhenaten (c. 1352–1336 BC). Of course, it was no surprise that this occurred in Thebes where the clergy had the greatest theocratic, totalitarian and theologically totalizing attitude.

Vital as it was to the development of monotheism, the Amun-Re monotheising tendency with Amunism was only a stage. A far more radical approach was required before authentic monotheism could be invented. The thrust of Amun theology, and all other chief god theologies, was always to totalize, to addition and to amalgamate gods in a worldview in which immanent diversity was the fundamental element. Amun was "one who made himself into millions (*heh*)," but it was "the millions" which counted most in this equation. The thrust of monotheism was spontaneously unitary. Even in the most extensive forms of chief god theology, this fundamental polytheistic gap with monotheism persisted — the simultaneous unity and diversity of the divine versus unity as a sole, indivisible divine reality, the totality achieved through temporary addition versus the permanent totality as a *unitary unity*.

Throughout the entirety of Egyptian religious history, the constant tendency was towards totalizing, towards the gods assimilating each other. Egyptian gods and goddesses did not have permanent characteristics or even permanent names and, as we have seen, were constantly subjected to synthesis and amalgamation with other gods and goddesses. No god was permanently a chief god, not even Re or Amun. Even the major chief gods like Horus, Re, Osiris, Ptah and Amun assimilated each other in addition to assimilating less important gods. There was a succession and simultaneity of chief gods rather than any permanent chief god. Moreover, it was characteristically polytheistic that these successive and/or simultaneous chief gods did not reject the existence of other gods, even the other gods in their own home nomes. Once the Hebrew Yahweh emerged from his polytheistic origins, he resolutely rejected all other gods as false and in a next stage resolutely denied their very existence.

No single Egyptian god, no matter how great his powers, including Amun, was ever authentically omnipotent and none was transcendental. Power, knowledge and functions were shared out among the hundreds of Egyptian national and local gods and the pharaoh-god. The Egyptian gods and goddesses and the pharaoh-god divided the universe among themselves and were immanent, material personifications of cosmic, natural, animal and human forces. They were material idols and emblem/totems and in the case of the pharaoh, a god incarnated in a human. Yahweh was truly omnipotent and transcendental; he did not share anything with any other god and was never immanent in nature. He was never a material idol. As to Jesus, despite his being killed and resurrected like Osiris, he was radically different from both Osiris and the incarnation of the pharaoh as a god by his voluntary self-sacrifice, his ethical nature and his eschatological promise.

Egyptian gods and goddesses were created in one way or another; they were not uncreated and existent outside time like Yahweh. Even when claims of being pre-existent or self-created were made for some of them, at best the context within which these claims were made (for Atum, Atum-Re, Ptah or Amun) had more to do with being self-existent rather than being self-created and outside time.

The primordial Egyptian creator god Atum emerged from Nun, the personification of the *waret* waters of chaos, before creating the other gods and the universe. The Hermopolis Ogdoad of gods and goddesses were concomitant to chaos. Ptah in the Memphis Ennead was described as pre-existent to the other gods and to the creation of the universe, but he was not, like Yahweh, pre-existent to chaos.

Of all the Egyptian creator gods, Ptah comes closest to the notion of a *First Principle*, or to the Aristotelian concept of the "Unmoved Mover," but there is a huge difference between Ptah who was concomitant to *Nun*, chaos, who was Ptah-Nun, and Yahweh who did not surge out of chaos, but existed before chaos, the "void," existed and who was the sole "Unmoved Mover."

Yahweh was the only god for whom claims of pre-existence to chaos and the power to create from nothing were made. There is only one example of an Egyptian god who was presented as the "Creator Uncreated" — Amun — and the context within the Stele of the Brothers Suti and Hor in which this claim is inscribed makes it doubtful that it was anything else but a superlative devoid of factual intention. The more usual claims made for Amun were that he was born of himself and had no mother or father, or that he was the *kamutef*, "the bull of his mother," or that he was "the unique," claims which were made for many other gods. Moreover, there was not a single Egyptian creator god, but many, depending on geographical locations and periods in time — Atum, Re, Khnum, Aten, Ptah, Amun and the goddess Neith were all creators of the universe.

All the Egyptian gods were born, even the primordial, self-created Atum and the pre-existent Ptah. They had consorts, brothers and sisters and children. They could be nurtured, assisted or maimed like Horus. They could be tricked, defeated, over-ruled, banished or castrated like Seth. They could become evil, like Seth. They could cringe in fear when threatened by Seth or Osiris. They could be enthralled by Hathor's strip-tease performance. They could get old and tired like Atum and Re. They could be poisoned or even need a remedy for a headache, like Re. They could be manipulated to destroy mankind and then be gotten stone drunk to prevent this destruction, like Hathor or Sakhmet. They could symbolize both humiliation and compassion, like Nephthys. They could even be murdered and then be resurrected by magical techniques, like Osiris. They could die and go to live in the afterlife, like the eight original gods and goddesses of the Hermopolis Ogdoad.

Some Pyramid Texts even suggest that the gods could be warned, threatened, deeply affected or rewarded according to their acts towards the pharaoh. Utterance 485, in Pepy I's (c. 2321–2287 BC) Sakkara Pyramid and in other pyramids states: "As for any god who will take me to the sky, may he live and endure; bulls shall be slaughtered for him, forelegs shall be cut off for him, and he shall ascend to the Mansion of Horus which is in the sky; but as for any god who will not take me to the sky, he shall not have honor, he shall not possess a leopard skin, he shall not taste *p3k*-bread, and he shall not ascend to the Mansion of Horus..." Utterance 310 states: "If I [the king] be smitten, then Atum will be smitten; If I be hindered on this road [to the sky], then Atum will be hindered..." Spell 175 in *The Book of the Dead* also suggests that the gods could be killed and expresses disgust with the gods who "have made war...done wrong...done slaughter..." and Atum calls on Thoth "to shorten their years, cut short their months, because they have done hidden damage to all that you have made." Even cannibalism among the Egyptian gods was possible — Isis threatened to eat a limb of Seth and although only a "small god," the pharaoh-god Unas, in Pyramid Text 273-4, actually "cooks" and "eats" the "big," "middle-sized" and "little" gods in the afterlife.[52]

None of this could even remotely apply to Yahweh. After Yahweh emerged from his probable polytheistic origins, he was theologically uncreated. Not only was he not "born," but in orthodox Hebrew theology it was impossible to imag-

---

52. Faulkner, R.O., *The Ancient Egyptian Pyramid Texts*, pp. 96, 172 and 80-81 and Faulkner, R.O., *The Ancient Egyptian Book of the Dead*, p. 175.

ine him being threatened, maimed, castrated, getting old and weak, being killed, or having a wife, brothers and sisters and children, let alone having a headache: The attempt to sometimes give him a wife — the Canaanite mother goddess Asherah — or to associate him with others gods — most usually the Canaanite Baal — by heterodox or heretical Israelites and Judahites tempted by polytheism between the tenth and fifth century BC resulted in frequent bloody battles among the Hebrews, Yahweh's elimination of heretical kings, and even the destruction of the nation-state before the final victory of orthodox Hebrew monotheism over polytheism.

Considerable evolution away from orthodox Hebrew concepts to pre-Christian and Christian concepts was also required before Yahweh could have a son, Jesus, in the first century AD. Moreover, Jesus was the son of Yahweh and was the Messiah only for the heretical Christians; for the orthodox Hebrews, the Messiah could not be divine, he could only be "the son of man" and a king/prophet, as he was more or less for the later Moslem monotheists. Moslem monotheism, which arose directly from Hebrew and Christian monotheisms, became the monotheism that most strongly insisted on the omnipotent, unitary nature of the sole god. This was so much so that Islam deemed Christian plural monotheism, the divinity of Jesus and the crucifixion of the God Jesus incomprehensible.

The possibility of duping their gods, which the Egyptians frequently used — and always used with the negative confession for the purpose of fraudulently winning an afterlife — was another huge loophole in the concept of omnipotence. Both the Zoroastrian and Christian ethical concepts of the afterlife as a reward and consolation were deeply at odds with this Egyptian manner of winning an afterlife.

Even the very notion of individual physical survival after death as practiced by the Egyptians was deeply incompatible with Hebrew monotheism until at least after the sixth century BC, since the early Hebrews were primarily concerned with the eternal survival of the collectivity, of the Hebrew people as a nation. And following their flirtation with the concept of individual physical survival, as inherited from the Persians, the Jews reverted to the traditional and orthodox view of a perishable body and an imperishable spirit which returned to God.

Quite simply the dominant, constant, internal and external thrust and spirit of the Egyptian system, like the Sumerian-Babylonina system and like animism, was multiple, composite, immanent, idolatrous, polytheistic and magical. It constituted the opposite of the monotheistic thrust of a transcendental, all-encompassing and all-knowing god, of a divine force with unitary omnipotence. This naturally led to extreme differences in the behavior attributed to Egypt's gods and goddesses and the Hebrew Yahweh, the Zoroastrian Ahura Mazda and the Christian Jesus.

Egypt's polytheistic gods and goddesses governed the universe and mankind with a mixture of gratuity, fickleness and cruelty, as well as law, order and justice. Rivalry, conflict and underhanded behavior among the gods, with serious theological and political consequences, were perhaps only slightly less widespread in Egyptian mythology than in Sumerian mythology. Eating, drinking, sexual intercourse, fighting, tricking, loving and hating other each other were usual occupations of Egypt's gods and goddesses.

The Egyptian gods and goddesses and the pharaoh-god were at best usually vaguely benevolent dictators and at worst, despots. At the end of the day, only magic, offerings and subservience could sway them.

Even if the early Yahweh's attitude to the government of mankind was similar to the gratuity, fickleness and cruelty of the polytheistic gods (the flood, the genocide of rival peoples, the temporary punishment of Job, etc.), it was seriously tempered by Yahweh's basic motive. The early Yahweh was "jealous," but "merciful," and his main concern was fighting with the Hebrews to make them better, rather than maintaining a status quo, a so-called natural, primeval, universal order. The later ethical, loving and universal Yahweh of the Judeans and the Christians constituted the opposite of the Egyptian polytheistic schema. In particular, the amplification of the ethical characteristic of Judaism from the sixth century BC and the addition of eschatological concerns and their crowning in the first century AD with the absolute ethical values of universal love and forgiveness of Christianity made the gap with Egyptian concepts unbridgeable.

Much the same can be said for the comparison between Ahura Mazda and the Egyptian gods and goddesses. Much of what Ahura Mazda saw as evil and against which he engaged a relentless battle which could only end in the victory of the good was considered by the Egyptians as part of the necessary duality of the universe which would always exist. Ahura Mazda was basically optimistic and merciful, even if he could be temporarily cruel — even sinners, after expiation, would one day be saved. For the Egyptians, there was only unchangeability for eternity; there would never be a *one day* which was different from any other day, either for so-called sinners or for the world.

Likewise, the monotheistic abstract thrust of a sole, invisible god was obviously radically different from anything the Egyptians had ever theologically invented. Even the "hidden god," Amun-Re, was always represented as a material idol and was directly immanent in the air and the sun and was immanent in everything through the other gods, as his *ba* aspects. With Akhenaten's Aten in the 14th century BC, the Egyptians did invent a sole god, but he was not abstract and invisible; he was the immanent sun and its rays, and he was represented in images. At whatever date Ptah/Memphite theology reached its plenitude — and this was probably the eighth century BC — it invented an abstract system of creation through the heart/mind and the tongue/word, but Ptah remained a representational god in human form. Moreover, although Ptah/Memphite theology represented a step towards sophisticated, abstract reasoning of the type central to monotheistic theology, its context of multiplicity rendered it incapable of drawing monotheism's abstract conclusion of a sole god to whom anything and everything could be linked, including human free will. The abstract concept of invisibility, born from intellectual speculation, was a key foundation of Hebrew monotheism. It was eminently compatible with the fundamental Hebrew option of transcendency and it opened the road to human free will and unbending ethical principles determined by the human mind and emotions; and it was a kind of halfway house to the invention of the non-mythological and rational approach by the Greeks in the sixth century BC.

Almost right from the outset and despite polytheistic relapses, both Hebrew Yahweh henotheism and then monotheism clearly took this road of an abstract, sole, invisible god and a revolutionary ethical approach. The first Hebrew decrees and myths, in the *Torah* (the first five books of the Bible), seem to already reflect a strong leaning towards very exclusive henotheism. Even in what is biblically described as Abraham's time (and Moses' time), Hebrew henotheism was already a near or pre-monotheism. There was more monotheism in the Abrahamic vision and in the so-called *Yahwist* henotheism, and even in the probably later *Elohist* henotheism — theologically, ethically and proto-democratically — than there was in Egyptian chief god monotheising theology. Only the short-lived primitive monotheism with Akhenaten's Aten religion constituted the beginnings of a monotheistic vision.

Of course, there are theories that much of the *Torah* was not composed, or even established as oral traditions, as early as the tenth century BC, but that it was almost entirely contrived in the late sixth century BC after the Babylonian Exile, thus rendering its early monotheistic credo doubtful. However, despite its contradictions and inaccuracies, the internal thrust and intricate structure of the *Torah* and other early books of the Bible, as well as frequent allusions to the battle waged by the Israelite religious leaders against polytheism among the people and many of the kings, seem to plead in favor of both early monotheistic literary fragments and oral traditions and a substantial body of monotheistic Biblical texts by King Josiah's reign (c. 640–609 BC), before a definitive composition of the *Torah* in the sixth century BC. It seems incontrovertible that at whatever date the *Torah* was actually finalized, pre- or near-monotheism was a central ambition of the Hebrews from the presumably Mosaic Period in the late 13th century BC, perhaps a key reality from about the eighth century BC, and the central reality from the mid-seventh century BC.

Hebrew near-monotheism, right from the descriptions of Moses' time, asserted that Yahweh was not of the same nature as the other gods. And this was also true of the descriptions given to us of Abraham's god, who still was not named Yahweh, or rather *Yhwh*. This Hebrew henotheistic or near monotheistic god was described as being more powerful and morally better than all the other gods in the universe. It was moreover a revolution of immense proportions to assert that a god could not be incarnated in an image, in sculpture, as both Abraham and Moses aggressively and fanatically imposed.

Yahweh was clearly not of the same nature as the polytheistic gods, just as the Sumerian and Egyptian polytheistic gods who had emerged from animistic nature religion and totemistic emblems were not of the same character as the nature religion and totemistic divinities. However, it must be reiterated that Yahweh almost surely emerged from the polytheistic gods. The unprovable likelihood is that Moses, or somebody like him, added several Egyptian and Babylonian attributes to Yahweh, including Amun's and Marduk's assimilation of the powers of as many gods as possible and Atenist sole god attributes.

By Moses' time, or the time the Israelites became a people in the late 13th century BC, Yahweh had no need of the other gods; he was assumed to be, and fictitiously assumed to have been from the outset, a unitary, omnipotent god. Yahweh was everything and while the existence of other gods was at first not denied, they were not to be "served." Yahweh was omnipotent and there was no need of other gods.

Obviously, there was no need for Yahweh to squabble or struggle with other gods as in Egyptian and all other polytheisms. Obviously, once Yahweh had "created the heaven and the earth" and gave the earth "form,"[53] an Egyptian-type eternal struggle between order, *maat*, and disorder, *izfeh*, was irrelevant. The Egyptian gods did not control disorder or evil; they fought them. Yahweh had eliminated chaos and used the forces of evil as he saw fit. This was utterly opposed to the Egyptian-type reasoning that the gods were personified in nature and together with the pharaoh-god ran the whole show according to an unchangeable schema.

However, the struggle to impose monotheism and its implications over polytheism was not an easy battle; it failed in Egypt and took centuries to impose in Israel. This struggle in Israel began almost immediately with the supposed constitution of the Israelites by Moses. At that time in the Sinai, according to the Bible, the Hebrew hankering for other gods — the golden calf episode —

---

53. Genesis 1:1, 2, 26 and 27.

was such a grave taboo that it resulted in one of the few occasions in which Moses was terrifyingly murderous. (The golden calf may possibly be linked to the many Egyptian bull and cow deities and notably to Apis as the animal manifestation of the god Ptah. It could also be linked to Hathor in her morning "golden calf" form; there was a major Hathor Temple in Serabit el-Khadim in the Sinai from about c. 1985 BC.)

Likewise, the Hebrew adoption of cults and worship of idols of other, foreign, gods and goddesses, like Baal, the Moabite Chemosh, the Ammonite Milcom, the Canaanite Molech (also a term for child sacrifice), the Sidonnite "Queen of Heaven" Ashtoret and of course Asherah (first El's and then Baal's consort and then a Hebrew tree goddess) were, according to numerous prophets, the main reason why Yahweh exercised fierce divine judgment against several polytheistic-leaning kings and destroyed the United Monarchy, then the Kingdom of Israel and then the Kingdom of Judah.

But Yahweh's divine justice was almost never enough to eradicate polytheism. Many Hebrew kings were not staunch monotheists; they would have preferred to pragmatically carry on business as usual in much the same way as the other countries of the Egypto-West Asian continuum did. Solomon (fl.c. 950 BC) tolerated polytheism, and kings like Ahab (c. 874–853 BC), Ahaz (c. 753–720 BC) and Manasseh (c. 686–642 BC) continued to practice polytheism and child sacrifice.

According to the Books of Judges and Kings, polytheism also seems to have been a usual practice among many ordinary Hebrews. Two eighth century BC inscriptions found on fragments of pithoi (large storage jars) in a Kuntillet Ajrud tomb in the Negev and the seventh century BC tomb inscription found in a Khirbet El-Qom near Lachish (in the Israel Museum), both referring to "Yahweh and his Asherah," indicate how strong such extreme polytheistic views must have been both before and even after Yahweh punished the Kingdom of Israel with total destruction. II Kings 23 also clearly indicates that there were idols of Baal and Asherah in the Jerusalem Temple and that polytheistic nature worship was common before King Josiah destroyed the idols and outlawed polytheism at the beginning of his reign (c. 640 BC).

The decisive step in the development of Hebrew full-blown monotheism did not come until the sixth century BC with the *nabiim* (prophets) Deutero-Isaiah and Jeremiah. Deutero-Isaiah proclaimed that Yahweh was the sole, permanent, universal god ("I *am* the first and I *am* the last; and beside me *there is* no God.") and that the idols which all the other peoples in the world believed to be gods simply had no real divine existence.[54]

---

54. Isaiah 44:6.

It is also probably only possible to speak about broad acceptation of monotheism by the Judean people from about this time. But even during this sixth century BC, Jeremiah's denunciation of polytheism, beliefs that the divine was immanent in elements of nature, and child sacrifice, indicate the continued existence of other beliefs. Even as late as the fourth century BC, the acceptation of monotheism was apparently not total. The largest Jewish settlement in the diaspora of that time, Elephantine in Egypt, was still practicing a heterodox, syncretic religion in which their Yaho was not only an odd version of Yahweh, but he was also sometimes coupled with worship of several other deities. These included the Canaanite/Egyptian love and war goddess Anath(bethel), a male deity called Ishumbethel and a Khn[ub] who may have been the local henotheistic ram-headed creator, sun and Nile flood god Khnum.[55]

Universal morality — so intimately linked to authentic monotheism and the culmination of the *tsadaquah*, righteousness, concept — also emerged with Jeremiah, who proclaimed that Yahweh practiced impartial, universal morality and justice for both individuals and nations. For Jeremiah, it was evident that if Israel sinned, Israel would be punished despite Yahweh's special relationship with Israel. Moreover, Yahweh would reward the *goyim* (the foreign nations) for their righteous deeds, as he rewarded Israel. Jeremiah and Deutero-Isaiah confirmed and amplified the universal monotheistic ethical tendency already evident with the prophets Jonah and Amos, who may have lived during the eighth century BC, when Yahweh was still a henotheistic or near-monotheistic god.

The Egyptian belief that the peoples of "the nine bows," the peoples of the foreign lands, the *khasut*, were "wretched" enemies who represented chaos became *caduc* with Jeremiah and the road was opened to Jesus' universal egalitarianism of love, morality and total forgiveness. At least the theoretical and idealistic end to the related *khasut/Goyim* concept was proclaimed by Jesus with his extraordinary proclamation: "Love your enemies, bless them that curse you, do good to them that hate you..." Even Akhenaten, who seems to have sincerely tried to temper the *khasut* principle and who probably could have gone along with Moses' "love thy neighbor as thyself,"[56] would not have been able to swallow Jesus' radical view.

After the sixth century BC, the monotheistic or near monotheistic gods, whether Hebrew, Persian or Christian, structurally ruled on the strict (but contradictory) basis of instinctive belief and fear, love and morality, rather than primarily on crude magic, offerings and animal sacrifices, even while these practices continued in various forms.

---

55. Ginsberg, H.L. in *Ancient Near Eastern Texts Relating to the Old Testament*, p. 491.
56. Matthew 5:44 and Leviticus 19:18.

From Jeremiah's time (c. 650–570 BC), a fundamental — and very un-Egyptian — switch took place, away from manipulating the gods with magic, offerings, trickery and insincere prayers for both individual and national salvation. According to Jeremiah, the god Yahweh saw no "purpose" in sacrifices made by unrighteous people: "...your burnt offerings are not acceptable, nor your sacrifices sweet unto me."... "I *am* the Lord which exercises lovingkindness, judgment and righteousness...for in these things I delight..."[57] Yahweh, according to Jeremiah, demanded *tsadaquah*, righteousness, true belief in the only god (himself) and moral justice for all, including foreigners. The punishment for not observing these precepts was the destruction of the nation.

Jeremiah's idealistic recipe for individual and national salvation marked a turning point in the history of religion away from the Egyptian type of magical thinking, but it also inaugurated a new type of magical thought. The belief arose that everything could be explained, including immense prosperity, but also immense national catastrophes, by God's will to reward good and punish evil. This is what monotheistic believers came to totally expect, and still expect, from their god. The Christian Calvinist Protestant ethic of the immense and justified prosperity of Protestant peoples is a direct consequence of this kind of thinking. Especially among the Hebrews, this kind of thinking produced incredible explanations of the worst catastrophes. If many eminent Jewish religious thinkers today see the *Shoah* as a baffling problem due to the evident failure of the Hebrew god to act morally and protect his people, many orthodox and fundamentalist Jewish rabbis (and some Christian theologians) have decreed that the *Shoah* was divine retribution for Jewish individual and/or collective sin.

The adage that horrible or accidental occurrences are instances when God does not reveal what he really thinks or does is applicable to Egyptian and other polytheisms; it is not applicable to Hebrew and other monotheisms where God supposedly always rewards goodness and punishes evil. In some ways, Christian monotheism (in the first centuries of our era) and Moslem monotheism (from the seventh century AD) even went further by the proclamation that their universal god rules on the basis of a moral plan, superior to any previous plan.

The Persian type of near-monotheism, which flowered in the sixth century BC, like the other monotheisms, also stemmed from henotheism and chief god theology, similar to the Egyptian chief god system. Ahura Mazdah was the "wise god," the chief god of a pantheon, perhaps connected to the Chief God Mithra, before becoming a chief god in his own right. However, Zoroaster (c. 6th century BC or c. 13th century BC?) radically transformed Ahura Mazda into the universal monotheistic God, probably before the Hebrews operated the same transforma-

---

57. Jeremiah, 6:20 and 9:24.

tion for Yahweh. In the final days, Ahura Mazda would ensure that justice and morality triumphed throughout the universe. Persian near-monotheism exercised a huge influence on the Hebrew way of thinking, but it somehow lacked the same radicalism as Hebrew henotheism and monotheism. It maintained a powerful force of evil, Ahriman, who had near divine powers; this was perhaps a key reason why Zoroastrianism quickly relapsed into disguised forms of national henotheism and polytheism in which the old gods and goddesses Zoroaster had tried to eliminate sneaked back into the Persian pantheon.

All the monotheisms, with the exception of the Christian, firmly rejected theriomorphism and anthropomorphism. Just as it was perfectly within the natural order of things for the Egyptians to perceive their gods as animal, combined animal-human or human idols, this was anathema to the Hebrews, the Persians and the Moslems. These religions used anthropomorphic terms to describe their god (with the Hebrews stating that man was made in the "image" and "likeness"[58] of god), but it was deeply anathema to them to represent God in an image or an idol.

According to Herodotus and Plutarch, it was the Persians who had the most extreme and savage attitude to idolatry and especially to animals being considered as gods in Egypt. Even if these claims are open to considerable doubts concerning their historic truth, it is certain that the Persian King Cambyses (c. 525–522 BC) and his predecessors and successors had little respect for Egypt's idolatrous religion and a complicity and special protective relationship with their fellow monotheistic, anti-idolatrous Judeans. Herodotus described Cambyses' disdain and mockery of the Egyptians for being "simpletons" who believe that an animal — the Apis bull — a "creature of flesh and blood that can feel weapons of iron" was a god. Herodotus also stated that Cambyses killed the sacred Apis and many Egyptians for rejoicing at the birth of an Apis. Plutarch says that Artaxerxes III Ochus (c. 343–338 BC) also killed an Apis Bull and "ate him for dinner." And if we are to believe the Elephantine Jews, who were mercenaries in Cambyses' army, Cambyses "knocked down all the temples of the gods of Egypt, but no one did any damage to this temple"[59] (the Yaho Temple, which of course had no idol).

---

58. Genesis 1:26.

59. Herodotus, *The Persian Wars, Books III-IV* (translated by A.D. Godley), Loeb Classical Library, Harvard University Press, Cambridge, Mass., 1920, 3.29.1-3 and 3.27.1-3, Plutarch, *Moralia, Volume V, Isis and Osiris*, p. 29 and Ginsberg, H.L. in *Ancient Near Eastern Texts Relating to the Old Testament*, Petition for Authorization to Rebuild the Yaho Temple, p. 491-492.

No Egyptian document claims that the savagery and sacrilege described by Herodotus and Plutarch — which have gone down in history as one of the saddest episodes of disrespect and insensitivity to the religion of other peoples — ever occurred, but this could been inevitable prudence and kow-towing to the Persian occupiers. It is also possible that Herodotus and Plutarch may have been retroactively reporting exaggerated Egyptian propaganda resentment against the Persians. Nevertheless, a document does exist in which the turncoat Egyptian naval commander Udjahorresne suggests that Persians had occupied and desecrated the Neith Temple in Sais.[60] And nevertheless, it was Persia and Emperor Cyrus II (c. 590–529) who enabled the re-establishment of monotheistic Hebrew independence in c. 538 BC and it was the Persian Emperor Artaxerxes II (c. 404–358 BC), and the head of his Egyptian satrapy, Arsames, who supported the demands of the Elephantine Jewish community to rebuild the Yaho Temple — where rams sacred to the Egyptians had been sacrificed — at the risk of making matters worse with the rebellious Egyptians of the time.

The Christian attitude to idolatry is of course more ambiguous. It is clear that the first Christians, the Judeo-Christians, were not idol worshippers, but by the end of the first century AD, the Christians believed that God had been incarnated in a man, as the Egyptians believed for the pharaoh. The early Christians struggled for centuries with the problem of the image, the idol, of Jesus, before the Eastern Church permanently authorized images in AD 843 and the Western Church authorized them in 1215 —stipulating that Jesus was not present in the images of him. However, Christian monotheism, like all the monotheisms, and even with ambiguities of the Eastern Church, firmly maintained that their god was not an idol or an image. This, of course, was in deep disaccord with Egyptian theology. Even when Akhenaten invented his sole god, Aten, in the mid-14th century BC, he deemed it necessary to represent him in a minimalist idolatrical image — the sun with human hands.

Another key characteristic of monotheism — a benevolent, personal, affectionate and moral relationship between the divine and man, which was strongest in Christian monotheism — was never generalized in Egyptian religion, either in relation to humanity as a whole, as we have abundantly seen, or even in relation to the Egyptian people.

Certainly, Re was not a benevolent, affectionate or moral god, even if attempts were sometimes made to picture him this way — such as the Middle Kingdom (c. 2055–1650 BC) Coffin Text Spells 1130/1031[61] tale of him creating man from his tears and his creation of equal social conditions which were per-

---

60. Lichtheim, Miriam, *Ancient Egyptian Literature, Volume III*, p. 38.
61. Wilson, John in *Ancient Near Eastern Texts Relating to the Old Testament*, pp. 7-8.

verted by man's creation of evil. In fact, aside from benevolence for the reigning pharaoh, any benevolence Re might have for humans was usually an after-thought, as in the tale of *The Destruction of Mankind*. Re was constantly entangled in power struggles and his reactions were usually human-like brutality, venge-fulness and scheming.

Certainly, many Egyptian gods and goddesses were fickle at best and evil at worst. A list of these gods includes the feared god of the waters, the fertility and the sun god, Sobek, his virgin mother and war goddess Neith and the *weret-hekau*, "great of magic," the fire breathing destroyer/benevolent and plague bringing/healer goddess Sakhmet, to say nothing about Seth and the mother and female principle goddess Hathor. Nut, the sky goddess and mother of the resurrected dead gave birth to Osiris, Isis, Horus the Elder, Seth and Nephthys by gambling with Thoth and cheating Re. Even Isis, the epitome of the perfect, protective mother, had ambivalent aspects notably in her relation to her "evil" brother Seth. Egypt's hundreds of ferocious demons also played roles in life and afterlife and in many cases were frequently referred to as gods, as *netjer*, who had powers which were close to those of the gods.

Relations with the gods in Egypt were a matter for the pharaoh and the priests and not the people. Only after the beginning of the First Intermediate Period (from c. 2181 BC), when afterlife privileges had been clearly extended to everybody, did a god, the afterlife savior god Osiris, play a personal role for every-body, or rather those people who could meet the material and magical require-ments for entry into the afterlife.

Egypt did however make many attempts in the direction of a moral, affec-tionate relation between the gods and man. In addition to Osiris, the goddess of order, truth and justice Maat, the consoling, protective and healing aspects of the Mother goddess Isis, the dutiful, justice-seeking son of Osiris and Isis, Horus, the wise, inscrutable god Amun and Pharaoh Akhenaten's brief Aten proto-monotheism all constituted attempts at inventing warm, affectionate gods. Dur-ing the New Kingdom (c. 1550–1069 BC), a major aspect of Amun-Re's personal-ity was compassion, especially for the poor. However, none of these attempts were comprehensive, consistent or conclusive. None of them basically changed the Egyptian framework of *heka*, magic. *Heka* magical appeasement and manipu-lation of the gods, and their idols or animal or plant fetishes, and the correct use of spells, incantations and *meket* and *wedja* (protective and welfare amulets) remained the ritual, materialistic and pragmatic *modus operandi* of the Egyptian religious system.

Hebrew monotheism aggressively rejected all this — without ever fully succeeding in eradicating it in practice — in favor of a subtler magic based on absolute belief in the powers of a sole invisible god who rewarded ethical behavior, both individually and nationally. *Tsadaquah*, justice and righteousness, was what Yahweh wanted and what the Hebrews struggled to achieve. *Asha*, truth and righteousness, is what the Zoroastrian Ahura Mazda sought to impose. A super *tsadaquah* was demanded by Jesus and the early Christians desperately struggled to achieve it. The affectionate, personal, moral, idealistic relationship between God and man which gradually became a central pillar of Judean, Persian and Christian monotheism constituted a huge difference with the pragmatic, magical, material Egyptian polytheistic attitude.

The monotheisms put the destiny of the individual into the hands of the individual. This was so, as we have seen in Chapter 9, with the sense of meaning which the Hebrew/Christian, Persian and Moslem monotheisms assigned to the history of mankind and its eschatological destiny. The fulfillment and paradisiacal reward of the individual through moral behavior, the end of suffering and evil and the end of ordinary history promised by the monotheisms implicitly rejected the Egyptian-type system in which man's destiny in the afterlife was part of a permanent schema practically solely determined by magical manipulation. Monotheistic eschatologies completed what, as we have seen in Chapter 4, was the Hebrew severing of the animistic connection to nature which was central to the Egypto-Sumerian system. Authentic, or integral, monotheism totally rejected animism, totemism, theriomorphism and the immanence of the divine in nature and postulated a clear domination of nature and the animals by a transcendental god. One of the key consequences of Yahweh's injunction to "man" to "have dominion...over all the earth" and to "replenish...and subdue it"[62] was a type of free will for man which was in deep conflict with polytheism. The monotheisms radically changed the rules of the ball game. I'm no great admirer of Pope John Paul II, but he perfectly expressed Christian monotheistic thought — so utterly opposed to that of ancient Egypt's permanent, unchangeable system — when he declared on Easter Sunday, April 15, 2001: "Rediscover today with joy and wonder that the world is no longer a slave to the inevitable. This world of ours can change."[63]

In the first centuries of the Christian and Moslem eras, it was perhaps the monotheistic eschatology with its ethical implications which the Egyptians

---

62. Genesis 1:26 and 27.
63. www.cin.org/pope/urbi-orbi-easter-2001.html

themselves perceived as the key point of difference between Egyptian polytheism and the monotheisms.

The overall conclusion is simple: unless one wants to change the standard definition of monotheism, nothing in Egyptian religion, except the Akhenaten/Atenist period of about 20 years in the mid-14th century BC, is sufficient to conclude in favor of any kind of monotheism, real, virtual or latent.

Yet despite all these restrictions, globally, the bottom line is a series of oxymorons. Despite its clearly polytheistic character, Egypt's monotheising tendencies were real. The gap between authentic monotheism and the advanced chief god phase of the Egyptian religion, notably Amun-Re theology, was small yet considerable. Small, because they were undoubtedly advanced stages in the evolution towards monotheism and a vague foretaste of what would occur, and considerable, because the plurality of gods and their functions was everywhere as the central substance of religion, politics, society and art. There is also the oxymoron of Ptah/Memphite theology and its abstract creation concept, which despite its context of polytheistic diversity and animism was certainly a monotheistic-like theological concept. Above all, the gap was unbridgeable in ethics and its eschatological implications.

Nevertheless, chief god theology in Egypt eventually led to the invention of monotheism, to the brief period of Atenist primitive monotheism. In the final analysis, chief god theology was the inner dynamic towards which Egyptian religion tended throughout its history. It was also the sacrosanct barrier in Egypt's vision that its theology was permanent and unchangeable which could not be crossed with impunity, as the failure of the Atenist primitive monotheistic revolution would prove. And yet, unless one adopts the extreme position of excluding the possibility of monotheising tendencies which contributed to forging the monotheistic revolution as well as excluding any Egyptian influence on Israel, it would seem that Egyptian chief god theology influenced Israel and that Atenism was an historical turning point of great magnitude — incomplete, but the beginning of the conceptual revolution which led to monotheism.

The polytheism/monotheising tendencies vs. monotheism debate is too complex to accommodate simplifications. Many possibilities and combinations of possibilities exist and unfortunately the surviving textual and archaeological resources are insufficient to make an exact, or totally comprehensive, evaluation possible. The analysis of some modern Egyptologists, like Frankfort and Hornung, that aside from the Atenist period there was never any real religious evolution in Egypt involving monotheising tendencies and that there was no more than a series of preferential gods within systems of multiple gods, can only be treated with extreme caution. Such views are misleading and perhaps they are even unlikely.

It should go without saying, but it goes better explicitly saying, that whatever value judgments one makes concerning polytheism and monotheism, whatever their failures and whatever their ultimately illusionary natures, none of this should affect a reasonable examination of their origins, their evolution and the influences they possibly exercised on each other.

CHAPTER 11. AKHENATEN INVENTS THE FIRST MONOTHEISM, ACCOMPANIED BY THE AMARNA ART REVOLUTION

THE ROOTS OF ATEN PRIMITIVE MONOTHEISM: HELIOPOLITAN SOLAR THEOLOGY, THEBAN AMUNISM, CHIEF GOD MONOTHEISING THEOLOGY, AND EGYPTIAN POLITICAL AND RELIGIOUS IMPERIALISM

As we shall now see, Atenism lacked many of the attributes of what can be considered full-blown or authentic monotheism, but at least on the theological level of the invention of a sole god, there can hardly be any doubt that Akhenaten invented a monotheism, mankind's first monotheism. Nevertheless, denials and doubts about this continue to be expressed among many historians and Egyptologists. Some of the reasons may be that the messy process of inventing monotheism is painfully clear in Akhenaten's career, in its failure and in its relation to pre- and post-monotheism in Egypt, while in Israel, as messy as the process also was, monotheism eventually succeeded. Quite simply, the propensity of our mindset is to focus on the Egyptian mess and not on the Hebrew mess.

The invention of Aten primitive monotheism was directly linked to the pivotal animistic and theological place of the sun expressed in Egypt from the earliest times and to Re and Heliopolitan "lightland" solar theology, assimilated and developed by Theban Amunism, the Amun-Re chief god theology.

Both the religious fervor for the sun and the theological amalgamating and unifying tendencies which finally resulted in Atenism were clearly present in the Re-Horakhte concept of the combined royal sun god of the Old Kingdom Fourth Dynasty (c. 2613–2494 BC) solar cult theologians of Heliopolis. Re was the godhead of the solar cycle and of the simultaneous diversity and ultimate harmony of the universe. Re and the nine gods and goddesses of the Heliopolis Ennead expressed the entirety of the universe. The pharaoh incarnated as a god, as Re's son, ruled on earth.

With ups and downs, the monotheising tendencies of the Re solar cult were amplified over about a thousand years and by the opening of the New Kingdom, and certainly by Amenhotep III's time (c. 1391–1352 BC), Egypt was on the verge of Aten solar cult monolatry, or monotheism, depending on how one interprets these terms.

Aten (*itn* or *jtn*) was a usual sacred term for the visible sun disk in the Middle Kingdom after 2000 BC. There are references to the Aten in Coffin Texts, in the very popular Twelfth Dynasty (c. 1985-1795 BC) *Tale of Sinuhe*, on the Abydos stele of Sehetep-ieb-Re, the Chief Treasurer of Amenemhat III (c. 1855– 1808 BC), etc.

Sinuhe notes that, "The god ascended to his horizon; the King of Upper and Lower Egypt: *Sehetep-ib-Re* [the apparently murdered pharaoh, Amenemhet I, c. 1985-1955] was...united with the sun-disc [the Aten]. The body of the god was merged with him who made him."[64] It is clear, here, that we are dealing with the traditional Heliopolis royal solar cult belief that the dead pharaoh ascends to the sun, to his father Re, merges with him and lives eternally. But it is the term Aten and not Re that is used, indirectly indicating that the Aten or Re had become interchangeable terms and that perhaps Aten was the preferred term.

The term Aten, with a phrase similar to that used by Sinuhe to describe Amenemhet I's passage into the afterlife, was used for the death of Amenhotep I (c. 1525–1504 BC). Thutmose I's (c. 1504–1492 BC) First Horus Name was "Horus-Re, Mighty Bull with sharp horns, coming from the Aten." Thutmose I was depicted wearing the Aten sun disk in the temple he built at Tumbos, north of Kerma in Upper Nubia. Frequent mentions of Aten can also be found in texts and art work during the reigns of Thutmose III (c. 1479–1425 BC), Amenhotep II (c. 1427 — 1400 BC) and Thutmose IV (c. 1401–1391).

At the beginning of the New Kingdom (from c. 1550 BC), the spells in *The Book of the Dead* also refer to the Aten. Spell 17 asks: "Who is he? He is Atum who is in his sun-disc. *Otherwise said*: He is Re when he rises in the eastern horizon of the sky."[65]

In Amenhotep II's time, the Aten was depicted as having rays ending in human hands. The sun disk Aten had become an object of worship, a god, in its own right, rather than just the term for the visible sun disk, and this may have

---

64. Wilson, John in *Ancient Near Eastern Texts Relating to the Old Testament*, p. 18.
65. Faulkner, R.O., *The Ancient Egyptian Book of the Dead*, Spell 17, p. 44.

the case at least as far back as Pharaoh Ahmose I (c. 1550–1525 BC), at the beginning of the New Kingdom.

These theological developments interconnected with political developments and with Egypt's political foreign policy aspirations and imperatives, which had been on-going from the start of the New Kingdom in c. 1550 BC. As we have seen in the preceding chapter, in the process of becoming an empire, Egypt had re-affirmed the universality of its solar theology and affirmed that Amun-Re created, ruled and maintained the universe. By Pharaoh Thutmose III's time (c. 1479–1425 BC), the universality and superiority of Amun-Re and his solar cult were being vaunted throughout Egypt's empire, from Nubia to the banks of the Euphrates River. Akhenaten's Aten not only inherited Amun-Re's Heliopolitan solar theology, he inherited its political and religious universality and imperialism.

Some 70 years after Thutmose III had begun establishing Egypt's political and religious domination in the West Asian *Retjenu*, the decisive steps towards transforming the Aten into a full-fledged and actively worshipped god were taken during the reign of Akhenaten's father, Amenhotep III.

Amenhotep III initiated the preferential trend towards Aten and instituted a cult for him. A stele from the Overseer of the Treasury Panehsy's house in El Amarna (now in the British Museum) not only shows him and his "great royal wife" Tiy bathing in the rays of the Aten, but also indicates a deliberate effort not to mention Amun in the royal cartouches surrounding the image of the Aten. Amenhotep III took the extraordinary step of not using his birth name, his nomen "Amun is satisfied" (Amenhotep), but only his royal throne praenomen *Nebma'atre* ("Re is the Lord of Maat — of order, of truth) so as to avoid any reference to Amun. His magnificent Malqata Palace, an elite unit of his army and his wife Tiy's royal *wia*, bark, were all called "The Aten gleams" or the "Dazzling Sun Disk." Amenhotep III himself was sometimes referred to as the "Dazzling Sun Disk."

Amenhotep III may have also built temples and shrines to Aten, but what is certain is that in the last years of his life he did not oppose the decision of his son and probable co-regent Amenhotep IV, the future Akhenaten, to build four temples to Aten in Karnak East, next to the Amun Temple, including the vast, 427 by 656 feet, *Gempaaton* ("Aten is found in the domain of Aten," or perhaps "the meeting place of Aten").

Political and economic motives can also not be excluded from Amenhotep III's preference for Aten. Like his father, Thutmose IV, he seems to have been concerned by the growing and excessive power of the Theban Amun clergy.

However, in general, Amenhotep III seems to have preferred Aten among all the gods rather than excluding the other gods. He also maintained both Aten's link to Re-Horakthe and to the Theban theologians' concept that the sun god Re-Horakthe was an aspect of the Chief God Amun. As late as year 31 of his reign, and year seven of his son's reign in co-regency, he honored Amun and Mut by building an Amun Temple in his Malqata Palace.

During Amenhotep III's time, it seems clear that the Aten was still a nature-religion-type divinization of the sun, much in the same way as the origin of Re was in the personification of the sun, the personification of star worship. The solar disk, which had always been an attribute of Re, remained as such, but the Aten sun disk aspect of Re's characteristics was now being accentuated. The emphasis was now on an Aten adaptation of the Re-Horakthe sun on the horizon concept, Re-Horakhte as the sun during the entirety of the day.

This amalgamated solar theological system was well illustrated by the text on the *Stele of the Brothers Suti and Hor*, the twin brother architects in the employ of Amenhotep III. The stele refers to Amun, Horakthe, Re, Khepri, Horus, Nut and Khnum and includes a section called "Hail to the Aten." All of these gods and goddesses are situated within an Amun solar cult, but it is a good guess that the premises of a conflict between Amun and Aten already existed.

A conflict between traditional Egyptian art and what has become known as Amarna art — and its religious consequences — also seems to have been in the making during Amenhotep III's time. At the least, it seems that the premises of Amarna art were sketched out in Amenhotep III's time before being radicalized by Amenhotep IV/Akhenaten. The artwork in several tombs which must have been begun during Amenhotep III's reign contains a mix of reliefs which are stylistically both classical and Atenist/Amarna. This is notably the case for the tomb in Thebes (TT55) for Ramose, who was a vizier under both Amenhotep III and Akhenaten, and Parennefer (TT188), who became Akhenaten's butler and one of his chief architects. The left rear wall of Ramose's tomb shows the coronation of Amenhotep IV depicted in traditional style without any of the body distortions typical of Amarna art, while the right wall shows Amenhotep IV and Nefertiti basking in the rays of the Aten and depicted in informal, naturalistic Amarna style including body distortions.

Amenhotep III's designated future pharaoh was his eldest son, Thutmose, the high priest of Ptah in Memphis. But Thutmose died at a very young age and disappeared from history, except for the story of him sending his beloved, mummified cat, "Meow," to the *Duat* afterlife in an elaborate stone sarcophagus. Amenhotep IV/Akhenaten (c. 1352–1336 BC) became pharaoh due to chance. Hardly any mention of him as a child has been found, indicating that he had not received any special education from his father and his entourage. It is mind boggling to speculate that had not Thutmose died, the course of history might have been different since Akhenaten would not have become pharaoh and the first monotheism probably would not have been established.

The term "Amarna Period" has come to designate the period from about 1352 to 1323 BC and includes the reigns of Pharaohs Akhenaten, Smenkhkara, Tutankhamun and Ay.

Although Amenhotep IV began his reign as a follower of the Chief God Amun with the title of First Prophet or Great Seer of Amun, it did not take very long for the conflict between Amun and Aten to emerge in the open. Amenhotep IV's motives in this conflict were undoubtedly basically of a theological order, but as for his father and previous pharaohs, political and economic considerations were included — how to stem the excessive power of the Thebes Amun clergy.

Amenhotep IV was anywhere from 11 to 16 years old when he apparently became co-regent, with 16 being the best guess. His first official task was probably that of Governor of Memphis and *Uer-kherep-hemutiu*, Grand Commander of the Artificers or craftsmen, that is High Priest of the Temple of Ptah, which he taken over from his deceased brother Thutmose.

The third *bekhenet*, pylon, at the south entrance of the Amun Temple in Karnak, built by Amenhotep IV's father in Thebes and decorated by the new co-regent, contains an image of the young co-regent worshipping the falcon-headed Re-Horakthe and in the standard pose of an Egyptian pharaoh killing a *khefty*, an enemy. But it also includes an image of the sun-disc, Aten. A lintel in Kharuef's tomb in western Thebes (TT 192), which also dates from the first years of Amenhotep IV's reign, depicts him worshipping Re-Horakthe, Atum, Hathor and Maat. The coronation relief in Ramose's tomb shows Amenhotep IV being blessed at his coronation by the goddess Maat.

It seems almost certain that, officially, Amenhotep IV's chief god during this first period of his pharaonic life — whatever the ideas he had in the back of his mind — was Re-Horakthe as embodied in Amun-Re and that he honored all the gods and goddesses as his father did. But during this same period, and right from year one of his reign, something must have indeed been stirring in his mind. In Gebel Silsila, north of Elephantine, where he quarried the stone for the temples he was building in Karnak East, a stele depicts him worshipping Amun-Re, but also describes him as the "First Prophet of Re-Horakthe Rejoicing in the Horizon in his name Shu (*Sw*, sunlight) which is Aten." The four sun temples he began building in Karnak East, around the central *Gemaapton*, were solely dedicated to Aten, even if they contained references to Atum, Shu, and Re-Horakthy and one of them, for Nefertiti's use, was called the *Hwt-bnbn*, "The Mansion of the Benben Stone," a reference to Re-Atum's primeval sun mound of creation.

Amenhotep IV, not yet called Akhenaten and not yet the son of the sole god Aten, was nevertheless well on his way to upsetting the powerful Amun clergy, engaging the Atenist revolution and even sowing the seeds of the future Amun-Re counterrevolution.

With the Karnak *Gemaapton*, the first works of art that can be qualified as representing the new "Amarna style" appeared. Given the traditionally strict principles and codes of Egyptian art and the centrality of the plastic arts as a form of expression and religious and social illustration, this was a considerable revolution. It surely added even more fuel to the fires of discontent burning among the Amun clergy.

Probably in year three, Akhenaten held a particularly ostentatious *heb-sed*, jubilee celebration, in his new *Gemaapton*. This was highly unusual since *seds* were organized for the first time only after a pharaoh had ruled 30 years. But more unusual still was that there were almost no polytheistic references in the ceremonies — aside from a hymn sung to the goddess Hathor, only Aten seems to have been named. Perhaps, this *sed* was in honor of Aten and not Akhenaten.

In year five of his reign, Amenhotep IV changed his nomen birth name to Akhenaten ("One who is useful to Aten"), dropping the reference "Amun is satisfied" (Amenhotep). He also changed his Horus name from "Strong Bull, tall of plumes" to "Strong Bull, beloved of the Aten," further indicating that he was no longer linked to Amun with his two plumed headdress or to the plumed *was* scepter nome emblem of Thebes. He then began revolutionizing his father's Aten deity, transforming Aten from being just the visible sun disk god and an aspect of Re into the declared sole god. Akhenaten, who had no doubt been married to Nefertiti (the *hemet nisut weret*, the "great royal wife") when he became co-regent, now gave her an additional name which illustrated her connection to the Aten and Akhenaten's immense love and esteem for her — Nefernefruaten, "Beauty of the beauties of the Aten," or perhaps "Perfect is the beauty of the Aten," or "Perfect is the perfection of Aten."

But some groping about, or concealment, must have still continued since there are documents from year five which refer to Aten as Hor-Aten (Horus-Aten). Nevertheless, the key to Akhenaten's revolution was already evident — Aten was no longer just a favored god among other gods and goddesses as he had been for his father Amenhotep IV, the other gods and goddesses were now being progressively diminished and eliminated and Thebes was now called "the city of the brightness of Aten."

Akhenaten, with a mixture of obvious sincerity and obvious fanaticism, then continued his revolution by abandoning Thebes and the Karnak Temple in year five or six of his reign, around 1348 BC. He built an entirely new capital and holy city called Akhetaten (today's Tell El-Amarna), on a vast empty plain about

200 miles downstream from Thebes and 150 miles above Memphis along the east bank of the Nile in the 15th Hermopolitan hare nome of Upper Egypt). Akhetaten is "the city of the *akhet*, horizon, of the Aten." This was an evident link to Horakhte (Horus, the sun in the horizon) and to Re-Horakhte. In year six, Akhenaten built 14 boundary steles around the city and one of the last to be erected — the "S" Boundary Stele — still included the names of other gods in his royal titulary. Horus was both in the first royal titulary name — "The living Horus; Strong Bull beloved of Aten" — and in the Golden Horus name, even if Horus "exalts the name of Aten." The "Two Ladies" title, the vulture goddess Nekhbet of Upper Egypt and the cobra goddess Wadjit of Lower Egypt, was also maintained and in his "son of Re" nomen, Akhenaten is the "Sole of Re"... "great in his lifetime, given life forever."[66]

But with these reserves, who can doubt that the "model" city of Akhetaten, largely finished by year eight in Akhenaten's reign, was indeed a city entirely and magnificently devoted to the worship of the new sole god, the sun-disk, the Aten. The House of the Aten, or central temple precinct, with its six open-aired courts, its focal point, the *Gemaapton* temple and two other temples, the House of Rejoicing and the Mansion of the *Benben* — was 2493 feet by 951 feet. It was surrounded on both sides by 365 mud brick offering altars, representing Upper and Lower Egypt and each day of the year. The city had two other major Aten temples, and notably the Mansion of the Aten (*Hwt-itn*) with its "window of appearance" where Akhenaten, together with his family, showed himself as a god to the people. Strung out along a five-mile "Royal Road" were an enormous palace for the King, including two harems, many shrines, spacious villas for the notables, administrative buildings, a records office ("The Place of the Pharaoh's Dispatches") storehouses and ritual slaughterhouses. On the southern end of the road stood a beautiful prayer garden known as the *Maru-Aten*, which probably also had a "window of appearance." In the eastern part of the city, there was a workmen's village. In the eastern cliffs of the city, construction had also begun of about 25 rock-cut tombs.

The *new* Aten, the cult of the visible sun disk, invented by Akhenaten and consecrated in his holy city of Akhetaten, took Re-Horakthe as a universal sun god and a concept and amalgamated him with the personification of sunlight and the god of the atmosphere between the earth and the sky, Shu. The principle of Shu, *Sw*, sunlight — the sun's rays — was elevated to the core reality of the universe and all life. Akhenaten also maintained the fundamental concept of the *maat* — rule according to the "truth" of primeval universal harmony. He assimilated the imperial and universal status that Egypt and its gods, and especially

---

66. Lichtheim, Miriam, *Ancient Egyptian Literature, Volume II*, p. 49.

Amun-Re, had solidly attained with the empire which Thutmose III (c. 1479–1425 BC) had consolidated and added concepts of brotherhood. Akhenaten adopted for Aten the principle of the political and theological universality of Amun-Re and attenuated its dominator aspects to an almost fraternal provider/ruler attitude towards non-Egyptians. Just as the earlier New Kingdom pharaohs since Thuthmose III's time had built temples and steles for Amun-Re and other gods in Nubia and Asia, Akhenaten now built temples for Aten deep in Nubia in the new city of *Gematen*, near Kawa, and in Syria at a still unknown location.

Primarily, the Aten sun god was a kind of compendium of the attributes of Re-Horakthe and Shu, but in practice, mention of Horakthe and Shu were eventually eliminated and the Aten became above all assimilated with the original Re and the entirety of his solar attributes. The central text of Atenism, *The Great Hymn to the Aten*, perhaps composed between year six and nine, still mentions "Shu-who-is-Aten" in its introduction, but proclaims: "O living Aten...Your rays embrace the lands...Being Re, you reach the limits..."[67] Between year six and twelve of his reign, Akhenaten's description of Aten became "Re lives, the Ruler of the Horizon...Re the father, who returns as the sun-god [the Aten]."[68] *Aten was Re*. However, in a clever sleight of hand, Re was also virtually eliminated, since it was Aten who was directly worshipped and not Re. Although an aspect of Re, even the main, totalized aspect of Re, it was Aten who counted and not Re. It was therefore Aten who came closest to monotheistic status, while Re's indirect ascension to near monotheistic status was purely theoretical.

This Aten solar monolatry/proto-monotheism embodied and expressed the Heliopolitan doctrine of composite divine harmony (Re and his ennead were the Universe) and universalism centered on the sun god Re and then on Amun-Re. Even though separated by more than a thousand years, it seems clear that the primitive Aten monotheism that Akhenaten first decreed was only a few steps away from the Heliopolitan solar cult centered on Re-Atum and Shu.

The strong tendency towards ultimate divine harmony expressed in Heliopolitan solar theology was the terrain in which Aten proto-monotheistic theology grew. But between Re and Aten, there was the theological evolution which had taken place with Amun-Re in Thebes. There seems to be no doubt that Re's super chief god status and Amun-Re's monotheising aspects influenced the elaboration of Aten proto-monotheism. Amun's assimilation of Re, all his powers

---

67. Ibid., pp. 96-97.

68. Aldred, Cyril, *Akhenaten, King of Egypt*, p. 278, Baines, John and Malek, Jaromir, *Atlas of Ancient Egypt*, p. 45 and Hornung, Erik, *Conceptions of God in Ancient Egypt, The One and the Many*, p. 246.

and all his aspects, and especially his incarnation as the sun, under the aegis of the powerful Thebes clergy, had further accentuated the movement towards super chief god status and proto-monotheism. In fact, Thebes did not just gobble up Re with Amun-Re, it gobbled up Heliopolitan solar theology and fervor. It had also transformed Amun into a monotheising god who was virtually the only god with real powers, the only one whom it was worth appeasing and honoring, even if all the other gods continued to exist as his aspects and continued to be served.

Amun was inherited from Re just as Aten was inherited from Re. Aside from the basic fact that Amun-Re as the universal god was clearly being pushed to the sidelines in favor of Aten as the universal god, there was nothing extraordinarily radical in Akhenaten singing the glory of the sun god Re as Aten, just as previous pharaohs had sung the glory of Amun as the sun god Re. In this sense and until this point, Akhenaten was behaving in a traditional Egyptian manner of amalgamating gods and had done nothing very different than his father Amenhotep III.

But by at least year five or six of his reign, and probably no later than year nine, Akhenaten had arrived at, or revealed, the revolutionary plenitude of his Atenist theology — the fundamental Egyptian concept of diversity was rejected; Aten was the sole divine reality and his sunlight — his rays — was the unique principle upon which everything in life reposed. A sole god and a sole explanatory principle now existed and all the other gods and goddesses, in singular or composite form, had been rejected. It remains unproven, but it was perhaps at this time that Akhenaten closed down all the temples in Egypt dedicated to gods other than Aten and engaged in a vast policy of destroying the statues of Amun and chiseling out his name everywhere. Some Egyptologists believe that this vast policy of destruction and erasure did not take place until towards the end of Akhenaten's reign, in year 14 or 15.

The Aten was the immanent, visible, beautiful and concrete sun disc. This new sole god was always represented much in the same way as already instituted by Akhenaten's father Amenhotep III — a red solar disk with the uraeus and the *ankh* emanating benevolent rays of sunlight which extended into human hands carrying an *ankh* amulet, or a few *ankhs*. The image of the Aten was therefore in no way totemistically animal, only very slightly anthropomorphic and closest to a nature religion representation, but nevertheless it was an image and was displayed as such wherever Aten was worshipped.

As a sole god, Akhenaten's Aten was theologically new, but not new in the form of its representation. And even theologically, the entire evolution towards the Aten concept, and notably the pivotal place of the sun's light, *Sw*, Shu, has to be taken into account. Akhenaten's theology has to be seen as both a revolution and the culmination of a long process. In short, Akhenaten made the leap to solar monolatry and proto-monotheism which the Heliopolitan and Theban theologians did not quite make with their Re and Amun-Re systems and which his father Amenhotep III did not complete with his preference for the Aten.

But many key questions remain — was the Aten the first monotheistic god and close to either or both the early Hebrew omnipotent, near-monotheistic henotheism and the later Hebrew Yahweh universal monotheism? Was the Aten either a unitary monotheistic god of the later Hebrew or Moslem type or a multiform monotheistic god of the Christian type? To what extent was the Aten different from the other gods in the Egyptian pantheons? To what extent was the Aten a personification of nature and an amalgamation of other gods? To what extent was the Aten a radically new type of god, an original, specific, sole god who was more than just the material sun?

None of the surviving Amarna Period texts or art works seems to satisfactorily answer the questions whether this sole divine reality, this sole god, was a material monolatry as the sun, a god who was omnipresent and omnipotent with his life-giving rays, or a god who was more than the material sun and its rays.

Of course, at the time, whether Aten was material or more than material or whether he was a radically new type of god probably did not have much significance compared to the rejecting and banning of Amun and all the other gods and the revolutionary monotheistic proclamation of the Aten as the sole god.

As we shall soon see, there are widely differing views on these questions among Egyptologists and historians. My own view is that the matter does not seem to be clear either way. There was a coexistence of many characteristics — some, monotheistic in a general way, and others not; and some similar to Judeo-Christian concepts and others not. To a modern mind, such a mixture appears contradictory and even impossible, but it was probably not seen as such by the supporters of Atenism in Akhenaten's time.

Aten is like other Egyptian gods and he is different from these gods. He has a material representation and he has characteristics that go beyond his material representation. He is theologically a sole god, yet other gods and goddesses hover in the background because they were amalgamated into Aten's functions. Akhenaten himself, much more than previous pharaohs in the framework of the divine kingship system, while in no way as divine as Aten, was somehow nevertheless greatly divine. It was to Akhenaten, rather than to Aten, that the people prayed in the shrines in their homes. This was also the case for Nefertiti, who was the incarnation of the goddess Tefnut (the eye of the sun and twin sister of Shu), just as Akhenaten's mother, Tiy, had been the incarnation of Hathor. With few exceptions, Amarna art clearly shows that only the divine Akhenaten and divine Nefertiti can be infused with the breath of the life force, the *ankh*, held in the ray-hands of the Aten. The exceptions sometimes concern Akhenaten's and Nefertiti's daughters, as in the "S" Boundary Stele.

The legitimate doubts about the integral soleness of Aten do not change the fact that Akhenaten at least glimpsed something essential about divine soleness and this 800 years before the Hebrew prophet Deutero-Isaiah unambiguously proclaimed it. And it seems certain that for the first time in history, a sole concept — sunlight (Sw, Shu) — was used to explain everything in existence, much as the omnipotent, benevolent will of the monotheistic Yahweh was later used for the same purpose.

Even though, at the zenith of its development, Atenism did not come near to the ethical and spiritual revolution eventually reached by the Hebrew Yahweh system and the later Christian system, Akhenaten did indeed invent the first monotheism. The structures, the modes of thinking and the feeling of monotheism had been invented, even if its most distinctive attributes remained to be invented — an invisible, abstract god, authentic soleness with no other gods or man-gods hovering in the background, universality, a link to this sole god and ethics and a final destiny for mankind.

Nevertheless, Atenism represented a huge ethical and spiritual advance in the Egyptian system. This advance was so fundamental that it had to be partially taken into account when Atenism was overthrown and Amun-Re chief god theology was restored. It was not until Egypt entered into religious decline with Amun priestly theocratic fundamentalism from the Twentieth Dynasty (c. 1099–1069 BC) that this advance was obliterated.

The brief 15-year period of Atenism represented one of the key periods in the history of mankind. It was the most untypical period of Egyptian history, but also the one which, even if it cannot be formally proven, perhaps had the most durable effects in the history of mankind. One man, Akhenaten, accomplished this almost single-handedly. One of the fundamental cultural changes operated by man with immense consequences had occurred.

The Several Sources for Atenism and the Amarna Period

Several sources give us insight into the Amarna Period and Atenist theology. The most important sources are the inscriptions of hymns and prayers to Aten and Akhenaten in several tombs of Atenist priests, scribes and officials. The most abundant inscriptions were found in the unfinished Akhetaten rock-cut tomb of Ay (TA25), whose construction began in year six of Akhenaten's reign. Ay was first the "Commander of all His Majesty's horses," a *sesh*, scribe/ priest, a "god's Father" (a temple title, also sometimes attributed to the pharaoh's father-in-law) and perhaps the father of Nefertiti. He then consecutively became the last vizier of Akhenaten, the vizier of Tutankhamun and the pharaoh (c. 1327–1323 BC). Upon Akhenaten's death, Ay renounced Aten and returned to the Amun-Re cult. The text on the west wall of Ay's tomb has come to be known as *The Great Hymn to the Aten.* It is the most complete version of *The Hymn to the Aten* and is considered to be the best description of Atenist theology. Another version of *The Hymn — The Short Hymn to the Aten* — has been found in Ay's and four other Amarna tombs.

The ruins of the city of Akhetaten itself are another major source for understanding Atenism and daily life during the Amarna Period. Despite the mass destruction of the site by Akhenaten's successors — foundations of structures rather than above-ground stone structures have been excavated — a very considerable amount of art and architectural ruins have been found in this city. Akhetaten had a population of at least 20,000 people and according to B. J. Kemp, the Field Director of the British Egypt Exploration Society's excavations at el-Amarna, perhaps as many as 50,000.[69] Sculptures, reliefs and decorated and inscribed *talatat* — the small limestone or sandstone blocks (always about 20 x 10 x 9 inches, one cubic foot) which Akhenaten invented to quicken the pace of traditional temple building methods — have been found in abundance. The ruins of about 25 rock-cut tombs (only two them completely finished) and the foundations of beautifully decorated temples, palaces, administrative buildings, the studio of the chief sculptor Thutmose (Djehutymose), the spacious 8000-square-foot villa of the vizier Nakht (Nakh-pa-Aten), as well as gardens, pools, wide avenues, artists' and craftsmen's workshops and a workers' village have been excavated.

It was not until 1824 that a major Egyptologist, John Gardner Wilkinson, visited the ruins of at Akhetaten/Tell El Amarna. Many others followed, including Karl Richard Lepsius, Robert Hay and Norman and Nina de Garis Davies, conducting notable exploratory, copying and epigraphic work. In our time, and especially since 1977, B.J. Kemp has considerably increased knowledge of the city and its inhabitants.

But once again, it was the brilliant, indefatigable and eccentric William Matthew Flinders Petrie who in 1891-92 was the first to begin elaborate excavations at Akhetaten/El Amarna. He uncovered the remains of the Aten Temples, Akhenaten's palace, the "records office," seven boundary steles, many private houses and three glass factories. He came up with a huge amount of art work and artifacts including sculptures and a mask of Akhenaten, images of Nefertiti and her children, murals, glazed pottery, amulets, tools and an extraordinarily beau-

---

69. Kemp, Barry, J., *Ancient Egypt, Anatomy of a Civilization*, pp. 305-306.

tifully decorated 25 foot square pavement which he considered to be the most important artistic find since the Old Kingdom. Petrie was also the first to evaluate Akhenaten's solar monotheism and art as revolutionary developments and to clearly demonstrate that Amenhotep IV and Akhenaten were not two different kings as some Egyptologists had supposed. He correctly established the Kings' List from Akhenaten to Smenkhkara to Tutankhamun to Ay to Horemheb.

The so-called *Boundary Steles*, a series of 14 steles which delimited the borders of the holy city of Akhetaten, despite their very damaged state, provide us with inscriptions and reliefs of Akhenaten, Nefertiti and infant daughters worshipping the Aten. They give us an important insight into Atenist politico-religious and theological doctrines and Akhenaten's iron will to build and eternally maintain this holy city.

The destroyed temple precinct that Akhenaten built in Karnak, east of the Amun Temple, has also yielded many important finds to excavators. This includes the series of strange colossi of an effeminate Akhenaten, which has led many people to conclude that he had a genetic disease, and a colossi which depicts a naked body without genitalia, which some scholars claim was Nefertiti and others claim was a hermaphrodite Akhenaten. Hundreds of decorated and inscribed *talatat* have been found in the ruins of East Karnak, especially by the Canadian Egyptologist Donald Redford (b. 1934). *Talatat* used as filling in temple gateway/pylons have been found in huge numbers — more than 45,000 in the Karnak and Luxor Amun Temples, 1500 in a Thoth temple in Hermopolis and hundreds more in several other sites. Many of these *talatat* have been re-assembled into coherent scenes which provide a considerable amount of information about religion and daily life in the Amarna Period. The Luxor Museum exhibits one of these re-assemblies, known as The *Talatat* Wall.

Pharaoh Horemheb's (c. 1323–1295 BC) Edict of Reform Stele in the Karnak Temple, his "prayer and hymn" statue from Memphis and his Gebel el-Silsila speos temple provide us with a fairly clear picture of the counterrevolution led by Horemheb which resulted in the end of the Amarna Period and the return to Amun-Re chief god orthodoxy. We can easily see why and what Horemheb destroyed in Atenism, as well as what persisted of Atenism in his time. The various inscriptions and art work in his two tombs, in Sakkara, near the Step Pyramid and in the Valley of Kings (KV57), indicate that several tenets of Amarna art were still in use. The art and inscriptions on steles and in the Valley of Kings tombs of two of Akhenaten's successors as pharaohs — Tutankhamun (KV62) and Ay (KV23) — and the tombs of two notables — Huy, Tutankhamun's Viceroy of Kush (TT40) and the vizier Ramose (TT55) — also indicate a partial continuation of Amarna art and Atenist concepts. A few scattered inscriptions concerning Akhenaten's immediate successor, Smenkhkara, have also been found.

Finally, the 382 *Amarna Tablets*, or *Letters*, are extremely valuable in the attempt to understand the situation of Egypt's colonies and vassal states, its foreign policy or lack of one, as well as the situation inside Egypt during the Amarna Period. These *Letters* were mostly written in cuneiform Akkadian, the lingua franca of the time, on clay tablets, by West Asian leaders and Egyptian vassal kinglets between the end of Amenhotep III's reign, during the entirety of Akhenaten's reign and during the beginning of Tutankhamun's reign.

The Amarna *Letters* were found in the ruins of Akhetaten's records office, "The Place of the Pharaoh's Dispatches," by a peasant woman digging mud-brick for use as fertilizer in 1887. Most of them are now preserved in the British Museum, with others in several museums including the Louvre and the Berlin Bodemuseum. E.A. Wallis Budge, then purchasing agent for the British Museum, was the first to understand the importance of the tablets and it was Petrie who rushed to Akhetaten only four years after the *Letters* had drawn considerable attention to the city.

Despite all these documents and art, knowledge about the Amarna Period is largely limited to what Akhenaten, his family and the elite ruling class did and believed. We do not know more about what "ordinary" people believed and how they lived in the Amarna Period than we know for most other periods in Egyptian history. B.J. Kemp, in *Ancient Egypt, Anatomy of a Civilization*, cautiously sees the city of el-Amarna as "Egypt in microcosm," even if "Amarna was not a typical Egyptian city. No royal city ever could be." He notes that the "Houses of the rich and poor are distinguished more by size than by design, although larger houses did possess features, such as an entrance porch, which denoted status in itself...If we remember that this was a time of great national prosperity, the gulf between rich and poor in this respect was not as great as we might expect. The rich and powerful lived in large houses, not in palaces. The great gulf was between the king and everyone else."[70] Despite Kemp's laudable attempts to fill the gap concerning ordinary people in el-Amarna, how ordinary Egyptians lived and what they believed remains one of the major unknowns, one of the blurriest issues, of Amarna and the entirety of Egyptian history.

On a more general level, we must note that even if the art, and especially texts, concerning Amarna are not as abundant as those which have come down to us for most of the other New Kingdom periods (and how could they be, when Atenism only lasted 15 years?), they represent a considerable amount of material. This leaves no valid explanation for all the loony theories which have arisen con-

---

70. *Ibid.*, pp. 261, 299-300.

cerning Atenism, except romanticism, manipulation and stupidity. Above all, it must be emphasized that none of the unknown or mysterious elements of the Amarna Period are sufficient to preclude a fairly comprehensive view of the central issue at stake — the core nature of monotheistic Atenism.

ATENIST SOLAR CULT THEOLOGY: A HERESY, A REVOLUTION, A MONOLATRY AND A PROTO-MONOTHEISM

Despite what we do not know about Atenism, *The Great Hymn to Aten* (or *The Hymn to the Sun*, as it is sometimes called) and the short versions of *The Hymn* and other hymns and prayers to Aten and Akhenaten, found in Ay's and other Amarna tombs, provide a relatively clear picture of Atenist theology, its background and origins.

Pharaoh Akhenaten, who seems almost certainly to have been the author of *The Great Hymn*, not only imposed the sun god Aten, incarnated in the solar disk, as the Egyptian royal and national god, but as the sole god of the world, the loving father, provider and ruler of all mankind: "O Sole God beside whom there is none! You made the earth as you wished, you alone, All peoples, herds and flocks, All upon earth that walk on legs, All on high that fly on wings. The lands of Khor [Syria] and Kush [Nubia], The land of Egypt. You set every man in his place, You supply their needs..."[71]

This notion of a loving, universal god was more advanced in this respect than the later Abraham's or Moses' notion of a sole national god. However, for both Akhenaten and Moses, questions about the "soleness" of god legitimately can be asked. For both Akhenaten, and Moses 150 years later, there was a "sole" creator of everybody and everything in the universe — the Aten, or Yahweh. Akhenaten's decree that the Aten was the "Sole God beside whom there is none," was ambiguous within the context that he made it, given Aten's assimilation of Re-Horakthe and "Shu-who-is-Aten" and his frequent references to them, especially in the early years of his reign. As for Moses, it is unclear whether Yahweh was the sole god in the universe or rather the most powerful god in the universe. Both the concepts of authentic "soleness" and universal and affectionate monotheism of the Atenist type does not seem to have appeared in Israel before the sixth century BC with the prophets Deutero-Isaiah and Jeremiah. It appeared in Persia somewhat earlier in a less advanced form with the prophet Zoroaster or his followers.

---

71. Lichtheim, Miriam, *Ancient Egyptian Literature, Volume II*, p. 98.

Read today, with retrospective knowledge, *The Great Hymn to the Aten* and the other hymns and prayers appear to take the sun, the sun god Re, as their metaphysical starting point, but metaphysics as Nature and not above Nature. Re is the universe and includes Horakthe as lord of "lightland" and Shu as the personification of sunlight, and Akhenaten in his capacity as *sa* Ra, the son of Re, is the beloved chief beneficiary of this situation. *The Great Hymn* states: "Aten...Being Re, you reach their limits, You bend them [for] the son [Akhenaten] whom you love..." Ay's Hymn *to the Aten and the King* states: "For the King [Akhenaten], *Neferkheprure, Sole-one-of-Re*...You [Aten] love him, you make him like Aten." Akhenaten accentuated this Re centrality by at least year 12 of his reign by describing Re as "the father, who has returned as the sun disk [Aten]."[72]

Aten can therefore be seen as somebody whom Re became. Aten can appear to be a mere difference in name with Re or an aspect of Re. Unquestionably, for Akhenaten, the son of Re/Aten, Aten was Re.

Nevertheless, there can be no question as to who was at the center of the stage — it was Aten. And Aten was the same as Re-Horakthe and Shu, and Aten was distinct from them. Aten's characteristics, and notably his moral and fraternal qualities, are also distinctly different from Re alone or from all these gods taken together as an amalgamation. All this is terribly confusing, except perhaps for an ancient Egyptian who habitually saw representations of the gods as both individual entities and aspects of other gods.

The surviving works of Amarna art, and their characteristic of greater concern for the real rather than the ideal, found in previous Egyptian art, perhaps provide us with a vague answer to the enigma of to what extent Aten was a distinct god and to what extent he was a composite god or an aspect of Re. All of this surviving art is similar when it concerns the worship of Aten. It usually shows the Aten sun disk with a uraeus, its rays ending in human hands (some of them carrying the *ankh*), and Akhenaten with his "great royal wife" Nefertiti standing behind him and some of their six daughters in various poses behind Nefertiti, all piously adulating and making offerings and bathing in the rays of sunlight — the goodness — of the Aten. The *ankhs* are close to the noses of Akhenaten and Nefertiti and are infusing them with the breath of the life force.

The clear feeling is that Aten is a distinct deity from Re. However, much as Re is the acknowledged origin of Aten, it is Aten who is present and not really Re. The Atenist sun disk and its hands are radically different from the traditional Re sun disk. The rays, sunlight, play a key role. There are no immediate thoughts and feelings about Re — at least for me — and it is only when one intellectually examines this art that the Aten sun disk can be acknowledged as an aspect of Re.

---

72. *Ibid.*, pp. 96-97 and 93 and Aldred, Cyril, *Akhenaten, King of Egypt*, p. 278.

However, if we can somewhat satisfactorily solve the problem of Aten's distinctness, or at least conclude that he virtually became a distinct god who had shed away the other gods, the problems of what he was beyond his material representation and whether or not Atenism was authentic monotheism remain.

J.H. Breasted (1865–1935), in *A History of Egypt* and many other works, expressed a firm belief that "...however evident the Heliopolitan origin [that is "Re as its source"] of the new state religion [Atenism] might be, it was not merely sun worship; the word Aton was employed in place of the old word for 'god' (*nuter*) and the god is clearly distinguished from the material sun." There was not a shadow of a doubt in Breasted's mind that Akhenaten was "the earliest monotheist and the first prophet of internationalism."[73]

Adolf Erman (1854–1937), in *La Religion des Egyptiens, Life In Ancient Egypt* and other works did not believe that Aten was a god distinct from the material sun. Erman saw Atenism as "the worship of the sun" as a "follow up to the Heliopolitan doctrine"..."In fact, it was not a sun god who was adored, but the material sun itself, which, by the hands of his beams, bestowed upon living beings that 'eternal life which was in him'."

Erman believed that Aten was not distinct from the material sun, but he also believed that Aten was utterly different from Egypt's old material gods and goddesses. For Erman, at the beginning of Akhenaten's system, the Aten had been a god alongside other gods, but by "year VIII" of his reign, "The god [Aten] no longer had anything in common with the old forms of the sun god, Atum, Khepri and Hor-akhti, and only the names of Aton and Re continued to be linked to him; in fact, he is now the star itself and not a god in the old way." Erman had no doubt that "the slates...of the past confused polytheism...had been wiped clean"...and that "an abolition of polytheism" had occurred. For Erman, Akhenaten was a monotheist who tried to set up the Sun god as "the sole god to the exclusion of any other," even if this "divinity" also "manifested itself in the king himself."[74]

A.H. Gardiner (1879–1963) believed that despite "contradictions" and "defects" in Akhenaten's "new faith," and while the Egyptian "system never ceased to be polytheistic, ...there was a powerful urge towards monotheism" which "temporarily replaced" "the main aspects of the traditional worship." Gardiner concluded that despite the fact that "His [Akhenaten's] deity was the great

---

73. Breasted, James Henry, *A History of Egypt, From The Earliest Times To The Persian Conquest*, p. 302 and *Ikhnaton, Encyclopaedia Britannica*, 1929 and CD 98 Multimedia Edition, 1994-1997.

74. Erman, Adolf, *La Religion des Egyptiens*, pp. 143, 152, 153 and *Life in Ancient Egypt*, p. 261-262.

luminary [the sun] itself, exercising its beneficent life-giving influence through the rays whose brilliance and warmth none could fail to experience," nevertheless "Atenism was no mere physical theory, but a genuine monotheism..." and even "a rigid monotheism."[75]

Cyril Aldred (1914–1991), one of the most noted specialists on the Amarna Period, in *Akhenaten, Pharaoh of Egypt* and in *The Egyptians*, emphasized the importance of the links between Aten and Re and Re-Horakthy cultivated by Akhenaten and saw a "reformed sun cult," a "sun worship," in which Akhenaten placed "...a little more emphasis upon the Aten, or visible manifestation of godhead, than he did upon Re-Herakthy, the hidden power that motivated it." For Aldred, "The power immanent in the disk is Re," but "...instead of incorporating all the old gods in his sole deity, he [Akhenaten] rigidly excluded them in an uncompromising monotheism." Aldred's conclusion is that, "The monotheism that Akhenaten proclaims is not the henotheism of earlier times, the belief in one supreme god without any assertion of his unique nature, but the worship of an omnipotent and singular divinity."[76] Aldred allied impeccable scholarship and the compilation of most of the known facts and most of the questions about Atenism in what may be the clearest and most neutral manner.

As for Erik Hornung (b. 1933), he believes that, "For the first time in history, the divine became one, without a complementary multiplicity; henotheism was transformed into monotheism. The mass of divine forms was reduced to the unique manifestation of the Aton and his rays....Akhenaten's aim was not only to dethrone Amon, but...to deny the existence of all the gods with the exception of the Aton....The new belief could be summarized by the formula: 'There is no other god but Aton, and Akhenaten is his prophet.'"[77]

Donald B. Redford (b. 1934) believes that "beyond a shadow of a doubt that Akhenaten's was an uncompromising monotheism that denied other gods," but wonders whether " 'religion'" is "the appropriate term" which can be applied in the same way to both Atenism and the Hebrew religion. Redford claims that "...the sun disk is a sophisticated symbol, a projection of kingship into the heavens on a universal scale"; and that "What Akhenaten put forward in no way involves a creed; it is more a royal statement regarding the king's relationship with his father than a religion of the people." He also believes that "...the sun disk crystallized in Akhenaten's thinking from an apotheosis of his own father Amenhotep III, whose sobriquet significantly was the 'Dazzling Sun Disk.'"

---

75. Gardiner, Alan, *Egypt of the Pharaohs*, pp. 227, 229, 216, 21 and 222.

76. Aldred, Cyril, *The Egyptians*, pp. 165-166 and *Akhenaten, King of Egypt*, p.240.

77. Hornung, Erik, *Conceptions of God in Ancient Egypt, The One and the Many*, pp. 246, 249 and 248.

For Redford, Atenism was monotheism, but not an authentic monotheism of the sixth century BC Hebrew type. He sees no similarity between the "Amarna 'religion'" and either the Hebrew "credal" religion of the later Iron Age "of faith in Yahweh"... "a wrathful, vengeful god...but also capable of compassion and forgiveness," or *a fortiori* in "the advanced (monotheistic) concepts of a Deutero-Isaiah of the sixth to fifth centuries..." For Redford, "the sun disk is a pale cipher, arousing little response in the worshipper...This deity could never be a *personal* god, except to his son (Akhenaten), and therefore was not imbued with the plebian quality of compassion. Nor did he demand any particular code of ethical behavior different from what had dominated Egyptian society from time immemorial." Redford even wonders whether it is "a waste of time" to compare Atenism and Hebrew henotheism or monotheism: "...a vast gulf is fixed between the rigid, coercive, rarefied monotheism of the pharaoh [Akhenaten] and Hebrew henotheism [Moses], which in any case we see through the distorted prism of texts written 700 years after Akhenaten's death."[78] In short, for Redford, there was no link, theological, moral, sociological, mythological or otherwise, between either Aten and Yahweh or the Egyptian and Hebrew Mosaic henotheism or later monotheistic system.

On the other hand, Sigmund Freud (1856–1939) had no doubt that Akhenaten had "introduced something new, which for the first time converted the doctrine of a universal god into monotheism." Freud also had no doubt about the link between Aten and Yahweh: "If Moses was an Egyptian and if he communicated his own religion to the Jews, it must have been Akhenaten's, the Aten religion." Jan Assmann (b. 1938) shares Freud's opinion. He believes that Atenism was "an authentic Egyptian monotheism," that "Akhenaten...is the first founder of a monotheistic counter-religion in human history" and that "mnemohistory (the history of cultural memory) is able to show that the connection between Egyptian and Biblical monotheism...has a certain foundation in history..." Assmann says that "There is only one possible conclusion to draw," and it is Freud's on Moses having "communicated...the Aten religion...to the Jews." For Assmann, "Akhenaten inherited the Heliopolitan concept of a universal god...but he turned a local cult into a general religion and gave it the character of an intolerant monotheism." Assmann also wonders if "...we may perhaps say that instead of founding a new religion, Akhenaten was the first to find a way out of religion...He rejected not only the polytheistic pantheon but even the theistic idea of a personal god. There is nothing but nature."[79]

---

78. Redford, Donald B., *Egypt, Canaan and Israel in Ancient Times*, pp. 377-382, and *Akhenaten, The Heretic King*, p. 232.

The French Egyptologist Nicolas Grimal (b. 1948) implicitly rejects almost the entirety of Assmann's views. Grimal, in *A History of Ancient Egypt*, states that it is "excessive" to talk about monotheism concerning Atenism. He acknowledges that Atenism "...suggests a universalist tone which has all the trappings of mono-theism," but he sees this as a "religious device" linked to "gathering all aspects of the creator into the person of the king himself." Grimal believes that Atenism "was not in itself revolutionary and was far from being the revelatory religion that scholars have occasionally claimed it to be." For Grimal, Atenism was "the continuation" of "the rise of the Heliopolitan cults"... "the sun — the ultimate creator — was evidently a fusion of numerous different divine attributes. Amen-hotep IV (Akhenaten) chose to worship the visible aspect of the sun — its Disc — the role of which had been clearly defined in Heliopolitan theology since the Old Kingdom."[80]

Another French Egyptologist, Claire Lalouette (b. 19??), takes a similarly radical and disconcerting view concerning Atenism and Akhenaten. Lalouette believes that Atenism was not a monotheism and in *Textes Sacrés et Textes Profanes de l'Ancienne Egypte* states: "The very popular and current fable that Amenophis IV...supposedly had a feeling for monotheism and supposedly provoked a 'reli-gious revolution' in this direction is hardly credible when one reads the Egyptian documents themselves, rather than modern interpretations. From the most ancient times (in Egypt), each god is the UNIQUE in the heart and spirit of the believer — something which does not exclude, with a goal of achieving greater magical efficiency, a possible recourse to other gods."[81]

(We shall soon see that the evaluations of Akhenaten the man are also sub-ject to widely differing and extreme views.)

As so frequently is the case in Egyptology, it is difficult to subscribe to a single view; there are useful insights in the theories of most of the Egyptologists who have attempted to see clearly in this debate on Atenism, on whether or not Aten was a sole god, a composite god, an aspect of Re, a god with other gods existing alongside him, or even a god who brought nothing radically new to Egyptian religion. But the diversity of these views should not blind us to the fact that some Egyptologists — like Redford, Grimal and Lalouette — adopt extreme positions which seem to defy common sense. It is certainly legitimate to postu-

---

79. Freud, Sigmund, *The Standard Edition of the Complete Psychological Works of Sigmund Freud*, Vol. XXIII, "Moses and Monotheism," pp. 22 and 24. Assman, Jan, *Moses the Egyptian, The memory of Egypt in Western Monotheism*, pp. 168, 169, 24, 153 and 189-190.

80. Grimal, Nicolas, *A History of Ancient Egypt*, pp. 228 and 230.

81. Lalouette, Claire, *Textes Sacrés et Textes Profanes de l'Ancienne Egypte, II, Mythes, Contes et Poèsie*, p. 125.

late that Atenism did not have the main theological and moral characteristics of later Hebrew monotheism, but it is terrifyingly incredible to hold that Atenism was not a monotheism when it is clear that a sole god, the Aten, finally emerged in this system.

The above is not meant to imply that there is no ambiguity — ambiguity does indeed exist. One of the major difficulties in evaluating the degree of monotheism in Atenism is that, in conformity with the traditional principles of the *maat* order, Akhenaten did not abdicate his role as divine king, as a pharaoh-god. It is likely that for Akhenaten, *maat* first of all meant that he, Akhenaten, as pharaoh-god was "Ruler of the *maat*," ruler and incarnation of the pre-ordained, primeval, harmonious, natural order of the universe as enunciated in Egypt perhaps as far back as 3000 BC. Akhenaten not only "lived by Maat" much like all the pharaohs before him, he accentuated and emphasized this role to unprecedented levels. Religiously, Akhenaten virtually proclaimed himself as a god alongside the Aten. Politically, he accentuated the absolute power of the pharaoh-god whose prerogatives had been progressively contested by the high priests and nomarchs

It has already been noted that Petrie, Breasted and Wilson in their translations of *The Great Hymn to Aten* mistakenly translated *ankh-em-maat* as "living by ("in" or "on") truth," something that Lichtheim and Aldred did not do, preferring the term "living by Maat," which primarily implied living according to the primeval universal order. Gardiner, like Rudolf Anthes, believed that for Akhenaten *maat* meant " 'orderly, well-regulated existence' with no reference to factual truth at all."[82] Nevertheless, and as we have seen, in the theological and societal terms of the time, the goddess Maat's *maat* code implied moral teachings even if they were not the basic aspect of the *maat* and it remains a good bet that Akhenaten paid more attention to this aspect than previous pharaohs did.

Akhenaten's was not only a particularly strong version of the Egyptian divine kingship system, a pharaoh-god and the First Prophet or Great Seer of Aten, theologically, he went even further with immense implications. Just as the god Aten was the Pharaoh of the universe (and even had a royal cartouche), Akhenaten was the divine Pharaoh of the earth, to whom the people prayed, or at least to whom they directed their prayers to Aten. He decreed himself as Aten's son and only intermediary: "You are in my heart, There is no other who knows you, Only your son *Neferkheprure, Sole-One-of-Re* (*wa-en-Re*, that is Akhenaten)..."[83] Akhenaten was therefore part of the Aten's divinity and even ate the offerings made to him.

---

82. Gardiner, Alan, *Egypt of the Pharaohs*, p. 223.
83. Lichtheim, Miriam, *Ancient Egyptian Literature*, Volume II, p. 99.

With such a decree, Akhenaten not only amplified the traditional dictatorial powers of the pharaoh-god, he increased the reverence and worship due to him as pharaoh-god, both from his entourage and the people. But as paradoxical as it might seem, it is just as obvious that he amplified the nearness of his god Aten to the people — the Aten loved and cared for his flock.

Akhenaten also virtually created two triads. The first consisted of a Christian-like Re the father, Aten the visible sun disk and Akhenaten as the incarnation of Re and Aten, as the son of Re and Aten, as the physical Re and Aten. The second triad extended holiness to his "great royal wife" Nefertiti, who was virtually decreed a mother goddess and was worshipped in a shrine dedicated to her. In this triad — Aten, Akhenaten and Nefertiti — Akhenaten and Nefertiti were decreed to be the perfections of Aten, pious optimistic and happy.

Akhenaten, like all the pharaohs before him, was the benefactor in this life, but he also decreed himself as the benefactor in the afterlife. On the whole, Akhenaten did not seek to reduce the Egyptians' obsession with death, mummification, resurrection and the afterlife; he sought to re-orientate it in favor of himself and to the detriment of the popular personal savior and afterlife god Osiris. An afterlife could only be obtained through the intercession of Akhenaten himself. Judgment in the Hall of Two Truths, the negative confession, and the monster Am-mut who devoured those whose heart did not weigh evenly with Maat's feather of truth were eliminated. Protective images of Isis and Nephthys on coffins were also eliminated in favor of images of Nefertiti. The "westerners," the dead, were supposed to worship both Akhenaten and Nefertiti. Osiris' role was eliminated.

It seems clear from all this that the Aten was not a personal god, like Yahweh and especially Jesus. More correctly, Aten was a personal god only for Akhenaten and to a lesser extent for his family. The personal god for the people, the god whom they were supposed to pray to, was Akhenaten himself.

Another difficult and important problem in Atenist theology is the elucidation of just what is exactly meant in real terms by the numerous references to what seems to be universal brotherhood. *The Great Hymn to the Aten* beautifully proclaims: "You [Aten] fill every land with your beauty...Your rays embrace the lands...The Two Lands [Upper and Lower Egypt] are in festivity...Who [Aten] makes seed grow in women, Who feeds the son in his mother's womb, Who soothes him [the son] to still his tears....The lands of Khor [Syria] and Kush, The land of Egypt. You set every man in his place. You supply their needs. Everyone has his food...Their tongues differ in speech...Their skins are distinct, For you distinguished the peoples. You made Hapy [the annual agricultural prosperity-giving inundation of the Nile, but also the god who personifies this inundation] in *dat* [the nether world]...To nourish the people... All distant lands, you make them live...A Hapy from heaven for foreign peoples...For Egypt the Hapy who comes from *dat*...Your rays nurse all fields..."[84]

The clear mutual affection between Aten and the ruling Pharaoh Akhenaten, the people in general — Egyptian and foreign — and animals and Nature is not found previously anywhere among the other Egyptian gods and goddesses, including in the words of the "the perpetually good and perfect" *Wennefer*, Osiris.

The Great Hymn to the Aten seems to indicate perfect equality among the Egyptians, among foreigners and among foreigners and Egyptians, regardless of differences of language, character and race. However, the pragmatic context is that universalistic brotherhood was something that was in deep contradiction with the traditional hierarchical, nationalist and arrogant Egyptian political and religious values. Before, during and after Akhenaten's time, Egyptian society was deeply hierarchical and class orientated. Concerning the *khasut*, the foreign lands, Amun-Re in the Egyptian mind was firmly established as the King of the Universe, as the composite godhead of the universe, but as we have seen, this did not mean brotherhood; it meant Egyptian supremacy.

Given Akhenaten's acts, which were often in contradiction to what he expressed in *The Hymn*, it remains a mystery as to just how far he went in his disagreement with prevailing Egyptian values. It is obvious that Akhenaten did not make any significant changes to Egypt's stiff hierarchical class system. It is just as obvious that he did not entirely go along with the view that foreigners were inferior to Egyptians. Despite the fact that Akhenaten did not undertake any foreign military campaigns, he clearly did nothing active to change the situation of Egyptian supremacy and domination in Egypt's vast empire; however, the people of the *khasut*, the foreign lands, were no longer systematically referred to as being "wretched" and "miserable."

It is also clear that for Akhenaten brotherhood and mutual affection concerning ordinary Egyptians and foreigners did not give them direct access to god, nor the right to enter the Atenist temples. The Aten temples, like the temples to the other gods in other times, remained reserved for the pharaoh, his entourage and the priests; ordinary people never were allowed beyond the gateway, the first *bekhenet*, pylon. On the other hand, it is only fair to note that it was surely historically too early to take the revolutionary step of allowing the people into the temple or a public place of worship, either in a country like Egypt where the ordinary people were fervently religious or, at first, among the Hebrews.

The Mosaic revolution, about 150 years after the start of Akhenaten's revolution, gave the ordinary people a direct access to god, but far from complete access to the temple. In Solomon's Temple (c. 958 BC), only the High Priest

---

84. *Ibid.*, pp. 96-99.

entered the Holy of Holies; the other priests had access to the Court of Priests; ordinary Hebrew males never went beyond the third courtyard of the Temple (the Court of Israelites); women never went beyond the fourth Court of Women; and gentiles were not allowed beyond the outer Court of the Gentiles. The Hebrew synagogue, where everybody freely gathered to pray and study, was only invented during the Babylonian exile (c. 586–538 BC), more than 750 years after Akhenaten proclaimed his ideal of universal brotherhood under the sole god who was the loving father of all mankind.

At about the same time (probably after about 1400 BC), the fervently religious Hindus seem to have totally excluded the *Panchama* (the *Dalit* untouchables), the outcastes, who constituted a huge number of people, from their shrines and then their temples, but admitted almost all other categories of society.

Nevertheless, around 1350 BC, no leader anywhere in the world whom we know about, except Akhenaten, appealed for brotherhood and mutual affection between a god and the people and between peoples. Despite all the limitations, it is simply beyond me how anyone can doubt that at least in Akhenaten's *Hymn*, we do indeed have a magnificent poem exalting differences among peoples and races, rather than systematically castigating or instrumentalizing them. Breasted was right to see the beginnings of a new tolerant, international attitude in *The Hymn* and many modern Egyptologists are quite simply wrong in their evaluation of this aspect of Akhenaten's religion. Despite its pragmatic shortcomings, Akhenaten's concern for universal brotherhood and affection was a huge step forward with many beneficial effects.

Akhenaten also certainly moved towards forms of a moral rather than just religious link between man and god (or the Aten) — something extraordinary for the 14th century BC — even if it may not really be possible to speak about an ethical code or precise moral obligations in the Aten system beyond what already traditionally existed in Egypt. This role was left to Judaism and Christianity, which anchored these concepts in coherent theory, at least, if not in practice.

The limitations concerning Akhenaten's monotheism are considerably fewer on the theological level. Both in religious texts and in his titulary names in the royal cartouches, Akhenaten progressively eliminated all the other gods not included in the amalgamation of Aten — Re-Horakthe and Shu — and in later years, as we have seen, also dropped references to Horakthe and Shu in favor of only Re as Aten, or Aten who was Re.

Akhenaten also ordered the elimination of the word *netjeru*, the plural gods. His attempt to wipe out, to literally hammer out, all the names and images of the other gods, beginning with the former chief god Amun-Re; and his order that all their temples be abandoned can only be seen as deeply anti-polytheistic. Akhenaten's zeal was such that he even erased the name of his father Amenhotep III, because it contained the name of Amun (Amen), and wiped out nine references to the *netjeru* in the vizier Ramose's splendid tomb in western Thebes (TT55); but his workers forgot two other mentions.

However, indirect references to some divinities continued. Hapy, as the Nile inundation god, persisted, and it would have been difficult to do otherwise since the annual Nile inundation and its personification in the god Hapy were inseparable.

No direct references were made by Akhenaten to Maat as a goddess and in year 12 of his reign, Akhenaten took the extraordinary step of ordering that the traditional hieroglyph for Maat (the kneeling goddess Maat with a feather in her hair) be replaced with a strictly phonetic sign. However, constant references were of course made to *ankh-em-maat*, "living by the *maat*," living by the goddess Maat's code. As for Hapy, Maat as a goddess and her code were virtually inseparable. Nevertheless, Akhenaten referred to *ankh-em-maat* more than any other previous pharaoh and if for no other reason than his changing of the glyph for Maat, it seems that *maat* for Akhenaten did indeed not only mean order, but also some kind of truth and morality, and even a morality which was revolutionary for his time.

It seems that Akhenaten partially succeeded in his anti-polytheistic project among the ruling and privileged elite. He himself had named these officials, paid them more than previous pharaohs (Ay stated that "He [Akhenaten] heaps my rewards of silver and gold")[85] and made them (unfulfilled) promises of luxurious tombs. It seems clear that he was not totally sure of the loyalty of these notables and army generals, since his palace guard was composed of Asian and Nubian soldiers. It is also clear that he had only very limited success among the people and of course no success at all among the thousands of Amun clergy and the clergy of the other gods who had lost their functions and their immense economic power.

The discovery of numerous objects dedicated to other gods in the ruins of the city of Akhetaten, including statuettes of Osiris, Isis, Ptah, Thoth and Bes and *wedjat* Eye of Horus amulets, attest to the fact that even in the holy Aten city ordinary people had not abandoned the traditional gods and beliefs. Even though the god of the people was supposed to be Akhenaten himself, neither the popular worship of the god Horus, the faithful friend of man, nor the extensive worship of the god Osiris as the savior god of death-afterlife, nor the worship of other gods seem to have been effectively eliminated. Even Akhenaten's mother, Tiy,

---

85. *Ibid.*, p. 94.

whom Akhenaten obviously greatly loved and respected, when she visited him in Amarna in year 12 of his reign, seems to have referred to Akhenaten's father as Osiris-Amenhotep. And even if prayers to Aten were inscribed on them, Re-Khepri scarabs were still placed on the hearts of mummies. The multiplicity of gods continued to exist in the minds and hearts of the vast majority of Egyptians.

The *Boundary Steles* around the city of Akhetaten also confirmed both the composite origins of Atenism and their persistence. Despite the proclamation of Aten as the sole god, references on the steles to other gods were frequent even if they were considered as aspects of Aten. Here too we find the same opening invocation as we do in The *Great Hymn to the Aten* and most of the other hymns and prayers: "Re-Horakhte-who-rejoices-in-the lightland In-his-name-Shu who is Aten, who gives life forever." One could suppose that just as for his cartouche, Akhenaten could have hammered out these references, but he did not, just as he does not seem to have ordered a change in the name of the second high priest of Aten from "Chief Seer of Re-Horakhte."

However, it must be emphasized that the *Boundary Steles* first of all illustrated Akhenaten's iron will to establish and eternally maintain the city as the holy city of Aten in the exact place where he built it and nowhere else (just like the intransigent Hebrew monotheists concerning Jerusalem) and to keep it as his royal residence: "Akhet-Aten...which his majesty...founded...as a monument to the Aten, according to the command of his father...I shall not violate this oath which I have made to Aten my father in all eternity...It shall not be erased. It shall not be washed out. It shall not be hacked out."[86]

Some Egyptologists speculate that the *Boundary Steles* could indicate that Akhenaten made a compromise with the Theban Amun priests that the domain of Aten's rule would not go beyond the boundaries of the city of Akhetaten. The fact that Atenism was the royal religion, that Aten temples existed even in Thebes and would be built in several other cities and abroad and that the temples to the other gods would be eventually shut down renders this theory unlikely, except perhaps as an early ruse or tactic.

The *Boundary Steles* also expressed several important theological points in a similar manner to the *Great Hymn to Aten* and in Amarna art — the main role of Akhenaten as the intermediary in the worship of Aten, the favors of eternal life he had granted to Akhenaten and his family and the declaration that both Aten and Akhenaten ruled the Two Lands according to the principles of maat order and justice.

In many other domains, Aten worship remained a materialistic, naturalistic monolatry marked by polytheistic characteristics. Above all, although Aten was

---

86. *Ibid.*, pp. 49 and 51.

a god, he was first of all the visible, material sun disk bestowing light, life, warmth and goodness, worshipped in open-air (roofless) sanctuaries with the sun in view, like the old Re sun temples at Heliopolis, Abu Ghurab and elsewhere. There was no statue of Aten in a *naos* sanctuary in the Aten temples, who had to be awakened, washed, anointed, dressed and put to sleep, but the walls of the temples were covered with images of Aten and the royal family and gargantuan offerings of cattle, fowl, game, vegetables, bread, fruit, beer, wine, incense and flowers were made to Aten. The god Aten was nature or part of nature, rather than above nature, even if he had created nature.

Despite his role as creator-provider and his fatherly and fraternal aura, it can only be one step away to conclude that the worship of the sun god Aten originated and was amplified to monolatry because the sun graciously provided man with the light and warmth needed to survive, that it was the central cosmological reality, that it was the instrument of order and justice and that in the political system the Pharaoh was the son of the sun.

Nevertheless, the Aten faith cannot just be limited to a form of solar monolatry, nor to solar cults within polytheism like the first *benben*, or the Atum, Re or Amun-Re solar cults. Atenism was substantially the worship of a sole god. As already noted, it seems hardly doubtful that the concept of sunlight (*Sw, Shu*) was elevated by Akhenaten to the status of the sole concept explaining existence and that this was the first known occurrence in history of a single concept being used to explain everything.

As can easily be seen from the preceding (and the following), I personally conclude that several realities coexisted in Atenism and that the likeliest possibility is that it was a confused situation. Atenism was simultaneously a heresy, a revolution, a monolatry (but somehow involving Aten as an aspect of Re) and a proto or primitive monotheism, both theologically and morally. It was also a logical conclusion of the predominance of the Heliopolitan sun cult and of Amun-Re chief god theology and universalism, a consequence of imperialism.

Perhaps, more than in words and in typical Egyptian fashion, it is in art where we most strongly and immediately get the overall feeling of Atenism and this impression is amplified by the central concern of Amarna art for the illustration of reality. The feeling of Atenism in Amarna art — for me — is of a representational, immanent, materialistic solar monolatry of the naturalist type, a form of worship which today we might say was imbued with both a pantheistic and adulatory spirit. The system of latria — worship — of Akhenaten and his entourage in dozens of Amarna works of art clearly indicate postures of extreme adulation which contrast especially sharply with the later mainstream Hebrew postures of sobriety. Nevertheless, a form of primitive monotheism can be intellectually superinduced to the immanent solar monolatric feeling in Amarna art, even if it is not immediately present. Minus the representational aspect, the feeling in Amarna art is also close to the warmth and love of the supposed c. tenth century Hebrew Psalm 104, a comparison usually only applied to the text of *The Hymn to the Aten*.

Atenism was clearly a revolution and a heresy of immense proportions within the Egyptian context. It briefly destroyed the very foundations of traditional Egyptian religion and art and altered its worldview.

There can be no doubt that the substance and context of Atenism were clearly insufficient to designate it as full-blown or authentic monotheism, but there also can be no doubt that with Atenism monotheism was invented, even if it was a primitive or proto monotheism. As such, Atenism represented an extraordinary development in the history of religion and although it cannot be formally proved, it is plausible that it contributed significantly to making the leap to authentic monotheism possible.

THE AMARNA ART REVOLUTION: A BRIEF OPENING FOR NATURALISM, REALISM, HYPER-REALISM, EMOTION AND CARICATURE (BUT ALSO IDEALIZATION)

A key aspect of the Atenist religion was the encouragement of informal, naturalistic, expressionistic, emotional art which included everyday secular subjects. As simple as this statement is, Amarna art nevertheless constituted a huge revolution in the history of art. For more than 1700 years, Egyptian art had operated within a strict theological and design framework in which the ideal essence of what should be, rather than reality, was the norm, and not only the norm but one of the central concepts of society. Atenist art (or Amarna art, as it has come to be known) partially smashed this system, both in content and in form.

There is hardly any doubt that the main thrust and cannons of Amarna art were dictated by Akhenaten himself, although its beginnings were during the reign of his father, Amenhotep III. In turn, Amenhotep III and his artists might have been influenced by the earlier naturalistic Cretan-Minoan art. Fragments of Minoan-influenced art have been found in the Tell el-Dab'a (Avaris?) ruins of the Hyksos Period (c. 1650–1550 BC).

Simultaneously, Amarna art portrayed Akhenaten and his family in a revolutionary, secular and relaxed manner and perpetuated, and even accentuated, the traditional Egyptian concept of the divinity of the pharaoh, using a revolutionary style to achieve this.

Even if it was not always the case, Amarna art encouraged a new type of art with secular, casual implications. Rather than primarily being an official, idealized art which praised the pharaoh and the gods, illustrated religious dogmas and served as "equipment" for the afterlife, scenes such as relaxed, warm family life, intimacy and affection, playing, preparing food, farming and hunting came more to the forefront. This form of representation clearly aimed at producing an effect of spontaneity and portraying the crux and mystery of everyday reality as it was, rather than illustrating perfect people, pharaohs or others, or illustrating conventional solemn scenes without emotion. The result was a mixture of naturalistic, emotional, realistic and hyper-realistic art. The heresy that it implied was as great as Akhenaten's religious heresy.

Amarna art violated the traditional code of sacred content and the stiff and pre-defined design code used by Egyptian art before and after it. However, Amarna art also used a code. If most of the old rules for depicting idealized people, and especially an idealized pharaoh and an idealized world, were broken, new design rules and a new content code of idealization were imposed. As heretical as it was, somehow the radically new naturalistic representation of Amarna art was a continuation of the traditional Egyptian artistic concept of idealization.

The violation of the traditional system of Egyptian art was of course most evident in the oversized, elongated heads, elongated bodies, exaggeratedly broad hips, fat, drooping bellies and spindly legs which Amarna art almost always used, even if a person did not correspond to this predetermined code as must have almost always been the case.

Amarna art also considerably altered the posture and gesture codes of traditional Egyptian art, producing a casual, immediate and real, rather than formal, eternal and ideal effect. The typical Egyptian combination of profile and frontal views did not change, but the 18-square grid design was revamped to accommodate the new depiction of the body. A single extraordinary example of how it would have been utterly impossible for Amarna art to operate with the old content, design and posture rules is the mural painting featuring two affectionate, serious, but playful daughters of Akhenaten (now in the Oxford Ashmolean Museum). This expressionist masterpiece of emotion, almost despite the central focus of the girls' elongated, over-sized heads, in many ways sums up what Amarna art at its best violated and achieved.

A mystery remains concerning the reasons for this style. Expressionism of this type could have been a technique to better portray *real reality* by deforming reality. In any case, the tendency to portray others, and not just Akhenaten, in this unusual fashion also points to a stylistic realistic and even hyper-realistic motive and *parti pris*. There could also have been a theological motive — the desire to incorporate opposites and, perhaps, male and female principles. However, Akhenaten's stylistic and/or theological *parti pris* also sometimes slipped into brutal caricature.

Some historians believe that this unusual body style had nothing to do with artistic or theological concepts. They believe that Akhenaten really had the strange — some say ugly — face and unusual body type portrayed by his sculptors and painters and that this was the reason which led to everybody, or nearly everybody, being depicted this way. Although it could be possible that at some point in his life, Akhenaten did have this strange facial and body type, images also exist in which he is depicted in a *normal* way, that is, without any of the Amarna style characteristics. (The several theories concerning to what extent the strange representation of Akhenaten was really a resemblance and whether or not Akhenaten suffered from a disease which may have produced these bodily characteristics will soon be examined.)

Beyond these considerations, the answer to the mystery of Amarna style may lie within the traditional Egyptian concept of the idealization of the divine pharaoh-god, of representing a king as divine, but doing it with new criteria, with a new style and content code. Like all previous Egyptian art, Amarna art remained an idealized representation of the divine forces, especially concerning the pharaoh. What had changed was the code, the style and content of instrumentalizing the representation of *the* pharaoh. As revolutionary a violation of all the design and content rules of the idealized pharaoh of traditional Egyptian art as were the depictions of Akhenaten, they may have been traditional in their purpose — depicting a divine king, a god above humans.

This is what appears to be the case in the series of colossi of Akhenaten found in the ruins of the East Karnak *Gempaaton* Temple. Sculpted according to the new design rules of the Amarna art code, they reveal a calm but self-satisfied pharaoh whose solemnity is accentuated by the effeminate and strange result produced by his wide hips, drooping stomach, elongated head and spindly legs. These statues probably aimed at consecrating the same traditional Egyptian concept of the idealization of the divine pharaoh-god, of representing a king as divine, but with the new criteria, in the new style code. The result is just as stiff, solemn and formal as the previous representation of the divine kings of Egypt; if there is anything that is really deeply changed, it is that Akhenaten appears as a tragic figure, something unheard of in the depiction of a pharaoh.

However, while the aim of the colossi seems to fit into the traditional intention, the same cannot be said for many other works of art depicting Akhenaten and his family. For the first time a pharaoh was portrayed in positions other than the idealized, conventional and solemn walking, sitting or fighting poses. Even more surprising are the well-known scenes of Akhenaten in prostrated, humble and happy poses, as well as in playful and kissing scenes with his children and in romantic scenes with Nefertiti, holding hands and kissing. This was the first time in Egyptian art that a pharaoh was portrayed with his family. There is even a scene on *talatat* which show a disgusted Akhenaten, obliged to strangle a duck in a ritual sacrifice and obviously unhappy about it. Perhaps most surprising of all is the grieving scene in his royal El Amarna tomb, where he is apparently mourning the death in childbirth of his daughter, Meketaten ("Behold the Aten," or perhaps "She Whom the Aten Protects"), who was also probably his wife (married in year 13 of his reign when she was about 11 years old) and the mother of their child Meriaten Tasherit (Junior, "Beloved of the Aten").

None of these types of behavior concerning a pharaoh — although most of them must have existed in private life, with the probable exception of grieving like a woman — were ever depicted before in Egyptian art and they were never depicted again. Such public behavior was quite simply not within the idealized depiction of a pharaoh-god. It was beneath the dignity of a perfect, idealized pharaoh, but it was not beneath the dignity of Akhenaten, who was clearly trying to show that, pharaoh-god as he was, he also experienced the same joys and sorrows as all the other people.

Apparently, using just as radical an approach in art as he used in religion, Akhenaten sought to free the artist from what he apparently saw as obsolete design rules and a narrow way of perceiving reality. Nevertheless, there were downsides to his system. Akhenaten seems to have restricted his artists to mainly relating the everyday life of himself and his family and some of the art he favored was no different in propaganda thrust than that which preceded it. A lot of it also adopted postures of extreme adulation for the sun-disc Aten, which even in Egypt had no pictorial precedent for any other god. Some of it even seems to anticipate the later popular syrupy, garish, artificially pious art of the Hindus and the Christians.

Nevertheless, it seems that the Amarna artist had more freedom than ever before to interpret — to seek the deep meaning and the best way of expressing a specific scene or person, including the pharaoh. This was so even if he had to obviously apply the new Atenist concepts and style to everybody and everything and fit his work into the mold of the new code of illustration, communication and propaganda. The Amarna artist did not have the total freedom that today we consider natural, but it seems that he was treated more as an individual than at any other time before or after in Egypt and that it was Akhenaten himself who granted the artist this new status. The artist was on the road to becoming an artist as we understand the term today. In retrospect, we can see that a breach in favor of secular, humanist and freer art was opened under Akhenaten and continued, in an attenuated manner, a kind of post-Amarna style, among the next pharaohs and right into Pharaoh Horemheb's reign, after c. 1323 BC.

There was enough freedom in the Amarna art system to escape from almost any rules from time to time, the new ones or the old ones. This seems to have been especially true towards the end of Akhenaten's reign. One of the great masterpieces of Amarna art, and indeed the entirety of Egyptian art, the unfinished quartzite head of Nefertiti or Meritaton, found in the studio of the sculptor Thutmose (Djehutymose) (and now in the Berlin Ägyptisches Museum), does not fit into the Amarna art code and stylistically could even qualify as a modern, realistic work of art. Both in content and style, this head is that of an individual whose individual qualities and unusual beauty are being emphasized. And Thutmose's most famous work, and one of the most famous works in all of Egyptian art, the limestone bust of a starkly beautiful Nefertiti who seems to be in an another universe (found by Ludwig Borchardt in 1911 and now in the Berlin Ägyptisches Museum), bears almost no stylistic resemblance to the numerous other "classical Amarna" representations of Nefertiti on steles, murals and *talatat*.

Nevertheless, the dichotomy between applying the new rules and individual artistic initiative must have been painfully real. It is notably evident in the depiction of Nefertiti over the years — she was variously depicted in a feminine, erotic manner with a narrow waist, broad thighs and buttocks and a protruding pubic mound, in a near modern "photographic" way and in Akhenaten style. An abyss separates the grotesque relief of Nefertiti with a huge misshapen head, big nose, thick lips and protruding chin (found by Petrie in 1892, Plate I-14 in his book *Tell el Amarna*) and the elegant limestone bust of Nefertiti in the Berlin Ägyptisches Museum; all that is evident about these two portraits is that they depict Nefertiti.

Thutmose was undoubtedly one of the major sculptors of the Amarna period and not a maverick or an exception — he was the "king's favorite and master of works," who had succeeded Bek as chief sculptor in Year Ten of Akhenaten's reign. In addition to his non-classical works, including preliminary plaster casts, many "classical Amarna" pieces were found in his studio including heads of Akhenaten, Nefertiti, Kiya (one of Akhenaten's lesser wives) and Akhenaten's daughters. Thutmose — with or without Akhenaten's permission — was one of the first cases in history of an artist who acted, and was apparently treated, as an individual and not as an anonymous, servile craftsman.

Amarna art, like previous Egyptian art, was not art for art's sake; it was not art as an independent activity and method of investigation and knowledge. However, Amarna art was a partial breach in the concept of art as a magical tool totally subservient to religious doctrines. The adventure of Amarna art was quickly closed, but it still stands as the first time that art was somewhat independent from religion. Although there are no links, Amarna art is part of the long adventure of wresting the independence of art from religion, an adventure which was partially reopened by the secular portraits of the antique Greeks and Romans, before flowering in the Renaissance in the 15th century and then culminating in total freedom of artistic expression from the late 19th century.

The style and the content of Amarna art give it a quality and a feeling which is not only strangely different from all the rest of Egyptian art, but also abundantly illustrate its radical and explosive philosophical underpinning. Its realism and hyper-realism, its emotion, its happy pantheistic solar, monolatric worship, its joyful floral and nature motifs and its overall humility, casualness and lightness (and frequently artificially exaggerated lightness) all contrast sharply with the formal, grave, heavy, essential, idealized, instrumentalized and frequently hypocritical forms of traditional Egyptian art.

Of course, this judgment takes nothing away from the grave, solemn greatness of so much in traditional Egyptian art and architecture, which was based upon a diametrically opposed theological and philosophical underpinning. At its best, Amarna art was Mozart and at its best, traditional Egyptian art was Bach.

We also should not forget the frequently misplaced caricature in Amarna and post-Amarna art. Belittlement of Asian and African prisoners and foreigners was standard practice in Egyptian art and continued during the Amarna Period. However, using the expressionistic tools of Amarna art, the caricature of Asians and Africans in some post-Amarna art became particularly vicious.

In many ways, it can be said that Amarna put art into art. Despite all its own conventions and rules, it partially broke the old Egyptian concept that art had to always depict an idealized essence rather that reality with its warts and beauties. Perhaps for the first time, emotion, individual feeling and interpretation rather than collective obligations were being given at least some free rein. The image and artists had never before had these dimensions. It is such terms of reference which now define art and artists.

What we now call art was put into art for the first time in the Amarna period.

THE COLLAPSE OF ATENISM AND THE COUNTERREVOLUTION LED BY HOREMHEB AND THE THEBES AMUN CLERGY

The radical Aten monotheistic digression collapsed after only 15 to 20 years. Akhenaten was perhaps only 30 years old when he died, no doubt a lonely man whose two great loves, Nefertiti and Kiya, at least four of his six daughters and most of his grandchildren and his mother Tiy had already been claimed by death, probably due to a plague which affected much of the Middle East at that time. He was certainly aware that Egypt's empire was falling apart and probably lucid enough to understand that the chances of his Aten monotheism surviving him were slim. He was apparently buried in the rock-cut tomb (TA26) that he prepared for himself in the eastern cliffs of Amarna, but nothing has been found in this unfinished, vandalized and looted tomb except for a broken granite sarcophagus with no mummy inside. In 1891, Petrie discovered broken canopic jars and *ushabtis* which had belonged to Akhenaten strewn in the streets of the ruins of Amarna.

Smenkhkara ("He Whom the Spirit of Re has Ennobled") ruled briefly from about 1338 to 1336 BC, probably in co-regency from year 15 of Akhenaten's reign. Probably, Smenkhkara ruled alone as a full-fledged pharaoh for only a very brief period. He was Akhenaten's son-in-law (through his eldest daughter Meritaten, "Beloved of Aten"), and was perhaps also his son (by Kiya), or his nephew (through one of his sisters), or his half brother through Amenhotep III and his daughter-wife Sitamun, or a cousin, or from an unknown lineage.

It is also possible that Meritaten briefly preceded Smenkhkara as pharaoh.

There is a further theory that it was Nefertiti who ruled, using the traditional attributes of a pharaoh like the false beard, much as Hatshepsut had done 150 years earlier. The name *Nefernefruaten* ("Beauty of the beauties of the Aten," "Perfect is the beauty of the Aten," or "Perfect is the perfection of Aten") was common to both Nefertiti and Smenkhkara before he changed his name. This theory is highly unlikely since Nefertiti seems to have died in the year 14 of Akhenaten's reign after being pushed into the background by Akhenaten during the year 12 of his reign, when his lesser wife Kiya and his daughter/wife Meritaten came to the forefront. Above all, it seems likely that the badly damaged mummy found in 1907 in the Valley of Kings tomb KV55 is that of Smenkhkara, although a controversy still drags on with some Egyptologists claiming that the mummy was that of Akhenaten himself.

But what would be extraordinary is that, if Smenkhkara was indeed a son of Amenhotep III, his birth name, his nomen, *Nefernefruaten*, would indicate that he was the first royal personage to have had an Aten name, before Amenhotep IV changed his name to Akhenaten. It would therefore be Amenhotep III and not Akhenaten who established the practice of giving Aten names.

In the brief few months that Smenkhkara ruled alone after Akhenaten's death, he timidly abandoned Atenism and adopted the old pantheon led by Amun-Re. This was carried out under the guidance of Ay, a supposedly firm believer in Aten, the man who in his Amarna tomb had carved the words: "I am one truthful to the King (Akhenaten) who fostered him, One who is straight to the Ruler and helps his Lord: A *ka* attendant of his majesty, his favorite..."[87]

---

87. *Ibid.*, p. 94.

However, Smenkhkara's efforts were considered insufficient by Horemheb, the top general in Akhenaten's Army (who had also, like Ay, had his "favors in silver and gold" doubled by Akhenaten), as Smenkhkara did nothing to destroy the Aten temples or at least outlaw Aten theology. Nevertheless, the restoration of Amun-Re as Chief God together with the entire Egyptian pantheon was underway.

The so-called "boy king," Tutankhaten ("Living image of the Aten," c. 1336–1327 BC), then became pharaoh when he was perhaps eight or nine years old. His coronation name, the existence of an image of Aten on the back of his throne and an image of Ay with a sagging Amarna style stomach in the "Opening of the Mouth" ceremony on the north wall of his tomb (KV62) clearly indicate that Atenism and its consequences were not yet fully eliminated.

Just as for Smenkhkara, nobody has ever been able to satisfactorily determine the origins of Tutankhaten. He was married to Akhenaten's third daughter with Nefertiti, Ankhesenpaaten ("Her life is of the Aten") when she was about 13 years old. Tutankhaten could have been Smenkhkara's brother or half brother (through Amenhotep III?), Smenkhkara's son, a nephew or a cousin of Akhenaten, or most improbably of all, Akhenaten's own son (by Kiya).

Once again, under the guidance and/or the constraint of the wily Ay, as vizier, and the watchful, suspicious eye of Horemheb, now *Imey-er-mesha*, "Chief Overseer of the Army" and "General of Generals," Tutankhaten changed his name to Tutankhamun ("Living image of Amun") and Ankhesenpaaten changed her name to Ankhesenamun ("Her life is of Amun"). They moved from Akhetaten/Amarna to Thebes, where the worship of Amun and the other gods had re-started in earnest. A complete restoration of the polytheistic system and its powerful Thebes clergy and temples were encouraged in Tutankhamun's name.

Tutankhamun, or his mentors, erected a stele in the Amun Karnak Temple (the so-called Restoration Stele, now in the Cairo Museum) outlining how everything had "gone to pieces," how "the land was topsy-turvy and the gods turned their backs upon this land" during Akhenaten's reign. He described everything which had been done in "service for his father Amun" and the other gods to restore the glory of the Two Lands, which "surpassed...went beyond, what had been done since the time of the ancestors."[88]

In addition to what appears to have been immense personal ambition, Horemheb fully understood the angry, unemployed polytheistic priests and especially the Theban priests supporting the popular "King of Gods" Amun-Re. With the clever, authoritarian Pharaoh-God Akhenaten dead, discredited and

---

88. Wilson, John in *Ancient Near Eastern Texts Relating to the Old Testament*, pp. 251-252.

out of the way, Horemheb and the Theban Amun clergy, the most powerful and numerous clergy of the time, now stepped up their counterrevolution. They do not seem to have met significant resistance.

The counterrevolution was not only concerned with religious and economic matters. Horemheb and many leading politicians and soldiers, who during Akhenaten's lifetime had apparently already been worried about his inability to keep Egypt united and prosperous and its vassal colonies in the West Asian *Retjenu* under control, were now apparently deeply concerned by the consequences, both at home and abroad, of continuing the Atenist politico-religious system. Both Horemheb and Ay, despite all their turpitudes, had no doubt correctly concluded that Egypt was in danger of political and economic collapse and that its empire was in danger of a breakup.

The Amarna Letters to Akhenaten indicate very troubled times, and notably complaints, warnings and appeals for military help, but the real crunch seems to have come only in Tutankhamun's time when the Hittite troops led by King Suppiluliumas (c. 1370–1330 BC) surged out of Anatolia, defeated the Mitanni at Carchemish and obliged several of Egypt's vassals in northern Syria to switch allegiance.

A final sad and extravagant event ended this period and humiliated mighty Egypt. Tutankhamun died young, at about 16 years old, perhaps in a hunting accident, perhaps in a military operation, but perhaps murdered by a power hungry Horemheb who seems to have wanted to take over as pharaoh at any price. Tutankhamun's widow, Ankhesenamun, the last surviving member of the royal family, was above all the royal heiress: that is, a future pharaoh had to marry her if the accepted rules of succession, established at the beginning of the Eighteenth Dynasty (c. 1550 BC), were respected.

Ankhesenamun (Ankhesenpaaten) was Akhenaten's third daughter, born perhaps in year five of his reign and married to her father at 11 or 12 years old in year 16 or 17, then married to Smenkhkara when Smenkhkara's first wife, her sister Meritaten, died, and then to Tutankhamun. Despite the fact that she had changed her name to Ankhesenamun, she may have still been attached to Atenism. In any case, she now seems to have been desperate to prevent Horemheb, the leader of the counterrevolution against Atenism, from becoming pharaoh.

Perhaps Ankhesenamun schemed with Ay, or perhaps she concocted the plan by herself, but she took the extraordinary initiative of sending a message to the victorious Hittite King Suppiluliumas requesting him, in her role of royal heiress, to send one of his sons whom she would marry, making a Hittite pharaoh of Egypt and the Hittites the allies of Egypt. This was a near incredible way of thinking — a foreigner invited to be pharaoh of Egypt! Perhaps Horemheb got wind of the plan, but in any case, the result was that Suppiluliumas' son Zan-nanza was killed on his way to Egypt, opening decades of armed conflict between the Hittites and Egypt.

Royal heiress Ankhesenamun married the more than 70-year-old Ay (c. 1327–1323 BC). If, indeed, Ay was Nefertiti's father and Tiy's brother, then Ankhesenamun married her grandfather and her grandmother's brother! Ay did not reign long enough to complete the destruction of the Aten cult. Curiously, he did not hammer out references to Aten and Akhenaten in the texts of *The Great Hymn to Aten* and in *The Hymn to the Aten and the King* in his unfinished Amarna tomb (TA25) after he had abjured belief in Aten.

When Ay died, Ankhesenamun disappeared from public view or died. Horemheb married Ay's daughter Mutnedjmet, who held the title of "Heiress," to ensure a legitimate claim to the throne and he was crowned pharaoh, supposedly by Amun himself in the presence of several other gods. "Her life is of Aten" (Ankhesenpaaten, who had become Ankhesenamun) had lost the battle to *Dejserkheprure*/Horemheb, the man who had done, and was still doing, most to destroy her father's reputation, the Atenist system, city, temples and the tombs in which her family were buried.

Horemheb (c. 1323–1295 BC), with the Horus name "Strong Bull with wise decisions," violently completed the Amun counterrevolution. The renunciation of Atenist monotheism and the reinstatement of Amun as *nesu netjeru*, the "King of the gods," and father of the pharaoh was clear from the beginning of Horemheb's reign even if he did not immediately outlaw the worship of Aten. He reinstated the Amun clergy, gave back their lands which Akhenaten had confiscated and confirmed the restoration of the former polytheistic system which Tutankhamun had already proclaimed. But he also was careful not to give Amun and Thebes total victory — he encouraged the worship of other gods and partially restored Memphis' religious and administrative role. While Tutankhamun was still alive, the prayer and the hymn on the statue of himself he erected in the Ptah Memphis Temple (now in the New York Metropolitan Museum) lauds Thoth, Ptah, Sakhmet, Osiris, Khnum, Re and Harakhte; it clearly indicates that Akhenaten's monotheism no longer had any meaning. Horemheb also named numerous loyal fellow soldiers to administrative positions in nomes and decentralized the political and economic system which Akhenaten had exaggeratedly over-centralized. He received many foreign delegations and made a limited attempt to restore Egyptian military control in *Retjenu*, but this attempt seems to have been largely unsuccessful and according to Hittite documents, Horemheb's claims of military victories seem to have been blatant lies.

Horemheb wiped out Tutankhamun's name and replaced it with his own on the Karnak Temple Restoration Stele which had re-instated Amun and the other gods. On the so-called Edict of Reform Stele in the Karnak Amun Temple, he proclaimed that he had "improved this entire land" by thoroughly reforming the administration, and especially the judiciary, and wiping out corruption and theft. Horemheb said that he sought to "[exp]el evil and suppress lying...delivering the Egyptians from the oppressions which were among them...seeking the welfare of Egypt..." He promised protection for the commoners and death for wrongdoers, including soldiers and "thievish tax-collectors." Wrong-doers would be severely punished, including "beating...with a hundred blows, opening five wounds..." or "his nose shall be cut off and he shall be sent [into exile] to Tha[ru] [in the Sinai]." [89]

Before the tenth year of his reign, Horemheb devastated the Aten temples in Thebes and the entire city of Akhetaten including the tombs (although the final demolition of the Atenist temples did not take place until Rameses II's time (c. 1279–1213 BC). Horemheb ordered the obliteration of Akhenaten's name wherever it could be found. Akhenaten's name was wiped out, hammered out. Spells were recited to destroy his name, destroying his *ren*, his name-soul, and in fact all of his souls. Horemheb also obliterated Ay's name for good measure, considering that Ay had been lukewarm. Akhenaten and Ay were condemned to what an Egyptian most dreaded — "the second death" — that is, no afterlife. And Akhenaten was no longer ever referred to by his name, but as "the criminal" who had invented an insane, hated system which had brought misery to Egypt.

Horemheb also embarked on an ambitious construction program, which included the renovation of many temples and especially the Amun-Re Temple in Karnak. Here he built three great *bekhenet*, the monumental temple pylon-gateways. For this purpose, he used 40,000 *talatat* blocks, which he *borrowed* from the destroyed Aten temples. Horemheb also took over for himself Ay's funerary temple in Djamet (Medinet Habu), western Thebes, abandoned his huge, almost finished tomb in Sakkara and built a bigger (345 feet long) and more beautiful royal tomb (KV 57) for himself in the Valley of Kings. He also built a speos (rock-cut) temple in Gebel el-Silsila, north of Elephantine, in which he included himself, alongside Sobek, the local crocodile god of the waters and the sun, among the seven gods represented!

Horemheb even tried to rule from beyond the grave by naming his vizier and fellow soldier Rameses I (c. 1295–1294 BC) as his successor.

All that said, it would nevertheless be simplistic to see Horemheb only in a bad light. He had his shady sides, but he pragmatically did what events commanded him to do and he did it energetically, notably his campaign to cleanup the administration and wipe out corruption and theft. Much of what today

---

89. Breasted, James Henry, *Ancient Records of Egypt*, Vol. 3, 50-67, pp. 25-33.

would be considered the behavior of a horrible human being was in fact standard practice for a pharaoh-god. During Amenhotep III reign, he had been a soldier-priest in the Amun-Re clergy and there is also no evidence that he was ever a staunch Aten monotheist. It can be supposed that even had he opted to continue monotheism, the groundswell in favor of polytheism would have probably rendered such an option untenable.

Aten, himself, after co-existing alongside the other gods for about 20 years after Akhenaten's death, lapsed into obscurity. As the visible solar disk, he now played a minor role as an aspect of Amun-Re. However, it proved impossible to totally wipe out the influence of Akhenaten's Aten proto-monotheism. It continued to play a role, both immediate, in Egypt, and in the future, most probably in Israel and perhaps in Persia.

The type of polytheism gradually restored in Egypt was Amun-Re chief god theology, in its strongest, most monotheising form and with an accentuated emphasis on Heliopolitan solar theology. As we have seen in Volume I, for almost a century previous to the Atenist primitive monotheistic experiment, Amun-Re chief god theology had already reached unprecedented monotheising heights and largely taken into account the concepts which had led to primitive monotheism. Now, it strongly continued along much the same road, gradually downgrading the role of the Aten to almost nothing and mixing chief god solar theology and monotheising tendencies within a polytheistic system.

And only about 70 years after *The Hymn to the Aten*, the previous monotheising, totalizing, chief god theology was even surpassed. Egypt's three main gods, Amun, Re and Ptah were merged into a triad of organic unity, with Amun as the *nb-tm*, the *nib-tem*, the Lord of All. And of course, Amun retrieved all his unitary and omnipotent titles which no other Egyptian god before him, except Aten, had received in such abundance — "The Lord of the Lords," "the UNIQUE," "the father of the gods," the god who "had created himself," "No god existed before him," etc.

Amun was now also a more affectionate and moral god. In the *Prayer to Amun*, in the Ramesside Papyrus Anatassi II, Amun is the "Helmsman of [the weak] Who gives bread to him who has none...My wealth is in the house of my [lord]. My lord is my protector...Amun who knows compassion, Who hearkens to him who calls him..." It is easy to see the influence of Akhenaten's concepts in all this. In fact, Jan Assmann, in *Egyptian Solar religion in the New Kingdom, Re, Amun and the Crisis of Polytheism*, traces "personal piety" and a "personal religion" emerging from "roots during the Amarna Period...eventually changing the whole structure of Egyptian religion, mentality and worldview." For Assmann, "The Ramesside Amun-Re is a god who becomes angry with evil and proceeds against it with implacable fury."[90] As we have seen in Chapter 8, the "penitential hymns" found in the Deir el-Medina workers' village tend to prove that there was indeed a generalized rise of feelings of personal piety and contrition during the post-Amarna Period.

But despite these feelings, which seem to be a prefiguration of monotheistic concepts, Amun-Re theology remained compatible with polytheism. In its restored form, Amun-Re chief god theology was no more opposed to polytheism than the pre-Aten Amun-Re chief god solar theology, or all the other previous forms of chief god theology. All the gods of the pantheon, including hundreds of minor local deities, flourished and praises were sung to them, but they were all aspects of Amun. Amun and his numerous aspects were once again worshipped together and separately. Re remained the old man of the gods and the key solar aspect of Amun-Re. Osiris was restored as King of the *Duat* nether world and benevolent provider of the afterlife. Ptah maintained a strong position, although of course with considerably lesser powers than in his heyday. Once again, the Egyptians showed that they were never upset by contradictions and extravagant theological constructions and always ready to make a synthesis without eliminating any previous layer of meaning.

Restored Amun-Re chief god theology stopped just short of the next logical step in the monotheising process, that is, declaring that Amun was the sole god and creating an irreparable rift with polytheism. This is what Atenism had done and what Hebrew monotheism would do.

And so, the Egyptian elite and people incorporated Akhenaten's influence in the acceptable form of the strongest ever chief god solar theology, laced with piety, and returned to an exuberant, and even an accentuated, practice of polytheism.

The two major annual festivals, which exuberantly celebrated Amun-Re and his system, and which had been established in Thebes at the beginning of the New Kingdom, were now restored and amplified. They perhaps show better than theological arguments how thoroughly Atenism had been rejected and how exuberantly Egypt had returned to polytheism. It is certain that economically, and probably also theologically, the bulk of the priests and notables preferred polytheism and certainly the quasi-totality of ordinary people could not grasp why they had been robbed of the many gods and goddesses of their polytheistic faith. Judging from various documents and pharaonic proclamations, it seems that the exuberant celebration of the *Opet* and The Beautiful Festival of the Valley were clear indications that the Aten period was seen as one of religious austerity and misery during which the gods had abandoned Egypt, and the return to

90. Lichtheim, Miriam, *Ancient Egyptian Literature, Volume II*, p. 112 and Assmann, Jan, *Egyptian Solar Religion in the New Kingdom*, pp. 140 and 203.

the traditional polytheistic religion was seen as a return to normalcy. This was partially an embellishment — Aten proto-monotheism could not match Amun-Re polytheism for exuberance, but it was not utterly austere; it had featured many joyful sides.

The *Opet* festival, in the second month of the *Akhet* inundation season, in Karnak-Luxor, which had already been one of the most extravagant and popular Amun-Re religious festivals in Egypt, was now celebrated with great ostentation. By Rameses III's reign (c. 1184–1153 BC), its duration had grown from the traditional 11 days to 27 days.

The triad of the gods Amun, Mut and Khons, in golden shrines, were taken in beautifully decorated boats from the Karnak *Ipet-isut* to the festival temple of Luxor, *Ipet-resyt,*" the "southern select place," about two miles up the Nile. Fervent and religious sexuality was expressed by Amun's aspect of male virility, the god Min, "the firm one," with his long erect penis and the supposed divine coitus of Amun/Min and the *hemet netjer nt Imen,* the "God's wife of Amun" — one of the wives or daughters of the reigning pharaoh — from whom the future pharaoh would be born.

The reigning pharaoh then entered the Luxor Temple's *ra per,* the *naos* sanctuary, merged with the royal *ka* spirit and double and his divinity was re-affirmed in a secret ceremony. He then re-appeared as a being who had been transformed and renewed in his status as a god, as the son of Amun-Re.

Animals were sacrificed. Free food and drink in immense quantities were distributed. Musicians, singers and dancers encouraged huge crowds of commoners and notables. The people used the statues of the gods in procession in their *wia,* barks, as oracles and asked for predictions and favors.

The bottom line was that Amun-Re, that is Amun, was now once again the uncontested all-powerful main god within a revived polytheistic system, the reigning pharaoh was his son, and the powerful priests of Thebes, the City of Amun, were once again the supreme theologians of Egypt and the country's main possessors of economic power.

But other imperceptible bottom lines may have also been present — radical theological evolution and reform now became impossible for the rest of Egyptian history...and yet, the role of Egypt, both as an influence and as a focus for rejection in the evolution towards monotheism as the religion of more than half the world's population, was far from over.

DID ATENISM INFLUENCE HEBREW MONOTHEISM, OR WAS IT A COUNTER MODEL?

We have seen — and shall see in detail in the following chapter — that there is no way of proving that Hebrew monotheism was influenced by Egyptian monotheising tendencies. We have also seen that while the differences between Egyptian monotheising tendencies, and notably Amun-Re chief god solar theology, Aten proto-monotheism and Ptah/Memphite theology and Hebrew monotheism were very significant, the possibility of Egyptian influence in the framework of a partially evolutionary process towards authentic monotheism cannot be discarded. But it is also necessary to note that the evolution towards authentic monotheism unquestionably involved what Israel rejected about Egypt on the theological, artistic and moral levels. Perhaps this rejection played almost as big a role as the possible influences. In any case, it can easily be demonstrated that Egypt in general, and even many aspects of Atenism, were counter models for Israel.

The centrality of the image, of art, in Atenism as throughout Egyptian history, was obviously rejected with the Hebrew prohibition of "graven images." The cult, the worship, of the immanent, material sun and its rays of light, the Aten, naturally providing life sustaining forces and representable in images was central to Atenism, while the almighty, transcendent, spiritual and non-representable *Yhwh* was the centrality of the orthodox Hebrew cult.

As we have seen, the opposition between immanence and transcendence is more basic than the difference between polytheism and monotheism, and that is what fundamentally defines the difference in the approach to the divine between the Egyptians, and indeed all other peoples, and the Hebrews.

Akhenaten, in describing Aten and in depicting him in art, remained within immanence, within the polytheistic context of visible, material nature gods and their personification in the universe and among man. The Sumerian sky god An was a behind-the-scenes god but he was immanent in the sky and had a father and a mother and children. The Hindu great father god, Brahma, created the universe and exemplifies its destiny, but Brahma originated in an immanent golden egg or lotus flower, first had five heads and then four heads, several wives (including a daughter), and several sons. Only Zoroaster's god, Ahura Mazdah (who probably emerged in the sixth century BC as a virtually monotheistic god), came close to forms of transcendence and omnipotence, although he too originated in immanence, in light, as the twin of Mithra, the sky god, had a son, was opposed by powerful force, Ahriman, and on the material level was closely associated with fire.

It must have been particularly shocking, at least for the early Hebrew monotheists fighting against frequent relapses into polytheism, that the Egyptian gods, including the Aten, were not only immanent but visible and materialistic. Abraham's god was already invisible and non-representational. Even after Moses, in the late 13th century BC, named this god *Yhwh*, presumably Yahweh, *Yhwh* remained abstract and invisible without any possible material representation. *Yhwh* was so thoroughly abstract that in answer to Moses' ardent request to reveal his name — and a name for the Hebrews, like the Egyptians, was revelatory of deep identity — *Yhwh* described himself as the "I AM" and "I AM THAT I AM."[91] In fact, *Yhwh* was as much or even more an activity than a name, linked as it was to the verbs "being," "bringing" and "becoming." It was a logical development that Hebrew theologians after the post-Exilic period (c. 539 BC) decided that *Yhwh* was an ineffable, unutterable term (*hashem*, the name). *Yhwh* was not only transcendental, above man and nature; he eventually became the first and only thoroughly abstract god ever invented by man and there was no possible way that he could be depicted in art.

Of course, it can only be supposition, but it also does not seem unreasonable that the Hebrew rejection of a human being incarnated as a god and of this man-god having a sole access to the supreme god, as Akhenaten, was influenced by the Egyptian experience. From a strictly theological point of view, what was perfectly coherent in a divine kingship system was perhaps most at odds and shocking in relation to authentic monotheism — the fact that Akhenaten not only did not abdicate his role as a pharaoh-god, but that he accentuated and emphasized his divinity. By maintaining his status as a god and by decreeing that he was the only intermediary, the sole way of access to Aten, Akhenaten locked himself into a system which could never be authentically monotheistic

Neither Moses nor Mohammed ever dared to claim as much. The mere ambiguous hint that Jesus might be the son of God was enough to condemn him for blasphemy by the Jews. The Moslems considered that the Christian Trinity was dangerously close to polytheism and the Koran declared that God has no child, partner or equal and is not "one of three."[92] Both Moses and Mohammed recognized that Yahweh, and Allah, needed a prophet, but certainly did not need an intermediary with sole access. On the other hand, there is a resemblance between Atenism and Christianity in that both Jesus and then Catholic dogma maintained that the way to the father was through the divine and human son — "no man cometh unto the Father, but by me,"[93] — much as there was no access to Aten except through his son Akhenaten.

---

91. Exodus 3:13,14.
92. The Koran, 5.76, 77.

The Hebrew moral system was too fundamentally different from every-thing that preceded it to have been anything but an original revolution, but the possibility that it had some roots in Egypt certainly cannot be discarded. From early Hebrew times (at least c. 1100 BC), it seems that the god Yahweh not only jealously demanded blind loyalty, but that equality and individual human rights were vital moral issues. Samuel (in Judges 17.6) states: "In those days, there was no king in Israel, but every man did that which was right in his own eyes." This stance might have been influenced by the rejection of the rigid Egyptian hierar-chical system, but also by the ethical concerns of the Egyptian *maat* system and Wisdom Literature and the inroads in favor of brotherhood that Akhenaten had made.

The strong and wide-ranging Hebrew rejection of incest and its couching in terms of self-evident respect and morality seems to be indisputably linked to a rejection of Egyptian practices. The taboo of incest, despite its being one of the earliest and most universal taboos, was widely flouted by the Egyptian ruling class, and particularly by Akhenaten. Yahweh clearly informed Moses and the people (in Leviticus 18.3, 6, 17 and 26) that "After the doings of the land of Egypt, wherein ye dwelt, shall ye not do...None of you shall approach to any that is near of kin to him...it *is* wickedness... abominations..." Such a Biblical passage clearly represented Hebrew disgust with Egyptian customs, but also a near total rejec-tion of Egyptian moral values.

It has often been pointed out that there are significant similarities between *The Great Hymn to the Aten* and Psalm 104, perhaps composed by King David (c. 1000–962 BC) and, if that was the case, then only about 300 years after Atenism. However, these similarities, like the similarities between Egyptian wisdom liter-ature and the Proverbs, can also be seen as a combination of influences and shared metaphysical and emotional conceptions with Atenism. Moreover, the Hebrews added elements which constituted a rejection of the Egyptian view.

Clearly, Psalm 104 exalted the "wise" role of Yahweh as benevolent creator of the universe, nature, man and the animals as in earlier books of the Bible and in *The Great Hymn to the Aten*. It also accentuated the affectionate, provider role and orderly relation between god and man and the animals which were key fea-tures of Atenism. David, or whoever was the author of Psalm 104, could also have been influenced by the key aspect of sunlight, the religion of the sun's beneficial rays as found in Atenism — "Who coverest *thyself* with light as with a garment..." But the final verse of Psalm 104 also contained the type of definite sanction for immorality which it is impossible to find in *The Great Hymn to the Aten* — "Let the sinners be consumed out of the earth, and let the wicked be no more." Contrary

---

93. John 14:6.

to traditional Egyptian theology and to Atenism, the Hebrews believed that Yahweh had given man a considerable degree of free will to model nature and man and that evil choices were widespread and had to be sanctioned.

Contrary to Atenism, authentic monotheism not only involved the undisputed existence of a single god, but its accompanying moral clarity, proto-democratic egalitarian principles, its plan for humanity and its desire to achieve human domination over primeval nature. Authentic monotheism laid great emphasis on the attempt to form a new kind of civilization in which there was very little that was primevally or naturally right, but rather what was right had to be established by man with the help of Yahweh. Yahweh existed not only to be worshipped as a national and personal god, but also to implement these pillars of Hebrew monotheism.

In still another key domain, especially for the Zoroastrians and the Christians — eschatology — Akhenaten not only added nothing to the pre-eschatology which had been developed in Egypt with the interconnection of the moral aspects of the *maat* system and the Osirisian afterlife system, but he downplayed Osirisian values and of course eliminated Osiris as a god.

And so, even if Akhenaten's worship of a sole god — monolatry — eventually shed connections to other gods, it remained a system of immanence, was theologically not as integral as Hebrew monotheism, was still morally far off from it and did not address the problem of man's free will and dominion over nature and primeval reality. The gap between Atenism and early Hebrew monotheism, and *a fortiori* sixth century BC authentic monotheism, remained large, even while it had been considerably narrowed compared to Egyptian monotheising chief god theology.

In short, and despite a considerable breakthrough towards forms of monotheism and despite the moral advances made by Atenism, Atenism and Akhenaten's behavior also could have constituted counter models for Israel.

CONFLICTING EVALUATIONS OF ATENISM AND AKHENATEN; LOONY THEORIES ABOUT AKHENATEN

Everybody, or nearly everybody, has an opinion about Atenism and Akhenaten and the consequences and influences they had or did not have. And it is true that aside from a few fundamental facts, it is possible to have widely differing evaluations. What are these minimal fundamental facts which many Egyptologists would accept?

Akhenaten set up a system which was inherited and developed from Heliopolitan solar theology. Atenism was anti-polytheistic heresy and revolution.

After the last references to gods like Re-Horakthe and Shu were shed away, its minimal core meaning was sunlight, solar monolatry, or proto-monotheism. The Aten was the material, immanent sun disc. Atenism was universalist, not only in the sense that Aten replaced Amun-Re as the dominant universal god, but also because Aten was the god of everybody. Akhenaten accentuated Egypt's traditional system of divine kingship to an unprecedented level, making himself the sole intermediary of the god, Aten. A new kind of art, more naturalistic and realistic than anything which preceded it, was a major invention of this religion and constituted a revolution in the history of art. Economic life in Egypt was deeply dislocated due to the shutting down of the temples of the other gods and their economic structures. Egypt's empire was endangered by Akhenaten's foreign and military policies. Atenism was not adopted by the majority of the people and after Akhenaten's death it was successfully combated by the political and religious elite as being heretical and miserable.

At the most, this nevertheless proved *a contrario* that a strong monotheising tendency and temptation coexisted alongside the dominant chief god/ polytheistic thrust of Egyptian religion. At the least, and even if some want to reduce Atenism to a form of henotheism, it proved that a radically new monotheistic form of religion was in the realm of Egyptian possibility.

Given Egypt's chief god and monotheising tendencies, Atenism can neither be considered as a total surprise nor as a total anomaly. Given the mainstream nature of Egypt's polytheistic spirit, the counterrevolution which overthrew it was also neither a surprise not an anomaly. Given that Egyptian polytheism had achieved a more sophisticated, complete and flexible state than any other polytheistic system in known history, it cannot be considered a surprise or an anomaly that it emerged from the Atenist Period with a re-affirmation of its polytheistic bedrock of religious belief and an even stronger chief god solar theology. In many ways, Egypt emerged from Atenism as it had always been and as what it would remain.

But everything else in between is open to debate, including the extent of the influence Atenism exercised on Hebrew monotheism and who exactly was the man, Akhenaten.

It can hardly be doubted that Akhenaten lost the battle for proto-monotheism due to a large combination of unfavorable factors and his knack for choosing forms of violence which exasperated powerful people and his inability to choose forms of probably necessary violence which could produce results.

Akhenaten actively encouraged Atenism by building sun temples to the Aten in many sites in Egypt beyond the city of Akhetaten — Karnak and probably Heliopolis, Memphis, Hermonthis and the Delta in addition to Nubia and Asia — but most of the people outside of Akhetaten continued to believe staunchly in polytheism. They seem to have agonized over the loss of their previous gods and beliefs and especially their afterlife beliefs linked to Osiris and they resented Akhenaten's persecution of the Amun and other clergy. They also certainly did not appreciate Akhenaten's version of universalism and fraternity — the very idea that Asians could have the same god as the Egyptians, rather than their gods dominating the world, must have been revolting and incomprehensible to the pretentious Egyptians.

Most of the priests also seem to have been staunch supporters of polytheism, but here Akhenaten simply posthumously lost a religious, political and economic power struggle led by Horemheb. The priests of Thebes, the City of Amun, had lost their privileges and Akhenaten no doubt had made a mistake in assuming that his revolution against Thebes could succeed permanently and that the Thebes clergy could be forced to swallow their loss.

Nevertheless, the self-evident characteristic of a revolution is to be revolutionary, and so despite the polytheistic bedrock in Egypt, it cannot be excluded that had Akhenaten been stronger and more astute, he might have swayed the country to his form of proto-monotheism. Supposedly, about a century later, Moses (c. 1250 BC) did not hesitate to order massacres to put down disbelievers and dissidents and staged a successful near-monotheistic revolution, despite a yearning for idolatry among the people, the weakness of his right-hand man Aaron, and the challenge to his leadership by Korah.

And to what extent was Akhenaten responsible for political and economic decline?

Clearly, he had created economic havoc by closing the temples of Amun and of the other gods and goddesses, as well as government offices in Thebes and Memphis. The temples were at the center of Egypt's economic life; their closure disrupted the local nome economies and encouraged corrupt parallel economic circuits. The transfer of the revenues of all the closed temples to the Amarna Temple administration created an over-centralized system that further aggravated economic dislocation. Akhenaten's huge temple building programs, first in Karnak and then in Amarna, Memphis and elsewhere, plus the building of the entirely new city of Akhetaten/Amarna and its 25 rock-cut tombs (not to mention the profuse and luxurious offerings made to Aten in the temples) must have literally drained the economy.

And why did Akhenaten not intervene to redress an increasingly troubled situation in Egypt's colonies in the West Asian *Retjenu*?

Clearly, Akhenaten lacked acumen not only in getting his proto-monotheistic message across and in economics and in methods of government, but also in military and foreign policies. Akhenaten was an autocrat like all Egyptian pharaohs, but somehow he did not manage to wisely use his authoritarian powers in any domain except art. He may not have staged a single military campaign (or even trading mission) into the *khasut* to gain more territory and booty, as had become standard practice for a pharaoh.

However, the accusations rendering him entirely responsible for the dislocation in Egypt's West Asian colonies and vassal states seem exaggerated. To begin with, the Hittites were in a period of ascension; they were on a roll, and nothing and nobody could have stopped them from squaring off with their rival Mitannis (Egypt's ally), trying to nibble away at Egyptian controlled lands in Amurru (northern Syria) and establishing an eminent position in West Asia. Moreover, the worm might have been in the apple since the reign of Akhenaten's father. The mighty, powerful and feared Amenhotep III had attenuated Egypt's traditional repressive policy in West Asia and had not reacted militarily to maintain exclusive Egyptian domination when it was beginning to be threatened. We shall also soon see that the mid-14th century BC was a time of great political, social and military disruption in Canaan — bands of wandering warrior-pillagers, the *Habiru* (who could have partially been proto-Hebrews), were constantly making stable life impossible for Egypt's vassal city-state kinglets.

Probably, a more standard pharaoh than Akhenaten would have intervened frequently in such a situation, if for nothing else than to preventively re-establish order, something which Horemheb later tried to do — although he succeeded less than the boasts of success he made. In fact, it was not until Rameses II (c. 1279–1213 BC) that Egypt more or less settled accounts with the Hittites at the battle of Kadesh in c. 1274 BC, where what was described as an Egyptian victory was seemingly a stalemate which led to a peace pact and a sharing of power between Egypt and the Hittites among the vassal states of the Levantine.

Akhenaten's foreign and military policies were deficient, but in retrospect it seems that containing both the Hittites and the *Habiru* was not within Egypt's capacities. These realities merged with Akhenaten's basic character as an apparent pacifist, absorbed by religion and not terribly concerned by foreign and military policy, but also his pretentiousness and self-assurance — qualities typical for Egyptians until they finally lost their empire. Perhaps, Akhenaten quite simply could not conceive of Egypt's superiority and domination really being threatened.

Although it is unfortunately understandable that Akhenaten's own people in his time and afterwards demonized him, it is indeed sad and odd that he has been frequently seen by some historians, and some smart aleck doctors, as being diseased, or half nuts, or dreadfully ugly, or all three. As to the frequent theories that Akhenaten was a eunuch or a woman disguised as a man, Petrie credibly dismissed these ridiculous views as early as 1894. [94]

However, it still commonplace to link Akhenaten's supposed unusual physical appearance as depicted in Amarna art and his supposedly strange behavior to abnormality, to madness, to a serious disease or to a genetic malformation. For some, beginning in 1907 with the eminent but controversial anatomist of Egyptian mummies, Grafton Elliot Smith (1871–1937), Akhenaten suffered from Froehlich's Syndrome. This disease leads to an under-developed chest, elongated head, neck, arms and feet, a big stomach and a generally androgynous appearance, as well as mental deficiency and emotional unsteadiness. A diagnosis involving mental deficiency in the case of a genius like Akhenaten is simply extraordinary. Attributing Froehlich's Syndrome to Akhenaten is perhaps just as extraordinary in that one of its symptoms is sexual impotency — Akhenaten had six and perhaps as many as nine daughters, also might have been the father of Smenkhkara and Tutankhamun, and was perhaps the only pharaoh in Egyptian history to have been depicted with his children.

Another ailment, the inherited Malfrone's Syndrome, has also been used to describe Akhenaten's "condition." This involves much the same physical deformities and weaknesses as Froehlich's Syndrome and adds weak eyesight and over-sensitivity to cold, but does not affect sexual potency or mental ability. A few really *great minds* have concluded that Malfrone's Syndrome fits Akhenaten right down to his adoption of the Aten sun disk as god because he was over-sensitive to cold!

Perhaps Akhenaten was abnormal; perhaps he did suffer from a disease, a genetic disorder or emotional instability. But the doctors and Egyptologists who adopt this view will have to come up with something more substantial than Froehlich's or Malfrone's Syndrome to make a credible case.

It is simply insufficient to conclude from the odd physical depiction of Akhenaten and the supposedly apparent lack of some secondary male sexual characteristics that he was either diseased or mad and that Amarna art was the product of a diseased imagination. While we will never know if he was considered ugly by the Egyptians of his time, it seems difficult today to apply this term to such an interesting, deep thinking and emotional face.

Moreover, as we have seen above, the case can be easily argued that the depiction of Akhenaten (and others in Amarna art) was a stylistic choice. Akhenaten may have somewhat resembled how he was depicted in Amarna art, but his facial and especially his bodily traits could have been hyperbolized for stylistic and perhaps theological reasons.

Perhaps, B.J. Kemp, in *Ancient Egypt, An Anatomy of a Civilization*, came close to hitting the nail on the head: "Most people have seen in the distortions to his

---

94. Petrie, W.M.F., *Tell el Amarna*, Methuen & Co., London, 1894, § 84-88, pp. 38-39.

body a faithful attempt to portray the effects of a serious disease from which the king suffered. It is a more plausible alternative, however, that it represents a bold attempt to represent kingship as a force with characteristics that place it outside the normal plane of human experience." This is an update of the view of a code for the "idealized representation of kings...above what is human," first expressed 70 years earlier by Heinrich Schäfer, with the essential difference that Schäfer saw the "naturalistic" *unhealthy* representation of Akhenaten as violating this code and Kemp sees it as embodying it in a new way. [95]

However, the tendency to physically depict many other personalities like Akhenaten widens the problem. Nefertiti, Akhenaten's children, Ay, Tutankhamun and many others were frequently depicted with sagging bellies, elongated heads and spindly legs. There is even an astounding stele (in the Berlin Ägyptisches Museum) showing Akhenaten's first chief sculptor, Bek, with a far bigger and more grotesque sagging stomach and breasts than Akhenaten. What are we to conclude — that all the sculptors obeyed orders to depict everybody like Akhenaten...that they voluntarily and subserviently copied Akhenaten's features...that all these personalities had Malfrone's, Froehlich's or Marfan's Syndrome...or that a stylistic choice and code, beyond even the depiction of Akhenaten, is the key to the matter?

As we have abundantly seen in Chapter 7, very marked stylistic choices and codes linked to religious beliefs are the self-evident characteristics of all Egyptian art, previous to and following the Amarna Period. The depiction of what was believed to be idealized essence and the design, color, gesture and body grid codes for the pharaoh and all others were obviously stylistic choices. Of course, it can also be surmised that Akhenaten broke this system and ordered his artists to strictly paint and sculpt reality, but the contextual evidence of Amarna art leans more towards a generalized change in the art code rather than to no code or to code only basically for Akhenaten.

And as we have seen, the Amarna art stylistic choice of hyperbole was not always followed. In addition to the "non classical" examples already cited concerning Akhenaten, Nefertiti and perhaps Meritaten, there are several examples of statues of Akhenaten, including at least one (now in the Louvre Museum) from the last part of his reign, which only vaguely correspond to Amarna tenets. It is clear that Thutmose, Bek's successor as Akhenaten's Chief Sculptor from year ten, attenuated Amarna artistic tenets, as best exemplified in the famous Nefertiti busts. And, needless to say, there are several "standard Egyptian" images of Akhenaten before the consolidation of Amarna art in year three or four

---

95. Kemp, Barry, J., *Ancient Egypt, Anatomy of a Civilization*, p. 265 and Schäfer, Heinrich, *Principles of Egyptian Art*, p. 16.

of his reign. Perhaps, what is most significant is the plaster mask which Petrie found in El Amarna, and which he mistakenly designated as Akhenaten's death mask; nevertheless, this mask, which was probably used as a model for *ushabti* portraits of Akhenaten, realistically shows a very "standard" or "normal" person without any distortions or deformities.[96] The mere existence of this realistic mask renders all hasty and imperious conclusions about a misshapen or diseased Akhenaten as open to considerable doubt, at the very least.

I do not know anybody who concludes that the great African artists, from the eighth century BC on, were mad because they exaggerated the size and the importance of certain parts of the body, like the head, the eyes, the breasts, the navel, the hips and the genitals. It is clear that this was done for symbolic and religious reasons. I do not know anybody who concludes that the great Buddhist artists, from the sixth century BC on, were diseased because for symbolic and religious motives they frequently depicted the Buddhas with oversized heads and ears, a bump on their forehead, sagging breasts and huge, fat bellies. I do not know anybody who concludes that Moses was mad because he imposed monotheism in a largely hostile environment.

And yet, it has to be admitted that if the likeliest explanation for Akhenaten's odd appearance is indeed the use of an artistic and divinity establishing code, we will probably never discover whether in fact Akhenaten's appearance was considered at the time as odd or non-average and we will probably never be able to determine whether there was some basis in real physical reasons for usually depicting him in a misshapen and hermaphroditic manner.

Akhenaten's seemingly wide practice of father/daughter incest has also been used frequently to paint him as some kind of a pervert. The evidence unquestionably leans towards this incest, although some Egyptologists continue to deny it. Two of the *Amarna Letters* (EA10 and 11), from the Kassite King of Babylon, Burnaburiash II (c. 1360–1333 BC) seem to establish in an independent, neutral manner that Akhenaten married his daughters, Meritaten and Ankhesenpaaten ("the mistress of thy house") when they were 11 or 12 years old. Another *Amarna Letter* from Abimilki of Tyre (EA155) also seems to indicate that Meritaten was Akhenaten's wife. A third daughter, Meketaten, may have also been his wife, and as we have seen, may have died while giving birth to Akhenaten's daughter. In year 16 of his reign, Akhenaten seems to have married a fourth daughter, Nefernefruaten Tasherit (Junior "Beauty of the beauties of the Aten") when she could not have been older than nine. In addition to his six daughters with Nefertiti, it seems likely that Akhenaten had three more daughters, one each from his daughters Meritaten, Ankhesenpaaten and Meketaten. It certainly

---

96. Petrie, W.M.F., *Tell el Amarna*, Frontispiece and § 90, p. 40.

seems that if he did not marry his two remaining daughters, Nefernefrure and Setepenre, it was simply because they both died at four or five years old.

It is obvious that all this was a disastrous situation, genetically, but what has to be repeated is that incest was more or less usual for an Egyptian pharaoh. What is not understood is why Egypt was one of the few examples in the history of mankind where although the pharaoh was a god and incest was usual among Egyptian gods, as it was in many other mythologies, the universal human taboo of incest was officially flouted. Some Egyptologists believe that incest was politically motivated, especially during the New Kingdom (from c. 1550 BC), since becoming a pharaoh necessarily meant having a connection to a royal female. Other Egyptologists have disputed this version and believe that it was merely a cover up to practice incest, noting that many pharaohs did not marry women of royal lineage.

Perhaps, and only perhaps, Akhenaten went further than most pharaohs in father/daughter incest since it was brother/sister incest which was the most common practice among the royal family, although Akhenaten's father, Amenhotep III also seems to have married at least one of his daughters, Sitamun. If we accept the theory of absolute royal female lineage — and there was indeed a marked increase in royal incest during the Eighteenth Dynasty — then perhaps Akhenaten married his daughters because they were "royal heiresses," thus politically reinforcing his legitimacy as pharaoh.

None of this excludes the possibility that Akhenaten could have indeed been some kind of a pervert. However, it is also clear that the context of pharaonic incest has to be considered, that Akhenaten loved his children, that it seems they loved him and always acted to further his political and religious goals almost to the bitter end and that in his mind, he was also marrying his daughters for political reasons. It of course remains impossible to imagine how anybody, even a pharaoh, can have sexual intercourse with and marry his daughters and at the same time exercise the normal function of a father.

Even the fundamental question of the extent of sincere belief and the extent of political and economic expediency — notably concerning how to limit or eliminate the power of the Amun clergy — in Akhenaten's religious motives can be legitimately posed. What really was in Akhenaten's mind is a question that has not been fully answered and will perhaps never be adequately answered.

The psychological impact of having such an imposing father as Amenhotep III, dubbed "the magnificent," might have also played a significant role in Akhenaten's motives. Akhenaten may have had an inferiority complex in relation to his father; he may have been driven to do more and better than his father. But unless one became an absolute radical, like Akhenaten, this was not an easy task in any domain. Amenhotep III ruled virtually uncontested from the Fifth Cataract of the Nile in Nubia to Syria; he was one of Egypt's greatest builders; the architecture and art of his period was on a very high level; the splendor of his court was perhaps unequalled in the history of Egypt and he apparently was a great hunter and a great womanizer.

Nevertheless, despite questions, failures and possible abnormality and perversity, saying that Akhenaten was one of the greatest (and strangest) pharaohs in Egyptian history is quite simply an understatement. Like it or not, the bottom line remains that he clearly was above all one of the major figures that the ancient world produced, a fabulous visionary in religion, the arts and society, and a forerunner of full-blown monotheism, secular art, universal values of brotherhood and more relaxed societal structures.

There has been no shortage of loonies in the past century who not only heaped magnified across-the-board praise on Akhenaten, but who credited him with all kinds of founding roles, achievements and knowledge which just could not possibly be true. The notions that the monotheistic Akhenaten was the founder of the Rosicrucians, the Freemasons, and other esoteric associations and sects cannot be supported by even the beginnings of credible supposition, let alone proof.

Still other theories hold that Akhenaten was a homosexual, despite his obviously enormous heterosexual appetite even if there is evidence in a stele carving of affection for Smenkhkara and therefore perhaps, and again, only perhaps, occasional bisexuality or repressed bisexuality.

The most incredible and looniest theory concerning Akhenaten was that he was Moses. A huge series of corollaries to this thesis "establishes" various degrees of identity between Atenism and Hebrew monotheism. These wild, but admittedly sometimes intriguing, views will be examined in the next chapter, on Egypto-Hebrew relations.

Among the serious Egyptologists, William Matthew Flinders Petrie was the first to go overboard on Akhenaten and to set the stage for a series of dithyrambic evaluations. With his usual mixture of flair, competence and eccentricity, Petrie wrote in 1894 in *Tell el-Amarna*: "...a revolution in art, in religion, and in ethics...No other king ever dedicated himself to an ethical idea as did Akhenaten...The attainment and the spread of truth was the object of his life. He is truely devoted to his one queen, is not ashamed of whatever is the truth...No king of Egypt, nor of any other part of the world, has ever carried out his honesty of expression so openly...Thus in every line, Akhenaten stands out as perhaps the most original thinker that ever lived in Egypt, and one of the greatest idealists of the world. No man appears to have made a greater stride to a new viewpoint than he did." Petrie regretted that "All the new ideals, the 'living in truth,' the veneration of the rays, the naturalism in art, the ethical views, all melted away, without leaving perceptible trace on the minds and ways of the Egyptians, and they rushed on into an age of warfare and decadence."[97]

Soon after Petrie, another dithyrambic evaluation of Akhenaten was made by James Henry Breasted. Despite his eminent scholarship and authentic greatness, Breasted also clearly got carried away in his evaluation of Akhenaten. He was convinced that Akhenaten was not only "the earliest monotheist and the first prophet of internationalism — the most remarkable figure of the Ancient World before the Hebrews," but also "...the world's first idealist and the world's first individual." Breasted admitted that "there is not here a very spiritual conception of the deity..." who was nevertheless "the beneficent father of all men"...and that it is "a gospel of the beauty and beneficence of the natural order...rather than the righteousness of the Sun-god..." Nevertheless, for Breasted, "Until Ikhnaton the history of the world had been but the irresistible drift of tradition...Consciously and deliberately...he...placed himself squarely in the face of tradition and swept it aside...He was...the world's first revolutionist, and he was fully convinced that he might entirely recast the world of religion, thought, art and life..."[98]

However, much more sober views about Akhenaten and Atenism have also been made by eminent Egyptologists. A.H. Gardiner (1879–1963), one of the most reliable and down-to-earth Egyptologists, recognized that Akhenaten's "religious revolution"; "was a genuine monotheism, and it is in the moral courage with which the reformer strove to sweep away the vast accumulation of mythological rubbish...that his true greatness lay; a negative greatness...but one that has been unjustly denied him."

Gardiner also recognized that "the reformer did everything in his power to rid [the sun god] of anthropomorphic associations," but that this "was impossible; the rays [of the sun god] had to be shown holding the symbols for 'life' [the *ankh*] and for 'dominion' or 'power' [the *was* scepter]..." Moreover, Akhenaten "was by no means disinclined to claim a share in his father's [the sun god] divinity; indeed...sometimes...this share approached complete identity."

And surprisingly, Gardiner believed that "A defect of the doctrine was its complete lack of ethical teaching," that "The texts lend little support to...the "supposition" that he wanted "to found a universal religion," rather than "a rigid monotheism of his own devising," but "On the contrary, the king's interests appear to have been almost parochial," that Atenist literature "is not wholly

---

97. *Ibid.*, § 93-95, pp. 41-42 and § 101, p. 44.

98. Breasted, James Henry, *Ikhnaton, Encyclopaedia Britannica*, 1929 and CD 98 Multimedia Edition, 1994-1997 and *A History of Egypt, From The Earliest Times To The Persian Conquest*, pp. 343, 342 and 339.

lacking in beauty, but is undeniably stereotyped in its expression" and that his (Akhenaten's) "representations...provide us with frankly hideous portraits the general fidelity of which cannot be doubted." Gardiner also suggested that neither Akhenaten nor his parents, Amenhotep II and Tiy, were "altogether normal."[99]

One of the most straight forward and to-the-point views of Akhenaten and his religion was made by Henri Frankfort (1879–1954): "...Akhenaten was a heretic precisely in this: that he denied recognition to all but one god and attempted to convert those who thought otherwise." "The Aten was more concrete, less spiritualized through mythology than any other god of Egypt...Akhenaten adored but one power and refused to accept a multiplicity of answers and, again, the Egyptians did not acquiesce. His monotheistic zeal offended their reverence for the phenomena and the tolerant wisdom with which they had done justice to the many-sidedness of reality." [100]

B. J. Kemp believes that Akhenaten was not concerned with "man's destiny or condition," but "in the source of life itself. In the Aten, he found a simple, unintellectual answer: the source was nothing but what he could see for himself, the disk of the sun...Akhenaten was telling the Egyptians something that they knew already, but in a way that made further serious speculation pointless. It is easy to understand why the Egyptians rejected the king's religion after his death; he had tried to kill intellectual life...It is as if one has to decide which actor would best play the part: an effete, limp-wristed dreamer, or a fearsome, despotic madman. If the religious idealism points to the former, his approach to his own position and the simple fact that he achieved what he did takes one to the opposite pole."[101]

One of the most extremely negative views of Akhenaten was made by Adolf Erman (1854–1937): "...the young king, who was physically ill as his portraits show, certainly had an anxiety stricken mind..." "The fury with which the reformer persecuted the old gods, especially the Theban god [Amun], finds its parallel only in the history of fanaticism." For Erman, it was "evident that a reformer who went so rashly to work as to try to set aside the whole history of a people with one stroke, could create nothing permanent." "The result...was the old faith grew still more rigid..." and "provoke[d] the reaction which would lead to the spiritual decadence of Egypt."[102]

---

99. Gardiner, Alan, *Egypt of the Pharaohs*, pp. 214, 227, 219, 228, 229, 230, 225, 214.

100. Frankfort, Henri, *Ancient Egyptian Religion, An Interpretation*, pp. 3 and 25.

101. Kemp, Barry, J., *Ancient Egypt, Anatomy of a Civilization*, p. 264.

102. Erman, Adolf, *La Religion des Egyptiens*, pp. 142 and 160 and *Life in Ancient Egypt*, pp. 262 and 263.

Perhaps the most negative view (although I'm sure that he would use the term realistic) is that of Donald B. Redford (b. 1934). Redford sees little to praise in either Akhenaten or in his "uncompromising monotheism." He almost writes off Akhenaten as basically being a sick fanatic whose pioneering role can be limited to the invention of some kind of inferior monotheism. Redford's evaluation, in *Akhenaten, The Heretic King*, includes: he was not a "humanist" nor a "humanitarian romantic." He "held up as a model, refined sloth." He was "deemed ugly by the accepted standards of the day," was "certainly close to his mother, possibly ignored by his father, outshone by his brothers and sisters, unsure of himself"; "no intellectual heavyweight." "Akhenaten in spirit remains to the end totalitarian...the champion of a universal, celestial power who demanded universal submission"; he "championed...in the truest sense of the word, atheism...." "The Roman world might well have called Akhenaten an 'atheist,' for what he left to Egypt was not a 'god' at all, but a disc in the heavens!" About the only thing Redford can say in Akhenaten's favor is that he "possessed unusual ability as a poet."

Redford and some other Egyptologists also wonder whether the Aten was just quite simply Akhenaten's father Amenhotep III. Redford goes as far as stating that, "What it was Akhenaten tells us plainly enough: the Disc was his father, the universal king...the king who sat on Egypt's throne bore as his most popular sobriquet the title 'The Dazzling Sun-Disc'...ubiquitously termed by Akhenaten 'my father.' I will not persue the implications of this, though they appear to me plain enough."

Well, I for one would have liked Redford to pursue his argument. Amenhotep III was indeed one of the pharaohs who went furthest in deifying himself beyond pharaoh-god status, notably in the Nubian Soleb Temple where he was worshipped, alongside Amun-Re, both as a moon god and as *Nebmaatra*, the pharaoh-god of Nubia, and there is a carving in this temple of Akhenaten making an offering to his father. However, there is no evidence to suggest that Akhenaten saw his father Amenhotep III as the Aten, except in that Akhenaten as all previous pharaohs believed that upon death the pharaoh becomes the sun in "light-land." Moreover, "The Dazzling Sun-Disc" was only one of Amenhotep III's titles and he did not reject his other titles. Perhaps, above all, the usual context of Akhenaten's use of the term "my father" indicates the sun personified as patriarchal father of the universe, a patriarchal father which minus the nature personification is much like the Yahweh of the later Hebrews and Christians.

It is no surprise that Redford feels "contempt" for "the king and his circle" and "apprehension" for his 'religion'" and that he "cannot conceive a more tiresome regime under which to be fated to live."[103] And it should be no surprise

---

103. Redford, Donald, B., *Akhenaten, The Heretic King*, pp. 232-235 and 170.

that, despite my great respect for Redford, much of the above is not only wildly too steep for me, but I do not even understand how such conclusions, in defiance of a reasonable interpretation of Amarna texts and art, can be reached.

If Petrie and Breasted were too extravagant in their evaluation of Akhenaten and insufficiently critical concerning the contradictions and limitations of his system, Redford, Erman, Gardiner, Grimal, Lalouette and others were strangely blind to the great historical peak in human endeavor reached almost single-handedly by Akhenaten. Breasted probably went too far in attributing qualities to Atenism and Akhenaten which in fact originated with Judeo-Christian monotheism, but he caught qualities about Akhenaten that many others missed. As outrageous as it might seem at first glance, Breasted's evaluation of Akhenaten as "the world's first individual" contained a grain of truth — Amarna art clearly shows individual characteristics that had never before been considered so importantly. And, perhaps above all, Breasted saw that "...under conditions so adverse... he...disseminate[d] ideas far beyond and above the capacity of his age to understand."[104]

---

104. Breasted, James Henry, *A History of Egypt, From The Earliest Times To The Persian Conquest*, p. 331.

CHAPTER 12. EGYPTO-HEBREW RELATIONS: SUPPOSED AND PROVEN EGYPTO-HEBREW CONNECTIONS AND THEIR CENTRAL ISSUE

THE CENTRAL ISSUE: THE ORIGINS OF MONOTHEISM

Egypto-Hebrew relations are extremely difficult to elucidate. Meager but clear evidence exists of Egypto-Hebrew relations and reasonable supposition about more extensive relations is largely within the domain of plausibility. However, there is only one single Egyptian textual reference to Israel which is certain, and several others from the third century BC to the first century AD which refer to supposed events from c. 1800 to c. 1200 BC, but which were in books now lost and are available only as quoted by other writers. There are many Egyptian references to sites in Canaan with typically Hebrew names, although these could have belonged to other Semitic groups. There are also several textual and pictorial references which are often interpreted to concern Israelites, but which are vague or uncertain. Finally, there are numerous Egyptian references to *Shasu* Bedouins and *Apiru* warrior-pillagers who may or who may not have been proto or early Israelites. In at least two certain cases, the references to the *Shasu* are accompanied by a reference to Y*hw*, which some Egyptologists and scholars interpret as a reference to the Hebrew god Yahweh.

That Egypt influenced Israel in countless ways — from dietary laws and circumcision to politico-geographic organization and divine kingship (as we shall see later, in Chapter 14 on Egypt's role as a hinge society) — is a plausible hypothesis. But the central historical issue in Egypto-Hebrew relations is the origin and evolution of monotheism.

Obviously, this centrality, if one accepts it as real, is a retrospective conclusion, since Egypt does not seem to have been in any way aware of the religious influence it might have had on Israel or the importance monotheism would have in the history of mankind. Just as obviously, the debate concerning Atenism and Hebrew monotheism has to be situated within the overall context of Egypto-Hebrew relations, the origins of the Hebrew people and its connection to monotheism.

Concerning Israel's awareness of Egypt, there is not only no problem, there is a staggering abundance. The Hebrew Old Testament contains 667 verses (and the New Testament, 27) that mention Egypt and the Egyptians. These include not only statements of deep disapproval of Egypt's morality and religion, prophecies that its cities and idols will be destroyed and descriptions of the Egyptians as superstitious, magically minded, proud and arrogant, but also frequent hopes that Egypt would intervene militarily on Israel's side and clear recognition that Egypt offered hospitality to foreigners, had great agricultural fertility, immense power, unparalleled wisdom and unequalled splendor. These descriptions of Egypt in the Bible are a mixed bag of verifiable information, credible statements, obvious inaccuracies and huge omissions.

As long as we only have fragments of the Bible from early dates — notably, two seventh century BC silver amulets inscribed with verses from Numbers and the Psalms (now in the Jerusalem Israel Museum) — and the quasi entirety of the Bible only from the first century BC, during the Essenian Period, the debate concerning the dating of the Bible will continue. Probability pleads most in favor of compilations and rewrites at various dates spread over centuries — the so-called Yahwist J-source, Elohist E-Source, Priestly P-source and Deuteronomist D-source and some kind of compilation of Biblical texts by King Josiah (c. 640–609 BC) — and a likely finalization of the *Torah* in the post-exilic period after the mid-sixth century BC. However, the paleo-Hebrew linguistic system used in its early parts, and its contents and thrust, are such that at the very least early extensive written fragments and oral traditions and customs, including those concerning Egypt and the struggle to impose monotheism, cannot be easily dismissed.

A prudent, interpretative use of the Bible is obviously required. Like all other ancient texts, including Sumerian, Egyptian, Hittite and Assyrian texts, its first goal was not to impartially relate history; it is a document whose thrust is propagandistic, but also one which contains probable facts. It has to be interpretatively read, read between the lines, in order to extract some probable "truth." Those who see conclusive evidence of extensive Egypto-Hebrew relations or conclusive evidence of almost no relations, and those who see no historical truth in the Bible or those who see extensive historical truth in the Bible, are usually loonies or people with axes to grind.

With all its shortcomings, the Bible remains one of the main non-Egyptian sources for the study of Egypt; and for some periods, notably during the 21st Dynasty (c. 1069–945 BC), it is practically the only available text. It is also evident that much of what the Bible states in relation to the battles Egypt fought in alliance with and against the Israelites, is not only plausible but can be cross-checked in Egyptian documents and art, even if the actual name Israel is only referred to once.

Biblical indications clearly point to Egypt being highly important for Israel, while Egyptian documents clearly indicate that the ideas of other peoples were unimportant for the Egyptians and could not have had much overt influence on them. It cannot be a surprise that except on rare occasions what counted for tiny, but lusty, Israel — from religion to politics — did not count much for great and arrogant Egypt. This was also obviously the case for Israel's Semitic cousin across the Dead Sea, Moab, which seems to have been mentioned only twice in Egyptian documents (both times by Rameses II, c. 1279–1213 BC, on topographical lists).

Egypt's largely impervious attitude to Israel was justified politically, economically and militarily. The Egyptian attitude to the Hebrews was not justified religiously, but there was no way that Egypt could be aware of the immensely important role which Israel would play in the history of religion. However, Egyptian intellectual indifference to Israel did not mean Egyptian absence from Israelite geo-politics, except in times of Egyptian political, military and economic weakness such as in the 12th century BC — factors which almost certainly facilitated the Israelites' campaign to establish their hold on Canaan.

Judah and Israel were among the many small and individually unimportant kingdoms of Syria/Palestine; but as a whole, this region had immense tactical importance for Egypt and for the Hittites and the Mesopotamian powers. Judah's and Israel's geographical position between Egypt and Egypt's great rivals for imperial power, Babylonia and Assyria, condemned the Hebrews for most of their history to alliances with either Egypt or Babylonia or Assyria. Egypt intervened in Judah and Israel almost systematically whenever Judah and Israel ceased to be vassals or *de facto* vassals of Egypt and leaned in favor of Assyria or Babylonia.

Egypt's frequent interventions in Judah and Israel took place long after the 14th century BC proto-monotheistic Atenist experiment was dead and buried in Egypt and mainly in times of greatly diminished Egyptian imperial power after the opening of the Third Intermediate Period in 1069 BC. However, even diminished, Egypt represented immense power for tiny Israel.

Whatever the problems involved both in the verification of Egypto-Hebrew connections and in establishing the dates of early Hebrew history, the comparisons between, and the evaluations of, Atenist monotheism and Hebrew monotheism made in the previous chapter are not affected in a core way by these problems. Nevertheless, it cannot be emphasized enough that no direct connection has ever been found between Atenism and Hebrew monotheism. And yet the historical context, the theological affinities and the indirect textual links are such that a considerable amount of supposition is not only possible, but unavoidable. This is true not only concerning possible influences between Atenism and Hebrew monotheism, but concerning the origins of monotheism within the entirety of Egypto-Hebrew relations.

Retrospectively, the main known elements of Egypto-Hebrew relations do not plead in favor of any kind of early Hebrew influence on Atenism, even if Hebrew or proto-Hebrew monotheising influences on Egypt theoretically could have existed. On the other hand, they plead in favor of Egyptian influence on Hebrew monotheism.

Given the Hebrews' mingled awe and disgust for Egypt, it seems highly likely that at several points in their history they were deeply influenced by the theological and moral atmosphere created by Egypt in the Middle East. It seems impossible to imagine how the Hebrews and/or a Moses in a period perhaps spanning the years from c. 1400 to beyond c. 1200 BC could not have been influenced both by Amun-Re chief god monotheising tendencies and Akhenaten's Aten proto-monotheism, despite the Egyptian attempts to erase Akhenaten and his religion from history. At the very least, the use of the most reasonable dates for the emergence of Israel renders it impossible to exclude a theological influence of the Akhenaten period on the Israelites and on Moses, or somebody like him.

As to earlier monotheising influences, theoretically, Egyptian chief god theology could have influenced Abraham (if he existed), and Abramhamic national henotheism could have influenced the Egyptians during a Hebrew sojourn in Egypt, but there is nothing solid to support these theoretical possibilities.

Facts concerning Egypto-Hebrew relations exist only from c. 1209. At this time, when Moses was supposedly establishing Hebrew monotheism and Joshua was supposedly conquering Canaan, Pharaoh Merenptah (c. 1213–1203 BC) staged a military campaign in Canaan. The Merenptah Stele (dated c. 1209 BC) indicates that the Egyptians were aware of the existence of an entity called Israel, which they claim to have defeated in battle: "Israel is wasted, bare of seed."[105] This is a conventional phrase, appearing many times and indicating the defeat of an enemy and not the total destruction of a people or even of its grain stocks.

Many scholars state that this is the only known mention of Israel in Egyptian documents, but such a view, as we shall soon see, is misleading. It does not sufficiently take into account the context of the topographical lists of conquered cities and peoples of several pharaohs which could be Hebrew cities and proto-Hebrew peoples.[106] It does not sufficiently deal with the possibility that the frequently mentioned *Apiru* nomad pillager-warriors and *Shasu* Bedouin "sand dwellers" could have been, or included, the Hebrews. It also does not acknowledge, or dismisses for various reasons, that Egyptian historians, including Manetho and Chaeremon, between the third century BC and the first century AD, frequently referred to the Jews and their Egyptian connections which they (unreliably) dated to the Hyksos and the 18th century BC. Moreover, Semitic names which could possibly be those of Hebrews, like Jacob, Joseph, Asher, etc., are frequent in Egyptian documents. There are even references to Menahem, Issacher and Asher as far back as Sobekhotep III's reign (c. 1745 BC) in a list of slaves on a papyrus (35.1446) now in the Brooklyn Museum.

Nevertheless, before the Merenptah Stele, we are reduced to speculation concerning Egypto-Hebrew relations. Did links exist in the Egyptian mind between proto-Hebrews and/or the *Apiru* and the *Shasu*? Did links exist between the Hebrews, the Hyksos, the Canaanites or the Sea Peoples?

Some scholars claim that the Rameses II (c. 1279–1213 BC) "Ashkelon Wall" at the Karnak Amun Temple, depicting a victory over the people of Ashkelon in a chariot battle, is proof of the first Egyptian intervention against a constituted Israelite nation. However, the "Ashkelon Wall" raises more questions than answers as to whether the people defeated by the Egyptians were Sea People, Canaanites, *Shasu* or Israelites or some of each. Despite some very affirmative statements, notably by the British Egyptologist David Rohl (b. 1950), that the people depicted are Israelites (but Israelites in the period between the late tenth century and first half of the ninth century BC), there does not seem to be any reliable way of settling this question and the likelihood is that there were no Hebrews involved. Unverifiable claims have also been made that a damaged portion of the Rameses II Beth Shan Stele contains the mention *t3 s3sw Yhw*, Yawe, or Yahweh, of the land of the *Shasu*.

On the other hand, Rameses II and Rameses III (c. 1184–1153 BC) topographical lists mention a place called Jacob-El, which could be the same site already mentioned on the Thutmose III (c. 1479–1425 BC) Karnak topographical

105. Lichtheim, Miriam, *Ancient Egyptian Literature, Volume II*, p. 77.
106. Wilson, John in *Ancient Near Eastern Texts Relating to the Old Testament*, pp. 242-243.

list. Rameses II also mentions a Joseph-El and Rameses III, a Levi-El. Joseph-El and Asher are mentioned in Amenhotep III's (c. 1390–1352 BC) temple in Soleb (Nubia). However, it has to be taken into consideration that by Rameses II's time, topographical lists frequently had as much to do with genuinely conquered sites as with a conventional, ritual and fictitious repetition of sites to signify the universal power of Egypt and the reigning pharaoh. Moreover, these sites might have been those of other Semitic peoples and not the Hebrews.

Once again, all this leaves us with a single certitude — the Merenptah Stele.

We now come to the relief found in Djanet (Tanis), which could be an depiction of a massacre of Canaanites or Philistines in Guezer in Pharaoh Sia-mun's reign (c. 978–959). Siamun supposedly wanted to both help his ally, Solomon (fl.c. 950 BC), and secure Egypt's border from Philistine raiders.

However, there is certainly no way of knowing whether, as the Bible notes, King Solomon "made affinity" with Egypt in order to get "rest on every side, so that there is neither an adversary nor evil occurent." To seal such a non-aggression pact, he is said to have married an Egyptian princess, presumably a daughter of Siamun. The Egyptian pharaoh is then said to have captured and burned the Canaanite city of Guezer in order to give it as "a present unto his daughter."[107] None of these Biblical statements are unreasonable.

We are still on shaky ground when we come to Pharaoh Sheshonq I's (c. 945–924 BC) Bubasite Portal in the Karnak Amun Temple and its several possible meanings. Pharaoh Sheshonq I invaded what were apparently Hebrew lands in c. 930 BC. He seems to have ended Siamun's alliance with Solomon and reestablished some kind of vague Egyptian vassalization over Judah, Israel and Canaan as depicted on the Bubasite Portal. However, it is unclear from the Bubasite Portal whether Sheshonq defeated Israelite armies or both Israelite and Canaanite city-states. The Biblical account of this war as well the events leading up it also lack clarity.

I Kings 14:25, 26 states that Shisak (presumably Sheshonq) sacked Jerusalem and Solomon's Temple in the fifth year (c. 925 BC?) of Rehoboam's reign, Solomon's successor. The rebel against Rehoboam, Jeroboam, after returning from exile in Egypt, sought and achieved the breakup of the United Monarchy, supposedly because of its polytheistic leanings. As Jeroboam I, he became the first king of the ten northern tribes grouped together as the Kingdom of Israel. An Egyptian attack against the United Monarchy in support of Jeroboam would certainly have made tactical sense for Egypt, even if it does not make retrospective religious sense. As Donald Redford has pointed out, the "belligerence" of

---

107. I Kings 3:1, 5:4 and 9:16.

"the chiefdom of Saul and the monarchy of David...toward the Philistines [the Sea People], Egypt's old enemies...could be viewed as beneficial to Egypt's interests...But, the battle won in Israel's favor, the peace and rising prosperity of Solomon's kingdom could only rouse Egypt's anxiety."[108] Therefore, the weakening of the United Monarchy as an independent power on Egypt's northwestern border, the breaking of the alliance between the United Monarchy and Tyre and the creation of an open passage to Byblos and beyond, could clearly have been logical Egyptian goals and clearly Egypt attained these goals.

However, if the highly damaged Bubasite Portal list of more than 150 cities vanquished by Sheshonq I ever mentioned Jerusalem and the Temple, it is among the many lines which were damaged beyond recognition. However, the Bubasite list does mention many Judean and Israelite cities cited in the Bible like Beth-Horon, Gibeon, Arad, Rabbith and Megiddo (where a fragment of a document mentioning Sheshonq has also been found) and perhaps the Field of Abram.[109] It is certainly within the domain of plausibility that Sheshonq defeated Hebrew armies in attacks against Edom, Judah and Israel. However, it remains baffling why such an Egyptian military campaign would have been engaged in favor of Jeroboam's Israel against Judah, while also attacking cities in Israel. Moreover, the scene depicted on the Bubasite Portal is vague — Sheshonq in a stereotyped, standard Egyptian pose is smiting 165 Asiatic prisoners from 165 towns with a mace-head and the inscription relates the usual tale of the pharaoh's inevitable victories. The accompanying list of captured cities also raises the usual doubts about the veracity of topographical lists.

There also must be considerable doubt that either David or Solomon, Kings of the United Monarchy, effectively controlled the vast zones attributed to them in the Bible. There are no references to such an empire — not only in Egyptian texts, but in the texts of other neighboring states — the geo-political situation of that time in the area would rather plead in favor of shifting alliances and states under shifting and loose vassalization. On the other hand, it seems certain that many Israelites of this time basically led a settled and agricultural existence, since the Guezer Calendar, written in this period (c. 925 BC) in paleo-Hebrew, was obviously intended for schoolchildren and links the months to agricultural tasks.

Several non-Hebrew and Hebrew relics provide relatively certain dating for Hebrew events and some kings after the mid-ninth century BC. These include the ninth century BC Tel Dan Stele (in the Israel Museum) which relates a vic-

---

108. Redford, Donald B., *Egypt, Canaan and Israel in Ancient Times*, p. 312.
109. Breasted, James Henry, *Ancient Records of Egypt*, Vol. 4, 719-722, pp. 355-357 and Wilson, John in *Ancient Near Eastern Texts Relating to the Old Testament*, pp. 242-243.

tory, apparently by Hazael of Damascus (fl.c. 840 BC) over the Kingdom of Israel and mentions what is most probably the royal "House of David"; the ninth century BC King Mesha (fl.c. 850 BC) Moabite Stone (in the Louvre) which relates a "victory" over Israel and King Omri (c. 884–872? BC) and mentions the god of the Hebrews, Yahweh; the ninth century BC Assyrian Black Obelisk (in the British Museum) showing King Jehu (c. 842–815 BC) paying tribute to Shalmaneser III (c. 858–824 BC) and referring to "Ahab the Israelite" (c. 874– 853? BC); and the enigmatic Hebrew ninth to seventh century *byt Yhwh* ostracon (in the Israel Museum) which refers to a gift to the "house of Yahweh." As to Solomon's Temple, built in c. 958 BC according to the Bible, the Jerusalem Israel Museum exhibits an eighth century BC one-inch ivory pomegranate inscribed in paleo-Hebrew with the words "sacred [to the] priests of the House of [Yahwe?]h" as possibly the sole object from the Temple which has been found. On the other hand, several hundred inscriptions in paleo, or early, Hebrew, from the late 10th to the mid-sixth century BC, have been found.

These relics attest Hebrew relations and conflict with Damascus, Moab and Assyria and constitute independent verification of some events related in the Bible. Nevertheless, these relics leave entirely open the question of Egypto-Hebrew relations during this period and make us almost solely dependent on Biblical accounts, even if it is almost impossible to imagine that there were no relations between Egypt and Israel when these events were occurring.

In 2 Kings 17:3–6, King Hoshea (c. 732–724 BC) of the northern Kingdom of Israel is reported to have revolted against his Assyrian vassal status and called for help from an Egyptian pharaoh mistakenly named "So" (Tefnakht, King of Sau [Sais], Osorkon IV, Piy, or an Egyptian general?). Help apparently did not come and Israel was destroyed in c. 724 BC by the Assyrian King Shalmaneser V (c. 726–721 BC).

In c. 701 BC, Pharaoh Shabitqo (c. 702–690) sent an army to support King Hezekiah (c. 715–686 BC) of Judah in his rebellion against the suzerainty of the Assyrians. Hezekiah and Shabitqo lost the war; and the Assyrians, who had pretensions to rule the world for the previous 200 years, finally invaded Egypt in 671 BC and occupied and vassalized it from 669 BC.

Pharaoh Nekau II (c. 610–595 BC) still paid lip service to Egypt's obligations to the Assyrians, but also attempted to take advantage of its decline. In 609 BC, he sent his new navy — built by Greek immigrants to Egypt — to northern Israel, presumably because Judah wanted to switch alliances from the Assyrians to the Babylonians. Nekau II killed King Josiah (c. 640–609 BC) and defeated the Judahite forces at Megiddo. He set up Jehoiakim (c. 609–598 BC) as the Egyptian vassal King of Judah.

Nekau II engaged the Babylonian Army of Nebuchadnezzar II (c. 605–562 BC) at Carchemish on the Euphrates River in 605 BC. Nekau II lost this crucial battle with the consequential loss of effective Egyptian influence in both Syria and Judah to the Babylonians. II Kings 24:7 notes how crushing this defeat was: "And the king of Egypt came not any more out of his land: for the king of Babylon had taken from the river of Egypt unto the river Euphrates all that pertained to the king of Egypt."

The Egyptian defeat incited the Egyptian Judahite vassal Jehoiakim to drop Nekau II in favor of an alliance with Nebuchadnezzar and then only three years later to revolt against Nebuchadnezzar.

The prophet Jeremiah (c. 650–570 BC) seems to have immediately understood that the Egyptian defeat at Carchemish was a watershed event signifying the end of the game for Egypt and the establishment of Babylon as the new super-power. He warned Jehoiakim not to rebel against Babylon, but to no avail; and in c. 597 BC, Nebuchadnezzar conquered Jerusalem and deported several thousand Judahites.

Nebuchadnezzar set up Zedekiah (c. 597–586 BC) as vassal king of Judah. At first, Zedekiah followed Jeremiah's policy of submission to Babylon, but after nine years he switched his allegiance to Egypt, perhaps with strong Egyptian encouragement, despite Jeremiah's warning not to rely on an alliance and military help from the weakened Egyptians.

The Egyptian forces, under Pharaoh Apries (c. 589–570 BC), momentarily relieved the pressure on Judah by attacking the Babylonians in Phoenicia, but when it came to the crunch for Judah, they did no more than deploy some forces near Jerusalem. In c. 586 BC, Nebuchadnezzar destroyed Jerusalem, the temple and the state and deported several thousand more Judahites. This conquest of Judah and the looting and destruction of Jerusalem was also noted in an Assyrian tablet, but we have only the Bible to tell us that Jeremiah was forced by a remnant of the Jews left in Judah to flee with them to Egypt, a country he thoroughly despised.

These frequent Egyptian interventions in the Hebrew lands must have led to contact with monotheistic ideas. Moreover, it seems clear that a heterodox Jewish community existed in Elephantine since at least the early seventh century BC and a Yaho (Yahweh) Temple seems to have been there well before the Persian conquest of Egypt in c. 525 BC. However, the Egyptians seem to have only become preoccupied or violently irritated with the theological consequences of Hebrew monotheism in the late fifth century BC. At that time, the Elephantine Jewish colony and its contingent of pro-Persian mercenaries with its temple sacrifices of lambs was seen as constituting a deep insult to their own

Elephantine ram god Khnum. The Elephantine Jewish community's alliance with the Persian masters of Egypt also certainly did not help matters.

From the late fourth century BC, with the settlement of a numerous Jewish community, notably in Greek Alexandria (after 332 BC) — which is often said to have numbered as many as a million people throughout Egypt, by Jesus' time — the Egyptians seem to have directly and violently accentuated their confrontation with both the Jews and Hebrew monotheistic concepts. The Egyptians developed virulent anti-Jewish feelings linked to resentment of this numerous, mainly prosperous, exclusive and monotheistic Jewish community. The excessive Egyptian attitude to the Alexandrian Jews was one of the root causes of anti-Judaism in Antiquity. In many ways, it was the beginning of anti-Semitism.

But there was also an attitude of disdain for the Egyptians among non-Hellenized Jews in Alexandria. These Jews frequently did not respect Egyptian and Greek deities and would not even share a meal with non-Jews. Great disdain was also rife among both Hellenized and non-Hellenized Jews for what they considered to be the primitive Egyptian religion. The temerity of the Jews in expressing their disgust for Egyptian-type idolatry and animistic polytheism seems to have been immense. The Apocrypha *Wisdom of Solomon*, probably written by an Alexandrian Jew between the 2nd century BC and the 1st century AD, stated that "the devising of idols was the beginning of spiritual fornication" and those who "deemed either fire, or wind, or the swift air, or the circle of the stars, or the violent water, or the lights of heaven, to be the gods which govern the world" are not "to be pardoned."[110] Even a gentle mystic and Hellenistic Alexandrian Jewish philosopher like Philo (c. 20 BC–AD 50) openly vaunted the superiority of the Jewish religion.

It was in such a conflictive atmosphere that the Egyptians apparently elaborated their own versions of a Hebrew stay in Egypt, that Greek, Roman and early Christian writers commented on this version and on the origins of monotheism and that Jewish writers largely rejected Egyptian, Greek and Roman views on these matters.

The first Egyptian records we have of these views were apparently contained in the lost *Aegyptiaca* of the Greek-influenced Egyptian priest/historian Manetho (fl.c. 300 BC), who may have partially gleaned them from the writings of his Greek contemporary Hecataeus of Abdera). The Judean first century general, turncoat to the Romans and then historian, Flavius Josephus (c. AD 37–100), in *Against Apion*, cited Manetho as "one of their [Egypt's] principal writers" who admitted that the Jews were "not originally Egyptian," but "had come into

---

110. *The Apocrypha*, Cambridge University Press, The Wisdom of Solomon, 14.12, 13.2 and 13.8.

Egypt...and subdued its inhabitants"(a reference to a supposed Hebrew-Hyksos link which will soon be examined), "went out of that country afterward, and settled in...Judea," were "mixed with Egyptians who "had the leprosy and other distempers"; that the Egyptians "joined battle with the shepherds and the polluted people, and beat them...pursued them to the bounds of Syria"; that Moses had not invented an original system, but had merely inversed Egyptian beliefs — "...had made such laws...as were mainly opposite to the customs of the Egyptians..." and that "the priest who ordained their polity and their laws, was by birth of Heliopolis, and his name Osarsiph, from Osyris, who was god of Heliopolis; but when he was gone over to these people, his name was changed, and he was called Moses."[111]

About 200 years after Manetho, the Alexandrian Greek grammarian Apion (fl.c. AD 85) and the Hellenized Egyptian historian Chaeremon (fl.c. AD 45) added their versions of the Hebrew sojourn and Exodus.

Josephus cited Apion as claiming that he (Apion) had "heard of the ancient men of Egypt" that the "forefathers" of the Jews were "of Egyptian original"; that "Moses was of Heliopolis...and offered his prayers...towards sun-rising" and that Moses "brought the leprous people, the blind and the lame out of Egypt."[112]

Chaeremon, according to Josephus, claimed that "Moses and Joseph were [Egyptian] scribes," had joined up with the people who "had pollutions upon them" and were finally all expelled from Egypt by Rameses.[113]

Josephus sternly refuted the claims of Apion that the Jews were of Egyptian ancestry and of both Apion and Manetho that the Jews had "leprosy...and were condemned to fly out of Egypt" and that Moses was an Egyptian Heliopolitan priest. Josephus added that Moses had rendered a great service to the Egyptians as the "General" of an Egyptian Army which defeated an Ethiopian (Nubian) invasion (a view already earlier held by the late third century BC Jewish writer Artapanus, who added that Moses the Jew had founded the Egyptian religion). Josephus also not only rejected the totality of Chaeremon's views, but also pointed out their contradictions and "ridiculous blunders."[114]

There does not seem any reason to doubt the correctness of Josephus' direct quotes of these writers in *Against Apion* and *Antiquities of the Jews* since his basic aim was not to warp them, but to angrily refute them as "false," "ridiculous" and "lies" proffered against the Jews and to prove the great antiquity and moral worth of the Jews. The conclusion is that by at least Manetho's time — the

---

111. Josephus, Flavius, *Against Apion*, 1.227 and 251.
112. *Ibid.*, 2.28 and 8.
113. *Ibid.*, 1.288 and 293.
114. *Ibid.*, 1.227 and 293 and Josephus, Flavius, *Antiquities of the Jews*, 2.238-243.

early third century BC — the Egyptian version of a Hebrew stay and an Exodus were well anchored and involved a link to the hated Hyksos, sun worship, the inversion of Egyptian beliefs and the expulsion of diseased Jews.

According to Josephus, an Egyptian attitude of thorough hatred of the Jews and their ideas had also been solidly anchored by Manetho's time — "Now the Egyptians were the first that cast reproaches upon us..."[115] Josephus seems to have correctly interpreted Egyptian texts as smacking of anti-Semitism (even if he did not use this term, which had not yet been invented). However, Josephus made very harsh comments about the Egyptian religion and probably could not even begin to understand that it was in fact the Hebrews who had *first cast reproaches* on the Egyptians. Even if it would have been near impossible to found the Hebrew religion on an inversion of the Egyptian religion as Manetho and others claimed, the Hebrew religion clearly instrumentalized Egypt as the epitome of what was negative, much in the same way that the early Christians would later instrumentalize the Jews.

In *Against Apion*, Josephus noted that "the difference of our religion from theirs hath occasioned great enmity between us, while our way of Divine worship did as much exceed that which their laws appointed, as does the nature of God exceed that of brute beasts; for so far they all agree through the whole country, to esteem such animals as gods." Josephus derided the "bad notions" the Egyptians have "concerning their gods" and wondered why they "could not think of imitating that decent form of worship which we [the Jews] made use of..." He also saw "envy" on the part of the Egyptians because the Jewish form of worship had been "approved of by many others..."[116]

It is possible, but unprovable, that Josephus, here, could be referring to Strabo (c. 60 BC–AD 38) who, while repeating the usual Egyptian view that "they [the Egyptians] were the ancestors of the present Jews" and that "Moses" was an "Egyptian priest," noted that Moses "being dissatisfied with the established institutions...left it [Egypt] and came to Judea with a large body of people who worshipped the Divinity." Strabo added: "He [Moses] declared...that the Egyptians and Africans entertained erroneous sentiments, in representing the Divinity under the likeness of wild beasts...that the Greeks also were in error in making images of their gods after the human form. For God, said he, may be this one thing which encompasses us all, land and sea, which we call heaven, or the universe, or the nature of things." Strabo had a positive attitude to the Jewish religion, which had "persuaded a large body of right-minded people," but eventu-

---

115. Josephus, Flavius, *Against Apion*, 1.223.
116. *Ibid.*

ally superstition and tyranny set in — "Such was Moses and his successors; their beginning was good, but they degenerated."[117]

Another "pro" Jewish version of early Egypto-Hebrew relations apparently originated with Hecataeus of Abdera (c. 290 BC) and was recounted by Diodorus Siculus (fl.1st century BC). Hecataeus, like most Greeks, thoroughly disapproved of the "strange" customs of the Jews and their separateness; but unlike most Greeks, he generally respected the Jews and much of their religion. This was perhaps linked to the fact that he wrote at a time when many Jews, perhaps a majority, were bending over backwards to adopt Hellenistic lifestyles and to create links between Hellenistic and Hebrew beliefs and values. Hecataeus supported this movement. Diodorus reported that Hecataeus believed that the Jews were expelled from Egypt in a time of pestilence because their religion had led the Egyptians to forget their own gods. Diodorus, who also believed that the Jews were originally Egyptian, noted that Moses had "ordained that they should have no images of the gods, because there was only one deity, the heaven, which surrounds all things, and is Lord of the whole."[118]

But as time went on, Greek and Roman writers generally adopted variants of the far less flattering Egyptian view that the Jews were descendants of the Egyptians who had been expelled because they had leprosy and usually coupled this with harsh descriptions of the Jews and their monotheism.

The Roman historian Tacitus (AD c. 55–117) was a prime example of this attitude. He subscribed to much the same analysis as Manetho: "Most writers, however, agree in stating that once a disease, which horribly disfigured the body, broke out over Egypt; that king Bocchoris seeking a remedy, consulted the oracle of Hammon [Amun], and was bidden to cleanse his realm, and to convey into some foreign land this race [the Jews] detested by the gods...Moyses...gave them a novel form of worship, opposed to all that is practiced by other men. Things sacred to us, with them have no sanctity, while they allow what with us is forbidden...They slay the ram, seemingly in derision of Hammon, and they sacrifice the ox, because the Egyptians worship it as Apis...the Jews have purely mental conceptions of the Deity, as one in essence...neither capable of representation, nor of decay...This flattery is not paid to their kings, nor this honor to our emperors...the Jewish religion is tasteless and mean...this vilest of nations."[119]

Several of the fathers of the early Church, from the late 2nd century AD, including Julius Africanus, Hippolytus and Clement of Alexandria, also stepped

---

117. Strabo, *The Geography*, 16. 2.34-38, 40 and 46.

118. Diodorus, Siculus, *Library*, 3. 1-3 and 3-6.

119. Tacitus, *The Complete Works* (Translated by Alfred John Church and William Jackson Brodribb) Random House, New York, 1942, *Book V: AD 70*, 5.3, 5.4, 5.5 and 5.8.

into the fray and assumed that the Hyksos were the Jews and that an Exodus, led by Moses, took place around 1550 BC.

THE ORIGINS OF THE HEBREWS

The origins of the Hebrews and their religious beliefs, like those of all ancient peoples and especially nomadic peoples, are difficult to establish. In addition to these usual difficulties, there is the specific handicap of the Hebrew interdiction of the plastic arts. Historical probabilities would obviously be much easier to establish if we had sculptures of Moses, Solomon, Amos, Isaiah, and Jeremiah, just as we have sculptures of Narmer, Djoser, Khephren, Akhenaten and Rameses II. We have seen above that there is only slim archaeological and independent textual evidence concerning the United Monarchy (c. 1020-925 BC) and no archaeological evidence concerning Solomon's temple, except, possibly, an eighth century BC priestly pomegranate. Even concerning the central means of Hebrew expression — writing — considerable difficulties and mysteries exist, notably the discrepancies between the Bible and available archaeological evidence and an absence of archaeological finds for many key events, especially those concerning Egypto-Hebrew relations.

However, many archaeological sites in Israel and Palestine have not been thoroughly excavated and more discoveries of writings, on ostraca, papyri, steles and utilitarian objects seem to remain possible. This would be especially true if one day it became possible to overcome both the Israeli religious and Palestinian political anathemas against excavating the Jerusalem *Har Habbayit*/Temple Mount under the Moslem *Al-Haram al-Sharif*/Esplanade of Mosques. Despite Josephus' report in *The Jewish Wars* that the Romans dug up the foundations of the temple, the Hebrew practice of *genizah*, the storing, or caching, of unused documents mentioning the word God, before eventually burying them, leaves open the possibility of more finds, like those made in 1896 in the Cairo Ezra Synagogue and between 1947 and 1956 in caves near the Dead Sea.

The early dates of Hebrew history are impossible to establish with any certitude. It is likely that, given the nomadic nature of the early Hebrews, the minor interest of the later Hebrews in architecture, the prohibition of the plastic arts, the widespread use of wood and the vast destructions which occurred, it will never be possible to clearly establish an abundance of archaeological facts concerning the United Monarchy, what preceded it and what was the nature of Egypto-Hebrew relations and the origins of monotheism during these times.

The evaluation of possible monotheistic influences between the early Hebrews and the Egyptians is evidently greatly hampered by the lack of any

Egyptian mention, before the third century BC, of a sojourn by Hebrews in Egypt. Moreover, the numerous Egyptian references to *'pr.w, Apiru* warrior-pillagers in Egypt and in Canaan as well as to *Sasw, Shasu* "sand dwellers," bedouins and their connection to a *ywh,* a *Yahwe* or a Yahweh, raise as many questions as answers, as we shall soon see.

The riddles of Hebrew history have to be accepted as such; but despite these riddles, it is very unlikely that the dates, both for their origins and their stay in Egypt, supposedly deduced from the Bible by some traditionalist rabbis and scholars, can be correct.

The traditionalist Jewish system places Abram in Canaan sometime between 2200 and 1900 BC, Joseph in Egypt sometime between 2000 and 1900 BC and the Hebrew Exodus led by Moses from Egypt around 1550 BC, that is about 200 years before Akhenaten. (Dates for Abraham and Joseph in the 18th or 17th century BC — when there were major migrations of Semites from Mesopotamia to the Levant and Egypt — have also been widely cited.)

In fact, a whole series of dates, beginning about 1500 BC in the Late Bronze Period and 1210 BC at the beginning of the Early Iron Age, are within the realm of reasonable possibility for Abraham, Joseph (and the sojourn of the Joseph and Jacob/Israel clans and their descendants in Egypt) and Moses, if they ever really existed and if the Exodus was at least partially factual and not myth.

It is also within the domain of plausibility, with or without an Exodus, but obviously unprovable either way, that some Hebrews were of Egyptian origin. On the other hand, and situating the matter within the sole Biblical references to Moses, it is doubtful that the leader of the "Egyptian" Hebrews, Moses, somebody so aggressive to Egypt, could have been ethnically Egyptian, even if his name "Mose" was clearly Egyptian.

Given the elaborate and frequently accurate description of Egypt in Genesis, it cannot be entirely ruled out that, as Genesis 41:43 claims, Joseph became "ruler over all the land of Egypt" (the Vizier of Egypt and the Chief Steward of a pharaoh's estate). If the Hebrew 20th century BC traditionalist date for Joseph in Egypt is used and if as Exodus 12:40 claims, the totality of the time spent in Egypt by the Hebrews "*was* four hundred and thirty years," then it follows, at least theoretically, that Joseph could have been vizier in Egypt in the 20th or 19th century BC during the Twelfth Dynasty and that Moses and the Exodus could be situated in the 16th or mid-15th century BC.

Obviously, there is something seriously wrong with these dates since they are not only in clear contradiction with some archaeological finds, but also with the early books of the Bible themselves. If, as I Kings 6:1 claims, the building of Solomon's Temple was begun "in the four hundred and eightieth year after the children of Israel were come out of the land of Egypt, in the fourth year of

Solomon's reign" (c. 958 BC is a possible date), then it becomes the inevitable conclusion that the Hebrew Exodus from Egypt took place in c. 1438 BC, more than 100 years before Akhenaten's reign. This in turn is notably in contradiction with Exodus 1:11, which indicates that the Hebrews were forced to build "for Pharaoh treasure cities, Pithom and Raamses," which in the case of "Raamses" places the early Hebrews without any doubt in Rameses II's time (c. 1279–1213 BC).

However, many other scenarios have their defenders, usually among religious historians and maverick Egyptologists and historians. The religious historians often systematically equate the Hyksos and their expulsion with the Hebrews and a c. 1550 BC Exodus. The mavericks often postulate a sojourn of the Hebrews in Egypt beginning from the 17th centuries BC, an Exodus in the 15th century BC and Egyptian battles with Israelites as described on the Merenptah Stele and supposedly on the Karnak Ashkelon Wall after 950 BC during the Hebrew United Monarchy.

Some of these frameworks have the advantage of reposing on some coherent archaeological possibilities and rendering the Bible account (too) marvelously coherent, but they have the great disadvantage of being in contradiction with a host of other and more plausible factors. Above all, the maverick frameworks frequently postulate a vast and non-credible fiddling of the usually accepted chronology of Egyptian history.

In recent years, such maverick views, by David Rohl, many Freemasons and others, in a widely touted so-called "New Chronology" school, have produced several different series of revised Egyptian and Hebrew dates. The Freemason United Grand Lodge of England has lent considerable support to the New Chronology School, including a 1447 BC date for the Exodus and a 1022–1006 BC date for Akhenaten. David Rohl, in *A Test of Time: The Bible: From Myth to History* (named *Pharaohs and Kings*, in the U.S.) situates Moses under Pharaoh Sobekhotep IV as a Prince of Egypt who then led the Exodus in 1453 BC, pushes the Late Bronze Age forward to 1220-820 BC, makes Akhenaten a contemporary of King David in the late 11th century BC, places Horemheb as a contemporary of Solomon around 977 who married Horemheb's daughter and identifies Rameses II with the Pharaoh Shisak of the Bible who plundered the Jerusalem temple around 925 BC, etc. Many Egyptologists, and notably K.A. Kitchen (b. 1932), have thoroughly demolished Rohl's theses.[120]

---

120. Rohl, David, *A Test of Time: The Bible: From Myth to History*, Century, London, 1995 and in *Biblical Archaeology: Time to Think Again?* at www.nunki.net/perRenput/Reaction/ReplyYurco.html. K.A. Kitchen in the 1995 Introduction to the reprinted *The Third Intermediate Period in Egypt*, Aris & Phillips, Warminister, England, 1986.

The impossibility of associating the Hebrews (or any other clearly defined people) with the Hyksos (as many do), the uncertainty concerning the link between the *Habiru* and the Hebrews (a link declared certain by some), the impossibility of lopping off almost 350 years from the probable dates of Akhenaten and Rameses II (as Rohl does) and the contradictions in the Bible all make these frameworks so exceedingly improbable that manipulation, romanticism, loony attitudes or glory-seeking have to be considered as their motives.

There are sufficient textual and pictorial certitudes in the chronology of the Egyptian Eighteenth to Twentieth Dynasties (c. 1550–1069 BC) and the Third Intermediate Period (c. 1069–747 BC) and too many proven concordances with the chronologies, kings' lists and wars of other countries, notably the Hittites, Assyria and Babylon, to render possible changes of 350 years in dates during these periods of Egyptian history.

For the Hebrews, a "reasonable" chronology implies that it is probably a good guess that the early Hebrews (perhaps led by the legendary Abraham) emerged, or arrived, in Canaan during the Late Bronze Age, in the late 14th or early 13th centuries BC. Archaeological evidence — utensils, jars and tools — found in the late 13th century BC Israelite settlements in the Samarian hills clearly indicate that the Hebrews were culturally and sociologically similar to the Canaanites, something which strengthens the hypothesis of an emergence of the Israelites from the Canaanite ethnic group.

If, on the other hand, the Hebrews came from Mesopotamia as the Bible states, then they would have carried a Late Bronze Age culture and a Babylonian chief god and proto-monotheising tendency, inherited from the system of the god Marduk and the moon god Sin, patron of the cities of Ur and Harran where Abraham is said to have lived. Within this scenario, the Joseph and Jacob/Israel Clans, and not the entirety of the Hebrews, would have probably lived in Egypt, notably in Lower Egypt (in Pithom: *Per-Atum?* and *Pi-Rameses*) at least from the 13th century BC. And then the best guess is that a Moses, or somebody like him, could have led these Hebrews out of Egypt in Pharaoh Rameses II's time (ruled c. 1279–1213 BC), or Pharaoh Merenptah's time (c. 1213–1203 BC). The Joseph and Jacob/Israel Clans would have then joined other Hebrew, Canaanite Semitic or proto-Hebrew clans in Canaan, perhaps including the *Habiru* and/or the *Shasu*.

This "reasonable" scenario most probably eliminates any direct contact between Moses and the proto-monotheistic Akhenaten (c. 1352–1336 BC). Above all, we should always keep in mind, as Jan Assmann has stated so well: Moses "grew and developed only as a figure of memory...Unlike Moses, Akhenaten...was a figure exclusively of history and not of memory."[121] But if one face-

---

121. Assmann, Jan, *Moses The Egyptian, The Memory of Egypt in Western Monotheism*, p. 23.

tiously wants to consider all the so-called possibilities, then Moses, who was said to have lived 120 years, could have known Akhenaten when he was 80 years or 90 years old and would have known Horemheb (c. 1323–1295 BC), who finished the job of overthrowing Atenism. Manetho's and Chaeremon's confused stories, related in an equally confused way by Josephus, also place Moses in the time of a Pharaoh Amenophis (Akhenaten?) and in a context of sun worship.

However, all this does not eliminate possible contacts between the Jacob/ Israel Clans and the Akhenaten period. Above all, it changes nothing concerning the overwhelming likelihood that Moses and the Hebrews would have lived in Egypt in the atmosphere of the restored Amun-Re Chief God theology with its own monotheising influences and the influences of Akhenaten's proto-monotheism, as well as memories of the Akhenaten period.

Beginning in the 1920s, two extreme views and a series of middle of the road options concerning the origins and dates of the early Hebrews, including the crucial issue of a Hebrew sojourn in Egypt, were elaborated. This research was carried out, and continues to be carried out, by a motley band of mainly American Middle East scholars. They include many serious and fabulous scholars, but also people with close, or formerly close, attachments to Christianity, unconditional Judeophiles, anti-Semites, anti-Zionists, extreme left wingers, extreme right wingers and a considerable number of loonies. Indeed, Hebrew/ Jewish studies almost rival Egyptian studies for both the great interest they have attracted and the varied and wild theories they have produced.

An American, William Foxwell Albright (1891–1971), is the foremost representative of the "fundamentalist" extreme view inherited from the 19th century. In *From the Stone Age to Christianity* and other books, he postulated that the Old Testament is fundamentally in conformity with historical fact and archaeological finds, including the stories of Mesopotamia, Abraham (and in Egypt c. 1800 BC), Moses, the Exodus from Egypt and a military conquest of Canaan by ethnically distinct Israelites in the late 13th century BC..

Very few modern scholars accept Albright's views and indeed they seem to be largely refuted or undermined, across the board, by archaeological finds, the sole Biblical mention of a connection between Abraham and Mesopotamia, the Biblical account of the Hebrew sojourn and Exodus, serious doubts concerning the totally distinct ethnic and religious characteristics of the early Hebrews in relation to the Canaanites, the contradictions of the Bible itself, etc.

Albright's insistence that the Mesopotamian 14th century Nuzi Texts and the c. 1800 BC Mari Letters and other Mesopotamian texts show a great similarity in Hebrew and Mesopotamian lifestyles, family customs and laws and therefore make the Mesopotamian origin of Abraham plausible is more than a little steep. It is one thing to correctly note such a similarity — even though all it might mean is that there were some common practices throughout the ancient Middle East — it is quite another matter to conclude from it that a legendary figure really existed. While the supposed Mesopotamian origin of Abraham cannot be dismissed outright simply because it only reposes on the stories in the Bible, it obviously has to be treated with far greater caution than Albright did. It also has to be weighed against the fact that Hebrew customs, laws and religion do not only indicate Mesopotamian influences; they indicate a mixture of Mesopotamian, Canaanite and Egyptian influences and the radical newness it built on these influences.

The German historian Albrecht Alt (1883-1956), in *Essays on Old Testament History and Religion* and other books, postulated the existence of a distinct Israelite nomadic group of shepherds living in the deserts near Canaan. They gradually and peacefully migrated into the Canaanite highlands before being joined by escaped slaves from Egypt and other groups and entering into armed conflict with the Canaanite city-states. It was this federation of groups which established the Israelite nation in Canaan and Jordan.

Some scholars, and notably the American George Emery Mendenhall (b. 1916), in *The Hebrew Conquest of Palestine* and other books, postulate that only a small group of Hebrews under Moses' leadership and with a new concept of a single god and a more egalitarian covenant came from Egypt in the Late Bronze Age. This covenant with Yahweh was based on the god's protection of every Israelite family and opposed to kingship of the Egyptian and Middle Eastern types. Mendenhall postulates that this group did not conquer Canaan, but mixed with a diverse population of Semitics, Indo-Europeans and Hurrians in Canaan and converted them to their Yahweh beliefs. This group, living outside mainstream society, became known as *Habiru* (with which the term *'ibri*, Hebrew, could be connected) — that is, rebel militias of transgressor warrior-pillagers opposed to the existing governments, economies and religions. Mendenhall makes what seems to be a very reasonable suggestion that the *Habiru/* Israelites used the god Yahweh as the central element in their struggle — in fact, a peasants' revolt — to establish a distinct identity as the Israelite tribe, but that this community was religious and not ethnic in its basic nature.

The American Norman Karol Gottwald (b. 1926), in *The Tribes of Yahweh, A Sociology of the Religion of Liberated Israel* and other books, accentuated Mendenhall's views, notably Marxist-type theories of a class struggle and liberation. He postulates that the Israelites were socially and politically oppressed Canaanite peasants, and that they became a confederation of rebel *Habiru* groups and successfully revolted against the authoritarian and aristocratically run Canaanite city-states. The liberated Israelites and Judahites then established a more egalitarian confederative system of politically equal tribes with a central government which had only limited powers and became small, emerging states.

Several other scholars include the *Shasu* Bedouins in their composite origin of the Israelites. The German Egyptologist Raphael Giveon (1916–1985), in *Les Bédouins Shosu des Documents Egyptiens* and other books, and the Canadian Egyptologist Donald B. Redford (b. 1934), in *Egypt, Canaan and Israel in Ancient Times*, postulate that the earliest Israelites were mainly *Shasu* in the central highlands of Canaan in the late 14th century BC. Redford postulates that "under Merenptah an entity called 'Israel' with all the character of a *Shasu* enclave makes its appearance probably in the Ephraimitic highlands (what is now the central area of Israel and Palestine)..."[122]

Redford believes that "...probably no part of the Israelites was even in Egypt during the New Kingdom in a capacity that later gave rise to the Sojourn and Bondage narratives" and that the Exodus tale was an Israelite adaptation of a Semitic Canaanite "origin story" based on "folklore" memories of the Hyksos conquest and then expulsion from Egypt. Redford's interpretation is that "ironically" this tale "lived on not in that tradition (the Canaanite) but among two groups that had no involvement in the historic events at all — the Greeks and the Hebrews."[123]

The American Egyptologist Frank J. Yurco (b. 1944), in *Merneptah's Canaanite Campaign and Israel's Origins*,[124] postulates a combined Canaanite, Sea Peoples and *Shasu* Bedouin origin for the Hebrews. He says that after an Exodus from Egypt involving a small number of people, the Israelites were a constituted people by c. 1209 BC as the Merenptah Stele notes. Yurco also holds that some of the battle scenes involving chariot warfare on the Ashkelon Wall in the Karnak Amun Temple, usually certainly attributed to Rameses II (c. 1279–1213 BC), should be attributed to Merenptah (c. 1213–1203 BC) and involved Israelite soldiers.

There are obvious shortcomings and a lack of sufficient evidence in all of the above theories. The most persistent element in them, bandied about for the past century, is that the Hebrews emerged from the *Habiru*, nomad-warrior-pillager people, referred to by the Egyptians as the *'pr.w*, *Apiru*, and in Akkadian as the *Sa-Gaz* (robber head-smashers). Despite the speculative nature of this theory, the origins of the Hebrews and early Egypto-Hebrew relations and influences are very dependent on the roles one assigns to both the *Habiru* and/or the *Shasu*.

---

122. Redford, Donald B., *Egypt, Canaan and Israel in Ancient Times*, p. 275.

123. *Ibid.*, pp. 378, 412, 422, 413, 422.

124. In the *Journal of the American Research Center in Egypt* –23, 1986.

The *Shasu* were hardy bedouins who sometimes had trading relations with Egypt, but who also consistently gave Egypt trouble, as nomads on their eastern border, as raiders, robbers, invaders and would-be immigrants and as foes in military battles. Asiatics, *Aamu*, including *Shasu Bedouins* from the West Asian *Retjenu* (Canaan and Syria), frequently sought refuge in fabulously fertile Egypt in times of drought and famine. The Biblical stories of Abraham, Joseph's brethren and finally Jacob/Israel's family voyages to Egypt are vivid reflections of this reality and also could indicate that the nomadic customs of Abraham's family resembled the customs of the *Shasu*.

Egyptian art and texts frequently referred to the *Shasu*, with the first mentions apparently occurring on the causeway between Pharaoh Unas' (c. 2375–2345 BC) Sakkara mortuary and valley temples where battles against the *Shasu* are described. Weni, an Upper Egyptian official and general in Pepy I's (c. 2321–2287 BC) or Merenra's (c. 2287–2278 BC) army, on his Abydos tomb wall, described his military campaign against the *Shasu* in which he "ravaged" and "flattened" the "Asiatic Sand-dwellers' land." Sinuhe in *The Tale of Sinuhe* describes the " 'Walls of the Ruler' which were made to repel the Asiatics and to crush the sand-farers (the *Shasu*)"[125] and which already existed around 1955 BC.

The trading mission depicted on the famous mural in Knumhotpe's tomb (BH3, c. 1925 BC) in Beni Hassan, north of Hermopolis, depicts bedouins from the *Retjenu*. Ibsha, or Abushei, leader of these 37 Asiatic bedouins, could be a Hebrew, or a proto-Hebrew — the military companion of David is named Abishai in the two books of Samuel. Ibsha is referred to as the *Heka-khasut*, "ruler of the foreign lands," in what seems to be one of the earliest mentions of this term (Hyksos) to designate the chiefs of foreign lands.

The Knumhotpe mural opens the vague possibility that seemingly mythological Hebrew personalities like the Bedouin shepherds Abraham and Joseph could have been among the Asiatic bedouins who frequently traveled to Egypt during the Twelfth Dynasty (c. 1985–1795 BC) and that they may have even been *Shasu* Bedouins, but as usual, it would be too simple to conclude at anything but vague theoretical possibilities. Judging strictly on Biblical descriptions, Abraham also could have been a *Habiru* from Mesopotamia who made good and settled down in the Hebron region.

From the New Kingdom (c. 1550–1069 BC), we get very full descriptions of the *Sasw*, *Shasu*, notably in Thutmose I's (c. 1504–1492 BC) description of his battles including against the *Shasu* "foreigners, abomination of God"[126] and espe-

---

125. Lichtheim, Miriam, *Ancient Egyptian Literature*, Volume I, pp. 19-20 and 224.

126. Lalouette, Claire, *Textes Sacrés et Textes Profanes de l'Ancienne Egypte, I, Des Pharaons et des hommes*, p. 91.

cially in the Rameses II so-called *Bulletin*, describing his "victory" at Kadesh (c. 1274 BC) and the *Shasu*'s wily ways. Many other texts, from the reigns of at least six other New Kingdom pharaohs and then Sheshonq I (c. 945–924 BC) and Pstamek I (c. 664–610 BC) mention the *Shasu*.

In the late Nineteenth Dynasty (late 13th, early 12th centuries), a letter from a border guard indicated that *Shasu* of Edom were allowed to go into Pi-Tum (the Pithom of the Bible) in order "to keep them alive and to keep their cattle alive..."[127] Once again, a Hebrew connection is theoretically possible, here. This Egyptian letter (as well as inscriptions concerning the presence of *Apriru* in this zone, the Wadi Tumilat), also casts doubts on Redford's analysis that there were no foreigners in this zone and that Egypt's eastern borders were too well guarded to allow the Hebrews (or presumably any others) out of Egypt during the late 13th century BC. Clearly, the borders were well guarded, but just as clearly there was an authorized willingness on the part of the border guards let to at least some people in and out.

Redford, and others, note that in the Soleb and Amarah-West temples, near the third cataract in Nubia, mention is made of a place name "*Yhw* in the land of the *Shasu*." In Soleb, a topographical list established by Amenhotep III (c. 1390–1352 BC) calls this place *Yhw3* (or *Yhw3w*) and in Rameses II's (c. 1279–1213 BC) temple in Amarah-West, it is inscribed as *Yhw*. Redford and Raphael Giveon cite these inscriptions to bolster their theory that the Hebrews emerged from the *Shasu* and later became, as Redford names them, "Shasu/Israelites."[128]

Redford states that "undoubtedly...we have here [the Soleb and Amarah inscriptions] the tetragrammaton, the name of the Israelite god 'Yahweh'...The only reasonable conclusion is that one major component in the later amalgam that constituted Israel, and the one with whom the worship of Yahweh originated, must be looked for among the *Shasu* of Edom already at the end of the fifteenth century BC." But Redford cautions that this does not mean that the "Israel...of the Judges or the early monarchy was already in existence in Edom at this time..."[129]

It is unquestionable that Redford is correct in assuming that these *Yhw* inscriptions are strong clues concerning the possible origins of the Hebrews. The maverick view that they refer to *Shasu*/Hebrews in Canaan after a 15th century BC Exodus from Egypt must be dismissed outright, although it is possible that the Egyptians sometimes lumped the Hebrews together with the *Shasu*. It is also probable that Redford is right in assuming that the statement on a Stele of

---

127. Wilson, John in *Ancient Near Eastern Texts Relating to the Old Testament*, p. 259.
128. Redford, Donald B., *Egypt, Canaan and Israel in Ancient Times*, pp. 272, 273 and 280.
129. *Ibid.*, pp. 272-273.

Psamtek I (c. 664–610 BC) to the " 'Shasu of the south' in the Delta" could refer to Hebrews, or Hebrews from Elephantine.[130]

All this certainly constitutes strong indications, but in no way does it constitute proof. The partially common cultural background of the *Shasu*, the *Habiru*, the Hebrews and other Semitic peoples must be considered before jumping to conclusions concerning both the origins of the Hebrews and the name and the attributes of the Hebrew Yahweh, which might have had sources among several ethnic groups.

We must begin with the fact that both the meaning of *Yhwh*, supposedly invented by Moses in the 13th century BC, and its authentic vocalization have been lost. Does it mean: I am that I am? I am who I was? I am who I will be? I will cause to be what I will? He brings into existence whatever exists? Is its pronunciation really "Yahweh" or is this, as seems more likely, merely the most logical supposition?

Yhw and *Yhwh* obviously stem from the same general Semitic, and notably Mesopotamian, Phoenician, Hebrew, Aramean and Arabian root terms, linked to gods with *Ya, Yo, Yau, Yah, Yar, Yahu, Yaho* and *Yam* in their names and to dozens of names of people and geographical locations. These terms were common to the Semitic peoples, probably including the *Shasu* and the Hebrews. A good case can also be made for the worship of a *Yo* among the Hebrews before the term *Yhwh* was decisively defined in Exodus 3:14 and 15. Moses' mother was named Jochebed, which seems to mean "the glory of *Yo*," and would therefore indicate that at least Moses' tribe, the Levis, seems to have known or worshipped a god in the *Yahophore* family, gods with names such as *Yo, Yahu, Yehoua*, or even Yahweh. At least a Midianite, or Kenite (east of Aqaba and in southern Canaan and the Sinai), awareness of *Yhwh* is also evident, since Moses was among these Semitic people of his father-in-law Jethro, the priest, when the term was defined and Jethro accepted Yahweh as being "greater than all gods."[131] The *Yhw, Yaho* or *Yahu*, of the heterodox Jewish community in Elephantine, southern Egypt, from the mid-seventh century BC, was clearly Yahweh.

A case can also be made for still another early candidate for the *Yhwh* tetragrammaton since according to the c. 1450 BC Ras Shamra Ugaritic Texts, a *Yw* reading for one of the names of the Canaanite sea god Yam is likely. *Yw* is linguistically close to Yam, the "favor(ed) and "beloved"[132] son of the god El. There is the temptation to read *Yawe, Yawu* or even Yahweh for *Yw, Yam*, and this is a temptation to which some have succumbed. In any case, we certainly have one of

---

130. *Ibid.*, p. 444.
131. Exodus 18:11.
132. Ginsberg, H.L. in *Ancient Near Eastern Texts Relating to the Old Testament*, pp. 129 and 134.

the earliest mentions — earlier than Soleb or Amarah — of a god who may have been a member of the *Yahophore* family and a forerunner to Yahweh. We also have the first description of the attributes of a possible member of the *Yahophore* family. However, on the theological level, there does not seem to be any substantial way to equate Yam and Yahweh; even their mutual relationship to the sea and storms on the sea is obliterated by the fact that Yam was the personification of the sea and Yahweh is not a personification of anything.

All these *Yahs* and *Yehs* may well be members of the *Yahophore* family of gods, forerunners or prefigurations of Moses' Yahweh or even primitive versions of Yahweh. While it cannot be proof of anything in itself, Kabbalistic doctrine holds that *Yh*, Yah, is the nucleus version of Yahweh.

The bottom line is that, despite Redford's adamant conclusion that the Egyptian inscription *Yhw* is the equivalent of the Hebrew tetragrammaton *Yhwh* for Yahweh, the matter is far from clear.

It may well be that the *Shasu* were among the first peoples to worship gods in the *Yahophore* family, but not necessarily a god named Yahweh. The Amarah-West *Yhw* inscription can perhaps also be vocalized as *Yehou, Yahue, Yahwe,* in the land of the *Shasu* rather than "Yahweh in the land of the *Shasu*" and some philologists claim that the Soleb *Yhw3* inscription should be vocalized as *Yehoua* (or *Yehouaw,* if it is read *Yhw3w*). There is also no description anywhere of the attributes of the *Yhw* mentioned at Soleb and therefore no way of determining how close or how far he was from the attributes of the later Yahweh.

At least on the theological level, it is presumptuous to totally equate the *Shasu Yhw* (or the Ugaritic *Yw,* for that matter) and the Hebrew *Yhwh.* The matter is not only one of linguistics, but also of context and content. Content and context overwhelmingly plead in favor of Moses' Yahweh, or the Yahweh of the early Israelites, being at least a god with new attributes. Even if Exodus 6:3 states that Yahweh is the same as Abraham's god, *El Shaddai,* "the almighty," the attributes Moses ascribed to Yahweh were clearly different than those of Abraham's god. And even if Moses' Yahweh did not signify integral monotheism, it took a revolutionary step in that direction, which was evidently not the case of all the *Yahs, Yos, Yehous,* etc. and even of *El Shaddai.* At the very least, even if Yahweh was not an entirely new god, he was a radically new interpretation of an older god or a combination of older gods.

Concluding that the Israelites were the *Shasu,* or only the *Shasu,* would almost surely eliminate the uncertain but seemingly substantial theory that the early Hebrews emerged from the *Habiru.* It is important to note that the Egyptians clearly distinguished between the *Shasu* and the *Apiru;* numerous texts prove that when they were designating *Shasu,* they said it and when they were designating *Apiru,* they said it. Where the two groups are mentioned in the same text, as in Amenhotep II's (c. 1427–1400 BC) Stele in Memphis (found by Ahmed Badawi in 1943 and now in the Cairo Museum), "3600 *Apiru*" and "15,200 Shasu"[133] are separately listed as having been taken prisoner in the *Retjenu*.

The *Habiru*, or *Apiru*, a people, or roaming gangs, seem to have wandered throughout the Middle East from Mesopotamia to Egypt and Anatolia from at least the 20th century BC until at least the late 12th century BC.

Although there are many etymological and semantic difficulties in establishing exact links between the terms *Habiru*, *Haberi*, *Eberi* and *Eber*, *Ibri*, *Ibrim* (Hebrews), these links are nevertheless possible. Beyond an inevitably inconclusive debate about words, there are good possibilities that some of the *Habiru* were proto-Hebrews, or the core group from which the Hebrew people developed. The matter is far from clear, but as long as no confusion is entertained about the *Habiru* definitely being Hebrews and as long as the usually accepted date of the emergence, or the arrival, of the Hebrews in Canaan is not altered from the 14th or 13th centuries BC, it seems a possibility to at least partially link the *Habiru* and the Hebrews rather than to exclusively link them to the *Shasu*.

Certainly, this possibility also implies difficulties. Is *Habiru* a generic term? Were the *Habiru* a social class of people or outcasts rather than an ethnic group? Did they belong, as it seems, to many ethnic groups, including Semitic and Indo-European Aegean and Anatolian?

Many scholars cite considerable evidence that the *Habiru* were social outcasts, but many of the Egyptian references to the *'pr.w*, the *Apiru*, seem to suggest they were more than just a social class of nomads. They are frequently referred to in Egyptian lists of prisoners and peoples as an entity rather than as individuals or a social category. For instance, it seems from these lists that the Egyptians considered the *Maryan* chariot warriors in the West Asian *Retjenu* as individuals and the *Apiru* as a constituted entity. Moreover, there is no fundamental incoherency in the possibility that the Israelites could have emerged from groups of multi-ethnic outcast *Habiru* in rebellion against the Egyptian overlords and their Canaanite vassal city-state kings.

There are many references to the *Apiru/Habiru* in Egyptian, Akkadian, Assyrian Anatolian, Canaanite and Levantine/Syrian texts. If the Hebrews were *Apiru*, Egyptian documents would push the early Hebrew (or probably, more correctly, proto-Hebrew) presence in Canaan, as well as relations with Egypt, back to at least the 15th century BC. The first Egyptian reference to the *Apiru* seems to be a tomb mural of Puymere (TT39, Thebes), Pharaoh Hatshepsut's (c. 1473–1458 BC) architect and later a high priest of Amun-Re, which depicts *Apiru* straining out wine. The Theban tomb (TT155) of Intef (c. 1479–1425 BC), the

---

133. Wilson, John in *Ancient Near Eastern Texts Relating to the Old Testament*, p. 247.

Royal Herald of Thutmose III, also portrays *Apiru* wine workers. The description of the capture of Joppa, in Canaan, in Thutmose III's time, refers to *Apiru* as notorious bandits, but the Papyrus Harris 500 on which we find it has been dated to about 1300 BC.

Around 1355 BC, *Amarna Letters* (EA287 and 288), written by the Canaanite/Jebusite (and Egyptian educated) Prince of Jerusalem (or rather the Canaanite *Urusalim*), Abdu-Heba, requested, and did not get, Egyptian help to repulse the *Habiru* who were threatening to take over the city. Other Amarna letters, in Akkadian and Canaanite and with a sprinkling of Hebrew words, from various Egyptian vassal city-states in Canaan, Amurru and Upi described military defeats and threats by the *Habiru* or *Sa-Gaz*.

It is clear that many of the Amarna letters found in the records office of Pharaoh Akhenaten's capital Akhetaten indicate a period of great political and military unrest and social disruption and even anarchy in Late Bronze Age Canaan during the 14th century BC. It is also clear that this disruption was largely due to warfare and pillaging by the *Habiru*. Considerable portions, and perhaps most, of Canaan were falling into *Habiru* hands, at least temporarily. EA288, from Abdu-Heba, the Prince of Jerusalem, notes that "The *Apiru* capture the cities of the king [pharaoh]. There is not a single governor remaining to the king, my lord — all have perished!" EA299, from the governor of Guezer, northwest of Jerusalem, states: "The *Apiru* are prevailing over us." EA273 states: "The land of the king is being ruined by going over to the *Apiru*." EA286 states: "...Let the king, my lord, send out troops of archers for the king has no lands left! The *Apiru* plunder all the lands of the king. If there are no archers here, the lands of the king, my lord, will be lost!" These and other Amarna letters have tempted some scholars, and many mavericks and loonies, to associate the 14th century BC *Habiru* with the Israelite conquest of the Canaanite Egyptian vassal city-states.

Some particularly audacious writers have concluded that the Egyptianized vassal king of Sishem, Labayu (EA244, 250, 252, 254) was the Hebrew/*Habiru* Saul (both being known as "The Great Lion"). Equating Labayu with Saul is a thesis which apparently can be entirely excluded by comparisons with the Biblical story of Saul. However, EA252 and 280 do indicate that Labayu attacked many Canaanite cities which were Egyptian vassals. EA289 (from Jerusalem vassal Abdu-Heba) even accuses Labayu of complicity with the *Habiru*, something which Labayu adamantly denies in EA254. The likelihood is that Labayu was an extremely aggressive and mercantile ruler, ready to team up with anybody if it served his purposes.

Maverick interpretations of EA256 also postulate that its writer, Mutbaalu, was Saul's son Ish-bosheth, the ephemeral King of Israel after Saul, that Taduwa (or Dadua) was the Hebrew David, that Ayab was Joab, one of David's key generals, that Ben-ilma was Benaiah, one of David's tribal chiefs, that Yashuya was David's father Jesse, or was Joshua, and that in EA292 and 294, Gulate was Goliath, etc., etc...[134]

Such views about a *Habiru*/Israelite Monarchy period of conquest in the 14th century BC do not tally with the fact that despite the frequent unrest and uprisings in Canaan at that time, Egyptian control over Canaan was firmly re-established by Sety I (c. 1294–1279 BC). The Sety I Beth-Shan Stele and inscriptions in the Karnak Amun Temple mentioned battles with the *Apiru* and the *Shasu*,[135] but not Israelites, nor any hint of some kind of centralized power in Canaan, nor *a fortiori* a Davidic Jerusalem. Moreover, there is also no mention of a Yahweh/*Habiru* connection in any Amarna letter.

As tempting as the maverick interpretations may be, to some, they also seem impossible unless one accepts a major upheaval in Egyptian chronology (*à la* Rohl and others). They all depend on situating the Amarna Letters at points between the late twelfth and the early tenth century BC (Rohl says between 1015 and 990 BC). It seems impossible to lift the Amarna Letters out of their 14th century BC international context. They also imply a hazardous revision of the Biblical names of Hebrew and Canaanite leaders as well as which cities were enemies of the Israelites.

After the 14th century Amarna Letters and the Sety I Beth-Shan stele, the *Apiru* were also referred to as transporters of stones at *Pi-Rameses* in Rameses II's (c. 1279–1213 BC) time (Leiden Papyrus 348), a date which corresponds to the Biblical description in Exodus 1:1 of the Hebrews executing forced labor for Rameses in this city.

However, when Pharaoh Mernepath (c. 1213–1203 BC) repulsed a Libyan invasion and then invaded the *Retjenu*, he did not refer to the *Habiru*, but to Israel, among other defeated peoples and cities. Pharaoh Merenptah's stele (c. 1209 BC) proclaimed that the Egyptian Army wasted Israel, indicating some kind of Egyptian control over the land.

The Merenptah Stele could also imply that by this date, the *Habiru*, or many of them, had become the Hebrew Israelites or that the *Habiru* and the Hebrew Israelites were two distinctly different peoples or groups. It also seems possible that the struggling Israel referred to by Merenptah were the people led by Joshua in the process of establishing the nation of Israel, just as it is possible that the

---

134. *Amarna Letters*, translated by Albright, W.F., Mendenhall, George, E. and Moran, W.L. in *Ancient Near Eastern Texts Relating to the Old Testament*, pp. 483-490. Also see Moran, William L., *The Amarna Letters*, Johns Hopkins University Press, Baltimore, 1992.

135. Wilson, John in *Ancient Near Eastern Texts Relating to the Old Testament*, pp. 251 and 254.

conquest of Canaan by Joshua was largely mythological — as the lack of archaeological evidence of a destruction of Jericho, at least in the late 13th century BC, tends to prove. Moreover, about 15 years after the Merenptah Stele mentions Israel, Rameses III (c. 1184–1153 BC) donated *Apiru* servants to the Heliopolis Temple and more than 50 years later, Rameses IV (c. 1153–1147 BC) once again refers to *Apiru* engaged in quarry work.

It is impossible to clearly affirm either that the *Habiru* were proto-Hebrews or that they were not, but it is possible to reject most of the maverick claims. As intriguing and meaningful as the *Habiru*/Israel/Egypt connections seem to be, and despite the fact that they would go a long way towards clarifying early Hebrew history and its Egyptian connection, the bottom line is that it is just as impossible to establish definitive links between the *Habiru* and the Hebrews as it is to establish such links between the *Shasu* and the Hebrews.

The most extreme views concerning the origins of the Israelites, Egypto-Hebrew relations and the establishment of monotheism are mainly held by the American Thomas L. Thompson (b. 19??) and the University of Copenhagen "minimalist" school (although revisionist might be a more appropriate term). The Copenhagen School and Thompson throw almost all the probabilities and possibilities concerning the origins of the Hebrews and Egypto-Hebrew relations into disarray.

Thompson, in *The Mythic Past: Biblical Archaeology and the Myth of Israel* and other books, postulates that the Semitic peoples arrived in Palestine from North Africa between 6000 and 4000 BC, that there was no Hyksos invasion of Egypt, that a Hebrew sojourn and an Exodus from Egypt could not possibly have existed, that there was no Egyptian influence on Hebrew myths, that there was no Israelite ethnic group distinctly different from the Canaanites in the 12th century BC, that a united Hebrew monarchy and kings like Saul, David and Solomon, could not have existed in the late 11th and early 10th centuries BC, that the northern kingdom of Israel emerged in the 9th century BC and that Judah emerged as centralized state under Assyrian vassalization only in the mid-8th century and early 7th century BC.

Moreover, according to Thompson, there was no such thing as Mosaic monotheism in the 13th and 12th centuries BC; Yahweh was a deity among many Canaanite and Hebrew deities and perhaps Jewish monotheism did not really exist until the early 2nd century BC. Thompson also claims that the Hebrews did not have a developed national consciousness and a literature until the post-exilic Persian Period after c. 539 BC and that the myth, traditions and writings of an old Israel were almost all created in the 2nd century BC under the influence of the Taliban-like Maccabees.

In short, according to Thompson, most of Hebrew history and religious development are myth and literature and it is ludicrous to make any use of the Bible as a possible source of history.

Some of Thompson's and the minimalist school's theories are indeed plausible, even if its basic thrust, methodology, lack of proofs and overall conclusions are extravagant. Thompson's and the Copenhagen School's work seem fundamentally flawed in being too selective in what they retain from the available archaeological record, too exclusive and definitive in how they interpret it and too certain that because archaeological evidence for certain events has not been found this necessarily means that these events did not exist. Nevertheless, exaggerated and distorted as Thompson's conclusions may be, he has drawn attention to the need to treat the Bible like any other document; but it serves no useful purpose to attempt to expose the magical thinking in the Bible by largely building another magical construction in which affirmations replace what should be questions and plausibilities.

Above all, Thompson is rigidly insensitive to the astounding, detailed content of the Bible. In itself, this powerfully points to a Late Bronze Age/Early Iron Age (13th century BC) origin of the Israelites and then to one of the most extraordinary examples of ethnic identity and original national consciousness in the history of mankind. Despite the probability that the Bible was rewritten, revised and re-revised and despite its myths, fantasies, errors, boastfulness and propaganda — things common to virtually all ancient religions — there is also much that can be corroborated by other sources, much that is reasonably likely and much that rings true.

It is simply extraordinary to postulate, as Thompson does, that the tales in the early part of the Bible were contrived virtually *ex nihilo* beginning in the late sixth century BC after the Babylonian exile. Thompson superbly ignores that, if the early parts of the Bible were entirely contrived in the sixth century BC and then finalized and written in the second century BC, the story line would not have portrayed a confused, gradual and difficult imposition of monotheism over polytheism from Moses' national henotheism with its rejection of Egyptian and Canaanite polytheisms to the sixth century BC authentic monotheism of Deutero-Isaiah and Jeremiah; it would have portrayed integral, authentic monotheism right from Moses', or even Abraham's, time with attacks against this monotheism. Monotheism and its radical break with all previous world visions, and especially the Sumero-Egyptian vision, was a revolution, but most of the Bible does not describe it as a *fait accompli*; it is rather presented as a divine ambition and proposal subject to many ups and downs and many difficulties. The achievement of the monotheistic world vision was too complex for it too have been composed *ex nihilo* at any date.

Thompson answers that, after the sixth century BC, the Jews created traditions and tales of good and evil, which warned people that they had to do the good — submit to Yahweh — or be condemned to the same evil consequences which had occurred in the past with the destruction of Israel. It is evident that that this type of archaizing, pessimistic warning literature was sometimes posteriorly created, as for instance in Egypt (*The Admonitions of Ipuwer* perhaps being the prime example), but it should stagger the mind of any reasonable person that this could have been the case for such a vast, varied and contradictory work as the Bible.

There is no reason to suppose that the Bible (Old and New Testaments) is utterly free of retrospective pessimistic warning literature and archaizing, manipulative texts. Manipulative retrospective writing was common in the ancient world (and of course still exists today). The story in II Kings 22:8–20 of the discovery of "the book of the law" in the Jerusalem Temple during Josiah's reign (c. 640–609 BC) is reminiscent of the discovery of the "worm-eaten" papyrus of Memphite theology in the Memphis Ptah Temple during Pharaoh Shabako's reign (c. 716–702 BC) and smacks just as much of the likelihood of manipulation. But manipulation or not, it seems difficult to exclude the possibility that King Josiah rewrote or wrote on the basis of earlier Yahweh monotheistic Biblical texts. And all of the Bible, or nearly all, of it, manipulation, an *a posteriori* myth created to justify Jewish national needs?!

Perhaps the view which is the most prudently realistic, while nevertheless taking into account many of the possibilities and memories concerning Egypto-Hebrew religious relations, the figure of Moses, and the Exodus, was made by Jan Assmann (b. 1938) in *Moses The Egyptian, The Memory of Egypt in Western Monotheism*: "I shall not even ask the question — let alone answer it — whether Moses was an Egyptian, or a Hebrew, or a Midianite. This question concerns the historical Moses and thus pertains to history. I am concerned with Moses as a figure of memory... the myth of the Exodus...the Hyksos sojourn in, and withdrawal from, Egypt was all that happened in terms of historical fact...The Egypt of the Bible symbolizes what is rejected, discarded, abandoned...Egypt's role in the Exodus story is not historical but mythical: it helps define the very identity of those who tell the story. Egypt is the womb from which the chosen people emerged, but the umbilical cord was cut once and for all by the Mosaic distinction."[136]

In the final analysis, the entire issue of the origins of the Hebrews and Egypto-Hebrew relations is open to so many interpretations that it is only possible to reasonably speculate. My personal speculation is that available archaeo-

---

136. Assmann, Jan, *Moses The Egyptian, The Memory of Egypt in Western Monotheism*, pp. 11, 7, 41 and 209.

logical evidence tends to show that there was no massive Exodus of Hebrews from Egypt and no massive, organized conquest of Canaan by the Israelites, but that the contextual situation — Biblical descriptions, memories and relics — indicates that something had indeed occurred, that there was a grain of truth in the myth. For me, if an Exodus of Hebrews from Egypt occurred, it was more a matter of emigration of a small group — perhaps the Joseph and Jacob/Israel Clans — rather than a situation of dramatic conflict with the Egyptians. Exacerbated conflict with the Egyptians could have been an embellishment which was added later by the Hebrews to dramatize their great national founding and origins myth, just like the Osiris/Isis/Seth/Horus tales which the Egyptians embellished into a founding myth of origins, theology and national unification. The possible legendary nature of the early Hebrew patriarchs like Abraham, Joseph and Moses is obvious. There is even less evidence to support the existence of a Moses who led the Hebrews out of Egypt and founded Israel than there is to support that of a Pharaoh Menes as the founder of the united Two Lands of Egypt. The best guess seems that the stay and bondage of some Hebrews in Egypt, their Exodus and the conquest of Canaan by the Israelites is a mixture of myth and fact. As to Egypto-Hebrew relations, they quite simply corresponded to Egyptian domination and indifference to relatively unimportant Israel.

Nobody can really answer the question as to whether the origins of the Hebrews were Egyptian, Mesopotamian, Canaanite, *Habiru* or *Shasu*, or whether they were a distinct ethnic group...or whether they were a mixture or a confederation of all these groups.

PREPOSTEROUS THEORIES ABOUT A DIRECT MONOTHEISTIC ATENIST/HEBREW CONNECTION AND A DIRECT MONOTHEISTIC HYKSOS/HEBREW CONNECTION

Despite both the reasonable plausibilities and reasonable doubts about the influence of Atenist monotheism on Hebrew monotheism, the Amarna Period has led to some of the most stupendously wacky theories about Egypt. There is no shortage of wacky theories concerning ancient Egypt, but those concerning Atenism, the Hebrews and the so-called Egyptian origins of Hebrew monotheism surely rank near the top.

These loony theories include a vast fiddling of dates, pushing them both forwards and backwards, usually in relation to Akhenaten as the founder of monotheism and his supposed links to the early monotheistic Hebrews.

Dates are pushed forwards, to place the Hebrew Exodus (myth or partial reality) in Akhenaten's time in the 14th century BC, or to situate Akhenaten in

Saul's, Solomon's or David's times in the 11th and 10th centuries BC, or even in the ninth century BC.

Dates are pushed backwards to situate Akhenaten and Moses around 1550 BC when the Semitic Hyksos (the *Heka-khasut*) were expelled from Egypt, sometimes linking Akhenaten, Moses, the Hyksos and the opening of the Red Sea to a tidal wave caused by the volcanic eruption in Thera Island in the Aegean Cyclades situated around this date, or even further back to the more probable c. 1628 BC date for the Thera eruption. These theories are sometimes accompanied by declarations that the Exodus was composed of or led by monotheistic Egyptians — and not Hebrews — escaping from the polytheistic counterrevolution.

There are also loony theories that Akhenaten was either Moses, Solomon, Jacob, or the legendary King of the Greek city of Thebes, Oedipus, described by Homer (c. eighth century BC?) and then by many others, notably the fifth century BC Greek playwright Sophocles. Other loony theories are that Pharaoh Ay (c. 1327–1323 BC) was somehow linked to the name Yahweh or the Yahweh concept, that Pharaoh Horemheb (c. 1323–1295 BC) was the Hebrew Joseph, etc.

Even Freud got into the act, by devoting a considerable amount of his time between 1934 and 1939 to thinking and writing about Moses and Akhenaten. Freud, who did not have an exhaustive knowledge about Egyptian religion and who relied heavily on the work of James Henry Breasted, admitted that his theses were "conjectures" (the first projected title of the book was *Moses, an Historical Novel*). Nevertheless, in *Moses and Monotheism*, he supposed that Atenism was rigorously monotheistic (it was not), that it rejected images (it did not), that Moses was an Egyptian (which is possible, but unlikely) and that Moses lived in Akhenaten's time, was linked to his royal family as a priest or a nomarch and after the collapse of Atenism became the leader of a people whom he created and named Israel and led into Canaan (all of which, except for the possibility that Moses created the Hebrew nation, is just simply fantasizing or preposterous if for no other reason than the evident discrepancy in the dates between Akhenaten and the Hebrew establishment in Canaan).

Freud further postulated that the Yahweh monotheism Moses preached was in fact Atenism (clearly, a simplification both theologically and morally). And even if Freud rejected simplistic conclusions about the similarity between the Egyptian term "Aten" and the Hebrew term "Adonai" for lord, it does not seem to have crossed his mind why Moses invented *Yhwh*, or Yahweh, instead of simply calling his god Aten.

In *Moses and Monotheism*, Freud also produced a fabulous psychoanalysis about the essence of Mosaic monotheism. Freud supposed that the Hebrews murdered Moses, largely rejected his Atenist monotheism and adopted a system hardly any different from Canaanite Baal worship, and only generations later did a second Moses arise who established authentic monotheism. This fits in well with his theory (first expressed in his *Totem and Taboo*) of the origins of religion and its supposed psychological links to the murder of the primordial father/leader because of his control over all the women in the group, the subsequent feelings of remorse and guilt, the link between feelings of guilt and ethics and their culmination in the deification of the father/ancestor and a peace pact in the group.

However, Freud's theories do not fit with any account in the Bible, including the frequently referred to story in Numbers 25 about Zimri (supposedly a guilt-ridden, disguised name for Moses), the prince of the Simeonites who was slain because of "whoredom" with a Moabite woman and worship of the Moabite god Baalpeor. It also does not tally with countless Biblical texts and several archaeological finds which clearly show an immense struggle between Yahweh/Mosaic henotheism/monotheism and Canaanite polytheism, which lasted centuries.

Freud's genial saving grace in relation to his many silly theories about Atenism and Moses is that despite his fictional presentation and his errors, he drew worldwide attention to the possible influence of Atenism on Hebrew monotheism and to the fact that Atenism was indeed a monotheism — something which was in sharp contrast to the loony theories of a secret or original monotheism in ancient Egypt. Moreover, on an implicit level, he demonstrated the evolutionary and syncretic nature of human beliefs as opposed to notions of divine revelation.

One must also consider the context in which Freud operated. He was one of the founders of modern atheism, but he was attached to his Jewish cultural origins and deeply appalled by anti-Semitism. He may have sought to abolish the singularity of Jewish monotheism and the problems this had created for the Jews by placing monotheism in an evolutionary framework begun in Egypt.

The obvious goal of most of the loony ventures to place Akhenaten, Moses and the Exodus in the same period is to render Hebrew monotheism a direct outcome of Akhenaten's monotheism, or even to make the two identical. Even more frequent have been attempts to assimilate the Hebrews and the Exodus with the mainly Semitic Hyksos immigrants and then conquerors of Egypt.

The Hyksos, who seem to have hailed mainly from Canaan, entered Egypt about 1785 BC and seem to have peacefully mingled with the Egyptians before forcibly establishing the two Hyksos dynasties of the Second Intermediate Period (c. 1650–1550 BC) and incurring the hatred of the Egyptians. Pharaoh Kamose (c. 1555–1550 BC) actively engaged the battle against the Hyksos and they were defeated and expelled from Egypt around 1550 BC by Pharaoh Ahmose I (c. 1550–1525 BC).

A major problem in dealing with the Hyksos is that Egyptians sought to wipe out any record of this detested period of foreign occupation. This was their usual practice — when a pharaoh, a notable or even an entire period of history did not please them, they destroyed everything attached to it and especially hammered out the name, the *ren* soul, of its key personalities. As we have seen, this practice perhaps reached its apex with the monotheistic Akhenaten.

In any case, only one possible contemporary Egyptian pictorial reference to the Hyksos has survived — reliefs in Abydos apparently depicting Ahmose I's war against the Hyksos — and only one contemporary inscription exists concerning the defeat of the Hyksos, that of Ahmose, the son of Abana, Pharaoh Ahmose I's navy commander's, in his tomb in Nekheb (Eileithyiaspolis). It mentions both the siege and destruction of the Hyksos Delta capital of Avaris and the Hyksos city of Sharuhen, near Gaza, in Canaan, but does not use the word *Heka-khasut*, Hyksos. The three earlier inscriptions of Taa II's (c. 1560 BC) and Kamose's battles against the Hyksos and notably the stele of the "Chief Treasurer Neshi," found in Karnak in 1954 by Labib Habachi, also do not refer to Hyksos, but rather to "miserable Asiatics." Neshi's stele also indicates that there could have been an alliance between the Avaris Asiatics and the Kerma Nubians.[137]

A century later Pharaoh Hatshepsut (c. 1473–1458 BC) inscribed on the walls of the Speos Artemidos Temple (dedicated to the "tearer," the lioness goddess Pakhet, near Beni Hasan) that things "had gone to pieces formerly, since the Asiatics were in the midst of Avaris of the Northland, and vagabonds in the midst of them, overthrowing that which had been made. They ruled without Re..."[138] Several texts, centuries later, notably the Sallier I Papyrus (c. 1220 BC) derided the Hyksos as having subjected the Egyptians to vile Asiatic values. However, the slim available evidence tends to prove the contrary — that the Hyksos in fact largely adopted Egyptian religion and customs.

Other related theories are that the Hyksos were monotheistic, or monotheistic Hebrews. The Sallier I Papyrus claims that Seth was the Hyksos' sole god, or at least that the Hyksos Pharaoh Apophis (c. 1555 BC) "served not any god that was in the whole land save only Sutekh (Seth)."[139] The controversial American historian Martin Bernal (b. 1937), in *Black Athena*, supposes it likely that the Hyksos version of Seth was the Jewish Yahweh and that the cult of Poseidon

---

137. Wilson, John in *Ancient Near Eastern Texts Relating to the Old Testament*, pp. 554-555 and 233-234.

138. *Ibid.*, p. 231.

139. Sallier I Papyrus (British Museum 10185), I, 2-3.

introduced in Greece during the 18th century BC corresponded to a Hyksos mixture of the Egyptian god Seth and the Semitic gods Yahweh and Yam.

However, despite these and other similar suppositions, available evidence, including scarabs and cartouches of some Hyksos pharaohs, shows that the Hyksos apparently promoted Seth as their chief god, but also worshipped other Egyptian gods as well as the Syrian god Baal and goddess Anat, imported into Egypt around 1800 BC, and the Syrian goddess Astarte, imported into Egypt around the same time as the Hyksos.

The main attributes of Seth had already been defined in the Pyramid Texts for at least 500 years before the Hyksos entered Egypt. It seems likely that the Hyksos revered Seth because he was a major god in their capital Avaris in the eastern Delta and because he was linked to deserts and foreign lands, rather than because of any link with a Hebrew monotheising influence or a god called Yahweh. Whatever date is used for the Hebrew Exodus — the 16th century, the 15th century or the 13th century BC — the Mosaic naming of the Hebrew god as Yahweh and his clear definition was posterior to the Hyksos conquest of Egypt and their adoption of Seth.

Resemblances between the attributes of Seth and the unnamed Hebrew Abrahamic god also hardly seem to have existed, either before the Hebrew henotheistic god was named Yahweh, or afterwards. In all likelihood, the tetragrammaton name *Yhwh*/Yahweh did not even exist during the Hyksos Period. Moreover, as we have just seen in the previous section, even the sometimes supposed forerunner to *Yhwh*/Yahweh, the *Shasu* Semitic god *Yhw*, cannot be dated with any certainty before the Egyptian pharaoh Amenhotep III (c.1390–1352 BC) and the Hyksos established themselves in Egypt almost 400 years earlier than Amenhotep III reign, around 1785 BC.

It also goes almost without saying that a Hyksos/Seth influence on Aten proto-monotheism, as captivating as it is to some, is a wild, loony theory. There is quite simply not a single mention of Seth in Atenist documents, and the use of this god who incarnated the forces of darkness, even as an example of monotheism, would have been anathema for the monotheistic Atenist religion based on sunlight.

Martin Bernal, using a "Revised Ancient Model" of history (which is almost as doubtful as David Rohl's "New Chronology"), also postulated, in the first volume of *Black Athena*, a probable early 16th century BC date for the Hebrew Exodus and assimilated the Hyksos conquest of Egypt and the sojourn of the Hebrews in Egypt, before postulating, in the second volume, that the Hebrew sojourn in Egypt was based on a folk memory of Hyksos rule in Egypt.

Many Christian and Jewish "historians" have frequently bandied about the theory that the Hebrews were the Hyksos, or a group among the Hyksos, and that they freed themselves or were expelled and then founded the new nation of Israel in Canaan. In order to make these theories work, the usually accepted dates of Egyptian history are fiddled by about 100 years to make the Hyksos expulsion correspond to a c. 1450 BC Exodus, or despite the contradictions in the Bible, the Hebrew traditionalist date of c. 1550 Exodus is used in conjunction with the defeat and the expulsion of the Hyksos from Egypt.

Early Egypto-Hebrew relations and the rise of monotheism would become uncannily clear if the Hyksos were tossed into the equation. We would even have some archaeological evidence of destruction caused by a war of invasion in Canaan. However, of all the numerous theories concerning the origins of Israelites, it is the one that can be most easily dismissed. The likelihood is that there was no direct link beyond possible Semitic cousinhood between the Hyksos and the Hebrews (who were in all probability not even a group with any easily distinguishable identity during the heyday of the Hyksos from the 18th to the late 16th centuries BC). Even assuming a *Habiru*/Hebrew connection, not even the beginnings of tangible proof can be found for a common ethnic identity between the obviously sophisticated Hyksos capable of ruling Egypt and the rustic warrior/bandit *Habiru*. Cousinhood between the Hyksos and the Canaanites seems to be far more evident than any Hyksos/*Habiru* link or Hyksos/Hebrew link.

The "Hyksos are the Hebrews" advocates frequently point to the use of the name Jacob by the Hyksos (and notably to the Hyksos Pharaoh Yaqub-Har, c. 1650–1633 BC), but this does not prove that they were Hebrews — merely that they, like other Semitic peoples, including the Hebrews, used this name. As to a monotheising Hyksos influence on Egypt, there is not much of anything except supposition, fantasy and even a loony attitude to support such views.

The fiddling, or inaccuracy, to associate the Hebrews and the Hyksos perhaps began with the postulations, errors or fantasies of the third century BC Egyptian priest/historian Manetho. As we have seen, Josephus (AD c. 37–100) cites Manetho as believing that the Jews were the descendants of the Hyksos who had defeated the Egyptians and were then in turn "driven out of the land...to the city called Jerusalem." Of course, Josephus adhered both to the Biblical tale of Joseph in Egypt and the Exodus and agreed with Manetho that the Hyksos were the ancestors of the Hebrews who had "dominion" over the Egyptians.

Josephus also believed that Hyksos, the Greek word for *Heka-khasut*, signified "captive shepherds" (i.e., the captive Hebrew shepherds). He also directly quoted Manetho as believing that the word Hyksos meant "shepherd kings" or "captives" and that they were the same people who founded Judea. In fact, there can be no doubt that Hyksos meant *rulers of foreign* lands, or *peoples*.

It is easy enough to see that Josephus' erroneous interpretation was obviously made to support his link between the Hyksos and the Hebrew people, who were then primarily a people of shepherds. On the other hand, Manetho's supposed description is mysterious at best. Although Manetho also noted that "some say [the Hyksos] were Arabians"[140] (which seemingly contradicts his own view that they were Jews), it remains difficult to understand why he called them "shepherds." Manetho must have certainly been aware that the term *Heka-khasut*, Hyksos, had been used by Egyptians since the Middle Kingdom (c. 2055–1650 BC), along with other terms, to designate the heads of the Asiatic nomadic groups along Egypt's eastern border, rather than to exclusively designate the two Hyksos dynasties of the Second Intermediate Period (c. 1650–1550 BC). It seems that the use of the term Hyksos to uniquely designate the Asian people of these two dynasties probably began with Manetho.

Many historians, would-be pundits and esoteric loonies have also used a probable fiddling of dates to postulate a link between various real or imaginary natural disasters and the Hyksos, the Hebrews, the Exodus and the parting of the Red Sea.

Until recently, it seemed that first prize in the field of fiddlers of Egyptian and Hebrew history went to the American Immanuel Velikovsky (1895–1979). In *Worlds in Collision* and *Ages in Chaos: A Reconstruction of Ancient History from the Exodus to King Akhnaton*, Velikovsky fiddled much of Egyptian chronology by about 600 to 800 years and postulated as historical facts that the Red Sea was opened in the mid-15th century BC in connection with the Hebrew Exodus from Egypt. This event was supposedly caused by a comet born in the Jupiter system which interfered with the Earth and Mars, causing widespread natural disasters in Egypt, Canaan, Greece and elsewhere and the sun to rise in the west and set in the east, before our solar system was stabilized with the comet from Jupiter giving birth to the planet Venus. In an extremely muddled way, Velikovsky also postulated that the Hebrews left Egypt a few days before the expulsion of the Hyksos, encountered and fought these Hyksos (who were the Amalekites) and liberated Egypt.

Perhaps the Velikovsky theory which most defies all available knowledge is that Akhenaten was Oedipus and lived in the ninth century BC and therefore was certainly not the first monotheist. This wild theory eliminates any possibility of Egyptian influence on Hebrew monotheism. It has been interpreted by some as a Zionist reaction by Velikovsky to enhance the Hebrew contribution to the history of mankind and to castigate what he considered as Freud's denigration of the Hebrew role in founding monotheism.

Many scientists have credibly refuted Velikovsky's "scientific" theories, notably Carl Sagan.[141] Velikovsky's serious discrepancies and contradictions

---

140. Josephus, Flavius, *Against Apion*, 1.14, 1.73, 1.223 and 1.227.

with ancient Egyptian, Mesopotamian and Hebrew texts have also been widely castigated by historians. In the final analysis, it seems that Velikovsky, a Jungian psychiatrist, employed an erudite system of transforming ancient mythological texts, fantasies and religious obscurantism into "facts," exacerbating the system used by Jung.

Since Velikovsky's death, a serious contender for first prize among the fiddlers of Egypto-Hebrew connections has emerged — the Egyptian writer Ahmed Osman (b. 1934), who has also fiddled Christian history. In *Out of Egypt, the Roots of Christianity Revealed* and other books, Osman goes right off the wall, postulating a marriage in the early 15th century BC between Pharaoh Thutmose III and Abraham's wife Sarah, which was the origin of a long series of mixed-blood Egyptian leaders whom the Hebrews later disguised as being strictly their own leaders. Thutmose III was also David; Yuya, the vizier of Thutmose IV and Amenhotep III, was Joseph; Amenhotep III was Solomon; Akhenaten was Moses; Nefertiti was Moses' sister Miriam who was the mother of Tutankhamun, who was Joshua, that is really Jesus.

Freud's phantasms concerning Numbers 25 are mere child's play compared to Osman, who claims that neither Zimri nor Moses was slain, but that it was Tutankhamun/Joshua/Jesus...and this is why there is no independent historical evidence of Jesus in the first century AD — Jesus had already been slain 1200 years earlier by Akhenaten/Moses' high priest Panehsy, who in Hebrew was Phineas, and in fact, according to Osman, the early Christians were expecting the second coming of Joshua/Jesus/Tutankhamun.

One might suppose that with Osman, the limits were reached in the fiddling of Egypto-Hebrew/Christian relations. In fact, the human spirit can always go further in this sad exercise — in September 2000, two Frenchmen, the brothers Messod and Roger Sabbah (b. 1935 and b. 1955), broke the sound barrier with *Les Secrets du l'Exode, L'Origine égyptienne des Hébreux*. They rehashed the ancient theories of Apion, Chaeremon, Strabo, Diodorus Siculus, Tacitus and others concerning the Egyptian origin of the Hebrews, added a dash of Freud's views concerning the direct link between Akhenaten's Aten monotheism and Hebrew monotheism, used Redford's theory of the Exodus/expulsion of the Hyksos appropriated by the Hebrew/Canaanite memory, applied it to an Exodus of Atenists to Canaan and adopted the pseudo-erudite pose of the recent authors of loony theories concerning the Egyptians and the Hebrews. They above all added a few new bits of nonsense by claiming that Abraham was not only an Egyptian, but that he was in fact Akhenaten! According to the "certitudes" of the Sabbah brothers, the Hebrews were the Egyptian monotheistic followers of Akhenaten/

---

141. Sagan, Carl, *Cosmos*, Random House, New York, 1980, pp. 90-91.

Abraham, who made a deal with the rulers of the restored Egyptian polytheistic regime to leave the city of Akhetaten and settle in the Egyptian province of Canaan. Moreover, Sarah was Nefertiti, Isaac was Tutankhamun but also symbolically Akhenaten, Jacob was also symbolically Akhenaten, Joseph was Ay, Joshua was Sety I, etc. Roger Sabbah says that he "is certain to have found the secret meaning of the Bible" (which had been) "re-written...during the sixty years of the exile in Babylonia...to camouflage the Egyptian origin of the Hebrews."[142]

All these loony cases would not be complete without adding a bit of abjectness. This indeed occurred in February 2001, when Egyptian authorities went back on a promise to allow two Japanese universities to extract DNA samples from Tutankhamun's and Amenhotep III's mummies in order to determine whether Tutankhamun was Amenhotep III's son. This decision came after a campaign in the Egyptian press denouncing a Zionist plot to expropriate the Egyptian heritage and attempts "to tamper with Egyptian history."[143]

None of this harsh condemnation of loony theories is meant to construe that the Amarna period and Atenist theology and their relation to Hebrew monotheism are crystal clear, nor even that there are not many unknowns about them. Just as there is no clear conclusion concerning many difficult questions about almost the entirety of Egyptian history, there are also quite logically no answers to many questions concerning the Amarna Period and especially such a complex problem as its possible relation to Hebrew monotheism.

None of the unknown or mysterious elements of the Amarna Period are sufficient to impede reasonable suppositions concerning the probable influences Atenism exercised on Hebrew monotheism. Nevertheless, almost all of the romantic, loony theories about direct Atenist/Hebrew links can usually be easily rejected — just as easily as the loony theories about a Hyksos/Hebrew link can be rejected.

THE TEMPTATION TO SEE A MONOTHEISING CROSS-FERTILIZATION BETWEEN EGYPT, BABYLONIA, THE *SHASU*, THE *HABIRU*, CANAAN/ISRAEL AND THE JUDEO-CHRISTIANS

It is tempting, and it would be very logically satisfying, to conclude that the development of monotheism — at least on the level of the reduction of many gods to a single god — was due to a kind of gradual cross-fertilization involving

---

142. www.soirillustre.be/3573egypte.html
143. Agence France Presse (AFP), 12/13/2000.

Egypt, Babylonia, the *Shasu*/Israelites or the *Habiru*/Israelites, the Canaanites and emerging Israelite religious concepts. Using this type of speculation, the culminating points in this evolution would be Judean sixth century BC exclusive monotheism and first century AD Christian multiform monotheism. However, the facts just do not exist to establish such a thesis.

Despite the archaeological finds of a huge number of Egyptian, Babylonian/ Assyrian, Canaanite and Phoenician and many Hebrew and Aramaic inscriptions and the descriptions in the Hebrew and Christian Bibles, a monotheising cross-fertilization can at best only be plausibly supposed; it cannot be proven.

References to monotheising influences between Egypt, Babylonia and/or the Hebrews have never been found. There are frequent references to Egypt's religious, ethical, political and social systems by the writers of the Old and New Testaments, but not a single reference can even be vaguely interpreted as awareness of Egyptian Amunism chief god theology and Aten primitive monotheism and only a single reference can be vaguely interpreted in the sense of an Egyptian monotheising influence.

This single vaguely possible textual concordance between Egypt and Judeo-Christian monotheism is Acts 7:22 — "And Moses was learned in all the wisdom of the Egyptians..." Without totally dismissing this possibility and its implications, it has to be very seriously tempered by the fact that the presumed author of Acts, Luke (fl.c. AD 70–90), placed this declaration within the context of a repetition of the essential elements of the myths of Abraham, the Hebrew sojourn, bondage and Exodus from Egypt. Was Luke merely repeating and amplifying the Old Testament tradition (Exodus 11:3) — true or false — that Moses "was very great in the land of Egypt..."? Or was he obliquely indicating that old Hebrew and emerging Christian monotheism were somehow based on Egyptian teachings?

Nevertheless, of all the possible monotheising influences, Egyptian influence on Hebrew monotheism is the one most difficult to reject; which of course implies at least an indirect Egyptian influence on Christianity (as we shall see in Chapter 14). It seems very difficult to assume that the Hebrews' and Christian Israel's detailed knowledge of Egypt excluded the domains of Amun monotheising tendencies and Aten primitive monotheism. If Moses, or somebody like him, existed and if the Moses tale is even just partially factual, it would indeed be likely that such a Moses would have been influenced by the chief god characteristic of traditional Egyptian religion as well as the Aten monotheistic heresy and indeed it would be possible that he would have incorporated some of these teachings in his new religion.

However, the contrary — Hebrew monotheistic influence on Egypt — seems highly unlikely, even though here, too, such a wild view has been postulated. The Swiss alchemist/physician Paracelsus (1493–1541) claimed that Abraham had transmitted monotheism to the Egyptians, who in turn transmitted it to Moses. As we have seen, the legendary nature of Abraham, the incertitude about early Hebrew dates and the single certain Egyptian mention of early Israel all plead against Hebrew monotheistic influence on Egypt. Moreover, the likeliest probability remains that the fruit of Egyptian monotheising tendencies — the Aten proto-monotheistic system — was largely established without foreign influence. As discussed above, Atenism seems to have been a logical consequence of the monotheising super Chief God Re solar cult Heliopolitan theology revised by Theban Amun-Re theology and radicalized by Akhenaten. Realistically, perhaps the only foreign element which played a role in Atenism was the rise of a more universalist attitude in Egypt during the New Kingdom, from 1550 BC, due to Egypt's conquests and increased contacts with foreigners; but even this has to be tempered due to the traditional Egyptian attitude of arrogance.

Despite the lack of evidence, the minimal likelihood, for me, remains that with or without Moses and with or without a major and long sojourn of Hebrews in Egypt, somehow Egyptian monotheising tendencies, Amun-Re chief god theology, Aten proto-m and perhaps Ptah theology influenced Israel on the theological level. The discovery of a huge amount of Egyptian religious objects in Canaan and the existence of several temples, notably an Amun-Re Temple in Beth Shan and a Ptah Temple in Ashkelon in the late New Kingdom, indicate continued early Hebrew proximity to the Egyptian religion at the very least, and possibly a direct monotheising influence. After the late eighth century BC, the monotheising aspects of the Ptah/Memphite theology could have also influenced the Hebrews and then the Christians.

However, it must be reiterated, as we have seen in Chapter 11, that the only prominent modern Egyptologist who believes that "the history of cultural memory" shows that there was a direct link between Atenism and Mosaic monotheism is German Egyptologist Jan Assmann (b. 1938). Most Egyptologists rightly believe that no Egyptian-Hebrew monotheistic cross-fertilization can be substantiated by firm evidence — and, as already noted, some Egyptologists like Erik Hornung do not see any monotheising influences in Egypt aside from Atenism; many Egyptologists, like Nicolas Grimal and Claire Lalouette, do not even believe that Atenism was a monotheism; and some Egyptologists like Donald Redford and Grimal postulate an entirely separate and exclusively Semitic development of authentic monotheism. Grimal notably and adamantly dismisses the supposition that "Atenism lies at the roots of Christianity, when in fact it does nothing more than reflect the common ground of Semitic civilizations." [144]

A series of similar problems arise when trying to analyze a Babylonian Marduk chief god monotheising influence on Israel or mutual chief god influences between Mesopotamia and Egypt. Here, aside from the Biblical account of a Mesopotamian origin of the Hebrews — which proves nothing in itself — and attested and frequent contact between Egypt and Mesopotamia from at least 3500 BC, there is even less possibility for reasonable speculation.

Nevertheless, it cannot be simply assumed that Israel was impervious to monotheising developments involving the amalgamation of gods practiced by the great powers of Egypt and Babylon/Assyria which surrounded and frequently vassalized it. The Egyptian Amun and the Babylonian Marduk were the foremost examples of this phenomenon and the early Yahweh operated in much the same way. Nor can it be simply assumed that the Aten sole god experiment in Egypt or the Ptah/Memphite theology could have been completely without effect on either the early Israelites or the Judeo-Christians, or even the Greeks. As we have also seen, and even though comparisons are not in themselves proofs, there are considerable similarities between Osiris and Horus and Jesus, Isis and Mary, and the Egyptian organic triad of Amun/Re/Ptah and the Christian Trinity. We shall also soon see that there are similarities between the Christian Trinity and Memphite theology and Genesis, Isaiah's and John the Apostle's teaching and the Greek concept of the *logos*.

It can also be reasonably assumed that, at the very least, chief god theological tendencies in Egypt and Mesopotamia made this option reasonably comfortable in both zones without overtly threatening polytheism. During the New Kingdom, the attenuation of Egypt's traditional religious arrogance of great assurance in its theology, also leaves open the possibility of influence — as the importation of several Asian gods into Egypt and the exportation of Egyptian deities and religious concepts throughout West Asia and notably in Canaan during this period proves. Egypt may well have been the center of gravity of chief god theology in the New Kingdom Egypto-West Asian continuum. On the other hand, the brief and unusual exception of Atenist proto-monotheism to the general polytheistic rule in Egypto-West Asia continuum may have influenced only the Israelites.

Concerning Canaan, direct Egyptian influence on this staunchly polytheistic society was primarily concerned with which of their gods were added to the Canaanite pantheon, usually with only limited or temporary success. Egypt's chief god theology may have also influenced Canaanite henotheistic and chief god theology based on the gods El and Baal.

---

144. Grimal, Nicolas, *A History of Ancient Egypt*, p. 228.

A Canaanite role in a supposed monotheistic cross-fertilization process does not seem to have been possible. Whether or not the Israelites emerged from the Canaanites, Canaanite influence on the Israelites was polytheistic and seems to have constituted one of the principal obstacles and temptations the Israelites had to overcome in finally establishing monotheism. The Israelites had to struggle for centuries with Canaanite gods and goddesses, especially Baal and Asherah, and with Canaanite religious practices such as idolatry, child sacrifice and temple prostitution before definitely rejecting them. Whatever the extent of Canaanite religious practices among the early Israelites, Yahweh henotheism or near-monotheism and its linked rigid morality were clearly the Israelite ideals and these ideals represented a radical religious break with the Canaanites, rather than a continuation.

Concerning the *Shasu* and the *Habiru*, we have seen that they had Mesopotamian links, that they were frequently in Egypt as nomads, traders, prisoners and slaves, that there could have been some kind of a Yahweh or pre-Yahweh connection to the *Shasu* and that some of the *Habiru* could have adopted a henotheistic Yahweh as a key element in their search for national (Israelite) identity. But none of this seems to have had much to do with the emergence of authentic monotheism.

Certainly, it is possible to assume a totally independent evolution towards monotheising chief god theology in both Egypt and Mesopotamia and a totally independent evolution towards monotheism in Israel.

It can be argued that the seed of monotheism was contained within the Semitic nomadic-shepherd mentality and that Israel carried it to its logical conclusion. In antique times, monotheism seems to have been more adapted to the Semitic mentality. It was Semitic Jews who first spread Christian monotheism and in later times, the Semitic Arabs enthusiastically adopted monotheism. However, a similar monotheistic type of logical conclusion was reached by the Indo-European Zoroastrians in the religion they brought to a flowering in the sixth century BC. They too operated under the influence of a shepherd culture, even if they became opposed to nomads and in favor of urban society. But it also must be noted that near-monotheistic Zoroastrianism switched back to forms of disguised henotheism and polytheism after less than 100 years.

And yet despite this possible independent chain of events, the lack of formal evidence, the unknown elements and even the improbabilities, it remains somehow impossible to dismiss outright some kind of mutual monotheising influence at least between the Egyptians, the Babylonians, the Hebrews and the Judeo-Christians. A cross-fertilization of this type could have taken place insidiously, inconspicuously, but its effects could have been nonetheless powerful in much the same way as there is no known trace of the life and concepts of Jesus in the Hebrew, Greek and Roman documents of his time, but the consequential influence of monotheistic Jesus on the Jews, the Greeks and the Romans was enormous.

The Israelites lived in a sea of polytheism and had to fight against the tide to establish monotheism, both within their nation and within their international environment. It remains reasonable to postulate that the final stage, the need to transform Mesopotamian and Egyptian polytheism and monotheising tendencies into authentic monotheism, including its fundamental moral aspects, first arose in Israel, but that this could not have occurred without influences.

It seems that the least that can be said was that there was a groping about and there were aspirations towards monotheism before authentic monotheism was actually established by Israel in the sixth century BC. This plausibly could have taken place through the intermediary of henotheism, chief god theology and proto-monotheism, notably with the Egyptian Re, Amun-Re, Aten and Ptah/Memphite theologies, the Mesopotamian gods Sin and Marduk, Abraham's nameless god, perhaps the Semitic Yahu and Moses' Yahweh. This groping towards monotheism even seems, to some extent, to have affected staunchly polytheistic Greece with notions like the *logos* and some temptations to see a sole pantheistic-type god. The triumph of monotheism involved many battles over thousands of years and although it may not have been inevitable, it was certainly not an illogical triumph.

Despite the dissenting voices, it is clear that the earliest known monotheising tendencies began in Egypt with chief god theology and the earliest form of monotheism began in Egypt with Atenism. Moreover, the monotheising tendencies of Ptah/Memphite theology could have exercised significant international influence after the late eighth century BC. The possible spread of these Egyptian tendencies largely remains mysterious and some kind of cross-fertilization cannot be dismissed simply because there is no evidence for it.

As much as there can be no doubt about the Hebrew influence on Christianity and Islam, the Egyptian influence on forms of Greek and Roman religion and notably the Isis and Osiris cults — or, in another vein, the Greek influence on Roman religion, or the Hindu influence on Buddhism — the influence of Egypt on Hebrew monotheism and a possible monotheising cross-fertilization in the Middle-East culminating in authentic monotheism must remain questions. Nevertheless, as long as one does not draw definitive conclusions, the main question that must be posed is, how could the Hebrews not have been influenced by the Egyptians?

Chapter 13. The Apex of Egyptian Power and Its Subsequent Decline

The New Kingdom — The Apex of Egyptian Power in All Domains

The New Kingdom, which had been opened by the Eighteenth Dynasty and the expulsion of the hated foreign Hyksos conquerors, rapidly became the apex of Egyptian power and inventiveness in all domains — political, economic, imperialistic, technological, religious, architectural, artistic, literary.

By the early years of his reign, Thutmose I (c. 1504–1492 BC) had stretched the borders of the Egyptian Empire to their greatest historical extent — from Kurgus below the Fourth Cataract of the Nile deep in Nubia to Carchemish on the Euphrates in Mesopotamia. From year one of his effective reign, in c. 1458 BC, Thutmose III (c. 1479–1425 BC) consolidated these territorial gains in 16 military campaigns over 20 years. With the exception of Nubia, which was directly ruled by Egyptians, Egypt ruled using a system of usually loyal, Egyptianized vassal city-state kinglets, sometimes supported by small detachments of Egyptian troops.

Egypt's strange concoction of an unbending polytheistic spirit and chief god solar theology had led to the rise of one of history's strongest chief, monotheising and universalist gods, Amun-Re. It also led to the constitution of the most powerful, richest and biggest temple and clerical complex ever seen, *Ipet-isut/Ipet-resyt*, Karnak-Luxor, as well as one of the greatest necropolis afterlife complexes ever built, the huge rock-cut tombs of the Valley of Kings and its annexed necropolises for royal wives, notables and craftsmen.

Just as the Old Kingdom (c. 2686–2181 BC) had been the time of great pyramid complexes, the New Kingdom was the time of great temples, rock-cut tombs and palaces. In addition to Karnak-Luxor, this age saw the building of such fabulous temples as Abu Simbel in Nubia, the Hatshepsut mortuary temple, the Amenhotep III mortuary temple; the Colossi of Memnon, the Malqata Palace and the Rameses II Ramessum mortuary temple on the west bank of Thebes/ Luxor; and the extension of the Ptah Temple in Memphis. The megalomaniac Rameses II not only completed the hypostyle hall of Karnak and built Abu Simbel and five other temples in Nubia, he also built a fabulous new capital in the Delta, Pi-Ramesse, with palaces, temples, lakes, granaries, warehouses and farms. Pi-Ramesse appears to have covered an area of nearly 2500 acres and was probably one of the largest cities in the world, in its time. The Sety I and Rameses II cenotaph temples in Abydos must also be mentioned, not only because of their particularly beautiful decorations but because they provide us with invaluable information about Osirisian rituals and two Kings' Lists of about 60 of the predecessors of Sety I and Rameses II, including tell-tale omissions like Akhenaten.

Much of the specificity of the Egyptian religion was brought to fruition in these New Kingdom developments — chief god solar theology within polytheism, monotheising tendencies, divine kingship, theocracy, monumental art and architecture as the key instrument of religious expression and, of course, mummification, afterlife beliefs, the complex system of several companion souls and an immense amount of funerary writings. With the 66-year reign of Rameses II (c. 1279–1213 BC), the longest in Egyptian history, Egyptians could even almost believe that individual eternal divine kingship was a matter of this world and not only the afterlife.

After the closing of the brief period of disorder created by Pharaoh Akhenaten's attempt to impose Aten monotheism, Pharaoh Horemheb restored order at home and Sety I (c. 1294–1279 BC) and Rameses II restored Egypt's imperial power, immense economic prosperity and splendor in the arts and architecture, especially in temple and tomb building. Aten proto-monotheism was the last attempt to rectify, or organize, the confusion of the Egyptian religious system; despite religious developments elsewhere in the world, Egypt would now stubbornly maintain chief god theology within polytheism until the end of Egypt.

By the mid-13th century BC Late Bronze Age, the immensity of Egyptian domination can easily be ascertained by a comparison with the rest of the world.

Since at least 1458 BC, and perhaps even from Thutmose I's reign (c. 1504–1479 BC), Egypt was the greatest imperial power and perhaps even for the first time in history it embodied the notion of a universal power.

In the entire developed world, polytheism was the religious system and Egypt's polytheistic system was the most sophisticated.

In art, architecture and literature, no people matched the production and splendor of Egypt.

In technology, Egypt together with Sumer and the eastern Mediterranean lands were the world leaders. Immense mastery had been achieved in bronze working, carpentry, glass making and faience. High yield agriculture and an extensive irrigation, canal and dam system were in vogue. The *shaduf* irrigation device, which had been introduced into Egypt in the 18th century BC by the Hyksos, was widespread. The Egyptians were also one of the world leaders in the strategic domain of the horse-drawn military chariot, the *wereryet*, also introduced by the Hyksos.

China became the world leader in the casting of bronze vessels, but both China and Japan were still not on the same overall level of technological and agricultural religious development as Egypt and both were still immersed in ancestor worship.

Meanwhile, the Mohenjo-Dara and Harappa civilizations in the Indus Valley had collapsed. The Vedic Iranian and Hindu civilizations were still in their primitive stages with the full flowering of the Hindu society and religion still 350 years into the future. Persia as such was not even on the map, but 800 years later it would constitute a great empire from the Indus River to Libya and would occupy Egypt for more than 125 years.

The Americas and Africa lagged behind in an overall way and much of Western Europe and North Africa were just beginning to become efficient in bronze techniques. The most famous Western European architectural endeavor of the time, Stonehenge (begun c. 2900 BC, completed c. 1500 BC), at 330 feet in diameter, could fit into a small section of any of several Egyptian temples and its rough-hewn stone technology was more than a thousand years behind Egyptian masonry technology.

And yet there were ominous, rumbling signs that Egyptian domination would soon come to an end.

The Hittite and Assyrian victory over Egypt's ally, Mitanni, between c. 1370 and 1365 BC, was a serious rupture in the balance of power in the West Asian *Retjenu*. Rameses II did not obtain a decisive victory against the Hittites at Kadesh along the Orontes River in c. 1274 BC. In face of growing Assyrian power, he needed allies of sorts and was eventually forced to share power in the Levant with the Hittites, allowing them to rule Upi and Amarru provinces, while Egypt ruled Canaan. Both the Egyptian and the Hittite versions of the peace treaty signed between the two nations clearly indicate that there was no Egyptian victory, but rather a non-aggression pact, a defensive alliance and power sharing.[145]

A new tool — a superior form of writing — was being developed by Minoan Crete and Mycenaean Greece. In turn, this would soon be surpassed by the invention of alphabetic writing by the Phoenicians in the 11th century BC. This development pushed Egypt into the rearguard in a vital domain.

Greece was in an early formative stage, but in the sixth century BC would invent the philosophical-scientific instrument which would destroy magical thinking and religion, which were the core realities of Egypt. And Greece would eventually occupy Egypt (c. 332 BC) and become the politico-military-cultural instrument which would destroy the Egyptian Egypt.

Israel was not yet born, but the Hebrews were at the beginning of a new, linked religious and ethical system — Yahweh monotheism and *tsadaquah*, righteousness and justice — which over the succeeding 1600 years would eventually sweep more than half of polytheism and almost all nationalistic ethics off the planet.

Perhaps the key to the end of Egypt's glory was that while Egypt was unquestionably influenced in all domains by the peoples of its empire, it was not influenced enough. As the world around it changed, Egypt stubbornly remained a curious mixture of an arrogant island unto itself, a crossroads, the self-proclaimed center of the world inhabited by a people favored and blessed by the gods, part of an Egypto-West Asian continuum, an imperialist power in the Levant, the annexionist of the African land of Nubia and a staunch supporter of theocratic polytheism which eventually skidded into religious totalitarianism, fundamentalism, fanaticism and extreme zoolatry.

For at least 250 years from 1458 BC, Egypt had been the world's greatest power. It remained a major, but shaky, world power for another 150 years until the closing years of the Twentieth Dynasty (c. 1186–1069 BC).

POLITICAL, MILITARY, RELIGIOUS AND ARTISTIC DECLINE FROM THE 12TH CENTURY BC

By the mid-12th century BC, Egypt was already in decline and by the closing decades and the collapse of the New Kingdom and the beginning of the Third Intermediary Period (c. 1069 BC), this decline became deeply embedded. This was the case not only from the standpoint of religious experimentation and innovation, but also politically, economically, militarily, architecturally and

---

145. Wilson, John and Goetze, Albrecht in *Ancient Near Eastern Texts Relating to the Old Testament*, pp. 199-203.

artistically. The way to the religious and political decadence of the Late Period (from c. 747 BC) had been opened.

Rameses III (c. 1184–1153 BC) was the last of the old-style powerful, imperial pharaohs, capable of great deeds in war and architecture and capable of more or less controlling or buying off the various powerful clergies. From the reign of Rameses IV (c. 1153–1147 BC), the power of both royalty and the civil administration gradually fell into disarray. A succession of pharaohs called Rameses rivaled each other in ineffectual rule. Perhaps, one of the key barometers of this decline was in Egypt's central way of expression, architecture and art — major construction activities became increasingly rare and art increasingly became an exercise of soulless repetition. Egypt also became increasingly dominated by a corrupt temple economic system, especially by the Theban Amun-Re clergy, who also wielded immense religious fundamentalist power.

Massive attacks and migrations led by Meshwesh and Libu from Libya and the Indo-European "Sea Peoples," including Greeks and Philistines, had been repulsed in c. 1209 and c. 1176, by Merenptah (c. 1213–1203 BC) and Rameses III, but the Egyptians were exhausted and lost their direct role as a world and colonial power. Eventually, they could not prevent the settlement of Libyan Meshwesh and Libu immigrants in Egypt and the Libyan prisoners they had forced to live in Egypt became a powerful community. These Libyan prisoners and immigrants may not have been barbarians and were certainly not "perverts," as Rameses III (c. 1184–1153) claimed, but they were certainly far less culturally evolved than the Egyptians and progressively dragged down the religious, political and social structures of the country.

In the reign of the last pharaoh of the New Kingdom, Rameses XI (c. 1099–1069 BC), Upper Egypt fell to generals led by Amun-Re priests operating from Thebes who were perhaps also of Libyan origin and who were assisted by Libyan Meshwesh troops. Herihor (fl.c. 1075 BC), who had been sent into Thebes by Rameses XI to put down a rebellion, went over to the rebels and got himself named First Prophet of the Amun-Re clergy. Egypt was *de facto* divided into autonomous zones with the weak Rameses XI controlling the Memphis region, his future successor Smendes in control of Lower Egypt and Herihor in control of Upper Egypt and of the Nubian provinces of Wawat and Kush.

Herihor, as the First Prophet of the Amun-Re clergy, already one of the powerful posts in Egypt for several centuries, was now unquestionably stronger than the reigning pharaoh. At several periods in Egyptian history, the Great Seer of the Heliopolis Re clergy in its heyday in the Fourth and Fifth Dynasties (c. 2613–2345 BC), or the First Prophet of the Thebes Amun-Re clergy, had sometimes been a close second in power to the reigning pharaoh; but now the priests seem to have become more powerful than the pharaohs. A.H. Gardiner has pointed out that the fact that Amenhotep, the Amun-Re First Prophet in the time of Rameses IXth (c. 1126–1108 BC), was depicted in an image as being as tall and as big as the pharaoh was already an indication that he was equal to the pharaoh and perhaps even stronger in the south.[146]

However, with Herihor, a new theocratic stage had been reached. He incarnated all the religious and political powers of the state and a considerable portion of its economic resources. Herihor even had his *shenu* cartouches with their royal titularies. Herihor also transmitted his title in a hereditary manner and one of his descendants as First Prophet, Pinudjem I (fl.c. 1050 BC) also put his nomen and prenomem in cartouches and virtually claimed status as a pharaoh.

Always the most totalizing and amalgamating (and, of course, the most monotheising) theology in Egyptian history, the Theban Amun-Re theology now degenerated into religious, political and economic totalitarianism, fundamentalism and fanaticism. Herihor, using Amun-Re theology and the military clout of the Libyan generals, virtually ruled Upper Egypt and Nubia as a quasi-independent state in which politics was strictly a religious domain.

During the beginning of the Third Intermediary Period (c. 1069-747 BC), the priests in the great temples of Karnak and Luxor continued ruling Upper Egypt as a quasi-independent theocratic state. They continued this tendency when pharaohs ruling from Tanis and Bubastis in the Delta were too weak to control Upper Egypt and with ups and downs throughout this period, the Theban clergy manifested its thirst for independent fundamentalist power.

In c. 945 BC, the descendants of Libyan Meshwesh and Libu prisoners of war, mercenaries and immigrants, who had become religiously Egyptian, took over in Bubastis in the Delta and reunited Egypt (and, of course, they particularly revered Bastet, the cat goddess of Bubastis). Their leader, Pharaoh Sheshonq I (c. 945–924 BC), opened the Libyan 22nd Dynasty. For the next 200 years, Libyan pharaohs ruled from Bubastis and Tanis in 22nd and 23rd dynasties, but frequently they did not rule the entire country. During Takelot II's reign (c. 850–825 BC), the Theban clergy resorted to civil war to impose their independence. During the 23rd and 24th Dynasties (c. 818–715 BC), Egypt was beset with phases of anarchy and was carved up into zones of influence run by ephemeral and rival pharaohs, priests and minor princes from several cities. Kushite invaders in c. 747 BC put an end to Libyan rule, ended the Third Intermediate Period and gradually reestablished the political unity of Egypt. The Kushite/Nubians, who believed that the origins of Amun were in Nubia, ruled in his name, but attempted to rule with a policy of conservative, restored, traditional Amun-Re values.

---

146. Gardiner, Alan, *Egypt of the Pharaohs*, pp. 298-299.

The year 945 BC was a watershed in Egyptian history. After more than 2000 years of power and innovation, Egypt had basically become a foreign-ruled or occupied country and only relatively brief periods of authentic political independence and relative cultural and religious recovery would occur in the future. On its own and under the rule of foreign occupiers, Egypt continued to play key roles among the world's political and economic leaders, but the great times of religious and artistic experimentation and innovation had ended.

THE KUSHITE AND SAITE DYNASTIES ATTEMPT TO REVITALIZE EGYPT

During the period of Kushite domination of Egypt from about 747 to 656 BC, with the 25th Dynasty ruling from Napata, in Kush, Egypt was a single state stretching from the Mediterranean Sea to Meroe in what today is Sudan.

The goal of the Nubians was the renaissance of Egypt, but they succeeded only very partially, and obviously, never came near to equaling the glory of earlier periods. However, the power of Egypt remained great and it continued to play a key political and economic role in the Middle East, rivaled only by Assyria.

The kings in Kush, beginning with Kashta (c. 770–747 BC), were even more culturally and religiously Egyptian than the Kushites in general had already been for centuries. Kashta battled with the Egyptians and his son, Pharaoh Piye (Piankhy, ruled c. 747–716 BC), founded the 25th Kushite Dynasty in Egypt. Piye had to put down resistance in Thebes, Heracleopolis, Hermopolis and Memphis and notably defeat the forces of Pharaoh Tefnakhte of the 24th Saite Dynasty before the Kushites were able to firmly establish their rule.

The *Victory Stele of Piye* (found in the Napata Amun Temple in 1862, and now in the Cairo Museum), shows that the Nubians' victory was not easy; and it illustrates how totally Egyptianized Piye was and shows that he had the best interests of Egypt at heart. On the *Victory Stele*, Piye said: "Hear what I did, exceeding the ancestors, I the King, image of god...Who left the womb marked as ruler...Piye beloved of Amun." Piye has to encourage his generals to fight ardently against Egyptian resistance and tells them to inform the Egyptians that "Amun is the god who sent us!" Piye usually forgave the kinglets who opposed him, but only after confiscating their belongings, treasures and horses; he even forgave the repentant and defeated Tefnakht, who gratefully acknowledged: "...you did not smite me in accordance with (my) crime."[147]

Now Piye ruled Egypt in the name of the Theban and national Chief God Amun. Like the Hyksos and Libyan pharaohs before him, he adopted all the

---

147. Lichtheim, Miriam, *Ancient Egyptian Literature, Volume III*, pp. 66-80.

usual Egyptian titles and customs. Above all, he made an attempt to revive Egyptian culture and religion rather than to impose Kushite cultural and religious variants.

The succeeding Kushite pharaohs also clearly wanted to maintain peace and the unity of Egypt, and stressed their role as legitimate continuators of ancient Egypt's history. This desire was perhaps illustrated with the episode of the Shabako Stone, by which the Kushites presumably attempted to document their role as continuators of Egypt's ancient culture of reconciliation as well as to promote peaceful Egyptian unity and reconciliation in the present. As we have seen, Pharaoh Shabako (c. 716–702 BC), Piye's brother and successor, claimed that he had found the text he inscribed on the Stone on a Memphis Ptah Temple papyrus dating to the Old Kingdom (c. 2686–2181 BC). And as we have seen in Chapter 4, there are good reasons to disbelieve this claim. By ascribing the writings of his time, lauding peace and reconciliation, to past times when the "great god" Ptah promoted peace and reconciliation between Horus and Seth, Shabako did no more than what Egyptians pharaohs and theologians had often done for more than 2000 years — change, transform and syncretize the Egyptian religion, gods and myths for purposes of political or religious necessity — or simply on a whim.

The Kushites fervently desired to be culturally Egyptian and to rule Egypt well and peacefully; but for the Egyptians, no matter what the Kushites did or did not do, they were foreigners — and so, could not get anything right. Resentment of the foreign Kushite rulers always remained strong. Moreover, despite their efforts at religious renovation, Kushite rule represented a further decline in the vitality of the Egyptian religion.

In c. 671 BC, the Assyrians invaded Egypt and, in c. 669 BC, Asshurbanipal (died c. 626 BC) set up the Saite Pharaoh Nekau I (c. 672–664 BC) as their vassal ruler in Lower Egypt. In 664, Asshurbanipal returned to Egypt and definitively defeated the Kushites. In the process, he sacked the great Amun Karnak Temple City of Thebes in 663 BC, an event which profoundly marked the Egyptian people and the state. The sack of Thebes was the supreme humiliation for the Egyptians.

Pharaoh Psamtek I (c. 664–610 BC) of the 26th Saite Dynasty became the ruler of a united Egypt. Officially, he was an Assyrian vassal; but, in fact, he was largely independent.

Psamtek I made further and stronger attempts to revitalize Egyptian religion and culture. However, these attempts had more to do with a repetition of ancient artistic forms and an accentuation of zoolatry than with a living, vibrant society. Perhaps, the major Saite artistic and architectural achievement was in temple building and especially in the renovation of the Neith Temple in Sais; and perhaps its biggest religious failure was in the extension of animal worship, despite the huge economic cost.

Attempts to reestablish Egyptian political power were partially successful, but Egypt remained in the shadow of both the Assyrians and the growing power of the Babylonians. Moreover, it relied more and more heavily on Greek and Anatolian Lydian and Carian mercenaries.

Nekau II's (c. 610–595 BC) attempt to re-establish Egypt as a major player in the political and military balance in the Levant dismally failed when his army was defeated by the Babylonian Nebuchadnezzar (c. 605–562 BC) at Carchemish in 605 BC. Once again, Egypt was forced to retreat back into its own land and Carchemish represented still another major defeat in Egypt's slide downwards.

Perhaps to prove that Egypt was still powerful, perhaps to show the Nubians who was the boss, and perhaps in revenge for the 100 years of Nubian occupation of Egypt, Psamtek II (c. 595–589 BC) attacked Nubia in 592 BC, but there could no longer be any question of Egypt permanently colonizing Nubia or any other country.

DECADENCE IN THE LATE PERIOD AND THE MOST ELABORATE SYSTEM OF ZOOLATRY EVER DEVISED

Egyptian cultural and religious decline was exemplified by the regression to fanatical zoolatry and an increased use of *heka*, magic, techniques and amulets. This took place in an atmosphere of economic prosperity but inner humiliation. Excessive zoolatry and *heka* practices had always been fundamental aspects of Egyptian religion and lifestyles, but from about the Late Period (c. 747 BC), they increasingly became tinged with fundamentalism and fanaticism. After the Persian conquest in 525 BC, the trend was extended further and probably reached its most excessive apex in the time of Ptolemy I Soter (c. 305–285 BC). The Egyptians seem to have made a desperate attempt to hang on to the vestiges of their religion and did so by accentuating their magical approach and especially zoolatric beliefs and practices.

One of the best independent descriptions of the extent of Egyptian fanatical zoolatry was made by Herodotus in *Histories*. Herodotus, describing what he saw around 440 BC during the Persian occupation, tells us that, "There are many household animals." "The Egyptians are the only people who keep their animals with them in the house." "All (animals)...are held to be sacred," that "for each kind [of animal] are appointed guardians....A son inherits this office from his father. [They] pray to the god to whom the animal is dedicated, shaving all or one half or one third of their children's heads, and weighing the hair...the weight in silver of the hair is given to the female guardian of the creatures, who buys fish with it and feeds them...Whoever kills one of these creatures intentionally is punished with death; if he kills accidentally, he pays whatever penalty the priests appoint. Whoever kills an ibis or a hawk, intentionally or not, must die for it."[148]

Zoolatry was always popular and widespread in Egypt, and at times became one of the main forms of religiosity. Linked to hunting magic, totemism, nature religion and animism, zoolatry seeped into Egyptian polytheistic religion (as it did into almost all early post-Neolithic religions), but the Egyptians went further than perhaps any people before them and certainly any after them in their cult worship and identification with animals. The combined animal-headed and human form of deities was Egypt's preferential way of depicting the gods and goddesses. However, it would be ridiculous to assume — as some do — that over the entirety of the history of Egyptian religion the veneration of animals was the pivotal theological concept or that venerating the gods in animal form was the main way rather than being just one of many variants.

Moreover, the vast number of texts and art works referring to animals give us a contradictory picture. It is clear that some specific animals were indeed divine, indeed gods — and not just symbolically, but in reality. However, it is frequently challenging to discern where the Egyptians were referring to a god as an animal and where an animal was being seen as the repository of the divine, as the house of a god, as an aspect, a manifestation, of its main form.

The absolute sacredness of an animal is only clear concerning single animals with special birthmarks and not all animals of the same species — the Apis Bull, as the incarnation of the creator god Ptah while alive and as the afterlife god Osiris when dead (in Memphis), the Mnevis Bull, as the incarnation of the sun god Re (in Heliopolis), the Buchis Bull, as the incarnation of the war god Montu (in Hermonthis), the *ahet* cow, linked to several mother goddesses and especially to the love and mother goddess Hathor (in Denderah) and the crocodile, linked to the god of the waters, fertility and the sun, Sobek (in Fayum).

It was only these animals, and especially the Apis Bull, who virtually became gods in their own right with only tenuous connections to the gods they were supposed to incarnate. They were worshipped in the temples with the same rituals and offerings as the idols of the gods and goddesses they theoretically incarnated. They were also used as oracles: there were ceremonies in which a question would be asked and if, afterwards, the Apis ate the food offered to him, it constituted a good omen and if he refused the food, it was a bad omen. On death, they and their mother-cows (seen as the goddess Hathor) were mummi-

---

148. Herodotus, *Books I-II*, 2.36.2, 2.65.2-5 and 2.66.1.

fied, given the same type of funerals as humans and became Osirises in the after-life, like humans. Some sarcophagi for Apis bulls were immensely elaborate and weighed 80 tons. A new bull, with a white triangle on its head and moon crescents on its sides, was then chosen to become the Apis. At the *Serapeum* in Memphis, the mummies of more than 60 Apis bulls and a million and a half ibises have been found. At the Hermopolis Gebel el-Tuna Necropolis, at least four million ibises were mummified. The implication is clear — the Apis bulls were full-fledged gods and the ibises were basically fetishes.

This state of affairs changed considerably during the New Kingdom (beginning c. 1550 BC). Thousands of animals were now raised in the temples. These animals gradually became confused with the gods themselves. Each temple raised hundreds and sometimes thousands of animals in special enclosures — ibises and baboons at Hermopolis, dedicated to the ibis or baboon-headed Thoth, moon god of wisdom; geese at Karnak-Thebes, dedicated to Chief God Amun-Re; crocodiles in Fayum, dedicated to Sobek; and one of the favorites, cats at Bubastis, in the Delta, dedicated to Bastet as a cat and the eye of the moon; but also falcons, dogs, scarabs, fish, etc.

In the Third Intermediary Period (from c. 1069 BC), the attitude of fanatical reverence concerning animals was a clear precursor of the relapse into the most extreme forms of zoolatry which took place in the Late Period (from c. 747 BC), long after most other societies had abandoned overt zoolatry.

Now, all the animals that were sacred to a god or goddess: all scarabs for Re-Khepri, all cats for Bastet and all ibises and baboons for Thoth were attributed sacred status, worshipped and mummified. All animals in a scared species became the incarnations of the gods they were associated with and were no longer just revered as fetishes, intermediaries or even aspects of the gods, but as the main manifestations of the gods themselves. Bulls, cows, rams, falcons, hawks, ibises, baboons, dogs, hares and cats became the most popular animal-gods, but fish, ichneumons (the mongoose), ostriches, crocodiles, gazelles, frogs and even mice were revered. There were so many types of sacred animals that almost all creatures, with the notable exception of the animals linked to the now evil god Seth, were considered as the main forms of the gods and goddesses themselves, in one place or another.

This gave rise to extreme forms of superstition, vehemence and hysteria. Great efforts had always been expended to determine which particular animal in a species was the actual incarnation of a god in its own right (especially the Apis and Mnevis Bulls), but in the Late Period, this practice became more akin to fanatical fundamentalism than to theology. Practices like drinking the water in the Fayum temple pool where Sobek was incarnated in a crocodile wearing golden earrings became general.

Although burials of bulls, cows and dogs can be traced back to prehistoric times in Egypt and considerable mummification and burial of animals continued afterwards, especially of Apis and Mnevis Bulls, now the raising of animals in temple enclosures was dramatically extended and huge animal necropolises arose throughout Egypt. This was accompanied by a cruel practice in which many of the bred animals were starved to death, mummified and expedited to the afterlife. In addition to the religious meaning and the link to the fact that it was a pious and worthy act to pay for the mummification and burial of an animal, the purchaser now had a hotline to the god represented by the mummy fetish and could communicate with the deceased in the *Duat* afterlife. Literally millions of animals were bred for sale, sacrifice, mummification and burial or for use as personal fetishes. This flourishing commerce was such an important source of income for the priests that it often led to the sale of fake mummies.

Hundreds of thousands of statuettes of animals, notably bronze cats and falcons, became not just fetishes but veritable gods. Amulets, which had always been extremely popular as talismans, were now produced on an industrial basis, usually in faience, and were sold by priests. This was especially the case for welfare and healing *wedjat* Eye of Horuses, life force *ankhs*, Osirisian *djed* "stability" pillars, *tiet* "protective knots" of Isis and Khepri resurrection scarabs.

Violence and even death was meted out to those who even unintentionally harmed certain animals or ate them, even because of extreme hunger. Fanaticism, violence and affection were especially rife concerning cats in the Late Period. The cat had become the favorite pet of the Egyptians and virtually every household had a cat that was supposed to bring a sweet, pleasant, fertile atmosphere to the home. The Egyptians used the affectionate and onomatopoeic term *miw*, meow, to designate cats. Cats were protected with ferociousness and temerity while alive and mourned by shaving one's eyebrows when dead. They were frequently mummified and entombed in the necropolis of Bastet's Delta city, Bubastis.

The protectress of cats and goddess of music and dance, Bastet, gradually became a benevolent cat-headed goddess, but she began her career in the Early Dynastic Period (c. 3100 BC) and the Old Kingdom (from c. 2686 BC) as a furious lioness-headed goddess and remained associated with Hathor and Sakhmet in their violent lioness-headed destroyer capacities. Her transformation from violent lioness to affectionate cat may have been particularly reassuring.

Wild cats had probably been deified before domestication as local emblem/totems and because they were mythologically seen as the killers of serpents. Re, in his role of killing the evil serpent Apophis, was often portrayed as a cat. The Egyptians, who were the first to domesticate cats, around 3000 BC, perhaps did so because they were particularly useful in protecting the granaries from mice.

After this date, domesticated cats dispersed from Egypt throughout the world and as all cat lovers know, the ambiguous attitude towards them continues unabated into our time.

Dogs (called *iwiw*, as the sound of their bark), and especially hunting dogs, were also favorite household pets and guards, especially among the notables. They were also used to clear homes of rats. However, there was even more ambiguity connected to them than to cats. Dogs were respected and given names linked to valor, like "Brave One," but were also seen as being excessively servile — royal slaves and prisoners were sometimes called "the king's dogs." The deities linked to dogs or jackals were numerous and revered, especially, the embalmment/tomb protector god Anubis and the "Opener of the Ways," Wep-wawet.

The Egyptians had not only maintained prehistoric concepts of divinity, fear and respect in relation to animals, but much more than most other peoples had obviously concluded that animals deserved affection. The Egyptians seem to have naturally loved animals in a way that many of our modern pet-loving and ecologically concerned societies can understand. They had tenderness for animals and were enthralled by communion and empathy with animals. But the downside, which eliminated much of the positive side, was that they obviously and frequently got carried away, especially in the Late Period.

Unless we frivolously assume that the worship of animals can legitimately constitute a form of evolved religion, the accentuation of zoolatry in Egypt has to be seen as a regression from more sophisticated and complex beliefs. It was already astonishing that the Egyptians were engaged in a kind of reverse evolution concerning zoolatry from at least 3000 BC by maintaining and even sometimes accentuating the representation of the divinities in animal and animal-headed forms, while other societies abandoned such representation. The simple fact is that, while most peoples gradually lessened or abandoned zoolatry, Egypt did not and in the Late Period, animal representations were only the tip of a religious iceberg which had become weighted with zoolatry and which continued right down to the end of Egyptian history as such.

In the first century BC, Diodorus Siculus reported that a Roman was killed for accidentally killing a cat. As late as the first century AD, Plutarch (c. AD 45–125), in *Isis and Osiris*, described widespread Egyptian fanatical zoolatric practices. He tells us that the neighboring cities of Lykopolis (Zawty) and Oxyrhynchus (*Per-Medjed*) fought each other because Lykolpolis worshipped wolf/dogs and Oxyrhynchus worshipped fish and ate dogs. Plutarch derided animal worship as "silly practices" which led the "cynical" to "atheism," but nevertheless curiously he expressed understanding for much of it, including the drinking of the water which ibises had drunk. In his zeal to defend religion and especially polytheism, the rational Plutarch tried to project beyond the irrational, beyond the exterior animal attributes in the Egyptian system of gods, in the forces of nature and in the deep characteristics of human existence — he rationalized Egyptian zoolatry as having great inner perspicacity, "usefulness" and "symbolism."[149]

There is no satisfactory explanation why zoolatry prospered in Egypt long after all other polytheistic religions scorned animal worship and had largely transformed zoolatry into the use of animal attributes as zoomorphic metaphors rather than reality. The simplest explanation remains that the Egyptians not only clung to their religious practices but accentuated some of them as a reaction to religious, political and military decadence and regression from the 12th century BC and to the invasion, beginning with the Persians from 525 BC, by foreign powers who mocked their religious practices. In any case, there can hardly be any doubt that Late Period simplistic hard-line zoolatry denatured the complex Egyptian religion.

PERSIAN RULE AND THE BEGINNING OF THE END OF EGYPT

Despite their defeat at Carchemish in 605 BC, the Saites had rebuilt a prosperous and centralized Egypt. But something was missing. The flame of the ancient religion was dwindling and was being replaced by decadent religious practices. The Saites fervently desired a renewal of the core of Egyptian life, of religion, but like the Kushites they presided over the beginning of the end of the extravagantly complex and comprehensive Egyptian politico-religious system.

By 525 BC, the Egyptian economy was insufficient to finance the war effort against the Persians. Moreover, the Greek mercenaries hired by the Egyptians turned out to be unreliable. The first period of Persian occupation of Egypt (525–404 BC) ensued.

If most Egyptologists and historians agree that by this time Egypt was a pale imitation of its past glory, there is wide disagreement as to when this all began and whether it signified decline, relative decline, or the end of ancient Egypt as such. John A. Wilson said that as early as after 1100 BC, just as the Assyrians claimed, Egypt had become "a broken reed"; that it was "a vast and impressive legend, a colossus slumbering in feeble old age." W. Stevenson Smith and Cyril Aldred took a similar view and assigned the beginning of the Late Period, with its grave problems and decline, to the Third Intermediate Period from 1069 BC. Nicolas Grimal refers to the Third Intermediate Period as the

---

149. Plutarch, *Moralia*, Volume V, *Isis and Osiris*, pp. 165, 167 and 171.

beginning of "the final phase." K.A. Kitchen takes a somewhat dissenting view — he prefers to characterize the period after 1100 BC as the "post-Imperial Epoch," but believes that the Third Intermediate Period (for him, 1100–650 BC) was "far from being chaotic...and so not merely 'intermediate,' but significant in its own right." A.H. Gardiner refers to "the last assertions of independence" in the 26th Dynasty (c. 664–525 BC) and says that with the reign of Pharaoh Apries (c. 589–570 BC), "The history of Egypt now becomes increasingly merged into that of the Middle East and of Greece..." and "Under [the Ptolemies, from 332 BC], Egypt was a changed land..."[150]

In any case, whatever its attempts and successes in playing an imperial role, Egypt was certainly largely "post-imperial" after 1069 BC, compared to its earlier imperial role. And even if much splendor remained, it was certainly in a "final phase" compared to its earlier across-the-board splendor. It had lost its empire, was incapable of military victory in Asia except over minor powers like Israel, had been progressively pushed back into its own land and frequently had to live under rival regimes of kinglets. It was also was increasingly controlled by foreigners or paid some kind of allegiance to foreign powers. Even if we include periods of some kind of foreign allegiance and thus not total independence, from 1069 BC until the Greek conquest in 332 BC, Egypt was ruled by Egyptians for only about half of this period.

Above all, Egypt was indeed a "broken reed" and was losing the very essence of its system: its vibrant, vanguard religious role. The Egyptian religion had become devitalized and centered on merely respecting and accentuating ancient beliefs, in an atmosphere which among other diversions had led to the relapse into extreme zoolatry and generalized fanaticism, typical of a decadent religion. Paradoxically, Egypt was now beginning to turn the fiction of eternally unchangeable religious and societal structures into reality. After than two thousand years, Egypt was beginning to lose its extraordinary flexibility, its capacity for change and for adaptation to any circumstances while cleverly claiming that no changes had been made.

Perhaps one of the sharpest views about Egypt's stagnation was that of James Henry Breasted, who absolutely situated the end of Egypt's "characteristic history" in 525 BC with the Persian conquest. Breasted reasoned that, "The fall of Egypt and the close of her characteristic history, were already an irrevocable fact long before Cambyses knocked at the doors of Pelusium [where the armies of

---

150. Wilson, John, *The Burden of Egypt*, pp. 289-291, 317, Smith, W. Stevenson, *The Art and Architecture of Ancient Egypt*, p. 231, Aldred, Cyril, *The Egyptians*, p. 170, Grimal, Nicolas, *A History of Ancient Egypt*, p. 309, Gardiner, Alan, *Egypt of the Pharaohs*, p. 352, 355 and 382 and Kitchen, K.A., *The Third Intermediate Period*, pp. xi-xii.

Psamtek III, c. 526–525 BC were defeated]...The Saitic state...had little or no connection with the past. They were as essentially non-Egyptian as the Ptolemies who followed the Persians...And if a feeble burst of national feeling enabled this or that Egyptian to thrust off the Persian yoke for a brief period, the movement may be likened to convulsive contractions...from which conscious life has long departed. With the fall of Psamtik III Egypt belonged to a new world, toward the development of which she had contributed much, but in which she could no longer play an active part."[151]

Some Egyptian texts of the time of the Persian occupation of Egypt, and notably the inscription on the Udjahorresne statuette, found in the Neith Sais Temple (and now in the Vatican Museum), at least partially corroborate Breasted's view. There is a mood of disenchantment in this text that indicates that the end is inevitably near, even if complete collapse has not yet taken place.

Udajahorresne (c. 550–510? BC) was a navy commander under Psamtek III and suffered defeat at the hands of the Persians. He was also a doctor, and after the defeat he became the Persian-appointed priest of the Neith Temple in Sais, "the Castle of *Bity*" (the Bee). At this time, the old Sais city, Lower Egyptian and war goddess Neith was generally seen as a divine mother, a mother goddess, a great celestial cow. Udajahorresne owed his livelihood to the Persians and had to be careful and respectful about what he said concerning them and their "Great Chief of all foreign lands, Cambyses," and his successor Darius, "ever-living" who was also "Great Chief of all foreign lands and Great Ruler of Egypt."

Despite this deferential sort of language concerning foreigners (people from the hated *khasut*), which must have driven more than one mummified New Kingdom pharaoh to wish for permanent death, we can read between the lines that Udjahorresne saw what was happening to Egypt as a catastrophe. Udjahorresne was a collaborator of the Persians — "I did as his majesty had commanded me" — and he obviously wanted the people to accept Persian rule because he believed that there was no other choice for the Egyptians. But he also wanted to have a clear conscience and wanted to be sure that good things would be said about him to Neith. Udjahorresne, like all Egyptian notables, wanted "his good name to endure in this land forever." He wanted to do everything he could to ensure that he would enter into the *Duat* afterlife. He claimed to have been "good in his town...defended the weak...rescued the timid...when the very great turmoil...happened in the whole land." "The very great turmoil" was a euphemism for the Egyptian defeat and the Persian occupation.

---

151. Breasted, James Henry, *A History of Egypt, From the Earliest Times to the Persian Conquest*, pp. 496-497.

Udjahorresne clearly saw the Egyptians as helpless and having to virtually beg favors concerning their religion. He was obliged to petition Cambyses to "expel all the foreigners [presumably Persians]...in the temple of Neith...demolish all their houses and all their unclean things...and return all its personnel to it..." He had to convince the presumably monotheistic Cambyses about "the greatness of Sais, that is the city of all the gods, who dwell their on their seats forever" and convince him that Neith deserved great honors because she is the "mother who bore Re and inaugurated birth when birth had not yet been..."[152]

Udjahorresne kowtowed to Cambyses (c. 525-522 BC), who — even if he did not profane King Amasis' (c. 570-526 BC) mummy or kill the Apis Bull, as Herodotus claimed[153] — certainly does not seem to have had any spontaneous sensitivity for the Egyptians' religious feelings. In any case, there is no doubt that Cambyses attempted to limit the revenues of the temples and that there was widespread hatred of the Persians. A notable like Udjahorresne must have been aware of all this; his expressed deference indicates just how much the "superior" Egyptian people (and despite their "superior" religion) had to put their pride in their pocket when dealing with the Persian occupiers. The general situation must have been humiliating indeed, unless of course Breasted was somewhat right — the end of Egypt was "an irrevocable fact" and the Egyptians no longer felt anything more than "a feeble burst of national feeling" from time to time.

Even if it is excessive to see the absolute end of Egypt with the Persian occupation (as Breasted did), even if this was anticipating events, it is not excessive to say that Egypt was by then an old-fashioned country and was being gradually excluded not only from international political power but also from the vanguard religious, philosophic, scientific and cultural changes which were sweeping the world at that time. Even if the Egyptian system was so all-encompassing and pervading that it continued to powerfully attract, impress, influence and repel, the original contribution of Egypt to the history of religion, art and architecture had virtually ceased. What the German philosopher Karl Jaspers (1883-1969) named the sixth century BC "Axis Age" was in full swing — and Egypt was not part of it.

In Greece, Thales, Anaximander, Anaxagoras and many other succeeding philosopher-scientists like Democritus were undermining the very basis of religion. They were ending the mythological, magical approach to physical reality and to mankind and were laying the foundations of rationalism, experimental science, materialism, free philosophical inquiry, atheism and the ideal of freedom. Soon, philosophers like Socrates would champion more *ethical* ethics, inde-

---

152. Lichtheim, Miriam, *Ancient Egyptian Literature, Volume III*, pp. 36-41.
153. See pp. 111-112 (refers to Herodotus and the Apis bull).

pendent of religion, and soon politicians like Pericles would be formulating systems of limited democracy.

In Judea, the prophets Deutero-Isaiah and Jeremiah were transforming Hebrew national monotheism and establishing true, or integral, universal monotheism, promoting impartial universal ethics and the priority of the individual over collective and temple ritual duties, postulating that suffering was a positive phenomenon and inventing the notion of the ideal messiah-king who would eventually set things right.

In India, Buddha was proposing a doctrine of fraternity, the possibility of enlightenment for everybody and a radical end to suffering through the suppression of all desire. He also taught doctrines of the non-existence of soul and an eternal god before these doctrines in the *Tripitaka* (the Three Baskets of Buddha's original teachings) were virtually overthrown by dozens of rival schools of Buddhist revisionists and in 200 short years evolved into personal salvation teachings that were often in contradiction to original Buddhism. And in India, the Jain teacher Mahavira was radicalizing the old and little-used Hindu doctrine of *ahimsa*, the non-harming of all living things.

In Persia, Zoroaster came to grips with the problem of the existence of evil. He invented the first true eschatology with an afterlife Paradise as a reward for authentic moral behavior and a Hell for evil behavior.

In China, Confucius was renewing the age-old political and social hierarchical system by lacing it with the inevitability of morality.

This mixed bag of progress and infantilism, which constituted fundamental changes in the way people viewed the universe, the world, the nation and the individual, gradually conquered the world. None of these changes, with the possible exception of Confucianism, were compatible with Egyptian religion and societal views.

Egypt had been the vanguard, the soul and the motor of religion and societal organization ever since the opening of the Old Kingdom (c. 2686 BC). As formally unprovable as it is, Egypt may have also been the role model in these domains. But in the sixth century BC, Egypt's exclusion and self-exclusion from the new, vast, modern movement accentuated its stagnation and decline. Using Breasted's terms, the end of a "characteristically" Egyptian history was in sight, even if to say that it occurred as early as 525 BC, as he did, seems incorrect.

It is clear that, after the first Persian conquest, Egypt did not have the resources to do anything else but more or less coexist with its conquerors, with only brief periods of revolt and independence. However, to say that there was just "a feeble burst of national feeling" for the Egypt of Persian times does not take into account that a good dose of Egyptian bluster still existed. On its own and under the rule of foreign occupiers, Egypt continued to play important roles among the world's political and economic leaders, even if the great times of religious and artistic experimentation and innovation had ended.

Through Herodotus' *Histories*, written after his trip to Egypt around 440 BC, during the reign in Egypt of the Persian Emperor Artaxerxes (c. 465–424 BC), we can easily see that the Egyptians had conserved their legendary feeling of superiority, despite their recent defeat in a major rebellion against the Persians (456 BC). But we also see that an ambiguous climate had set in that was no doubt linked to cultural decline and to nostalgia for their ancient periods of glory.

The Egyptians had now become boastful, which was perhaps a sign of confusion and an inferiority complex. Herodotus reported that the Egyptians believed that they were "the oldest people on earth" (until c. 664 BC, when after a secret, surrealistic experiment involving two newborn children and the word *bekos*, bread, they attributed this status to the Phrygians). For Herodotus the general context was that of all countries, Egypt "has the most wonders and everywhere presents works beyond description," that the Egyptians "are religious beyond measure, more than any other people," that they claimed to be "the first [who] used the names of twelve gods" and that "the names of nearly all the gods came to Hellas from Egypt," that they "were the first people to establish solemn assemblies, and processions, and services" and "the first [who] assigned to the several gods their altars and images and temples, and first carved figures on stones," that they were "the first [who] reckoned by years and made the year consist of twelve divisions of the seasons...[which] they discovered...from the stars," and that more portents have discovered by them than by all other peoples."

Here we have a mixture of truth, falsehood, ignorance and fantasy. The "oldest people on earth"? — certainly the oldest constituted nation. "The names of twelve gods"? — Herodotus may in fact be referring to the nine deities of the ennead, but in any case, if this means the first designation of divinities, certainly not; the Sumerian gods were named before; and certainly the Greeks "borrowed" some gods from the Egyptians. "The first images and temples"? — certainly not; without mentioning any other previous divine image-makers and temple builders than the Anatolians and the Sumerians. "The first carved figures on stone"? — what about the Magdalenians, 30,000 years earlier? "The 12 divisions of the seasons," that is the solar year — most probably. As to "wonders," "portents" and "religious beyond measure," there hardly seems to be any doubt that all this was true.

Even in 440 BC, Egypt and especially its static culture, if not its living culture, deeply impressed Herodotus, and rightfully so; although perhaps when he says, "I think that their [the Egyptian] account of the country was true,"[154] he is making a judgment which is more than a bit steep.

The Egyptians did recover full political independence from 404 to 343 BC, between the two Persian occupations. This was a period of no great achievement, although it seems to have been prosperous and the renovation of many temples was undertaken. It was marked by a further extension of animal worship in what was probably still another attempt to promote typically Egyptian religious customs. Two Persian invasions, in 386 BC and 350 BC, were repulsed before the Persians under Artaxerxes Ochus (c. 343–338 BC) finally defeated Egypt and occupied it for another eleven years, before being defeated themselves by the Greeks.

The Stele of Nectanebo I (c. 380–362 BC), who usurped the throne and founded the 30th Dynasty (now in the Neith Temple in the great Greek Delta city of Naucratis), indicates a pharaoh very concerned with his status: "Mighty monarch guarding Egypt," conscious that he has "to maintain everything done by the ancestors" and perhaps worried about what the people expect of him: "Who [Nectenebo] does good to him who is loyal, They can slumber until daylight..."[155]

The last indigenous pharaoh of Egypt was Nectanebo II *Senejemibra*, (360–343 BC). The Persians then re-occupied Egypt, this time using far more severe repressive methods to break the Egyptian spirit. But what was yet to come, at the hands of the Greeks, and far more with cultural than military means, is what spelled the real destruction of Egyptian Egypt.

GREEK AND ROMAN RULE — THE END OF EGYPTIAN EGYPT

Perhaps the most convincing date for the end of Egyptian history is 332 BC, with the Greek occupation and the progressive infiltration and then the domination of Hellenistic influences.

Nicolas Grimal (b. 1948) sees the defeat of Nectanebo II (360–343 BC) by the Persians as "the end of Egypt as an independent entity," the period from which "The Egyptians were no longer masters of their own fate"; he believes that from Alexander's conquest of Egypt, "the history of Egypt after 332 BC was inseparable from that of the Greek world," but he does not believe that "Egypt actually lost its identity" at that time; rather that the "desire to preserve the original purity of Egyptian culture eventually reached a state of stagnation." With

---

154. Herodotus, *Books I-II*, 2.2.1-5, 2.35.1, 2.37.1, 2.4.2, 2.50.1, 2.58.1, 2.4.2, 2.4.1, 2.82.2 and 2.5.1.

155. Lichtheim, Miriam, *Ancient Egyptian Literature, Volume III*, pp. 86-89.

"the civilization that grew up in Alexandria...Egypt might not yet have been reduced to the purely exotic role that it was to play with regard to Rome, but it was certainly already a thing of the past. Appearances were assiduously kept up...But it would not be a history of the Egyptian people..."[156]

After the Macedonian Greek defeat of the Persians in 332 BC, Alexander captured Egypt virtually without any Egyptian resistance. Alexander was welcomed as a liberator from Persian occupation and persecution, and the priests of the Amun Karnak Temple proclaimed him as the god-ruler of the world. The Egyptians surely did not realize what they were letting themselves into — an insidious Greek policy which would eventually destroy their culture and language and religion, which, despite the allegations concerning Cambyses, the Persians had never consciously practiced in a widespread manner. Persian occupation and repression were overt; Greek repression of Egyptian societal values was covert, but far tougher than anything the Persians had practiced. The Greeks destroyed Egyptian Egypt.

Under Ptolemaic rule, from 305 BC, Egypt was independent from Greece but was ruled by the Greeks for the primary benefit of the Greek settlers and was an integral part of the Hellenistic world. Antagonism between the Greeks and the Egyptians grew steadily and the Greeks had to put down periodic uprisings. It took more than 150 years, well into the 2nd century BC, before antagonism between the Egyptians and the Greeks had significantly diminished. From then on, the Egyptian approach to life became more and more Grecianized.

Egypt was a major agricultural exporter, but more for the economic benefit of the Greeks than for most Egyptians (with the notable exception of the clergy, who exchanged acquiescence to Greek religious dictates for material advantages). Politically, the Greek Ptolemies, in Egypt's name, held sway over vast areas from Abdera in Thrace to much of the coastal zone of Anatolia, Syria and Palestine, parts of Libya and a part of Nubia. But once again, this had more to do with the Greek elite in Egypt than with the Egyptian people.

Greek became the official language of Egypt and remained so for more than the next 900 years.

During the Ptolemaic and Roman Periods (after 332 BC), great temples continued to be built, notably the huge Horus Temple in Edfu (called Apollinopolis Magna by the Greeks), the Isis Temple complex in Philae and the Hathor Temple in Denderah. But as magnificent as these temples were, and notably Philae, they were not comparable to the great achievements of ancient Egyptian temple architecture like Karnak, Luxor, Abu Simbel, Memphis or Heliopolis.

---

156. Smith, W. Stevenson, *The Art and Architecture of Ancient Egypt*, pp. 381, 383, 385 and 386. ˙

Paradoxically, for all their splendor, the Ptolemaic temples were sure signs that Egypt had gone into an era in which it was gradually losing its religion and culture. The building of these temples was commanded and overseen by Ptolemaic rulers who could not even speak Egyptian, let alone read the hieroglyphic inscriptions on the temple walls. It is usually assumed that only a single Ptolemy, Cleopatra VII (51–30 BC), bothered to learn how to speak and write Egyptian. In addition to the Egyptian gods, the temple murals depicted the Ptolemies and then the Roman Emperors. Philae, Edfu and Denderah were not indicators of the vitality of the Egyptian religion in Ptolemaic and Roman times; they were remarkable leftovers of what once were the fabulous traditions of ancient Egyptian architecture.

The production of art and the writing of religious texts, including new versions of the old myths, wisdom texts and hymns, continued but were substantially influenced by Greek philosophy and styles. In fact, as we shall soon see, from the late 2nd century BC, Greek philosophy was insidiously completing the process of the destruction of the very core of the Egyptian religion and world-view.

Practically the only real religion-related advance was a substantial improvement in mummification, coffin and sarcophagus techniques. Here, too, there was a merger of traditional Egyptian and realistic Greco-Roman styles, notably for the mummy masks and the decoration of the sarcophagi.

The Ptolemy was now a god and married his sister, like the former Egyptian pharaohs, and deified his wife and all the previous ptolemies and their wives. The first Greek head of the Satrapy of Egypt, Ptolemy I Soter ("the savior"; ruled as Satrap from 323 and then as king from 305 to 285 BC), invented a new god, the human-headed sun, fertility and healer god Serapis. This was a combination of several Greek gods including Zeus, Dionysus, Helios, Hades and Asclepius and the Egyptian Osorapis, that is the Ptah-Apis Bull after its death who became Osiris-Apis. The Greek-influenced Egyptian priest/historian Manetho (fl.c. 300 BC) may have played a key role in setting up the cult of Serapis for the Greeks. Many other Greek gods and goddesses were imported into Egypt, notably Demeter, who paraded as Isis. However, on the whole, Greek policy was to paternalistically allow the Egyptians to practice their own religion as they saw fit while infiltrating their own customs, beliefs and artistic styles.

When the Romans conquered Egypt in 30 BC, it is certain that the Egyptian religion and traditions were already a mixed bag of Greek and decadent Egyptian religious practices and art rather than a flourishing affair.

The very popular first century AD wisdom text, *The Instruction of the Papyrus Insinger* (in the Leiden Rijksmuseum), shows how severely traditional Egyptian religious and social values had been eroded. Significantly, the type of virtue and morality preached in this text have far more to do with austere Greek philosophy than with the traditional optimistic, joyful and physical Egyptian traditions. It is now "the god who sends...fate and fortune," rather than observance of the *maat* order, obedience to the pharaoh or ptolemy and behavior according to one's hierarchical status. Greek-type philosophical disdain for the body and sexuality is lauded: "He who is abstemious with his belly and guarded with his phallus is not blamed at all." It now also seems that sin exists and that magical salvation doctrine is of no importance: "Nor is there anyone who listens because of your praying to the sky"; and "Neither the impious nor the godly man can alter the lifetime that was assigned him."[157]

The translator of the above text, Miriam Lichtheim (b. 1914), rightly notes that "Its ethics is one of endurance rather than of action...Greeks and Egyptians alike were participating in, and being transformed by, the currents of Hellenistic universalism, syncretism and pessimism which were undermining all the polytheistic cultures of the Mediterranean world and paving the way for the new gospel of the kingdom of heaven."[158]

Indeed, *The Instruction of the Papyrus Insinger* clearly showed how deeply Greek philosophy had transformed the traditional Egyptian religious, ethical and worldview. The main Greek influences on later Christianity — high, but austere moral values, freewheeling, lucid but pessimistic metaphysics and anti-worldly, anti-material, anti-physical and anti-feminine attitudes had taken hold in Egypt. The foundations for a conversion to Christianity in Egypt were being laid. The Egyptian magical view centered on the good life here on earth and the optimistic Osirisian solution to the problem of death was slipping beneath the horizon. Take out the few rare mentions of Egyptian gods in *The Instruction of the Papyrus Insinger* and this text could be almost attributed to any Greek Platonist or Stoic philosopher.

One can legitimately ask what was left of an Egyptian Egypt. Egyptian society, religion and art became less and less vibrant as the Roman grip was strengthened, as Egyptian participation in the running of the state, its politics, economics and culture was eliminated and as the Egyptian religion was progressively subdued by the Hellenistic view. Whatever date is adopted for the end of Egypt, its agony had been quasi-permanent from the first Persian conquest in 525 BC and probably long before. The *Instruction of the Papyrus Insinger* rendered this agony transparent and announced what was to come. From now on, in the house of traditional Egypt, the lights were on, but nobody was at home.

---

157. Lichtheim, Miriam, *Ancient Egyptian Literature, Volume III*, pp. 186-213.
158. *Ibid.*, pp. 9-10.

Thus, the Roman defeat of the Greeks in 30 BC opened a new era of cultural decline for the Egyptians but one of economic prosperity, albeit mainly for the Roman masters. Egypt was the wealthiest of all the Roman colonies and with its huge grain production became the breadbasket of Rome. The Roman colonial system was basically a continuation of the Greek colonial system, but it was far more severe and exploitative. It bled Egypt white. The population of Egypt decreased due mainly to plagues, disease and harsh conditions. It also became more and more mixed — in addition to the Greeks and the Romans, according to Philo (c. 20 BC–AD 50), Jews lived in two of Alexandria's five districts and there were also large populations of Phoenicians, Syrians and Anatolians, especially in Alexandria.

The Roman emperors, as was their policy everywhere in their Empire, adopted a relatively moderate attitude to the local religion and even continued the temple building projects begun by the Greeks. However, as was also their policy throughout their Empire, the Romans were always wary of their subjects' religious sentiments and always ready to brutally put down any religious-political uprising.

Little by little, the Romans completed the task, begun by the Greeks, of disintegrating the Egyptian core of Egypt. Roman Emperor Diocletian (284–305) dealt the decisive blow, fully integrating Egypt into the Roman Empire. Not a single civil servant was Egyptian; Roman law prevailed; Roman coins were the only legal currency; Roman influence in art and religious images was extensive and Greek influence in religious doctrines, rituals and art continued.

Hieroglyphic writing, the *medu netjer*, the sacred words of the Egyptian gods, which was supposedly eternal, was also on the wane. Paradoxically, it had been the Greeks and the Romans who, over the centuries, had added thousands of signs to the original Egyptian system, but hieroglyphics increasingly fell into disuse both because of the devitalization of the Egyptian religion and the emerging Christians who considered its pictorial aspect as idolatrous and polytheistic. The Romans also gradually phased out the use of Egyptian cursive demotic, which had been in common use from about the 26th Dynasty (c. 664–525 BC) as the norm for writing in administrative, literary, everyday and even religious use. It was replaced by a new Greek script named Coptic, using a basic Greek alphabet plus six Egyptian demotic letters; it bore only an approximate resemblance to the Egyptian language.

The real Egypt, *Ta-Wy*, the Two Lands, had sunk beneath the sands and had been replaced by *Aigyptos*.

The majestic falcon, *bik*, Heru/Horus was no longer on the horizon. The creator Tum/Atum was no longer perched on the *benben* primeval mound. The horrible Setekh/Seth would no longer thunder and rage. The ideal mother Aset/ Isis had no more need to nurture and protect her dimpled baby Harpakhrad/ Horus; the hundreds of animal, human and animal-headed human "great gods," *netjeru-ah* or *wer*, and small gods, *nedsew*, had disappeared; there were no more *sa Ra*, no more omnipotent pharaoh-god-sons of Re, who *ankh-em-maat*, who lived by the goddess Maat's divine order and kept *izfeh*, disorder, at bay. Artists no longer had to sculpt and paint idealized gods and humans. The *hery seshta*, "the overseer of mysteries" priest no longer spent 70 days stuffing bodily organs into canopic jars and mummifying bodies for eternity with material techniques and great *heka* magic. There was no more "Opening of the Mouth" ceremony so that a sculpture could become alive or the deceased could breathe and eat in the *Duat* afterlife. The good *Wennefer* Asar/Osiris, in "The Hall of Two Truths," no longer graciously let people sneak into the *Duat* for *wehem ankh*, happily repeating life, and then letting their *ba* roaming souls sneak out for visits. There was no need to use *meket* and *wedja* amulets, to ward off the terrible Crusher of Bones or the Red Fiends in the *Duat*. There was no need for convoluted amalgamations of several gods into the aspects of a single god. There was no need to hunt down and obliterate any mention of the heretic monotheistic Akhenaten's and his beloved *hemet nisut weret*, "great royal wife" Nefertiti's names, their *ren*, their soul names. Amun-Re was no longer the *nesu netjeru*, "King of the gods" and the "UNIQUE." The larger than life Rameses II, "Strong Bull, beloved by Maat, Protector of Egypt, he who strikes the foreign countries," dashing across the walls of the Karnak, Luxor, Abu Simbel and Abydos Temples in his chariot and striking down the Hittites no longer had meaning...

There was simply no more *Ta-Shema* and *Ta-Mehu*, the land of the sedge reed and the land of the papyrus clump, Upper and Lower Egypt, no more *Kemet*, the black land, no more *Ta-Wy* the Two Lands, no more *Ta-Mery*, the beloved cultivated land. All that remained was *Aigpytos*, the Egypt that the Greeks and Romans had made

THE END OF EGYPTIAN POLYTHEISM, THE RISE OF CHRISTIAN MONOTHEISM AND THE SEARCH FOR A NEW RELIGION FOR EGYPT

The rise of Christian monotheism and the fall of polytheism were ambient possibilities throughout the Middle East and Western Europe in the first centuries of our era. In retrospect, it could appear that the victory of monotheism was logical given the groping about and the evolution towards monotheism over thousands of years. In fact, the imposition of Christian monotheism was a struggle and not a fatality. In this struggle, Egypt resisted far less than Europe, and especially Greece, in the attempt to maintain its indigenous beliefs or to adopt new syncretic beliefs with a polytheistic thrust.

The lack of any great resistance by the Egyptian people to the rise of monotheistic Christianity in the first centuries of our era can be explained by many factors. Their own polytheistic religion had been denatured and subdued by the Greeks, the Romans and even their own priests for several centuries. Their own religion had not preserved them from centuries of foreign occupation, exploitation and humiliation. And the Greek and Roman polytheisms (including their savage aspects, like the Bacchic cults) frequently appeared to them as pale images of their own ancient polytheism, which had become devitalized. The people, first individually, then massively, now sought individual and ethical salvation, rather than collective and political power, and found it, as so many other peoples and individuals in the Greco-Roman world did, in Jesus and Christianity.

Beginning in the late second century AD, there was a movement towards Christianity in Egypt, as elsewhere, notably among the oppressed poor and women. Tradition holds that Saint Mark introduced Christianity into Egypt in the first century AD; but it seems certain that only small numbers of dissident Jews and Greeks in Alexandria were involved in Christianity at that time, often in emerging Gnostic views. In these early decades of Christianity, it was perhaps the small number of Christians in Egypt which largely preserved them from the type of virulent persecution they faced in Europe. It was not until the early third century that Christians were numerous in Egypt.

Jesus was both a majestic god and close to ordinary, persecuted, suffering people, somebody who proclaimed that "the last shall be first"[159] — this could only have had immense appeal for the humiliated Egyptians who, even in this time of decline, were conscious of the fact that they had been the first but were now among the last.

Jesus also represented the enhancement of the old Hebrew idea, invented by Isaiah and Jeremiah in the sixth century BC, that suffering was positive. This was an important aspect of emerging Christianity which could only find favor among the humiliated Egyptians.

It can be reasonably assumed that the Egyptians had been familiar with this concept of suffering and other Hebrew ideas for many centuries, notably the invisibility of god, non-magical ethics, an intransigent anti-idolatrous attitude and the abhorrence of the multitude of gods and their frequent animal representation. However, as we have seen in Chapter 12, the Egyptians developed virulent anti-Jewish feelings during the Ptolemaic Period (after 332 BC). In practical

---

159. Matthew 20:16.

terms, anti-Judaism eventually meant that it was probably more acceptable and attractive for the Egyptians to accept monotheism, ethical clarity and the concept that suffering and morality would be eventually rewarded in their Christian, rather than Jewish, versions, accompanied as they were by anti-Judaism and the visibility of Jesus as a god. Moreover, even in the first centuries of our era, although Christianity in Egypt came from Rome and the lands of the Roman Empire, it was not Roman; it transcended Rome and the Egyptians did not feel that they were adopting a Roman religion.

Contrary to the great struggle, persecution and martyrdom required to establish Christian monotheism in Europe, the transition to monotheism went off relatively smoothly in Egypt. There was only scattered persecution, notably with the Roman Emperor Diocletian (AD 284–305), who tried unsuccessfully to destroy Christianity in Egypt and elsewhere. Had the struggle to impose Christianity been lost in Europe, it inevitably would have meant the end of emerging Christianity as a separate religion and not just a Jewish sect, throughout the world and of course in Egypt.

The Romans did not have the theological and metaphysical capacities to renovate polytheism and make it more credible; the Greeks theoretically did. They tried to do it, and failed. Many Greeks put up a determined fight to maintain a renovated polytheistic system and appealed for tolerance from the Christians, something which they generally did not get.

Plutarch (c. AD 45–125), highly impressed by the Egyptian religion and especially its Osirisian and Isis aspects, tried to reconcile Egypt, Greece and Rome and polytheism and monotheism, arguing that there were many ways to view the same divine reality and many names for the same gods who had a common origin. For Plutarch, as for many other Greeks in his time, religion was universal, even if different names and terms were used in different places.

Plotinus (AD 204–270), a Greek born in Egypt, founded Neoplatonism, which was an austere and heroic attempt to merge Greek ethical and introspective philosophy and vaguely polytheistic and naturalist Greek religion. In fact, Plotinus best illustrated the losing battle being fought against emerging Christianity; he became known as the last original "pagan" philosopher and only succeeded in providing a Greek philosophical and metaphysical basis for Christianity — which it is uncertain he would have appreciated.

Perhaps the Greeks lost the battle for the preservation of polytheism in Europe and the Middle East because deep down they, themselves, doubted the credibility of their religion and had become apologists. The type of arguments they frequently used implicitly confirmed the superior ethical view and more coherent theological view of Christianity. Greece's own atheist and agnostic philosopher-scientists had set the stage for such an outcome at least six centuries earlier and over the succeeding centuries many of their philosophers and especially Xenophanes (fl.c. 520 BC) had succeeded in simply, thoroughly and permanently discrediting polytheism as an immoral and disreputable system.

Greece lost the battle to maintain polytheism in Europe and the Middle East, but it paradoxically served as a vital bridge between polytheism and monotheism. The Neoplatonist view of the one and the many, of hierarchically numerous intermediaries, was a vital bridge between Egyptian polytheism and Egyptian Christianity. And in the end, the Greek adoption of Christianity for themselves and for the world was accompanied by the incorporation of numerous transformed Greek philosophic doctrines, notably the Neoplatonist anti-worldly concept that the earth and mankind were blemished or evil and only the divine was perfect and good. Philo (c. 20 BC–AD 50), the Alexandrian Hellenistic Jewish philosopher, merged Platonism and Judaism and deeply influenced the early fathers of Egyptian Christianity. He notably held the very Greek idea that god and the soul were the supreme values and that it was the soul which united man to god.

The Greek Alexandrian theologian Clement (c. AD 150–215) firmly believed that knowledge and other-worldliness, as in Greek ethical philosophy, was the highest goal of Christianity. He propagated the belief that Greek philosophy had been an ethical stage towards Christianity and could still serve as a path towards the Christian form of faith. Certainly, Clement's analysis was pertinent at least concerning Egypt.

Greek polytheistic doctrines and customs, including the adoption of feast days linked to the cycles of the sun and the moon, also played a major role in popularizing early Christianity in Egypt.

The pragmatic Romans — great engineers, politicians, lawmakers and soldiers — were wretchedly poor theologians. As far back as the fourth century BC, they had basically copied and assimilated their pantheons and religious systems from the Greeks. Rome became more and more triumphant everywhere on the battlefields, but more and more uncertain of itself in matters of religion.

As early as the end of the first century AD, Rome was being torn asunder by a struggle between several religions. By the middle of the third century, Rome was an extraordinary *bric-à-brac* of rival and frequently contradictory beliefs and practices. Their state religion had become an imported and transformed version of the Syrian Sol sun cult, the Sol Invictus ("The Unconquered Sun") religion, and coexisted with official Emperor worship. Many other religions and cults vied for supremacy, including the old Greco-Roman pantheon led by Jupiter, a version of Persian Mithraism as a religion of light, Manichaeism, the Roman-Syrian Jupiter-Dolichenus cult, the Phrygian Attis castration cult, Babylonian and Greek divination and astrology, mystery cults such as Bacchus, Demeter and Isis,

Judaism and of course Christianity (which the Romans first believed was merely a form of Judaism).

By the fourth century, Greek polytheism and all other "pagan" cults were seen as inferior to monotheism for the Romans as for the Greeks themselves, precipitating a vast groundswell that engulfed polytheism. In the end, only the Jews in the Roman Empire successfully resisted Christianity and maintained their own ancient brand of monotheism.

In 312, the decisive step towards imposing Christianity was taken with the decree by the Roman Emperor Constantine allowing Christians to freely practice their religion. Constantine was merely accepting a reality — the Christians had become too numerous and powerful to successfully repress. Nevertheless, this decree greatly favored the flourishing of Christianity in Egypt in the early fourth century, where it rapidly became the majority religion. Emperor Theodosius dealt the decisive blow to the moribund Egyptian polytheistic religion, and other polytheisms, by a decree in 384 establishing Christianity as the official religion of the Empire, outlawing "Paganism" including unchristian animal sacrifices, animal mummification and magic, and closing down almost all of the Egyptian temples.

In 391, the *Serapeum* in Alexandria, the temple of the Greco-Egyptian god Serapis, was attacked and burned down by Christians under the inspiration of Theophilus. The symbolism here was extraordinary — at one and the same time, polytheism was being destroyed via what was probably the biggest temple in the world at that time; one of the last meager remnants of Egyptian theological influence was erased; and all this was being carried out with the participation of Egyptians converted to Christianity. What was left in Serapis of the beloved Egyptian god Osiris and the powerful creator god Ptah was now destroyed by Egyptians, themselves.

In c. 415, another deeply symbolic blow to "unchristian" concepts was struck with the horrific torturing and murder of the Neoplatonist Hypatia (born in Alexandria in c. AD 370). Hypatia was probably one of the last scientist-philosophers working in what remained of the great Alexandria Library and in what remained of Greek science, which had been persecuted out of existence. For Egyptian Christianity and its Patriarch of the time, Cyril (d. AD 444), Hypatia epitomized the Greek "pagan" and suspicious ideals of science and philosophy as values which were more important than the Christian faith. Christian fanatics ripped her flesh from her body and burned her and her books. As late as the mid-fifth century AD, there is evidence that fanatical Christian monks attacked "pagan" temples and destroyed statues.

By this time, the Egyptian people were an integral part of the movement towards the adoption of Christianity that had spread throughout the Roman

Empire and cut across political and cultural nationalisms. There were many aspects in Christianity — in addition to, or despite, its fanatical militancy — which the Egyptians could easily grasp and appreciate: the Christian "triad" of Father, Son and Holy Spirit, the Neoplatonist multiple approach to the sacred, the Jesus savior role like Osiris, the Mary consoling mother like Isis, the similarity between "The Virgin and Child" and Isis and Horus, and the Christian Paradise concept which was a clear improvement over the *Duat* afterlife. Moreover, several of the magical aspects of Christianity, like the use of idols (even if this remained controversial within the emerging Church) and the Eucharist sacrament were much like their own ancient *heka*, magic system.

Egyptian Christianity also exercised a particularly important influence on world Christianity with the development of a monastic movement in desert locations from the early fourth century. The first major monastery in Christianity — Saint Catherine's — was built on Mount Moses in the Sinai between 527 and 565. The Egyptian monastic movement was exemplary concerning piety, abnegation and anti-political and establishment behavior, both for Egypt and the Early Christian Church.

After the split of the Roman Empire in 395 and the incorporation of Egypt into its East Roman (or Byzantine segment), Egypt became more and more part of an eastern Mediterranean Christian religious and cultural zone, albeit in almost constant rivalry with the other great Christian zone of the time, Syria and its Church of Antioch. It is this date — 395 — which is the usually accepted date for the formal end of ancient Egyptian history. It was under East Roman rule in the succeeding years that Christianity took a firm hold in Egypt and ended the slightest semblance to an Egyptian Egypt. Emblematically, this deep change was marked a year earlier, in 394, in the Philae Isis Temple by the last carving in hieroglyphs, in the *medu netjer*, the sacred language of the Egyptian gods.

However, the agony over what new religion best suited the needs of the Egyptian people was far from over. The search for what was the deep substance of Christianity and monotheism continued among the Egyptian Christians for another 250 years before the collapse in favor of Islam.

Egyptian Christianity — run by Greeks and Romans — not only participated in the numerous theological and political quarrels which embroiled the Early Christian Church, but it was frequently the turbulent center of this debate concerning the nature of Christianity. It is difficult to say to what extent, or even whether, the Greek and Roman leaders of Egyptian Christianity were directly influenced by ancient Egyptian religious attitudes. Egyptian Christian leaders right from Clement's time (c. AD 150–215) claimed that they had considerable knowledge of the ancient Egyptian religion, including its "secret" elements. They usually took great care to emphasize that these Egyptian religious views were false. However, it is nevertheless certain that they championed several theological options that were reminiscent of ancient Egyptian beliefs and they manifested the same frenzy for theological experimentation, contradiction and change without change that had been a hallmark of the ancient Egyptians.

The liturgical function of images — their veneration, promoted by the Egyptian Christian monks — was a central aspect of Egyptian Christian doctrine just as it had been for the Egyptian polytheists. Egyptian Christians from at least the early fourth century were (and still are) "icondules," worshippers of images. They believed that icons of Jesus and the saints were alive, could be influenced to produce miracles, and deepened the faith of those who kissed, prostrated themselves and prayed to them. It was perhaps the Egyptian Christians who were the first to make icons and they believed them to be "written" as well as "painted," or even done "without hands," that is miraculously. All this is very reminiscent of the traditional Egyptian beliefs that a work of art is not real or complete unless it is named by an accompanied, identifying text, that an image is a "guide," an "opener" and that the statues of the gods and goddesses are magically the gods and the goddesses, that the *ka* soul of the god, the double, is within the statue.

This Egyptian Christian view created immense conflict within the Church because it clearly contravened the Hebrew, and now Christian, second commandment against the worship of religious images. It also largely contributed to the hostility that the western leaders of the Church felt against Egypt. The Hieria Synod in AD 753 ruled that image worshippers were Christological heretics and ordered all images of the saints destroyed. But only 24 years later, in 787, the Nicea Ecumenical Council authorized the veneration of images, nearly 150 years after most Egyptians had converted to Islam. This was confirmed and amplified in the Byzantine Empire in 843 by Methodios, the Patriarch of Constantinople. In the Western Church, the matter of icons was not definitely settled until the fourth Lateran Council in Rome in 1215, which decided that Jesus was present in the Eucharist but not in the images of him. This constituted a final break between the Roman Catholic Church and the centrality of image worship that was so much a part of both ancient and Christian Egypt.

Above all, and at the same time, Alexandria was a major center for the debate within the Church concerning Christology, that is, the nature of Jesus. Perhaps more than any other single factor, the Christological debate deeply affected Egyptian Christianity, with the term "Alexandrian theology" eventually signifying heresy. As we shall see, this played a significant role in the acceptance of Moslem rule in Egypt from 642.

Origen (c. AD 185–254), an Alexandrian theologian, supposedly self-castrated, was the first to rock the Christological boat. While he was opposed to images and idols, which he said represented things which do not exist, he held that although the Trinity was a unity, the Son Jesus was a less important god than the Father. This split the Trinity into unequal parts and virtually created a polytheistic situation in which there were indeed three gods. Arius, another Alexandrian theologian (c. AD 250–336), with Arianism, claimed that only God the Father was completely divine and that the Son Jesus was a created being who was not god, but was more than a man and should be worshipped: another quasi-polytheistic situation. Perhaps, both Origen and Arius represented a subconscious Egyptian nostalgia for polytheism.

Linked to Christology, Origen held that Mary was the *Theotokos*, the "Godbearer" — "the Mother of God." This attribution, obviously similar to Isis' role as "mother of all the gods" from the New Kingdom (c. 1550–1069 BC), had not been used before by the Early Church, but despite opposition it became official doctrine at the Ecumenical Council of Ephesus in AD 431, presided by Cyril (d. AD 444), the Patriarch of Alexandria. Cyril was usually fanatical in fulfilling his duties in Alexandria — whether this concerned persecuting Christians who did not agree with him, persecuting scientists and philosophers, expelling Jews, or protecting the Egyptian Church from domination by Constantinople.

At the Council of Ephesus, Cyril had Nestorius (d. AD c. 451), the Patriarch of Constantinople, overthrown and banished to Upper Egypt. The apparent, but uncertain, reasons were that Nestorius refused to accept the *Theotokos* concept and supposedly claimed that Jesus was incarnated in virtually two separate persons, one divine and the other human.

Cyril was the inventor of the Monophysite view that Jesus had only one nature, that he was a single divine being, God, or rather more precisely that the union of God, the Word (the *logos*), with the flesh at the instant of incarnation in Jesus created a divine union which was impossible to break. Here, there seems to be almost as much Ptah/Memphite theology as Saint John's doctrine of the logos/word. The orthodox Christian view of Jesus as two beings, God and human in one hypostasis, was mainly championed by the Syrian Church in Antioch and the Monophysite view was championed by Alexandrian Christianity.

Cyril now attempted to reconcile the antagonists in the Christological quarrel by insisting on the unity aspect of the Monophysite view — that Jesus' single nature was the fruit of the union of the *logos* and the flesh. The Egyptian Christian, or Coptic views, in all their forms, including Cyril's, were rejected by the Chalcedonian Council in AD 451.

Many other Christological doctrines, each more subtle (or incredible) than the last, were developed by Alexandrian and other theologians. The apotheosis was perhaps reached with the monotheltic view, invented in AD 638 by Sergius, the Patriarch of Constantinople, that Jesus indeed had two natures but that he had only one *monos*, one will. But the Egyptian Copts stuck to their hard-line Monophysite views and increasingly were seen as heretics and increasingly were persecuted by Constantinople.

On the one hand, the Coptic view seemed to be in contradiction to ancient Egyptian religious traditions that a god could be incarnated simultaneously in several forms, notably in animal and/or human forms. On the other hand, it was in accord with the Egyptian religious concept that a leader, a pharaoh, was a god and that the pharaoh, like Jesus, had a divine father and a human mother. In any case, whether or not the Egyptian Christian theologians had been affected by the remnants of the religious atmosphere of old Egypt still floating about, it seems certain that the ancient Egyptian priests of Heliopolis, Memphis or Thebes would have loved this Christological debate in which any contradiction could be absorbed into a synthesis without losing its contradictory nature.

In the final analysis, the Egyptian Monophysite version of Christianity, while it was certainly a monotheism and perhaps even a stronger monotheism than the orthodox version, nevertheless maintained a vague link to polytheism since a man, Jesus, was a god. Origen's and Arius' theories even went further towards polytheism.

The Greek polytheistic influence on Christian theology and social mores, and especially the Neoplatonists, were additional values which meant that the Egyptian (and European) transition from polytheism might have been less abrupt and total and something of a transition than it could seem at first glance. But if, theologically, Christianity was something of a transition as well as a revolution, it was clearly perceived by many Egyptians (and Europeans) as bringing essential spiritual, ethical and social progress and comfort.

The last vestige of the Egyptian polytheistic religion — the cult of the goddess Isis, which was extremely popular throughout the Greco-Roman world — was outlawed by another Christian decree in 535. The closing down of the Philae Isis Temple, which had already been partially a church for nearly 200 years, by the Byzantine Emperor Justinian I (AD 527–565), was accompanied by the transformation of the entirety of the temple complex into a church with a resulting massive defiguration of the reliefs and sculptures of the Egyptian gods and goddesses. Justinian reiterated the prohibition of so-called "paganism" he had made in 529 when he closed down all the Greek philosophical schools. He now also outlawed anti-Christian blasphemy and obliged the people to be baptized and attend church.

In taking such extreme measures, Justinian was in fact merely applying the militant, intolerant Christian attitude of the time. In addition to political reasons, he might have even sincerely believed that unity was necessary before the second coming of Jesus. In Egypt, the practical result of his policies was the deathblow to the moribund Egyptian polytheistic religion. Strangely, a single Egyptian religious practice — mummification — continued sporadically among Egyptian Christians, right to the Moslem conquest.

THE MOSLEM CONQUEST AND CONVERSION OF EGYPT

Christianity might have won in Egypt, had its mainly Greek leaders not had such an obsessive propensity towards defending minority theological views together with an odd nostalgia for polytheism, matters which eventually put Egyptian Christianity on the fringes of Christianity and opened a highway for the Moslem conquest.

The question of what monotheistic religion was best for Egypt was re-launched by the emergence of the Moslem version of monotheism in the early years of the seventh century and was settled by the Arab conquest of Egypt in 642. The new and eventually stable Moslem version of monotheism was gradu-ally adopted in Egypt, together with maintenance of a minority Monophysite Christian religion.

The Moslem conquest and conversion of Egypt went off relatively smoothly. It took place in troubled times of wars between the Christian Byzan-tine Empire and Zoroastrian Persia (604–628) and then between the Arab Mos-lems and the Persians (632–651) and the Arab Moslems and the Byzantine Empire (from 632 to the unsuccessful siege of Constantinople from 674 to 678).

This time, Egypt's "old friends," the Persians, had once again occupied Egypt from 618 to 628 and engaged in widespread persecution including the massacre of Christian monks. Byzantine rule was restored after the Persian withdrawal, but it remained shaky and was an easy prey for the Arab Moslem forces who had tremendous momentum, both theologically and militarily. Noth-ing, and nobody, could stop the triumphant Moslem sweep, and certainly not the docile Egyptians.

From 632, the Moslem army concurrently attacked the Zoroastrian Sasa-nian Persian Empire and the Christian Byzantine successors of the East Roman Empire. In less than 20 years, the Moslems destroyed the Persian Empire and in less than 50 years plunged the Byzantine Empire into disarray, leaving it in con-trol of only Anatolia and parts of southeastern Europe. By 651, the Arab Moslems had fought and preached their way out of Arabia and into Mesopotamia, Persia, the Levant and North Africa. By 733, in a little under a century, they had consoli-dated their rule from Spain in the west to the Oxus River and India and China in the east.

In 639, a small Arab army led by Amr Ibn al-As invaded Egypt. By 641, the exhausted Byzantines sued for peace and in 642, Egypt was captured. Perhaps the majority of Christian Egyptians almost welcomed the Moslem invaders; in any case, they certainly did not resist much and surrendered quickly. The Moslem army was preceded by its reputation of having massacred tens of thousands of Christians and Jews, notably in Syria and Arabia, who had resisted or refused to convert or submit. This must have had a fearful effect on the morale of the Copts.

However, many other factors came into play. The loyalty of the Egyptian Monophysite Christians had been severely weakened over a long period. They had not only been subjected to heavy taxation and a weak military defense by Constantinople, but as we have seen they had also been subjected to hostility and persecution by the strong anti-Monophysite Chalcedonian elements in the Constantinople Byzantine Church, who treated them as heretics.

Moreover, the Moslem invaders and then occupiers committed very few errors. In many ways, they were more tolerant than the Byzantines. There was no immediate attempt to massively convert the Egyptian Christians or to persecute them. The churches were not closed. The Monophysite view, as almost any Christian theological opinion, was irrelevant to the Moslems, and that enabled the Egyptian Copts to stabilize it. The Byzantine tax system was more or less maintained, but not aggravated. The change of language from Coptic and Greek to Arabic was a slow process with Arabic only becoming the official language of Egypt in 705 and only totally replacing Coptic and Greek in the ninth century, with exception of the use of Coptic as a liturgical language which continues in our time.

The Egyptian Christians became *Dhimma*, protected but specially taxed people and second class citizens, with severe restrictions on church building and political activity (which still exist today). The Egyptians, who since Greek times had called themselves *Aigyptioi* (westernized as Coptic) now left this term to the exclusive usage of the Egyptian Christians. The Copts in Egypt accepted what many Christians and Jews in Syria and Arabia had refused. But the Arab Moslem leaders of Egypt now preferred to allow the Egyptian Christians to gradually understand by themselves what was religiously best for them, that is, conversion to Islam.

The conversion of the Copts was a slow process; but when a Copt converted to Islam, he was treated in the same manner as a Moslem anywhere, whatever his origin. A Copt newly converted to Islam became a full-fledged member of the world family of Moslems, the *Umma*. For the ordinary Egyptian, who had never been an entirely respectable member of the Greek or Roman families and was frequently a marginal member of the Christian family, this feeling of belonging was something entirely new.

Just as the Egyptians had once seen spiritual progress and comfort and equality in Christianity, they now gradually saw them in Islam, with the added quality of tolerance. The Moslems also offered even greater religious certitude and an even more all-encompassing system of daily life than the Christians. In the Moslem system, like the ancient Egyptian system, there were no "maybes." There was also great comfort in being part of a new powerful empire rather than part of the Byzantine world that was dwindling and had not protected them from the Persians. Furthermore, the theological transition from polytheism to monotheism that the Egyptians had begun with Christianity was now logically crowned by the adoption of the most integral and rigorous brand of total monotheism, which Islam represented.

Not surprisingly, the question of Jesus as a god was the most difficult problem that the Egyptians had to confront during their conversion to Islam. On the one hand, there was a certain coherency and modernity in the monotheistic Moslem view that no man, not even Jesus, could be a god and given the dynamism and power of the Moslems, it was possible to assume that Islam and the prophet Mohammed were indeed the "seal" of monotheism, God's final word. On the other hand, the Jesus savior figure and the Mary consolation figure remained powerfully attractive in Egypt and remained somehow attached to the beloved Osiris and Isis of old. Moreover, although Allah was a single divine nature and therefore just as monotheistic as the Egyptian Monophysite view of Jesus, Allah was transcendent and therefore not as close to suffering humanity as Jesus. However, this transcendence was considerably attenuated by the powerful rule played by Mohammed as the sole prophet of Allah.

The result of all this soul-searching was a split among the people, with the vast majority converting to Islam and the survival of a minority Monophysite Christian Coptic Christianity. Despite later and abundant persecution that still goes on today (and which since the 1980s has become terrifyingly endemic), the Coptic Church has maintained itself in Egypt as a minority community of at least five million people, under ten per cent of the Egypt's total population.

Over the centuries, despite the persistence of Coptic Christianity, and into our time, Islam became Egypt's stable religious system. Just like the Christians before them, the Moslems gradually destroyed anything that smacked of ancient Egypt or, at best, simply neglected it. The monuments and art of ancient Egypt had become meaningless and useless to the Egyptian people and this gradually led to the total disappearance of the ancient Egyptian religion and its architecture and art beneath the horizon and the sands. Even the Great Sphinx in Giza, the *shesep ankh*, "the living image," became buried in sand up to its neck. The

Egyptians no longer cared about ancient Egypt and would not begin timidly caring again until the 19th century.

The final disintegration of the Egyptian polytheistic religion and traditions confronted with monotheistic Christianity and Islam therefore occurred with minimal conflict, but the Egyptian religion, together with the later Hindu and Hebrew religions, had lasted longer — more than 3000 years — than any other in known history. Egypt had truly been at the leading edge of religion for at least 1500 years until the rise of Hebrew near-monotheism in the late 13th century BC and had survived until the Christian religion became official and popular in the early fourth century AD. What had been destroyed — the religion which Egypt had founded around 3100 BC — was the most complete and influential religion mankind had ever seen until its time.

Egypt did recover its full political independence in 1953, but, of course, this modern Egypt has very little in common with ancient Egypt, except for its people, who still live on a narrow strip of land bordering the Nile and in the Delta, and who are probably ethnically much the same, although culturally and socially light years apart. The only remains of its ancient culture are static; the language and the religion are not Egyptian and the landscape is dominated by fields covered with cotton rather than emmer wheat and barley. Even the central geographical character of the ancient Two Lands, *Ta-Wy*, the *iteru*, the Nile River, has been altered with the opening of the Aswan High Dam in 1973 and the end of the annual inundation (which should not be regretted, because of the economic improvement it has induced).

The world's great and unceasing interest in ancient Egypt, coupled with tourism, have considerably amended modern Egypt's frequently indifferent views to its heritage. Egyptology is now taught in the universities by Egyptian Egyptologists and there is a spectacular project to build a 125-acre museum near the Giza pyramids to replace the marvelous, but hopelessly cluttered, Cairo Museum. However, the history, art, literature and religion of ancient Egypt remain insufficiently taught in Egypt's schools, almost all of the world's top Egyptologists are not Egyptian, the vast majority of books on ancient Egypt are Western and, aside from the Cairo Museum, all the major Egyptian art collections are in Western museums.

During the hundreds of years it took to destroy Egyptian Egypt, an imaginary and mangled Egypt, *Aigyptos*, emerged in European religion, esotericism, philosophy and science. Ancient Egypt became passionately more important for the West than it was for Egypt. This led to an Egypt in which its authentic role as a hinge, a link, and a turning point, and a role as an imaginary hinge society, emerged simultaneously.

Chapter 14. Egypt as a Hinge Society, a Link and an Influence — Authentic and Imaginary

The Egypto-African Connection — Convergences between Egyptian and African Divine Kingships

Much remains to be explored concerning Egypt's influence on African religions and African influence on Egyptian religion. This is a difficult task due to the quasi-absence of surviving Neolithic and Early Bronze Age African works of art and architecture and the lateness of African written documents and history. African oral traditions do not fill this gap. It difficult to evaluate what was the result of Egyptian influence and what was the result of independent African development. It is just as difficult to evaluate what was the result of African influence on Egypt and what could have been elements of a common culture between Egypt and Africa.

For the most part, non-African knowledge of African religions and societies began with Arab historians in the 11th century and was further constructed during the European colonial period, beginning in the second half of the 15th century AD, from available art, religious practices, oral traditions, observation and speculation. African priests, usually grouped in secret societies, did not greatly cooperate with these efforts. Moreover, the first Arab and European accounts were obviously tainted by racism and the need to justify colonialism and slavery.

It is only recently that African scholars themselves, like the Malian Amadou Hampate Bâ (1900–1991), especially concerning oral traditions, the Senegalese historian Cheikh Anta Diop (1923–1986), the Congolese writer Théophile Obenga (b. 1936) and the historians who worked with J. Ki-Zerbo (b. 1922) on the Unesco *General History of Africa* (to name only a few scholars), undertook to depict ancient African societies and religions from a non-European point of view. This type of African studies is flourishing in the U.S., but one of its consequences has been the ambiguous Afrocentric school founded by Molefi Kete Asante (b. 1942), which sets some things right but fundamentally promotes the erroneous thesis that Egypt was a black African civilization. (This imaginary side of Egypt will soon be examined.)

Aside from Nubian culture, it is difficult to draw many conclusions, or even to speculate, about any ancient African culture earlier than the Nok culture of Nigeria which dates to the 9th century BC Iron Age and for which sixth century BC terra cotta sculptures have been found. These sculptures — as well as most succeeding African art — do not seem to belong to the same family of expression as Egyptian art. We have very little knowledge about Africa before the Nok period except for Egyptian references in art and texts concerning Nubia, notably Nubian soldiers and slaves and African prisoners and slaves, and the African goods which were much sought by the Egyptians as luxury products: incense, gems, ebony, animal hides and live animals such as giraffes and monkeys. The most extensive Egyptian descriptions of African lands other than Nubia concern a land of Punt, which seems to correspond to the coastal areas of what is now Sudan, Eritrea, Djibouti and Somalia. Of these descriptions, the fullest are the carvings and paintings of an expedition to Punt on the walls of Pharaoh Hatshepsut's (c. 1473–458 BC) Deir-el-Bahri mortuary temple, but they are insufficient for the drawing of cultural and theological conclusions.

These gaps make it unfortunately impossible to verify countless suppositions about the links between Egypt and Africa. Although comparisons between ancient Egyptian culture and theology and what we know about African cultures and theologies only for the past few hundred years can provide some clues, it is a haphazard process.

Despite all these difficulties, the issue of a possible African connection to Egypt's origins has become a burning question, partially for legitimate historical reasons, partially for natural motives of curiosity and partially for socio-political reasons.

The general thrust of mainstream views by historians, Egyptologists and Africanists, operating on the basis of scanty demonstrable proofs, provide some answers, but also continue to pose questions. As we have seen in Chapters 1 and 3, the usual, prudent conclusion is that in the early Naqada I Period (c. 4000–3500 BC) a common cultural and technological background was shared between Egypt, Libya, at least northern Nubia and perhaps Nilotic East Africa and that there was an ethnic black Nubian element in the population; and then, after about 3500 BC, a separate Egyptian development with a fusion of North African,

Semitic and black elements into the Egyptian Mediterranean type and the persistence of darker complexioned people south of Thebes. It is also usually assumed that as the centuries and millennia unfolded, Egypt's development became both largely independent and more and more subject to significant West Asian influence.

It is likely that the Egyptian religion was imposed on Nubia, perhaps as early as the Fifth Dynasty (c. 2494–2345BC). Egypt also could have been one of the main influences in the Horn of Africa (Punt) from as early as about 2300 BC. During Thutmose III's military campaigns after c. 1458 BC and the Egyptian conquest of land well beyond the Fourth Cataract of the Nile, direct Egyptian influence on the Bantu people of this region could have occurred. It is certain that after the defeat of the 25th Kushite Dynasty (c. 747–656 BC) in Egypt, the Egyptian religion played a direct role in the constitution of the specific Nubian religion. Egypt, directly or via Nubia, also probably influenced the religions of southern Sudan, the Horn of Africa and East Africa and in all likelihood played a role in the elaboration of many other independently developed African religions.

In addition to this scenario, there are basically two radical views concerning relations between Egypt and Africa. E.A. Wallis Budge, in *Osiris & The Egyptian Resurrection*, postulated that the early "Egyptians...are Africans [like] the people...in the Sûdân are Africans..." and that "Egyptian beliefs...are of indigenous origin, Nilotic or Sûdânî in the broadest signification of the word...[and that] foreign influences first modified...then checked their growth and finally overthrew them." Within this schema, Budge believed that "it is wrong to class the Religion of Ancient Egypt with the elaborate theological systems of peoples of Asiatic or European origin." Nevertheless, Budge somehow distinguished three categories of Africans — Egyptians, Nubians and Blacks.[160] The Senegalese historian Cheikh Anta Diop, in *The African Origin of Civilization, Myth or Reality*, held that "Ancient Egypt was a Negro civilization" which "descended from that of Nubia, in other words, Sudan," that the "Ethiopians" (Nubians/Sudanese) and the Egyptians were the first people to attain what we call "civilization" and then influenced other African societies and the world.[161] All the other radical views about the Egypt/Africa relationship are more or less variants of these views.

Budge listed an impressive number of similarities between ancient Egyptian beliefs and modern African beliefs, but he omitted many key differences and

---

160. Budge, E.A. Wallis, *Osiris & The Egyptian Resurrection, Volume I*, pp. 361, vii, xxvi, 200 and *Volume II*, p. 222.

161. Diop, Cheikh Anta, *The African Origin Of Civilization, Myth Or Reality*, pp. xiv, 150, 244 and 151-152.

drew his conclusions from a very personal interpretation of the residual religious and societal practices of the African religions during his time.

Diop's thesis that the Ethiopian/Egyptian religion was the core of the entirety of Africa's religions, including the rise of great societies in West Africa from about 700 BC, seems far too radical and unverifiable. (Diop's views will be dealt with more fully in the Afrocentric section.)

There are similarities in Egyptian and many African creation myths, cosmogonies and magical behavior patterns. One of these similarities is the concept that a creator god organized the universe, created and provided the life force to all forms of existence — nature, humans, animals and the afterlife — and must be constantly appeased. The similarity here is in tone, more than in content, since creator god notions of this type can be found nearly everywhere in the world. The notions of a constant threat of disorder if magical rituals and sacrifices by divine leaders and sorcerers to appease the gods are not correctly carried out or if an individual's or a collectivity's behavior are not in conformity with the divine design are either common to Egyptian and African religions or are influenced by Egypt.

However, there are a great variety of African creation myths, some similar to the Egyptian concept of original chaos, such as one variant of the Yoruba (Nigeria) creation myth which starts the world with a watery chaos similar to the Egyptian Nun and *waret*, or the Boshingo (central Africa) myth in which darkness and a watery realm preceded creation. Many other African creation myths, including Yoruba myths, have very little resemblance to the Egyptian creation myths. The Yoruba ancestor of mankind, Oduduwa, came down to the world on a chain with a cock, a bit of earth and a palm grain. The Fang (Gabon and the Congo Brazzaville) believed that nothing but the god Nzame existed before creation, as did the Dogons (Mali) with their god, Amma. The Ngbaka's (northern Congo-Kinshasa) supreme god Gale sent the brother and sister team Seto and Nebo to earth where they copulated and created the Ngbaka people.

The concept of a supreme, omnipotent and omniscient sky god among many other gods in many African religions resembles Egyptian chief god theology and notably the god Amun-Re. The South African Zulu Unkulunka — the ukqili, "the wise one" — the East African Ganda people's Katonda — "the big eye in the sky" — the Ghanaian Akan's Brekyirlhunuade, who "knows all and sees all," the distant, concealed Baule's (Ivory Coast) Alura, the Nigerian Isoko's Cghene who sends all good things and his anger, but is never seen and cannot be understood, and many other African gods resemble the all-knowing, wise, hidden (and from whom nothing is hidden) Egyptian Amun. However, one of the main characteristics of the Egyptian chief gods was that they amalgamated many gods as their aspects into a single unit, a practice absent in Africa.

There is also a great divide between Egypt and Africa when it comes to the representation of the divinities. African sculptures and masks almost never depicted the gods; they were not idols of the gods. They alluded to the gods as fetishes empowered by the spirits that mediate with the gods, in sharp contrast to the direct and detailed Egyptian depiction of the gods as idols. The African divinities were immanent in the elements of nature, but they were ethereal and described in words; they were not idols; the Egyptian divinities were the epitome of both immanence and of physical representation.

In the central domain of the afterlife, the Egyptian notion of the *Duat*, the "Other Land," and the generalized African-animist notion of the constant invisible and mediating presence of the spirits of the ancestors in an invisible realm, but in this life, in this world, as well as the link between the visible and invisible worlds, are considerably different. The gap is huge between visits of the Egyptian *ba* and *akh* souls to the living (to perhaps settle some minor family problems), and the usual African concepts of the ancestors constantly and deeply immersed in the daily life of the living, on the land where they were born.

The convergence between many aspects of Egyptian and African divine kingships seems to indicate the likelihood of both direct and indirect Egyptian influence. In the Kushitic zones of Nubia, Ethiopia, the Horn and Kenya, it seems evident that there was an early and direct Egyptian divine kingship influence. Elsewhere in Africa — from the Congo to West Africa to East and Southern Africa — the probable dates for the establishment of divine kingships are relatively late, during the first millennium AD and usually even later. Nevertheless, the similarities between divine kingships in many African civilizations and in Egypt were strong and suggest a single origin.

The coronation ceremony of the Egyptian king and many African kings involved a magical ceremony in which the throne, the king's seat, was a source of his divinity. The Egyptian and the African king were then invested with divine powers, considered as sons of gods, the providers of all forces which rendered the good life possible and in charge of maintaining cosmic order and preventing or correcting disorder.

However, there was a fundamental difference in thrust between the African ritual murder of the old, feeble king and the Egyptian *heb sed* jubilee, ritual. The *heb sed* theoretically took place for the first time after the pharaoh had reigned 30 years; African kingly ritual murder took place whenever it was thought that the king was too weak and in some African societies was systematically organized after the king had reigned only for a couple of years.

For the Egyptians, the *heb-sed* was designed not only to prove that the pharaoh-god remained physically strong, but above all to procure resurrection and renewed strength for him in this life. For the Africans, the ritual murder of an old king took place because his powers had waned and he therefore no longer physically mirrored divine order and prosperity and was no longer able to ensure it. Ritual murder of the African king, usually together with a huge number of his servants and entourage (and sometimes the eating of the murdered king's heart, as among the Yorubas), ended the king's ordinary material life on earth, put him into the realm of the spirits and constituted a system of royal succession — the opposite of the goals sought by the *heb-sed.* The Egyptians sought to regenerate their old pharaoh; the Africans sought to expedite their old king into the invisible world.

The Nubians, sparked by Egyptian colonization and influence, adopted their own national version of divine kingship whenever they had autonomous power and naturally perpetuated the Egyptian divine kingship system when they ruled Egypt (between about 747 to 656 BC). From about at least the sixth century AD, perhaps much earlier, divine kingship was a frequent form of government in many parts of Africa. Egyptian divine kingship could have spread from Nubia to much of Africa after the eighth century BC. It was clearly flourishing when the Portuguese explorers and colonizers arrived in Africa after 1460 AD.

Given the overall similarity of the strong divine kingship institution in Egypt and Africa, one could expect similarities in clerical institutions. In fact, these are radically different. This is notably the case for the absence of organized African clergies and shrines and temples that were of such central importance in Egypt. However, it is possible that the secret societies, so prevalent in Africa, which assisted the priests in their ritual duties, were the African equivalent of the elaborate and complex Egyptian clergies. On the other hand, like the Egyptians, the African sacred kings had luxurious palaces, a large number of wives, big administrative staffs and a huge number of slaves.

The probabilities lean towards an Egyptian influence on African divine kingship institutions rather than the contrary; but it is theoretically possible to inverse the problem. It is possible to see the origins of divine kingship in African countries like the Sudan or simultaneously in East and Central African countries and Egypt, in times before 3500 BC, when these zones were culturally similar. The African practice of ritually killing sorcerer/rain-makers when they became old or when they failed to produce results can be seen as a forerunner of the ceremony that the Egyptians attenuated with the *heb-sed* jubilee.

There are many other aspects of African religions that can be ascribed to a common origin, to Egyptian influence or to autonomous African development which came up with beliefs similar to the Egyptians'. One of the most spectacular of these convergences is the Ghanaian Ashanti *Kra*, the life force. It clearly resembles the Egyptian *ka*, not only phonetically but also as a life force and as a part of the soul of the creator god in each person.

It is also evident that there is a similarity between many ancient Egyptian and African everyday objects. This includes braided wigs, combs, mirrors, beds, stools, headrests, baskets, jars and boxes. On the other hand, Egyptian jewelry and textiles differ considerably from the oldest African examples of these objects found and no early African glass or faience has been found.

The bottom line seems to be that, once the characteristic Egypt emerged after 3000 BC, its culture and religion were defined by their distinctiveness. The tendency of this early Egypt was to be an island unto itself. Gradually, over the centuries and millennia, despite the persistence of some African cultural influences, Egypt predominantly became part of an Egyptian/West Asian continuum in political, cultural, commercial and technological terms. A continuum of similar technological and societal structures developed from the Egyptian Nile to the Mesopotamian Tigris; it did not extend into black Africa, except, of course, for Nubia. Writing, monumental architecture, advanced agricultural and irrigation systems and urban values were common aspects of the Egyptian/West Asian cultural continuum after 3000 BC; they did not exist in Africa during the same timeframe. Characteristic Egypt and characteristic Africa, as we know them, are basically the expressions of different cultural contexts.

THE PROBABLE EGYPTIAN INFLUENCE ON THE HEBREW MESSIAH-KING, JESUS, SON OF GOD, AND OTHER DIVINE KINGSHIP CONCEPTS

Can Egyptian influence on forms of divine kingship be assumed concerning the Hebrews, the Christians and Rome and Europe? The major hurdle to such a view is the absence of direct references attesting that these peoples adopted, or adapted, divine kingship from the Egyptians. This does not categorically mean that such influence did not exist. The double possibility that there was insidious Egyptian influence in some zones and a wholly independent emergence of this concept among many other peoples is an attractive option.

The Hebrew attitude to divine kingship might have been as much a direct result of their supposed Egyptian experience as a result of their monotheistic hostility to anybody but Yahweh having any kind of divine attributes. It is obvious that the Hebrews were at first reticent concerning the very notion of kingship and utterly opposed to divine kingship, the deification of a human being. For the early Hebrews, preponderantly immersed in religion rather than politics, the only king was Yahweh, the *melech haolim*, the King of the universe. Despite the defeat of this religious reticence by the political leaders, Hebrew kingship was always subject to extreme tension between the political and the religious, with the result being that the Hebrews eventually adopted systems which closely linked their kings to Yahweh.

The Hebrews began by preferring judges (*shophetim*) to kings. Deeply pious, but without any divine attributes, the judges were essentially religious leaders — contrary to the system of Egyptian theocracy, the mix of religion and politics. The judges may have ruled Judah and Israel from about 1200 BC to the establishment of Saul as King of the United Monarchy about 1020 BC. The Judge Samuel reluctantly named Saul as king, but continued to reserve divine attributes to the sole God Yahweh.

Saul had a frenzied, trance-like prophetic relationship with Yahweh which seems to owe something to both the Egyptian oracle priests and the emerging Syrian-Hebrew system of *nabiim* (prophets). Saul's establishment of a political kingship was controversial. On the one hand, the people wanted "a king... like all the nations" and the military necessity of combating the Philistines pled in favor of the unifying factor represented by a king. On the other hand, the Hebrew religious leaders seem to have considered the period of the judges as a golden age of personal freedom and righteousness uncontaminated by politics and the inception of political royalty as the possible beginning of corruption.

Yahweh himself did not like the idea and told the Judge Samuel that he considered himself "rejected." For Yahweh, the institution of kingship was an encroachment on his divine kingship powers,[162] something which *a fortiori* indicated that the leap from pharaoh to pharaoh-god was a logical theological step, that kings were indeed divine.

All this was so logical that, although by about the sixth century BC the Hebrews had developed the world's first system of absolute and exclusive monotheism, they also no longer had an aversion to divinely linked kings and went further still by developing the radical messiah-king concept.

The messiah-king concept seems to owe something to the Egyptian pharaoh-god concept and especially his status as an ideal personage and his role of ensuring cosmic and worldly harmony and peace. The Hebrew messiah-king to come, while not theoretically divine, in practice would carry quasi-divine attributes, notably that of establishing universal peace and brotherhood. The Hebrew messiah, son of King David, was therefore a kind of ideal personage with similarities to the pharaoh and his role in Egyptian theology, even if the messiah was a more spiritualized and ethical variant of the Egyptian concept.

The Buddhists traveled a similar road to the Hebrews concerning the rejection of divine kingship, but succumbed to a form of deification of humans from at

---

162. I Samuel 8:1-22.

least the 2nd century AD by declaring that their *bodhisattvas*, their potential Buddhas, who had refused extinction in Nirvana in order to share the lives of the people, were gods.

The Romans came closest to the Egyptian concept of a powerful superhuman being, capable of being a god and directing the affairs of humanity. But the Roman application of divine kingship was a pale reflection of the Egyptian system. Nevertheless, the reasons for a Roman Emperor declaring himself a god were much the same as those of the pharaohs — acquiring absolute political and military clout by putting oneself in the league of divinities rather than humans. The situation which rendered divine kingship possible, both in Egypt and in Rome, was also the same — the exploitation of the people's overwhelming need not only for superhuman protection, but for immanent superhuman protection, for a god incarnated in a human, or a superhuman presence in the world of humans. Octavian/Augustus (63 BC–AD 14) as divi filius, son of god, and the first to name himself Emperor of Rome (27 BC), seems to correspond perfectly to this schema..

After Augustus, the Roman emperors continued to be considered as gods incarnated in humans. A first apex in this system was reached with Aurelian (AD 270–275), who was virtually a substitute, a viceroy, for the god Sol Invictus (the unconquered sun). Diocletian (AD 284–305) probably went furthest of all in setting up an absolute divine right monarchy and virtual theocracy while claiming that he was not a king.

He supposedly came to power by divine will, was "son of the gods," "creator of the gods," Jovius (Jupiter, the Roman Chief and sky god) and the *Domini Noster* (Our Lord). Diocletian adopted an Egyptian-type system in which a Divine Plan made him the Great Provider, the provider of all good things which made life possible, much like the Egyptian pharaohs. He was one of the most dreadful persecutors of Christians. He was in Egypt in AD 296 to put down a revolt by Achilleus, and thus became the last Roman Emperor to visit Egypt.

The Christians, after getting more than a little help between about 200 BC and AD 100 from Hebrew apocalyptic writers and sects, extraordinarily, incredibly and imaginatively carried the concept of divine kingship even further. The Christian heirs to the Hebrews transformed the messiah-king concept and deified Jesus. They also eventually allotted a quasi-divine status to Mary as mother of God.

Despite his short stay among humans, Jesus eventually became the most successful of both the dying/resurrecting and incarnated-in-a-human gods. The path opened by the Egyptians with the pharaoh-god culminated with the Christian concept of Jesus' superhuman presence on earth as the unblemished savior, the comforter and the consoler — the Good Shepherd.

Jesus became an example of a traditional Egyptian-like son of a god/man-god system, and at the same time a son of the only God, ruler-king of the universe, and God himself within the trinity which is also a unity. These aspects of the Jesus concept are so similar to the Egyptian pharaoh-god/man-god, son of Re and Amun/Re/Ptah organic triad concepts that it seems impossible to exclude some kind of Egyptian influence.

The Jesus concept seems to owe even more to the god Osiris. Osiris began his career as the god ruling the earth, as the heir to his father (the earth god, Geb) who had also exercised this role. But somewhere down the line, Osiris was also like Jesus, something of a man/god, a god and a man, participating in the life of man and sharing his joys and sorrows. He was the god mythically credited with propulsing Egypt from ignorance to knowledge, from primitive religious beliefs to advanced religious beliefs. And Osiris' resurrection and his promise of resurrection after death to all was the supreme gift a god could give to man.

Osiris' resurrection, together with the generalized West Asian theological-agricultural transfer of spring renewal to human resurrection and notably the Sumerian Inanna and Dumuzi ("the flawless young" Tammuz, in later Babylonia) and the Canaanite Baal and Adonis, may have played roles in evolving the resurrected Jesus concept. At the very least, the context of resurrected gods in the Greece of the time with Persephone/Kore and Dionysus, the temptation of Son of God/Son of Man theologies in the Judea of the time and wide general knowledge of the Osiris, Tammuz and Adonis sagas may have exercised considerable theological influence on the elaboration of Christology.

Osiris' national and personal savior role, accompanied by warmth, affection and a meaningful afterlife, were clearly prefigurations of the roles which Jesus later assumed. Jesus supposedly fulfills the promise of the alliance made to Israel and he is also a universal, personal, forgiving savior, using the concept of love in this life and salvation in the afterlife.

The question which can be legitimately asked — and which can never be answered — is: could two such similar gods have arisen in a totally independent manner? However, even if Egyptian mythology and theology and West Asian concepts were perhaps sources of inspiration for some of Christian theology, the distinctive concepts of early Christianity such as egalitarian universalism (except for women) love, fraternity and the lofty concept of total forgiveness could not have owed much to previous theologies.

In medieval and later Europe, political and religious rule by divine right was both a heritage of Antiquity (including Egyptian antiquity) and a perversion of Jesus' clever principle — "Render to Caesar the things that are Caesar's, and to God the things that are God's."[163]

The absolutism of the monarch, apparently begun with Charlemagne (AD 768–814) as Emperor of the Holy Roman Empire, evolved into the medieval concept that God gave absolute political power to the king and absolute spiritual power to the Church. But, of course, both the kings and the popes wanted both powers; in short, without necessarily being aware of it, they wanted an Egyptian-type system. By the 17th century, the concept that the Christian king ruled absolutely by divine right and could do no wrong — politically or religiously — had reached its apex.

The monarchical divine right concept was in almost permanent conflict with the concept of papal divine right, the divine rights of the "Prince of the Church." The pope was not only divinely infallible in religious matters, for centuries, but many popes did their utmost to extend this infallibility into the political realm or to prevent kings from naming bishops. As a political concept, royal divine right survived until the English Civil War and the execution of Charles I in 1649, the American Revolution in 1776 and the French Revolution and the execution of Louis XVI in 1792.

The separation of the Church and State outlined by the first amendment to the American Constitution in 1791 and decreed in no uncertain terms by the French in 1905 put a virtual end — at least in the West — to the monarchical divine right concepts first established in Egypt. However, papal infallibility still stumbles along in the Roman Catholic Church with the affectation that it remains a part of the Pope's divine mandate.

Strong divine kingship systems, with no evident connection to Egypt, and which produced various types of divine kings within widely different systems of religious belief, are found throughout the world — from the theoretically and benevolent and righteous system of the Chinese "Sons of Heaven" after Confucius (c. 551–479 BC) to the omnipotent Shinto "Sons of God" in Japan after the fourth century BC, to the extraordinarily cruel human and animal sacrificing "Sons of the Sun God Inti" of the Inca emperors and the Aztec emperors of the war and sun god Huitzilopochtli and the creator/sun/wind god Quetzalcoatl among the military Indian societies in the 14th and 15th centuries AD.

Unquestionably, divine kingship and the deification of humans in its various forms was a need shared by nearly all of humanity at different times. Unquestionably, the ravages of divine kingship and the deification of humans were immense. Unquestionably, no one can affirm whether another system was possible at any given time before divine kingship was rejected. Unquestionably, divine kingship arose independently in most parts of the world. Unquestionably, the origin of deification of humans — in this life or as ancestors — is lost in the

---

163. Mark 12:17.

night of time. Unquestionably, the first known people who coalesced their beliefs into an elaborate theology of divine kingship were the Egyptians. The unanswered question is — did Egyptian divine kingship insidiously and indirectly influence West Asia and Europe?

EGYPTO-HEBREW CONTACT: A CONNECTION AND A MASSIVE REJECTION

Even if we accept the reality of frequent Egypto-Hebrew relations at least from the late 13th century BC, the central problem remains that very little credible verification of Egypto-Hebrew influence seems possible. Nevertheless, an Egyptian role can be deemed reasonably plausible in several critical domains among the Hebrews, notably the emergence of monotheism, the partially real, real, or at least supposed Egyptian realities in the establishment of the Hebrew national founding Exodus myth, and the adaptation of divine kingship.

It is in the domain of non-magical ethics, a domain in which the Hebrews made the first and one of the most original contributions, that intriguing questions can be asked about the role of the link to Egypt. Yahweh's proclamation to Moses in Leviticus 18:3, that, "After the doings of the land of Egypt...shall ye not do" clearly indicated awareness and explicit rejection of Egyptian practices across the board and especially in regard to ethics. But was this rejection in ethics as complete as it might seem?

The Egyptian *ankh-em-maat*, "living by *maat*," stripped of its crude magical and primeval aspects, shared the same common concern as the Hebrew *tsadaquah* ideal of righteousness for decent behavior in society — doing the ethical thing. The ethical aspects in the Ten Commandments and in the *maat*, as described in the "Negative Confession" in *The Book of the Dead* and especially in the *sebayt*, the Wisdom Texts, do not differ greatly. Moreover, righteousness and justice remained linked to the divine for both the Hebrews and the Egyptians. The Egyptian gods and goddesses and the Hebrew god both desired righteousness, justice and order — even if they imputed very different contents to these concepts.

The key difference between the ethics of Hebrew monotheism and the ethics of *maat* was that the problem of the existence of human evil had central meaning for the Hebrews and the Christians, while the Egyptians were usually content to pay only lip service to an ethical interpretation of the *maat* as a human struggle and duty. Ethical behavior was the law for the Hebrews and the later Christians; it was only recommended decent behavior in society for the Egyptians.

The Bible amply illustrates that Hebrews fervently struggled with the *tsadaquah* principle and with the Ten Commandments and succeeded in at least now and again in applying them. The Egyptians did not understand the centrality of the problem of evil on the human level; evil was assimilated with disorder and necessary and inevitable primeval dualism. It was the job of the pharaoh and the gods, rather than all individuals, to fight and defeat the evil of disorder. The Egyptians pretended that they had behaved ethically and did not feel guilty about this pretence. They sincerely clung to the use of magical manipulative techniques of the gods and magical spells to prevent or overcome any evil and earn the right to an afterlife. The Egyptian gods did not control evil and disorder; they were obliged to combat them in a never-ending daily struggle. Yahweh controlled evil and disorder. The Ten Commandments, supposedly given to Moses by Yahweh, expressed Yahweh's will and were consubstantial with belief in him as the sole god. It was up to man to struggle with and apply the Ten Commandments; Yahweh's only struggle was to find ways to encourage man to love *tsadaquah*, righteousness.

It seems possible to assume that, from very early dates, and perhaps even by the 12th century BC, the law, linked to Yahweh, was sacred for the Israelites. The Ten Commandments represented a coherent attempt at rule by law, independently of an individual's or a society's respect for ethics, and was frequently in opposition to the aggressive side of individuals and society. The Ten Commandments also represented an attempt at egalitarian law linked to human needs and the human thirst for justice. This attempt at egalitarianism radically distinguished the Hebrew ethical code not only from the Egyptian *maat* and Egypt's stiff, sanctified hierarchical society, but also from the hierarchical legal code established by the Babylonian King Hammurabi (c. 1792–1750 BC). By the sixth century BC, with the prophets Deutero-Isaiah and Jeremiah, the Hebrews had developed a system of universal, non-magical and impartial ethics. In the first century AD, the early Judeo-Christian ethical code culminated this evolution with the invention of a super *tsadaquah*, which radically differed from Hebrew ethical values by proposing the unsurpassable ideal of forgiveness, something which places Christianity at the apex of the history of religiously inspired ethics.

And so the plausible conclusion is that the Hebrew leap, and *a fortiori* the Christian leap, to non-magical and egalitarian ethics was a type of leap the Egyptians could not make; but *another* plausible conclusion is that Hebrew ethics emerged from a complex magical magma which it shared with Egypt.

If the radically different systems of Egyptian and Hebrew ethics strangely share some common roots, there seem to be no strange reasons for the large number of magical and ritualistic similarities between the Egyptian and Hebrew religions. The explanation of these similarities strongly seems to be Egyptian and

Sumerian influence. It can be argued that both Hebrew and Egyptian rituals and magic largely derive from the same type of nature religion sprinkled with totemistic concepts common to almost all prehistoric and ancient societies. However, there are far too many striking and detailed similarities to rule out the probability of Egyptian influence. A major magical and ritualistic Egyptian influence on Judaism is likely. In many ways, Israel seems to have made both a selection and a radical break in its Sumerian and Egyptian magical heritages.

There are startling Hebrew resemblances to the Egyptian system in the domain of magical amulets, despite the Hebrews' firm theoretical rejection of magic and especially of Egyptian magic. Like the Egyptian system, the Hebrew amuletic system combines the use of the amulet with the reciting of spells (*keshaphim*), the inscription of "words of power" inside or on the amulet and the naming (the Egyptian *ren* soul name) of demons and evil powers which are being fought or charmed. For the Hebrews, the letters of the alphabet were powerful amulets, just as the hieroglyphs were the *medu netjer*, the words of the gods, for the Egyptians.

The Hebrews, like the Egyptians, were extensive users of amulets and talismans and their amulets (*kam'ea*) were similar to the Egyptian *meket* and *wedja* protection and welfare amulets. The *kam'ea* included the *tefillin* (phylacteries), leather boxes worn on the forehead and left arm during morning prayer; the *tallit* prayer shawl with *zitzith* fringes knotted in such a way to form the numerical value of the word *zitzit*, 613, which is also the number of *mitvot*, the ritual commandments and obligations, the *zitzith* themselves being worn at all times by devout adult males; the *mezuzah* case containing scriptures, placed on the right doorjambs of houses and rooms; the *saharon* protective crescent worn by kings, women and camels; the *hamsa*, hand of God and the *Magen David*, Star of David, as a protection against the evil eye, evil spirits and demons; the *lehashim* snake charms to protect women giving birth against Lilith; the *rimmown*, pomegranates, used by priests in the temple, etc.

Many ancient peoples throughout the world attached strong, magical significance to names, with the Egyptians and the Hebrews going particularly far in this domain. Here again, the Egyptian and Hebrew magical name systems reveal great similarity. The Egyptian name, the *ren*, and the Hebrew name, the *shem*, very clearly have religious attributes. In the Egyptian system, the *ren* is one of a person's five main souls and in both systems, knowledge of a person's name means understanding of the identity of a person and opens the possibility of manipulating and dominating him. As Abigail says in I Samuel 25:25, "for as *is* his name is, so *is* he." Yahweh, in Exodus 3:14, concealed his real name behind the abstract *Yhwh*, "I AM THAT I AM." Moses, in claiming this, perhaps learned a lesson from the Egyptian practice of concealed, real names for their gods and demons. The

Hebrews changed the name of a person who assumed new responsibilities — in Genesis 17:5, Abram became Abraham, when he was destined to become "a father of many nations," just as the pharaoh when ascending to the throne, took four new names in addition to his nomen, birth name. Among the early Judeo-Christians, Jesus in Matthew 1:23 also became Emmanuel — "God with us" — before he himself, in Mark 14:36, instituted the most radical name change of all, with Yahweh, who became *abba*, "my father." Mohammed, in the seventh century BC, continued in this vein, naming Yahweh/ *abba*, Allah.

The Egyptian soul system (in which several souls link up with the body, upon death, and animate it) could have played a role in the definition of the Hebrew *nefesh* or *neshamah*, soul concept. The Hebrews, like the Egyptians, believed that there could be no soul without the body. Ultra orthodox Jews still believe this, even if during the late *Talmudic* Period (before AD c. 500), the Jews introduced some kind of separation of the body and the soul and while acknowledging the standard Hebrew view that the soul left the body at death to return to God, they speculated that the soul was reunited with the body at the final resurrection (which was in many ways similar to what the Egyptian *ba* and *ka* souls did).

Perhaps more astonishing, among Jews in the *Talmudic* Period and among the later Kabalists (from AD c. 12th century), there was a belief, like the Egyptians', in the existence of more than a single soul; this was the *neshamah yeterah*, a temporary, additional soul which was given by God for the Sabbath day.

The Hebrew *ruach ha-Qodesh*, the breath of life principle, with which Yahweh created the world and manifests his presence in the world resembles the Egyptian *ankh*, the force and breath of life principle, including how the *ankh* amulet was placed next to the nostrils to inhale its force.

The Hebrew belief in the presence of Yahweh, the *shekhinah*, in the ark of the covenant, in the tabernacle, the *mishkan*, which contained the tablets of the Ten Commandments, and was later placed in the temple Holy of Holies, the *Kodesh Kodashim*, could have been inspired by the divine presence of the *ka* soul of the statue of the Egyptian god in the *naos* temple sanctuary, or tabernacle, and in the bark (boat) shrines which transported the statues of the gods in processions.

The tabernacle itself, as the portable sanctuary for the ark of the covenant, built by the Hebrews in the wilderness after their escape from Egypt, bears a startling resemblance to the *wia*, bark shrine, as a floating temple, a mobile shrine, for the transport of the divine statue of a god. And of course, both the Holy of Holies and the later synagogue tabernacle, where the *Torah* is kept, resemble the Egyptian *naos*, the *ra per*.

Perhaps, too, the key Hebrew principle of man being created in the image of god, while it probably owes more to the Sumerian concept of seeing the gods as superlative humans, owes at least something to Egypt. The reigning pharaoh as Horus, the son of Re or the son of Amun-Re had always been considered as the image of the gods on earth, and the frequent Egyptian term for mankind, "the noble cattle," used as far back as Pharaoh Khufu's (Cheops, c. 2551–2528 BC) time by the magician Djedi, seems to indicate a groping towards anthropomorphism.

The Hebrews' attitude to animals also could have been very strongly influenced by the Egyptians, both in direct opposition and positively. Animal sacrifice was a central element in the ancient Hebrew religion, but according to many verses of the Bible it was explicitly opposed to the Egyptian type of sacrifices practiced in favor of "idols" and to the eating of the blood of animals, that is, the eating of their souls. However, the Hebrew magical, ritual sacrifice of the unblemished red heifer (*adom parah*) as a purification of sin and defilement resembles Egyptian practices and the extravagant criteria for its identification resemble those used for the Egyptian *apis* and *mnevis* bulls. The vast Hebrew system of protection of animals crowned by the general concept that animals have "souls" had its general origins deep in prehistory, but it could have also received a powerful boost from zoolatric and animal-loving Egypt.

Early Israel's tribal organization, involving a head for each of the twelve tribes in delimited geographical zones, distinctive totemistic standard-banners and a system of military conscription resembled Egypt's *sepat*/nome system.

Some of the Hebrew *kosher* pure food and utensil laws could owe something to the Egyptian nome alimentary taboos. The Hebrew obsessive abhorrence and prohibition of the pig could have its origin in the Egyptian abhorrence of the pig as the most impure animal, as the animal related to Seth and responsible for the blinding of Horus. The Hebrew prohibition of certain types of fish and crustaceans may also owe something to Egypt's general rejection of some fish and crustaceans as unclean and evil.

Although, according to the Bible, circumcision was ordained by Abraham before the Hebrews' stay in Egypt, and although the Hebrews seem to have been the first known people to attach such great importance to circumcision by imposing it on all males, this practice may have in fact been adopted by the Hebrews after their stay in Egypt. At the least, it may have been reinforced by the Egyptian practice of the circumcision of the sons of royalty, the clergy and the notables.

In any case, this is the opinion of Herodotus, if we assume — as seems correct to do so — that in his time (c. 484–420 BC) the "Syrians of Palestine" were the Jews. Herodotus says that, "the Syrians of Palestine acknowledge that they learned the custom [circumcision] from the Egyptians..."[164]

A dissenting view was expressed by Strabo, in the first century AD, who believed that it was the Jewish descendants of the Egyptian priest Moses who had established the practice of circumcision.[165] This view is impossible to accept, given that circumcision is depicted as far back as a relief in Ankhmahor's Sakkara mastaba (c. 2300 BC) and described on the First Intermediate Period (c. 2181–2055 BC) Naga-ed-Der Stele. Strabo also believed that the Jews instituted female excision, but there are no known Jewish references to excision.

It is essential to emphasize once again that, despite many plausible Egyptian influences, Israel in its main religious thrust — in ethics, as in the beginnings of abstract, non-mythological thinking, strict monotheism, and above all, in transcendence, in the break in the concept that the divine was in nature — constituted a massive rejection of Egyptian religious principles; no doubt, the first such massive rejection.

The Egypto-Greek Link

Egyptian magic and Greek rationalism are two of the most contradictory systems in the history of mankind. In this sense, Egypt and Greece were deeply opposed, as we shall soon see; but this implicit opposition did not affect a probable and considerable Egyptian influence on Greek religion, mythology and esotericism, and especially Orphism, and the spread of an Isis cult throughout the Greco-Roman world.

There are certainly other opinions, notably that Greek religion developed independently from Egypt. This is theoretically possible, but it implies that the numerous similarities in religious concepts and myths between Egypt and Greece were fortuitous or came from other sources. It also implies that the Greek identification of many of their gods and goddesses with Egyptian gods and goddesses and the belief by several Greek authors that the Egyptian pantheon was a model for their own pantheon are totally misleading. All this would be a lot to swallow, and renders Egyptian religious influence on Greece the likeliest possibility.

Egypt, over at least 1500 years, was a link between purely Egyptian and West Asian religions concepts and Crete and the antique Greco-Roman world. The religious influence here, notably in the type of gods created and their functions and powers, may have been direct and considerable. In fact, one of the outstanding roles played by Egypt in the history of religion may well have been the

164. Herodotus, *Books I-II*, 2.104.3.
165. Strabo, *The Geography*, XVI.2.37.

early transmission of many Egyptian and West Asian polytheistic religious values and rituals to Greece and from there to Rome. The Egyptian religion unquestionably played such a role and powerfully influenced the Mediterranean world after the Late Period (from c. 747 BC).

This transmission could have begun with Pharaoh Mentuhotep-Nebhepetre II (c. 2055–2004), who reunified Egypt, founded the Middle Kingdom (c. 2055 BC) and opened a great period of commercial expansion, artistic renewal and widespread contacts and conquests in the Mediterranean continuum. The Minoan civilization, which was established in Crete around 2000 BC, may have taken significant elements from Egypt and West Asia at a time when mainland Greece was largely a backwater, just beginning to embark on urbanization and soon to be plunged into disarray for centuries by the invasion of barbarous Indo-European tribes.

Egyptian contact with Crete (*Keftiu*, in Egyptian) is attested by fragments of Minoan-influenced mural paintings at the end of the period of Hyksos occupation of Egypt (c. 1600–1550 BC) and was apparently accentuated from about 1555 BC during the struggle against the Hyksos. Egypt apparently negotiated naval protection from the Minoans, which led to frequent visits of Minoan sailors, diplomats and traders to Egypt. It would seem that the Egyptians and the highly advanced Minoan civilization exercised a mutual influence on each other.

There are pictorial and textual evidence and pottery relics indicating considerable trade and frequent contacts, including diplomatic missions between Egypt and the Greek Aegean world from the 15th century BC. Beginning with Hatshepsut's reign in c. 1473 BC, these visits are attested by bas-reliefs and paintings depicting Minoans and perhaps other Greeks paying tribute in several tombs (notably, Menkheperra-seneb, TT86, Senemut TT71 and Rekmira, TT100). The Mycenaean invasion of Crete around 1450 BC led to the adoption by the Mycenaeans of a considerable portion of culture and religion and then the Greeks incorporated many aspects of Mycenaean-Cretan religion.

By about the reign of Psamtek I (c. 664–610 BC), Egypto-Greek intermingling became direct and intensive with the encouraged presence of skilled Greek immigrants, ambitious traders and increasing numbers of mercenaries serving in the Egyptian Army. Daphnae (Tel Dafana), west of the Sinai, and Naukratis (Piemroye), south of the future Alexandria, became the main cities of Greek settlement. Ahmose II (c. 570–526 BC) attempted to confine the Greeks to Naukratis after a revolt by his Greek mercenaries in 570 BC.

In the succeeding years and centuries, Egypt had to confront growing Greek power and influence both inside and outside its country. It is certain that by the 7th century BC, Greece had extensive trading relations not only with Egypt but also with Phoenicia, Babylonia, Persia and perhaps even beyond. As

Greece rose to the status of world power after they defeated the Persians in 490 BC at Marathon, Egypt was caught between Persia and Greece. Egypt rarely had anything to gain from this situation, even when it allied itself with Greece against the Persian occupiers. The culmination of Egypt's relations with the Greeks came with the Greek conquest of Egypt in 332 BC and the ensuing Greek rule for 300 years, which turned out to be even more culturally repressive than Persian rule.

Clear and stark differences existed between Egypt and Greece, right from the establishment of the network of Greek city-states around the eighth century BC and the virtual establishment of what can be called the nation of *Hellas* in the seventh century BC.

Over the succeeding centuries, the differences between the two countries became radical, with the inventions in Greece of independent — unlinked to religion — science, philosophy, history, literature and plastic and performing arts. Greek sculpture was especially exemplary of this difference, with its search for both realism and perfect forms in the human figure, in contrast to Egypt's main thrust of an official art depicting mythological values and things the way they should be and not the way they are. Non-religious based ethics, democratic institutions for the aristocrats and the centrality of the practice of sports completed a landscape which made Greece a very different country from Egypt.

Perhaps above all, while both the Egyptian people and elite continued to tend towards the mythological and magical, a split occurred in Greece with the people tending towards mythology and magical religion and much of the elite tending towards a search for clarity, for critical rationalism, even when they rebelled against the consequences of rationalism or used rationalism to justify religion.

Over the centuries, the Greek attitude to Egypt was not consistent, except for great awe for Egypt's technical and political achievements and its great antiquity. Broadly speaking, the Greek attitude to Egypt ranged from a sixth and fifth century BC acknowledgement of Egyptian religious influence to a zestful mockery and scorn of what were seen as primitive Egyptian religious values, especially concerning animal worship, and to the development of a self-sufficient attitude of superiority from the late fourth century BC during the Greek occupation of Egypt.

During the period of Greek conquest, the Egyptians referred to Greece as *hau-nebu*, a term which had previously been used in conjunction with *wadj wer*, "the great green," to designate the Mediterranean and the countries beyond its northern shore.

Judging from what we know of the writings of Hecataeus of Miletus (c. 540–490 BC) and from the writings of Herodotus (c. 484–420 BC), the early

Greeks saw a kind of across-the-board excellence in antique Egypt — climatic, agricultural, artistic, architectural, military and above all, religious. The Greeks saw Egypt as a country which had produced a great civilization more than 2000 years before they themselves had even established a semblance of a loosely linked state. For the early Greeks, this awesome Egypt was the forerunner of their own and superior greatness

It is impossible to clarify whether Homer, Pythagoras, Thales, Solon, Plato and other Greek writers, philosophers and politicians actually did visit Egypt and learn from Egyptian sages as some ancient Greek writers (notably, Plato, c. 428–347? BC, Diodorus Siculus, fl.1st century BC and Plutarch, c. AD 45–125), would-be pundits and even historians claimed. What seems certain from a comparison of Egyptian and Greek texts is that Egyptian mathematics, geometry and medicine were primitive and pragmatic compared to what the Greeks discovered, understood and developed. This seems so, despite Aristotle's belief that mathematics and geometry were discovered in Egypt and then came to Greece. As we shall soon see, there is also no way of attributing any substantial Egyptian influence on Greek philosophy.

In an overall way, it is plausible to say that Egyptian influence on Greece was basically religious and that traditional Egyptian society did not accept Greek views, although Egyptian priests made sporadic claims that Greek philosophy was adapted from Egyptian wisdom.

Hecataeus of Miletus (c. 540–490 BC) seems to have been the first major Greek personality whose visit to Egypt and writings about Egypt are verifiable. However, we only know his book concerning Egypt, *Ges Periodos* or *Periegesis* (usually translated as *Circumnavigation of the Known World*), through some fragments and references by later authors.

The visits and writings of Hecataeus of Miletus, Herodotus (in the fifth century BC), Hecataeus of Abdera (in the late fourth century), Diodorus Siculus and Strabo (in the first century BC) and Plutarch (in first century AD), among many others, all illustrated a desire by cultured people to visit Egypt as later peoples desired to visit vanguard Rome, London, Paris or New York. Even if most of these writers were appalled by Egyptian superstitions, the "Egyptomania" of our modern times had its equivalent in Greece from at least the fifth century BC.

These authors, and especially Herodotus and Strabo, were among the few historians and geographers of those times who aimed at some kind of objectivity (even if their standard of objectivity bears very little resemblance to what we call objectivity today). Moreover, Herodotus and Strabo made "honest" errors and misinterpretations due to a lack of knowledge that we now have retrospectively corrected.

Herodotus sometimes acted like an over-enthusiastic tourist ready to swallow anything in an exotic land. He was frequently subject to fantasies and romanticism and frequently was derided by later Greek and Roman writers, including Aristotle who called him "a story teller," Hectaeus of Abdera who believed that he "preferred marvelous tales and the invention of myths" rather than "truth," Manetho who faulted him "for his ignorance and false relations of Egyptian affairs," Cicero who named him "the father of lies" and Plutarch who labeled his work "fictions and fabrications." Modern historians almost unanimously reject considerable portions of his writings and it is obvious that much of what he reported could not be true, but were things told to him rather than things he saw. Strabo, for his part, was unduly harsh and disdainful and clearly seems to have been more familiar with Lower Egypt than with Upper Egypt.

With these correctives, Herodotus and Strabo were among the non-Egyptian antique writers who simultaneously illustrated both Greek "Egyptomania" and the implicit, radical differences between the Greek and Egyptian views and contributed most to helping us understand Late Period and Roman Period Egypt in all domains. Despite his shortcomings, Herodotus, especially, is invaluable for understanding Egypt, much in the same way that the Bible despite its inaccuracies is invaluable for the study of Egypt. Herodotus was the father of what has come to be known as Egyptology; he did not deserve the virulent criticism which was directed towards him — or, at least, he also deserved resounding praise for his pioneering role.

A western-Greek-Macedonian city in Egypt, Alexandria (Raqote, in Egyptian), the city that Alexander founded in Egypt in 332 BC, and Ptolemy I developed, eventually became not only the greatest Greek city of science, scholarship and culture but one of the greatest cosmopolitan cities of the western world. By the third century BC, at a time when Athens was persecuting its own scientists, Alexandria was the greatest city of scientific inquiry in the world. Alexandria survived into the fifth century AD as a city elaborating and anticipating much of what became the modern western outlook.

The paradoxes here are enormous: the greatest city of the emerging new sciences and philosophies was situated in Egypt, the country which had developed religion and magic to its most extensive degrees; and the great Alexandria Library was perhaps destroyed by the early members of the Christian religion who would later become the paragons of modernity, but who at that time considered science and scholarship as "pagan." What was, however, in character in Alexandria was the non-participation of almost all the Egyptians in the intellectual life of this city — most Egyptians thoroughly rejected everything Alexandria stood for.

The Greek settlers in Egypt amassed great wealth, frequently to the detriment of the Egyptians and like all colonizers this was one of their major goals, but this aggressive attitude of exploitation did not take away from the lingering awe the Greeks felt for Egyptian civilization. Greek philosophers, scientists and politicians in Alexandria expended considerable efforts studying traditional Egyptian lore and encouraged Egyptians like Manetho (fl.c. 300 BC) to write about Egyptian history and religion.

At the maximum, Greek (and also Roman) infatuation with Egypt suggests both an inferiority complex, especially in relation to religion, and a direct Egyptian religious inspiration of Greece. At the very least, the similarity in many religious and mythological concepts between Egypt and Greece suggests significant influence because of Egypt's anteriority.

This could appear outrageous for many who consider that the Greeks were the inventors of the epitome of polytheism and the master myth inventors of history. There can hardly be any doubt that the Greeks, perhaps together with the Hindus, were indeed the most masterful and prolific authors of mythology, but there is also hardly any doubt that Egyptian mythology obsessed and influenced the Greeks.

Above all, conventional wisdom needs revision concerning who invented the most elaborate and universal polytheism — it was the Egyptians, and not the Greeks. The Greek approach to polytheism was not at heart an original religious development; the overall approach is the same as in Sumero-Egyptian polytheism, even if there are, of course, differences. The antique Greeks, for most of their history and despite some monotheising temptations of the pantheist type, certainly practiced one of the purest and most vigorous and unbending polytheistic systems, but a system in which there was no amalgamation of gods and very little zoomorphism. It was the Egyptians who first set up the most comprehensive polytheistic system, even if they flirted with monotheism.

Although Greek religion and mythology bear many of the distinctive marks of Indo-European culture and although pre-Greek and Greek religion seem to have been directly influenced by other West Asian religions, notably the Indo-European Hittite, Egypt's influence on the Greek pantheon of gods and on Greek rituals and religious concepts seems to have been extensive. In esotericism, as we shall soon see, Egyptian beliefs and techniques, both real and imaginary, played a basic role in the elaboration of Greek Hermeticism.

Herodotus believed that most of the main Greek gods were originally Egyptian and that Egypt inspired most of Greece's religious practices. He saw only a difference in names — Egyptian or Greek — for the main gods rather than differences in origin, identity, meaning or functions, with the Egyptian names coming first. This seems to be still another exaggeration on the part of Herodotus, but he was right in assuming that many Greek and Egyptian gods and goddesses represented the same forces, or personifications, of nature, even if their names were different — something which Plutarch later amply demonstrated.

Just as there were immense similarities in the roles of the Sumerian and Egyptian gods, in much the same way these similarities existed between Greek and Egyptian gods and, later, between Roman and Greek gods. The Greeks were particularly disdainful and sarcastic concerning the zoolatric aspects of the Egyptian gods. Perhaps, this was because there was very little zoomorphism in their own religions and only some in their mythology, with the deities being able to transform into animals — but not being primarily animals. Aside from the problem with Egyptian zoomorphism, the Greeks clearly had an obsessive need to compare, identify and position their own gods, mythology and religion in relation to Egypt. Herodotus' systematic desire to identify the Greek gods with the Egyptian gods was indicative of the Greeks' awe for Egyptian religion and mythology.

In short, even if the specific, original aspects of both Cretan and Greek religion seem stronger than the Egyptian influences which jolted them, at least some (and perhaps many) aspects of Cretan and Greek mythology and religion were based on the Egyptian and West Asian models. The minimal reality seems to be that the influence of Egypt on Greek religion and mythology generally has been vastly underestimated.

Harpocrates, the god of silence, was an adaptation of Horus the child; Hecate, the moon and witchcraft goddess, seems to owe much to Heka, the god of magic; Pan, the playful fertility god, seems to owe something to the ithyphallic Min, and might have also an ithyphallic version of Amun; Silenus, the drunken Greek satyr resembled Bes, as the god of joy and sexuality; the "Seven Hathors" who could predict the future and notably when a person would die prefigured the Greek *Moirai*, "fates," the three goddesses and in later times old women who spun the tale of human destinies noting who would suffer and how much and when the person would die; and so on.

The Greeks also identified many of their gods and goddesses with Egyptian divinities. This was especially the case for Isis, who was identified with the virgin wisdom goddess Athena, the mother goddess Hera, Demeter, the vegetation goddess, the resurrecting Persephone, the goddess of love Aphrodite (who was also identified with Hathor) and also sometimes with the virgin huntress and moon goddess Artemis; Dionysus, the vegetation and ecstasy god, with Osiris; Typhon, the monster, with Seth; Apollo, the god of shepherds, crops, medicine, music, archery and divine secrets with Horus; Leto, the Titaness, with Wadjit; Zeus, the supreme father-sky god, with Amun; Heracles, the deified hero god, with Khons and Harsaphes; Hephaistos, the blacksmith god, with Ptah; Artemis with Bastet; Athena with Neith; Nekhbet with Eileithyia...Pan and Priapus with Min; Asclepius, the healer, with Imhotep; Hermes, as the messenger of the gods' wisdom and possessor of secret knowledge with Thoth as *Hermes Trismegistus* and Hermes as the guide of souls to *Hades*, with Anubis as Hermanubis; etc.

On the other hand, and as we have seen, the sun, fertility and healer god Serapis, combining several Greek gods and Osorapis, the combination of Osiris and the afterlife Apis Bull, was invented by the Greek Ptolemy I Soter (c. 305–285 BC). He built several magnificent *serapeums* (temples) to Serapis, the biggest in Raqote, the original Egyptian part of Alexandria. Ptolemy I's goal was to encourage joint Egyptian-Greek worship. Serapis was connected to the beloved Osiris at a time when Osiris' popularity was at a very high level, but eventually Serapis had greater success elsewhere in the Mediterranean world and especially in Rome. Ptolemy I used a trick, later also widely used by the Romans — the claim that the gods of occupied countries were in fact the same as those of the occupiers, with different names. This usually worked to some extent, but failed miserably when the Romans after 32 BC tried to convince the Jews that Yahweh was Jupiter.

The Greek myth of the birth of Apollo, the molesting of his mother Leto by a snake and Apollo's revenge bear a similarity to the Isis-Horus tale, while the Greek fertility and dying-resurrecting cults like Persephone/Kore and Dionysus seem to owe much to Egyptian-influenced Minoan Crete and to West Asia in general. The Greek myths of the ripping into pieces of Zagreus and of Pelops resembled the ripping into pieces of Osiris. The parts of the myth of Jason and the Argonauts involving the ripping into pieces of some of its characters and their possible resurrection by the use of magic also resembled the Osiris tale and resurrection beliefs. The Cretan/Greek Minotaur myth, the bull-headed man/ monster, might have been influenced by the Egyptian Apis, Buchis and Mnevis bull cults and bull-headed gods in general — although the cult of bulls goes far back into the early Neolithic in many places including Anatolia, and Sumer, where Gilgamesh fought the divine bull much as Theseus fought the Minotaur in the Greek myth.

The Greco-Roman world was particularly impressed by Egypt's ancient and vast afterlife system and its religious architecture, notably the pyramids. However, the mainstream Greek and Egyptian concepts of the afterlife were fundamentally different. The Greek approach to the afterlife was neither a continuation, a repetition, of this life — as the *Duat* was for the Egyptians — nor a place for a reward. *Hades* was a dark, meaningless place like the Sumerian *Kur* or the Hebrew *Sheol* and even the Elysian Fields of the Blessed Souls could in no way compare to the good life in the *Duat*.

On the other hand, Egyptian magical rituals and mysteries seem to have been one of the main influences on the Greek mystery cults centered on esoteric afterlife concerns such as in the Orphic, Eleusinian and Dionysiac traditions. The origins of Orphism and Orpheus seem to be in Minoan Crete and perhaps, before then, in Egypt, notably the great preoccupation concerning immortality and the afterlife, the consequences in the afterlife of this life and instructions on how to behave in the afterlife.

The original Greek paradise, Elysium, to which heroes went (before it became a place of reward for moral conduct in the late sixth century BC) seems to be a development from Minoan concepts. In turn, the Minoan concept seems to be a development of Egyptian concepts, notably the pleasant *Aaru* Fields of the Egyptian *Duat* "Other Land." The Orphic obsession with morality, sin and guilt might have had part of its origin in a literal interpretation and exaggeration of the moral aspects contained in the Egyptian *maat* code of universal order.

The beliefs involved in the Eleusinian mysteries (probably dating from before 1000 BC) on how to win immortality, the fundamental importance of the correct performance of rituals if one is to have an afterlife and the belief that death for the initiated is a blessing are all similar to Egyptian theology. In fact, they are so similar that it seems reasonable to conclude that they largely stem from Egyptian beliefs, even if some Hellenists deny any Egyptian influence in the Eleusinian mysteries.

This does not mean that there were no other influences, or independent inventions, in the elaboration of the Eleusinian mysteries. The framework for the Eleusinian mysteries — the enactment of the story of the vegetation goddess Demeter who sought the resurrection of her daughter Persephone/Kore — might be a variant of the old Sumerian Inanna/Dumuzi and Egyptian-Osiris agricultural myths, and they seem to owe much to the annual Egyptian temple festivals and especially those of Abydos Osiris Temple. As depicted in the Eleusinian mysteries, Demeter's ardent quest to bring Persephone/Kore back to earth also clearly resembled Isis' ardent quest to resurrect Osiris more than it could be linked to fickle Inanna's abandonment of Dumuzi. However, the Eleusinian emphasis on searching for the truth seems to have been particular to the Greek philosophical genius.

The Dionysiac mysteries and festivals, which took place throughout Greece, seem to have had both an agricultural/theological connection to Egypt and West Asia and a resemblance to the populist joy, including the sexual orgies, which the Greeks believed were characteristics of the Egyptian temple festivals.

Numerous other Egyptian inspired mystery cults of salvation, resurrection and the curing of illnesses were widespread throughout the Mediterranean world in the last few centuries BC and the first few centuries AD. Tales of the death and resurrection of Osiris were particularly popular and gave rise to strange rituals of transubstantiation and even castration in which the supplicant could earn salvation and immortality.

It was probably the Isis cult which was the prime example of this salvation influence, as well as of the concepts that Isis was Mother Nature, that she pantheistically embodied the entirety of nature and that she was the essence of great wisdom and magic. Isis cults were practiced throughout the Greco-Roman world. At least until the end of the 2nd century AD, Isis was the Roman goddess/ Queen of the World, the mother of everything, the "goddess of 10,000 names," the ultimate divinity who merged all the divinities. In Alexandria, she was the goddess of sailors and the harbor. In Sais, on the Rosetta branch of the Nile, the inscription on the Isis/Athena statue stated: "I am all that has been, and is, and shall be, and my robe no mortal has yet uncovered."[166] In Delos, Rome and Pompey, her statue was washed, clothed and fed every day and her annual quest for Osiris was celebrated. This Isis cult was perhaps the supreme example of how many elements of the Egyptian religion, even if mangled by the Greeks, had penetrated throughout the Mediterranean world.

Special mention has to be made concerning the extraordinary influence of some of the most frequent Egyptian magical practices on the antique Greco-Roman world. The interpretation of dreams, divination, the foretelling of events and propitious days and oracles where allegedly secret knowledge was revealed — all widespread in Greco-Roman World — seem to have been extensively influenced by Egypt. On the other hand, astrology seems to have seeped into Egypt from Greece during the Greek occupation of Egypt.

Greece and Rome were then prime examples of peoples who took the mumbo-jumbo of Egyptian magic and mystery cults deadly seriously and persisted in seeing deep occult knowledge in so many of the crudely magical Egyptian religious texts. Greece, and especially Rome, were in such desperate need of religious dogma that they swallowed a lot of Egyptian junk food. As we shall soon see, Plato (c. 427–347? BC), either because he believed it or was engaging in his pedagogical technique of "the noble lie," was a particularly strong reflection of this tendency. But the ancient Greeks and Romans were not alone in gobbling up dubious Egyptian notions; as we shall soon see, so-called Egypto/ Greek *Hermetica* even played a curious role in the European Scientific Revolution from the 16th century.

---

166. Plutarch, *Moralia*, Volume V, *Isis and Osiris*, p.25.

GREEK RATIONALISM AND THE REJECTION OF THE EGYPTIAN MAGICAL AND MYTHOLOGICAL VIEW

However, while Greek and Roman awe for Egypt were great and while Egyptian influence on Greek and Roman religion is demonstrable, it was of course rationalism which was the vanguard characteristic of ancient Greece, the hallmark of the typically Greek genius. The central aspect of rationalism was an implicit and massive rejection of the Egyptian type of magical and mythological view based in animistic nature. The Greek critical approach to man, the materialist and mechanist approach to the universe and the intellectual freedom to experiment, to search for intelligible meaning and to speculate constituted the utter opposites of the Egyptian view based on mythology, magic, animism, emotion and intuition presented as the original, only and permanent situation of man and the universe. Even the Greek philosophers who opted for belief in the gods did so using, or misusing, rationalism.

This second massive rejection of the Egyptian view, after the Hebrew religious and ethical rejection, was begun by Greece's scientist-philosophers in the sixth century BC. It had far more historical significance than the first Hebrew rejection. It constituted one of mankind's most radical adventures and greatest revolutions.

Eventually, Greek philosophy, science, politics, historical method, literature, theater and art eliminated the pillar constituted by Sumero-Egyptian-type thinking. Greece established the domination and the supremacy of both abstract reasoning and practical, experimental science. It established the exigency of clarity. It established the humanist centrality of man as the source of knowledge. And eventually, after the Greek conquest of Egypt (c. 332 BC), Greek philosophy became a direct instrument inside Egypt for the destruction of the old Sumero-Egyptian view. The Egyptians themselves used much of the new Greek view when they massively rejected their own religion and traditions and adopted Christianity beginning in the late 2nd century AD.

It seems impossible to imagine anybody in the magical Egyptian society even vaguely flirting with atheism and entirely plausible to think that a vanguard rational part of Greek society opened the road of atheism. It was impossible for the magical Egyptians to ask the final questions paradoxically latent in the very invention of religion — do the gods really exist or does a god really exist, does something called the soul really exist, can there be a religion without gods, and can ethics have an existence independent from religion and god?

The Greek scientist-philosophers (and the sixth century BC Indian Buddhists) raised these questions and started the first revolt against religion and the beginnings of atheism. The Greek experience — together with a paradoxical and imaginary Egyptian influence — then largely influenced the 16th, 17th and 18th century European philosophers and scientists and led to the war against God in 18th and 19th century France.

To what extent the Pre-Socratic Greeks were actually aware that they were radically rejecting the Egyptian magical, animistic and mythological view and to what extent they were rejecting the ambient vision of the entire antique world will never be known. The surviving fragmentary quotes of most of the Pre-Socratic philosophers clearly convey the domination of an anti-magical, non-mythological, critical, mechanical, materialist, secular search for truth and for ethical meaning, but make no mention of any foreign society.

On the other hand, it seems certain that the Greeks understood that there was very little or no connection between their new methods of investigation — philosophy and science — and the "wisdom" of earlier peoples, notably the Egyptians. The Greek philosophers who succeeded the Pre-Socratics made no mention of the later — and still bandied about — notion of an Egyptian origin for Greek philosophy. Even Herodotus (c. 484–420 BC), who believed that Greek religion stemmed from Egypt, made no similar claim concerning Greek philosophy. Plato admired many aspects of Egyptian society and even seems to have believed that the Egyptians with their great wisdom knew how the land of Greece had been founded, but he made no mention of Egyptian links to Greek philosophy. In *The Phaedrus*, Plato has Socrates saying (but wondering and doubting that it was true) that "Teuth" (Thoth) had invented arithmetic, geometry, astronomy, letters (writing) and draughts and dice. Only Aristotle (c. 384–322 BC) in *Metaphysics* clearly saw a scientific link to Egypt, (wrongly) believing that mathematics and geometry had come into Greece from Egypt where they were founded. Hecataeus of Abdera (c. 290 BC), as reported by Diodorus Siculus (fl.1st century BC), seems to have made a vast description of legends, rather than facts, which attributed Greek borrowing from Egypt in many scientific, philosophical and political fields. However, this did not stop Hecataeus, like most of the succeeding Greek writers including Diodorus and Strabo, from expressing very negative views concerning what they saw as primitive Egyptian beliefs and attitudes.

No people anywhere until sixth century BC Greece interpreted the universe, existence and ethics in anything but a magical religious context. Everybody was spontaneously religious. The societal values which Egypt had pioneered were eventually credibly replaced by Greece. Even religion as a value, as truth, would eventually go by the boards as an ultimate result of the experiments and speculation begun by the Greek scientist-philosophers.

An extraordinary sense of temerity, of individual freedom to speculate and criticize, of the elevation of the soul, animated the ancient Greeks. Thales, Anaximander, Democritus, Aeschylus, Euripides, Socrates, Plato Aristotle, Pericles, Epicurus and an army of other thinkers, writers and politicians turned old world values around. The tragedy of life, the sense of the human in art, the search for a rational, provable, mechanical, material, non-mythological meaning of nature and man, the search for an ethical pleasure principle, the search for a valid ethical system, the search for justice and a democratic form of government — in short, the reckless search for intelligibility and truth at any cost set the Greeks apart from the Egyptians, or any other people. The cliché that the world was never the same after the Greek revolution is the simple truth, just as the world was never the same after the Sumero-Egyptian polytheistic revolution.

Of course, this does not mean that the Greeks invented a perfect system, but rather that they operated a major advance over anything preceding them. The entirety of their system was notably flawed by the fact that it was only applicable to so-called free men, to male aristocratic citizens. In particular, Plato's doctrines were flawed by a near fascist vision of ethics and of political power and a strange mixture of the rational, the religious and even magical hocus-pocus.

The peak of human endeavor reached in Greece was of a completely different nature from the peak reached in Egypt. Just as modernity in Egypt had been the perfecting of highly organized polytheism, mythology, *heka*, magic, monumental architecture and irrigation technology, modernity in Greece was clarity, rationalism, logic, skeptical philosophy and science. Greek religions were elaborate, powerful and popular, but they did not make significant original contributions to the history of religion. Greece was not a land that produced religious innovation.

Aside from a few similarities, this mainstream Greek philosophy and science were obviously antagonistic to the Egyptian way of thinking. Much has been made about one of the most startling of these similarities — the Egyptian Ptah/Memphite notion of heart (mind), word and thought as the origin of creation and the Greek *logos*, the "word," or "reason" which governs the universe. Among many others, the eminent Egyptologist James Henry Breasted, using this similarity, was tempted by the romantic view of an Egyptian origin of Greek philosophy. He thought that "Early Greek philosophy...may...have drawn upon [the Egyptian Ptah/Memphite notions of the] mind, the heart...the idea of a single controlling intelligence...[whose] efficient force...[was the] spoken 'word', and this primitive 'logos' is undoubtedly the incipient germ of the later logos-doctrine which found its origin in Egypt."[167]

---

167. Breasted, James Henry, *A History of Egypt, From the Earliest Times to the Persian Conquest*, p. 300.

Aside from the probability that Ptah/Memphite theology as revealed on the Shabako Stone dates from the late eighth century BC, as we have seen in Chapter 4, and with all due respect to Breasted, this is a confused and fragmentary method of evaluation. Even if parts of the concept of the *logos* may have seeped into Greek philosophy from Egypt, in its Greek version it originated as a mixed bag of traditional and modern concepts. At one and the same time, it was a triumph of logical, deductive reasoning in Greek philosophy and the continuation of an irrational concept of Greek religion; and irrationality was exactly that from which vanguard Greek philosophy was trying to free itself.

The *logos*, as invented by Heraclitus (c. 540–480 BC), was a triumph of logic, of the independent power of thought to understand the world and the individual, but it was also entwined in an obscure near mythological system. For Heraclitus, the *logos* was true forever and everything occurred because of the *logos*, all things were one, all things fire; God took many shapes, even if the gods had not made the world which was in constant flux; the lord had an oracle at Delphi who showed meaning by signs; and souls smelled in *Hades*. The term *logos* has come to epitomize logic and rationality, but within Heraclitus' system, it was far from being just that. Moreover, despite Heraclitus' rational side, he also believed that gods, strife, war, slavery and free citizens were all permanent, necessary realities. Heraclitus was an anti-democratic religious thinker, even if he had dissident religious views.

Certainly, there is a possibility that Ptah/Memphite theology influenced the religious aspects of the *logos* concept, but it does not seem that Heraclitus' foray into logical thinking, into logic as a way of understanding the world, had much to do with Memphite theology or with Egyptian lore in general. The Memphite doctrine did indeed postulate an extraordinary abstract notion of the power of the word and will, but it was entirely enveloped in a magical religious view. This was not the case for Heraclitus' *logos*, despite its religious aspects. Moreover, Heraclitus' notion that the only permanent aspect of things was change was entirely anathema to the Egyptian notion of permanency without change, ever since creation, since "the first time."

The *logos* is obviously linked to religious concepts in Christianity and Judaism, but it is not its religious aspects which are essential to the overall thrust of Greek rational philosophy. Whether the notion is Egyptian, Hebrew, Greek or Christian, creating something — and *a fortiori*, the universe — by the word, by naming it, is the epitome of magical religious thinking, albeit more sophisticated than crude material magic.

It is simply silly to assume that rationalist Greek philosophy and science grew from Egyptian foundations and especially silly to use the entirety of the *logos* concept as a proof of this. In a broad sense, there is no way of denying that the Egyptian and Greek approaches to understanding man and the world were radically different. Above all, Greek rationalism was the epitome of abstract reasoning, it was the system which the Hebrews had begun to use imperfectly when they invented an invisible god above nature and its consequences and which the Greeks carried to its logical secular philosophical and scientific consequences; aside from Memphite theology, there is practically no example of abstract reasoning in Egypt. Quite simply put, most of mainstream Greek logic, philosophy and science implicitly rejected the Egyptian view.

For most Greek philosophers, virtue in this life was the supreme good and could only be obtained by control over the body by the highest substances, which were the *nous* — the mind, reason — and the *psykhé*, the soul. The *nous* and the *psykhé* were not only fundamentally different and separate from the body but also opposed to the superficial pleasures of the body. While it is true that the *nous* was more than the mind and often included the spirit and in a sense, the will of god, the thrust of Greek philosophical values was rationality, skepticism and freedom to speculate. At least for free citizens, the Greek goal was virtue and freedom, freedom in this life, rather than in a hypothetical afterlife. For the vanguard Greek philosopher-scientists, the magical, primeval order was mythological and erroneous and man had the rational capacity to understand the material mechanisms of the universe and the freedom to search out and choose the best laws and the best course of individual and societal behavior.

Such Greek concepts would not have even crossed the Egyptian *nous*!

The very basis of the Greek way of thinking was in utter contradiction to the Egyptian way of thinking. Freedom, freedom to speculate about nature and man, and to criticize, were not Egyptian ideals. The fundamental Egyptian ideal was not freedom, but to seek conformity to what was perceived as the permanent, divine and natural order in the *maat* code. For the Egyptians, man was a part of the *maat* primeval natural order and his place and possibilities within this order had been had been settled long ago at the *zep tepey*, "the first time," the time of creation, and codified by the Heliopolitan, Hermopolitan, Memphite and other clergies after 3100 BC.

It would not have even crossed the *nous* of most Greek philosopher-scientists (with the notable exception of Pythagoras) to situate themselves within a system dominated by magic and immanence, that is, an Egyptian-type system. What had been natural for the Greek priests, theologians and myth-makers in the centuries prior to the sixth century BC rationalist revolution — polytheistic religion and magical theology and rituals — became anathema to most of the Greek philosopher-scientists. This remained the case even for the Greek philosopher-scientists who thrived in Alexandria from about 320 BC to well after AD 200.

287

Greek views were especially in contradiction with the Osirisian concepts of the centrality of the afterlife as a goal and the eternal survival of the body and souls which need each other to remain immortal. It is significant that Greek philosophy (or religion) made no significant contribution to afterlife theory. They were also deeply opposed to the Egyptian emphasis on the body in this life and usually to its survival *per se* in the afterlife. For the Greeks, the body was an inferior substance and the goals for this life were the virtuous elevation of the soul and freedom. Except for the followers of esoteric mystery cults, the afterlife had no central meaning or hope for the Greeks.

We know that at least from Herodotus' time (c. 484–420 BC), Greek philosophical notions were so irrelevant to the Egyptians that they not only never took them into consideration, but they disdained them and regarded them as childishly foolish. It was not until the late 2nd century AD, when Greek ideas and ethics had been incorporated into Christianity and when the Egyptians were no longer really Egyptian, that the Egyptians accepted some Christian/ Greek ideals.

Most of Greek philosophy quite simply horrified the Egyptians when they first came into contact with it. Many Greek writers, in addition to Herodotus, noted from the fifth century BC on that the Egyptians looked upon Greek culture with condescension from the heights attained by their own ancient religion. Plato, in *Timaeus*, cites "a very old" Egyptian priest as telling Solon (c. 639?–559 BC): "...you Greeks are all children, and there is no such a thing as an old Greek...you are all young in mind...you have no belief rooted in old tradition and no knowledge hoary with age." The "very old priest" in Sais admired the "power, courage, bravery, military skill and generosity" of what he described as "the finest and best race of men that ever existed," the Athenians who had lived nine thousand years earlier, but as for the Athenians of his time, "writing and the other necessities of civilization have only just been developed...so you have to begin again like children, in complete ignorance of what happened in our part of the world or in yours in early times."[168]

But what the Egyptians considered worthless in Greece's Golden Age of philosophical and scientific achievement was at the same time a sure-fire indicator of what they themselves represented in religious terms, but also of the sclerotic state they had fallen into. The paradox, or perhaps the result, of the sclerosis of the Egyptian religion was that after condescendingly rejecting Greek culture for centuries, by about the beginning of the 2nd century BC the Egyptians

---

168. *Plato, Timaeus and Critias*, Translated with an introduction and an appendix on *Atlantis* by Desmond Lee, Penguin Books, London, 1977, *Timaeus*, 22, pp. 34-35, 25, 38 and 23, p. 36.

docilely allowed Greek philosophical and religious ideas to denature their own religion and worldview.

The seemingly inexhaustible fount of Greek philosophers and scientists ran almost the entire gamut of investigation into the nature of the universe and of life and especially of ethics. Practically all of these views were in sharp contradiction to traditional Egyptian views, in that they practically all lacked or rejected mythological and magical thinking and often contained no theology.

Thales (fl.585 BC) probably started the Greek scientific and philosophical adventure. From the little we know about him — most of which originates with Herodotus — it seems that he sought clear material, mechanical causes for everything and implicitly contested anything that was mythological and could not be rationally determined. This seems to have been notably true in his probable prediction, using rational observation, of a solar eclipse in 585 BC; his maritime navigation technique using the pole-star Ursa Minor; and his determination from winter astronomic conditions that there would be an abundant olive crop. Above all, Aristotle credits him with postulating that water is "the primary entity," the "first cause" of everything, and that everything contains water and that the earth "floats" on water.

Thales seems to have laid the foundations for non-mythological, materialist, secular thinking. Even if he may not have been aware that he was doing it, this inevitably led to a separation between knowledge and religion, and to atheism. The inner dynamic of Thales' approach implied the ruin of the central concepts of Egyptian polytheism: that nature was animistic, and that it had a divine personality and will. Thales' approach also implicitly ruined the monotheistic claim of a creator god being at the origin of nature and man, and of him having a purpose and organizing a definitive plan for nature and man.

The debate over whether Thales really said that "everything was full of the gods," as Aristotle reported, will probably go on forever. Such a statement would certainly have been out of character with his materialist, mechanical, non-animist view of nature, with water as its origin and with his non-naming of a god of water.

The debate over whether Thales actually visited Egypt and postulated a theory concerning the annual inundation of the Nile and devised a system of calculating the height of a pyramid by its shadow, as well as the tradition, or legend, that he brought geometry into Greece from Egypt will also probably never be solved.

In any case, the three or four statements and acts which plausibly can be attributed to Thales and what followed among the philosopher/scientists in Miletus was nothing less than the first attempt in history at understanding based on a materialist, secular, rationalist, critical, open-ended stance as opposed to the ancient, and especially Egyptian, mythological, magical, animistically immanent, unchangeable approach. Knowledge as we understand the term today began with Thales. Churchill said that, "Never...was so much owed by so many to so few"; for Thales, it can be said that never has so little led to so much.

Anaximander (b.c. 510 BC) believed that there was a basic, material substance — the Infinite — from which our world and other worlds floated freely in space and evolved. Animals, according to Anaximander, were born from moisture as it evaporated under the warmth of the sun, and then man evolved from the animals. In both the physical world and the human domain, he held that opposites struggled with each other and led to the periodical correction of injustices, a kind of automatic ethical mechanism. Such a system eliminated the role of the gods and the need to appease them, concepts which were utterly foreign to the Egyptian system.

Xenophanes (fl.520 BC) decried the immoral and disreputable behavior of the polytheistic gods and concluded that they were anthropomorphic figments of man's imagination. Xenophanes opted for the existence of a sole pantheistic-type god who was identical to the entirety of the universe, understood everything and influenced everything; but he believed that it was impossible for any man to comprehend the truth concerning the gods. Obviously, the nature of Xenophanes' god was fundamentally opposed to the Egyptian concept of the gods.

Above all, Egyptian mythology and religion were less impregnated than the earlier Sumerians' and later Greeks' with the concept and feeling that humans were playthings in the hands of omnipotent gods, who were not necessarily moral. There are very few pessimistic texts of this nature in Egyptian literature — *The Admonitions of Ipuwer*, *The Dispute Between a Man and his Ba*, a few *Harpers' Songs* and *The Instruction of Papyrus Insinger* — and they all concern untypical times of disorder or decline. There is also no trace of the Egyptians ever judging the behavior of their gods, even when the gods acted savagely in relation to man or did not follow codes of behavior which were the acceptable norm for humans. For the Egyptians, the essential point always remained that the gods had given man correct, natural religious, moral and societal structures. As disreputable as the behavior of many Egyptians gods was, no Egyptian would have dared to challenge them as Xenophanes did.

Anaxagoras (c. 500–428 BC) declared that *nous* is autonomous and has power over everything. He was tried for atheism and in any case denied that there could have been a divine origin of the world, opting for some kind of mechanical process of creation. Anaxagoras' views struck at the very heart of Egyptian-type thinking which had put everything in the hands of the gods and almost nothing in the autonomous hands of man and his superior *nous*.

Protagoras (b.c. 500 BC), the first sophist and perhaps the first agnostic, simply concluded that there was no such thing as objective knowledge and that only the individual and society could set norms: "Man is the measure of all things..." Here, too, we are dealing with a type of rational, humanist speculation that the Egyptian mind could not even begin to grasp.

Socrates (c. 469–399 BC) elevated personal doubt, inquiry and self-knowledge into the supreme search for ethics, clarity and truth. Virtue, in the sense of the search for knowledge, and the control of the mind over the body were the values that Socrates seems to have practiced. Needless to say, Socrates was not even on the same planet as the Egyptians. The type of moral high ground and other-worldliness adopted by Socrates, and which seemed so natural to later Greek Stoic philosophers and even to fundamentally religious Neoplatonists, could only have appeared ridiculous to the Egyptians. However, and paradoxically, it was the Neoplatonist view introduced into Egypt by the Greeks, especially during the 2nd century AD, which played a key role in the final destruction of the Egyptian view.

Perhaps some Egyptians, even well before Socrates' time, like the legendary Ptahhotep (c. 2400 BC?, c. 2345–2181 BC?) might have understood the value of the Socratic type of virtuous conduct in relation to some people, but he would have nevertheless been dismayed by its total application, right up to preferring truth and morality in the face of threatened death. Ptahhotep would have probably recommended servile, expedient behavior to Socrates in relation to his political superiors and to his judges, to say nothing about the use of magical spells. On the other hand, Ptahhotep would have applauded Socratic virtuous behavior towards people who could accept such behavior or towards people who were poor.

Democritus (fl.420 BC) postulated that everything was made of material atoms and that the world operates according to mechanical laws without purpose or finality, and that if a creator god exists, something would have had to create the creator. The goal of life for Democritus was much like that for other Greek philosopher-scientists — virtue, pleasure and moderation which ignored or suppressed bodily satisfactions. Both Democritus' view of the goals of life and of a mechanical, non-animistic nature without purpose, will or divine personality would have been considered insane, in Egypt. He would have probably been sent to a Temple House of Life for treatment with a universal remedy like *degem* or seen as a demon trying to impede the maintenance of *maat* natural order and truth.

Plato put a good, creator god above everything, but believed that rational laws not directly related to the creator governed existence. Austere Socratic virtue and reason were his touchstones. With all his genius for reasoning and his belief that moral behavior did not depend on the will or the approval of the gods, Plato nevertheless reversed the Pre-Socratic tendency towards atheism and firmly put the gods and mythology back into Greek philosophy. He believed the world and goodness were eternal and that absolute virtues could not be understood by man; but that the mind could gain knowledge, that the body was an obstacle to knowledge and that the soul was immortal. He envisaged an authoritarian utopia ruled by superior people, that is, male aristocrats by birth and reasoning ability who were rich enough not to work and able to devote themselves to philosophy.

Plato's mixture of politics and religion and his disdain for experimental science were, of course, partially in accord with the traditional Egyptian religious attitude and the politico-social hierarchical system. Plato, although he never attributed philosophical capacities to the Egyptians, was indeed a believer in the idea that ancient Egypt had possessed great religious wisdom as well as knowledge about the origins of nations, including Athens and the mythical Atlantis. He was an admirer of the Egyptian priest-king system, the educational methods for youth, and mummification. He also believed that Anaximander and other Greek philosophers and Solon had visited Egypt.

And yet, with his extreme emphasis on the mind and rationalism, Plato, perhaps, together with Democritus with his totally mechanical system which left no tangible place for the divine, represented the supreme examples of the Greek difference in approach with the Egyptian primacy of the magical, the divine, the body and the forces of nature.

Aristotle (c. 384–322 BC), in *Metaphysics*, believed that there was a "first principle," a primary substance and reality which is "eternal and immovable" and which is the source of everything. This "Unmoved Mover" was god, but Aristotle also subscribed to the "traditional" belief that the heavenly bodies (the stars and the planets) were divine and so according to his calculation of the number of heavenly bodies (47 or 55), there were presumably 47 or 55 "Unmoved Movers" and supposedly 47 or 55 gods.

Aristotle postulated that the *nous* was rational intuition and that contemplation and voluntary virtue which checks bodily desire were the highest goods. Like Plato, he believed that high virtue was for the few and that slavery was justified. Aristotle's concept of moral virtue — the *meson*, the virtuous mean between deficiency and excess, not doing too much of anything, but not too little, either — was strikingly similar to the prudent, but high, moral views expressed by the vizier Ptahhotep, perhaps some 1800 years earlier, if one makes allowances for Ptahhotep's insistence on pragmatic, expedient behavior based on hierarchical values.

Epicurus (c. 341–271 BC) reduced ethics to practical considerations of intellectual pleasure and pain in general. He reasoned that the problem of suffering and evil in this world could neither be solved nor justified, an afterlife could not possibly exist and if gods existed they played no active role. Needless to say, such views seemed both heretical and stupid to the Egyptians.

Perhaps no other school of Greek philosophy than the stoics was more typical of the Greek hyperbolic rational view, and more opposed to the Egyptian magical view. Zeno (c. 336?–264? BC), built on Socrates' and Plato's heritage of the supremacy of reason, totally repudiated emotions and passions, elevated reason and logic to the status of the highest good, democratically decreed that everybody had the power to reason, decided that there was a universal moral law unlinked to gods and declared the gods to be human ancestors who had been deified because they had been heroes and benefactors.

No Egyptian, even after many Greek ideas had seeped into their lives, could have coped with the stoical system. The stoics' grim resolve to calmly endure any kind of misfortune would have been particularly incomprehensible for the individual Egyptian who always actively sought, notably with amulets, to magically manipulate the gods for protection and to eliminate misfortune and to cast spells on others. This central stoical belief would have probably been even more incomprehensible for the Egyptian state theocratic system, which depended on magical manipulation of the gods to achieve imperialist domination over its neighbors.

It was perhaps in the domain of ethics that the divide between Greek philosophical speculation and the Egyptian way of thinking and feeling was greatest. Most Greek ethical speculation was largely autonomous and occurred long after the Egyptian struggle with ethics had sunk beneath the surface of their preoccupations, but it was nevertheless a *de facto* rejection of most of Egyptian theology concerning the nature of ethics. In the main, the Greeks implicitly and massively rejected the Egyptian magical view that correct human behavior, or ethics, was part of a primeval natural order which man did not and could not determine. The Greeks opened the road to a pragmatic, non-religious approach to ethics, to some kind of answers based on man's search for truth. Greek philosophers turned ethics topsy-turvy by imagining what seemingly were all the ethical possibilities open to man. They came up with views ranging from the predetermination of ethical behavior, to voluntary selective morality, to divine morality and to ethical behavior determined by man alone.

Like the Persians, the Hebrews and the Christians, ethics — virtue — was a goal of life for the Greeks, but the genius of the Greeks was to attempt to establish ethics as an independent value in itself and frequently as the main value of life. Ethics were so fundamental for the Greek philosophers that most of them could not conceive it being dependent on any other domain, including religion. Ethical behavior for the Greeks was based on human understanding. This view was held by Socrates, for whom ethics was the supreme value rather than religion and the gods of Athens, but also by philosophers like Plato and Aristotle, who had strong religious options, by Zeno and the Stoics, who saw virtue as the only good and something solely dependent on an individual's free will, and by Epicurus, who reduced ethics to the perception of what was painful and pleasurable. Even one of the implications of the thinking of early philosophers like Thales and Anaxagoras is that a man-made ethics is possible.

There were, however, a few Greek philosopher-scientists who were close to Egyptian views. Among the Pre-Socratic philosophers, Pythagoras (fl.530 BC) postulated a view almost identical to the Egyptian idea that magical religion was the central structure of life and close as well as to Egyptian-type totemistic superstitions. In addition to his fabulous discoveries in geometry and astronomy, he was the inventor of a wacky system of transmigration of souls, rebirth, superior people, the love of wisdom and the evil of stoking a fire with an iron rod. Pythagoras was also adamant about not eating beans, just as Herodotus tells us that the Egyptians "priests cannot even endure to see them, considering beans an unclean kind of legume."[169] Except for his (correct) declaration that the earth is a sphere and his scientific talent, he could have almost been an ancient Egyptian with magical thinking and emotions at the center of his life. However, the legends that he acquired his knowledge in Egypt have to be taken with more than a grain of salt, lacking as they do any evidence or even probability.

Parmenides (fl.c. 500–450 BC) was a kind of a curious halfway house between the Egyptian and later Greek ways of thinking. He radically postulated that only what *is* is real, that it is impossible for it not to be real and that existence could not have come from inexistence. But he also postulated that everything remains constant, is eternal, that nothing changes and that birth and death are merely phases, names, illusions. He said there was only truth and illusion, and that truth seems to have come from "the one" —which he seems to define as both a god-like being and a pantheistic material reality.

This brought Parmenides close to the Egyptian method of describing the universe and existence rather than developing them, rather than seeking progress. However, it left Parmenides considerably removed from the Egyptian view of the creation of the universe from a watery chaos, from Egyptian afterlife doctrines and from the Egyptian notion of truth as something which was strictly linked to order rather than something which *is*, which is a kind of metaphysical way of life. In some ways, Parmenides was like Heraclitus — he embodied

---

169. Herodotus, *Books I-II*, 2.37.5.

aspects of the Egyptian mythological religious view and, with his doctrine of what *It is* and *It is not*, reached a typically Greek, exacerbated rational view with a high degree of strictly logical reasoning that went over the brink into religious metaphysics.

Perhaps both the radicalness of the Greek view and its deep opposition to the Egyptian view lies between Protagoras and Socrates: between Protagoras' claim that no sure answer is possible, that "man is the measure of all things" and that a reasonable, or pragmatic, path has to be determined solely using human means; and Socrates' hint that an individual has to muddle through in his metaphysical search for clarity, truth and ethics. These Greek views, and especially the attempt to establish morality as the touchstone of everyday life — which became the pillars of the Western way of thinking — are utterly antagonistic to the basic Egyptian tenets of control by the gods within a predetermined and permanent order.

EGYPT AS A HINGE BETWEEN THE ANCIENT AND CHRISTIAN ERAS

The Christians fused the Hebrew, the Greek and the Egyptian views. The Christians diluted Hebrew monotheistic concepts and amplified Hebrew ethical concepts. Greek metaphysical influence is particularly strong, notably through Plotinus (AD 205–270), born in Egypt, who founded Neoplatonism and postulated the idea that the earth and mankind were tarnished and only the divine was perfect and good — a concept which became a central Christian dogma. Greek and Egyptian roots in rituals, customs and theology are numerous. A comparison of the Egyptian and Christian religions in many domains inevitably — and despite an almost total lack of formal proof — leads to speculation that Egypt played a pivotal role in the elaboration of Christianity, both through Judaism and on its own. Many key Christian beliefs and rituals may have been established using a curious combination of Egyptian influence, a stance of strong rejection of Egyptian practices and the development of theological concepts originating in Egypt. As we have seen in Chapter 9, Egyptian traditions and early Egyptian Christianity in the opening centuries of our era also constituted a direct influence on Christianity in many domains, from the nature of Jesus to the adoration of images of Jesus, Mary and the saints and to monastic life.

Christianity, like Judaism, in its main thrust, and notably its ethical content, was deeply opposed to the Egyptian view. The early Christian Church was indeed as ethically opposed to traditional Egyptian practices and centrality of magic and as verbally opposed to the Egyptian way of thinking as the Hebrews were. However, like the Hebrews, the Christian rejection of Egypt was paradoxically and largely effected alongside the maintenance of many transformed Egyptian magical beliefs and rituals. The considerable Egyptian influence on Christianity has not been sufficiently studied and is usually vastly underestimated.

Possible Egyptian influence is evident concerning the almost magical link between belief and salvation, between Jesus-the-savior and future afterlife bliss, and also between the Jesus-Mary duo and the Horus-Isis duo. It seems impossible not to accord a role to Osirisian savior, salvation and afterlife theology in Christian theology. It seems highly probable that Osiris, together with the concept of the divine pharaoh, were prefigurations of both the Hebrew Messiah/King concept and its Christian transformation into the Jesus, dying/ resurrecting Son of God concept. Somewhere down the line, Osiris and Jesus were offering the same thing — magical salvation in the afterlife. Even the dreaded Egyptian afterlife "second death" was perhaps echoed by John in Revelation 21:8. As we have seen in Chapter 9, the chief Christian difference with the Egyptian system was ethics, works, even if Christian theology never clearly solved the mixture of faith, works and predestination involved in earning a Christian afterlife.

However, in addition to their immense difference in ethical conceptions, there were other significant differences between Osiris and Jesus. Osiris was a father image; Jesus was a son image. Jesus was incarnated as a god without sexual desire; Osiris had immense sexual desire. A god or a goddess without immense sexual desire was totally unheard of in Egypt or in any other antique society before the Hebrew invention of the asexual Yahweh and the epitome of this concept with Jesus.

Another key Egyptian theological influence on Christianity could have been the Memphite theology of the creation of the world through the heart (the mind), intelligence, and the tongue/word of the god Ptah. This theology bears a startling resemblance to the theology of the Christian apostle John at end of the first century AD: "In the beginning was the Word, and the Word was with God, and the Word was God....And the Word was made flesh [the incarnation of Jesus] and dwelt among us...And his name is called The Word of God."[170]

As we have seen, despite lingering doubts, it is improbable that the Memphite/Ptah theology dates to the Egyptian Old Kingdom (c. 2686–2181 BC), but nevertheless it is quite possible to assume that it exercised international influence from the eighth century BC. It is within the realm of possibility that Ptah/Memphite theology influenced the Hebrews, notably in the creation myth ("And God said, Let there be light: and there was light") and Isaiah ("So shall my word be that goeth forth out of my mouth...it shall accomplish that which I

170. John 1:1 and 1:14 and Revelation 19:13.

please...")[171], influenced the Greek notion of the *logos*, the word, or "reason" which governs the universe, and seeped into Christian theology.

The Christian transformation of the Hebrew sole invisible god system into multiform Trinitarian monotheism, with a temporarily visible, immanent son of the invisible god playing a central role, may have been influenced by the Egyptian triadic system, and notably by the Amun/Re/Ptah unitary organic triad. This could partially explain the rapid success of Christianity in Egypt from the third century AD, albeit eventually in an Egyptian version — the Egyptian Christian Monophysite concept that Jesus, the Son, has only one nature, divine, which absorbed the human (like the ancient pharaohs!). In any case, the Trinity and its consubstantiality was something that would make the Egyptians, with their numerous triads, amalgamated gods and gods as aspects of other gods, feel at home. An eminent Egyptologist like John A. Wilson (1899–1976) even claimed that the ancient Egyptians were Monophysites from very early times, recognizing "different beings" but feeling "those beings to be of a single essential substance..."[172]

The Holy Spirit, or Holy Ghost, the third person of the Trinity, was derived from the Hebrew *ruach ha-Qodesh*, the holy breath of life principle, which itself may have been influenced by the Egyptian *ankh* force and breath of life principle. In the early centuries of Christianity, Egyptian Christianity rejected the idea that the Holy Spirit was equated with God. To them, and especially to the Alexandrian theologian Origen (AD 185–254), it was a spirit which animated the Church, but not the entirety of creation. As a spirit, a guardian, an ally, a ghost, such a view is close to the concept of the Egyptian *ka* soul.

The Holy Spirit as a power which bestowed many gifts, including "other tongues" and spiritual guidance when it descended inside an apostle or a believer could have also been influenced by the ghost, ally, guardian and power aspects of the *ka*.

Curiously, the dualistic soul-body concept, so fundamental in Christianity, may owe something to the Egyptian *ba*, the roaming soul, despite the basic Egyptian concept that the soul cannot survive without the preservation of the body. The *ba* lived with the gods but visited his deceased body, indicating that a separation between body and soul was possible.

The Christian Tabernacle, where the bread and wine for the Eucharist are kept, seems to have derived from the Hebrew Tabernacle which, in turn, as we have seen, probably owes much to the Egyptian *ra per*, the *naos* tabernacle and the *wia*, bark (boat) shrines used to transport the gods.

---

171. Genesis 1:3 and Isaiah 55:11.
172. Wilson, John in *The Intellectual Adventure of Ancient Man*, p. 66.

It was probably G.I. Gurdjieff (1866?–1949), whose own teaching is mainly a kind of esoteric Christianity, who went furthest in the rapprochement between the ancient Egyptian religion and Christianity; but he did it in a way which was simultaneously contradictory, intriguing and unprovable. In some of his writings, Gurdjieff adopted the usual view that "...the Christian religion, having taken the Judaic doctrines as their basis, changed only its outer details," but in other texts he held that "The Christian Church, the Christian form of worship...was all taken in a ready-made form from Egypt, only not from the Egypt we know, but from one which...existed much earlier. Only small bits of it survived...and...we do not even know where they have been preserved." Gurdjieff then went on to state that this "prehistoric Egypt was Christian many thousands of years before the birth of Christ...its religion was composed of the same principles and ideas that constitute true Christianity." The only concrete element Gurdjieff cited for this Egyptian link was so-called "schools of repetition" in Egypt which became "a model for...the form of worship in Christian churches..."[173]

The problem is that the closest we can come to the concept of "schools of repetition" in ancient Egypt would be the Abydos Temple secret Osirisian death and resurrection "mystery" ceremonies — ceremonies which at the earliest could have been elaborated in the Sixth Dynasty (c. 2345–2181 BC), about 750 years after the end of prehistoric times. The Christian liturgical telling of the story of Jesus may owe something to the Abydos Temple Osirisian commemorative ceremonies, but these ceremonies appear to be largely insufficient to justify the total origin of the Christian Church in Egypt as Gurdjieff seems to do. And, of course, the entirety of Gurdjieff's argument is flawed by his reference to a superior kind of Egypt in prehistoric times, something which archaeology has abundantly proven to be incorrect. Yet Gurdjieff seems to be pointing to a general Egyptian influence on Christianity which cannot easily be dismissed.

In the final analysis, when dealing with Egyptian influences on early Christianity, the same problem of credible proof is frequently posed as it is with Judaism; but, as with Judaism, the similarities are so great that it is impossible not to consider the plausibility of considerable Egyptian influence on Christianity — that is, once again, as long as we do not lose sight of the essential differences between the two and especially the revolutionary nature of Christian love, forgiveness and ethics.

---

173. Gurdjieff, G., *All And Everything*, Routledge & Kegan Paul, London, 1962, p. 1002 and Ouspensky, P.D., *In Search of the Miraculous, Fragments of an Unknown Teaching*, pp. 302-303.

EGYPTIAN DREAM INTERPRETATION AS A LINK TO THE HEBREWS, THE GRECO-ROMANS AND FREUD

It seems likely that the central magical role of dreams, provoked dreaming and controlled dreaming in Egyptian society influenced the Hebrews, the Greeks and the Romans and had an indirect influence on Freud's theories.

The probable use of dreams by many peoples to conclude that a more perfect, more complete self, or a soul, exists and that it is the soul which dreams could go back to Neanderthal times. The linking of the function of dreaming to orders and advice from the divine, healing, premonition and the afterlife are all too widespread, before and after Egypt, to conclude at any kind of original Egyptian influence. However, it seems certain that, at the very least, the elaborate Egyptian system of provoked and controlled dreaming and their grid or code of dream meanings had an influence throughout the Mediterranean world.

Joseph, Moses, Samuel, Daniel and many other Hebrew prophets used dreaming as the means to supposedly understand God's will and to interpret and predict events. Some of the most famous Egyptian dreams, and their interpretations by the Hebrew Joseph, notably the dream of the seven years of plenty and the seven years of famine, are vividly described in the Bible.

Despite the Biblical description of Joseph as a better dream interpreter than the Egyptian priests and notables, it seems logical to assume that there was Egyptian influence on the Hebrews concerning the importance, the function and the interpretation of dreams. Given the anteriority of Egyptian civilization, it is difficult to imagine how such an essential domain as the dream world could have been excluded from the probable across-the-board influence the Egyptians exercised on the Hebrews.

The influence of the Egyptian magical dream system on the Greeks and Romans also seems to have been considerable. During their occupation of Egypt (332–30 BC), the Greeks used the Egyptian system to provoke and control dreams in the temples they built in Egypt dedicated to the Greco-Egyptian god they invented, Serapis. The dream interpretation system described by Artemidorus Daldianus of Ephesus (fl. 2nd century AD) in *Oneirocritica*, seems to owe much to the Egyptian system. The provoked and controlled dreaming practices in Delphi, Memphis, Delos and in later Roman temples were similar to what was practiced in the Egyptian temple Houses of Life.

The Roman Emperor Constantine's famous dream about Jesus in AD 312 was similar to the premonitory dreams of many Egyptian pharaohs before major battles. Jesus appeared to Constantine in a dream, at the time when Constantine was a believer in the god Sol Invictus, the Unconquered Sun, informing him that he would be victorious in battle if he placed the first two letters of Jesus' name on his soldiers' shields. The official conversion of Rome to Christianity began in a dream.

The links between the Egyptian and Hebrew emphasis on the deep meaning of dreams and the central aspect it played in Sigmund Freud's (1856–1939) work may appear to be tenuous, but Freud did acknowledge the great influence on his work of his Jewish subconscious and background, and he had made at least a cursory study of Egyptian religion and had read Artemidorus. There are some startling analogies between his descriptions of the dream world and those of the ancient Egyptians. In any case, Freud, in *The Interpretation of Dreams* (1899) and later works, agreed with the Egyptians, Hebrews and other ancient religious peoples that dreams had deep meaning and played a central role in life. This was in sharp contrast to most of the scientists and doctors of his time, who imputed dreams to strictly chance physical stimuli.

The key difference between Freud and the Egyptians and Hebrews was that the atheist Freud designated the non-religious unconscious and psychological spheres — the mind, the libido — as the sources of the deep meaning of dreams, rather than the religious sphere or any kind of magical premonition, domains which Freud totally rejected.

For Freud, dreams were among the realest, most instinctive parts of a person's unconscious being, the part in which he expressed his truest feelings, desires and fears in coded language — "dream-work" — so that his civilized ego and alter-ego were unable to exercise censure. For the Egyptians, the dream world was the magical world of the gods, the demons, original chaos and where an individual met his *ka* guardian soul his true or best self, in a prefiguration of the afterlife.

Freud used the usual situations, fantasies and objects of his time in which the dreamer constituted his coded "dream-work," the *mise en scene* of his deep, unconscious desires and fears, while the Egyptians used the usual situations, fantasies and objects of their time in a basically premonitory system.

The correct interpretation of Egyptian-type premonitory dreams — in modern Freudian terms, the interpretation of the dream code — was obviously capital. The similarities between the Egyptian and Freudian systems in this domain are startling. Freud did not believe that a code of symbolic meaning for the situations and objects in dreams could be exclusive, but much like the Egyptians he did believe that dreams were a "kind of cryptography" which could be "decoded" and that some phenomena could be almost universally and unequivocally interpreted in a symbolic manner.

The emphasis on sexuality was just as basic in the Egyptian system as in the Freudian system. As we have seen in Chapter 8, the Egyptians used sexual situations in dreams to predict events in life: a man who dreamt that he was looking at a woman's vagina would suffer great misfortunes; dreaming that one made love to a cow meant that the person would have a pleasant day; if a woman dreamt she made love to a horse, it meant she would be violent with her husband, etc. Freud used a grid of symbolic or coded dream meanings in an inverted sense to the Egyptians, with sexual meaning imputed to usual objects and seemingly ordinary situations — ladders, staircases, elevators and flying for sexual intercourse, long and pointed weapons, trees and sticks for the penis, cupboards, chests, cars and pouches for the female body, entries and exits for the bodily orifices, rooms for women, kings and queens for fathers and mothers, etc.

Freud's choice of dream symbols made sense; they were not arbitrary, even if the basic thrust of his overall system was, and still is, contested. On the other hand, to a modern mind, the Egyptian choice of dream symbols seems arbitrary and even comical, but this might quite simply be because we are no longer aware of the context that made such choices sensible. In many ways, Freud's dream world and dream code had their roots in the industrial and secular world and were a version of the Egyptian agriculturally and magically, religiously, based dream world. In much the same way, one can suppose that new dream symbols, codes and interpretations based on the computer-age culture will one day emerge.

Freud's *id*, seen by him as the primitive, illogical instincts driving the unconscious, can also partially be seen as a modern definition of the *ka*. For the ancient Egyptians, the *ka* guardian soul, the true or best self, was met in dreams; for Freud, the *id*'s instinctive, inherited, unconscious needs and wishes were expressed in dreams.

EGYPT AS AN INSPIRATION FOR ESOTERICA — POSSIBLE TRUTHS AND INCREDIBLE IMAGINATION

Most Western esoteric groups consider that mankind's first elaborate esoteric system originated in ancient Egypt; however, very little is known about any such system of so-called secret knowledge. Yet, on a strictly historical basis, all the modern esoteric systems, with the notable exception of the Hindu, seem to have been influenced by the Egyptians in both real and imaginary ways.

A first distinction has to be made between esoteric systems that seek to explore and develop human potential and loony theories and magic, including so-called satanic magic. This distinction is not easy to establish either for Egypt or for any of the succeeding esoteric systems — all of them seem to mix authentic systems of comprehension and development and incredible magic.

It is obvious that all societies which built major temples and/or developed priest castes produced esoteric systems or secret societies. Well-known examples are Sumer, Israel, Greece, India, Africa and the shamanistic societies in Siberia and the Americas. It is also clear that the Egyptian temple system, together with the Sumerian, were the earliest elaborate temple organizations and that by the New Kingdom (c. 1550 BC), the Egyptian network of temples was by far the biggest, involving literally hundreds of thousands of priests.

It seems possible, and even likely, that from at least the Sixth Dynasty (c. 2345–2181 BC), major Egyptian temples like Heliopolis, Memphis, Hermopolis and Abydos organized secret ceremonies. During the New Kingdom (c. 1550–1069 BC), Karnak and other temples professed doctrines which can be called "secret" and numerous temple Houses of Life probably dispensed at least some so-called secret knowledge, that is, "knowledge" which was not for everybody, nor even everybody in the priest caste. It is also obvious that numerous Egyptian concepts such as the systems of nine gods and five souls seeped into many esoteric systems as the enneagram and the pentagram and that the Egyptian organization of its priest caste and its sacred temple architecture became models.

How much conscious intention went into conceiving these Egyptian systems of nines and fives and how much artificial symbolism was later added will never be known. As the symbol for totality, the Heliopolitan *pesedjet*, ennead, could have been applied to countless phenomena which have survived in several esoteric systems right into our time. These include a hierarchy of nine spiritual levels, sacred enneagram dance movements based on perpetual intertwining movement from nine sources, esoteric *mandala*-type and especially enneagram symbols representing universal knowledge and the completed, sacred whole based on nine levels, nine sides, nine angles and nine occurrences. As to fives, five united souls in the afterlife constituted a unified person in the Egyptian system. This Egyptian system of five was probably at the origin in various esoteric systems of the pentagram representing perfect, harmonious unity of man's supposed five functions.

Many claims have been made, spanning more than two thousand years, concerning the existence of elaborate Egyptian wisdom. It is often difficult to determine whether this meant wisdom based on esotericism or rather great knowledge and ability in domains ranging from architecture to agricultural technology, to art, to mummification, etc. We have seen that the Greeks perceived very few or no links between their philosophy and science and the "wisdom" of the Egyptians. Nevertheless, a fantasy arose of Egyptian wisdom that had influenced everything Greek. This view was largely first nourished by some Greeks themselves — Herodotus, Plutarch and to some extent Plato and Aristotle, all of whom credited the Egyptians with occult religious knowledge. Over the centuries, the implication became that Egyptian knowledge and esotericism had influenced everything Greek, even when this was not necessarily the belief of many of the Greeks who first wrote of Egyptian influence.

The person who seems to have gotten the ball rolling in this direction was Herodotus (c. 484–420 BC). His *Histories* seems to have been the first vehicle for the idea that there was immense and secret knowledge in Egypt and that neither the Egyptian priests of his time nor himself wanted to talk too much about this to ordinary people. Plutarch (c. AD 45–125) derided the Egyptian practice of "treating...animals...as gods," but nevertheless believed in Egyptian "wisdom touching all that had to do with gods...an enigmatical sort of wisdom" in Egyptian "symbolism and occult teachings."[174]

Plato (c. 428–347? BC) also played an unwitting decisive role by either inventing the lost island/continent of Atlantis and its emblematic defeat by the original Athens or by supposedly relating real Egyptian beliefs about an Atlantis. According to Plato, in *Timaeus* and in *Critias*, Solon (c. 639?–559 BC) had been told by "a very old" Egyptian priest in the Neith/Athena Temple in Sais about the huge, beautiful, fertile, technologically advanced island of Atlantis which had existed 9000 years earlier. Critias' great-grandfather had supposedly told Solon that Atlantis was a powerful and fabulously prosperous civilization whose people "obeyed the laws and loved the divine to which they were akin...[and] retained a certain greatness of mind...wisdom and forbearance." However, "when the divine element in them became weakened by frequent admixture with mortal stock," the Atlanteans sunk into "degeneration" and "attempted to enslave" Greece, much of Europe, and Africa "up to the borders of Egypt" before being defeated by Athens, which "rescued those not yet enslaved...and generously freed all others living within the Pillars of Heracles [beyond the Strait of Gibraltar]. At a later time...earthquakes and floods of extraordinary violence...all your [Athens] fighting men were swallowed up by the earth, and the island of Atlantis was similarly swallowed up by the sea and vanished..."[175] Plato's purpose in inventing or relating this myth seems to have been to describe a great, wise, ideal (and near-fascist) prehistoric Athens which could serve as a model for the Greece of his time. Other Greek and Roman and then Western writers, priests and personalities right into our time enthusiastically transformed Plato's myth into a tale of how so-called Egyptian esotericism and technical knowledge were linked to the heritage of the lost continent of Atlantis and of how Egypt had transmitted its Atlantean heritage to Greece.

---

174. Plutarch, *Moralia*, Volume V, *Isis and Osiris*, pp. 165, 25 and 27.

175. *Plato, Timaeus And Critias*, translated by Desmond Lee, *Timaeus*, 22, p. 35, *Critias*, 121, p. 145 and *Timaeus*, 25, p. 38.

With or without the Atlantis angle, the Egyptians, probably beginning with Manetho (fl.c. 300 BC) made precise claims of the existence of Egyptian esotericism, of a "hidden" knowledge, in ancient times. Major personalities in Late Antiquity, like Josephus (c. AD 37–100), Saint Clement of Alexandria (c. AD150-215), Eusebius, Bishop of Caesarea in Palestine (c. AD 260–340) and Horapollon (fl.5th century AD) made similar claims. The idea of an Egyptian esotericism was relayed by Greek *Hermetica* to Marsile Ficin (1433–1499), Bruno (1548?–1600), Kepler (1571–1630), Newton (1642–1727), Ralph Cudworth (1617–1688), Friedrich Schiller (1759–1805), and many other Renaissance scientists and philosophers and to the Freemasons, the Rosicrucians and other esoteric groups like that of Gurdjieff (1866?–1949), and to many artists and musicians, notably Mozart (1756–1791).

The unsolvable problem is: to what degree did claims concerning an elaborate Egyptian esoteric system correspond to a real Egyptian reality and to what degree were they imaginary? There are no doubts about the vastness and intricacies of the Egyptian system of magic, *heka*, from very early times, from well before 3000 BC, and the secret teachings and ceremonies in later times. There can also be no doubts about the complexity of the Egyptian soul and afterlife systems, even if they can perhaps be better qualified as naive illusions rather than elaborate esotericism.

However, two fundamental questions cannot be answered: was *heka* merely what we consider it to be today — crude magical practices and naive beliefs — and were Egypt's secret teachings and ceremonies really elaborate esoteric systems of understanding and human development or mere hocus-pocus or conventional wisdom? In other words, did ancient Egyptian teachings contain a layer of sophisticated so-called esoteric doctrines which were equivalent to the elaborate systems which were later developed in India, in the Greek world, among the Jews and among the Moslems?

The overall probability points to Egypt having been the first known society to possess a highly organized system of secret teachings and rituals, as reflected in the Abydos Temple Osirisian "mystery" ceremonies. Sety I's (c. 1294–1279 BC) cenotaph temple in Abydos included a room which was apparently out-of-bounds, although its exact purpose has never been determined. The Osireion Temple (or cenotaph), which Sety or Merenptah (c. 1213–1203 BC) built and the Hermopolis Tuna el-Gebel necropolis maze of catacombs and Thoth Temple (c. 525 BC–AD 395) are also candidates for secret teachings or rites. The overall probability also points to this secret teaching system having been a mixture of a real attempt at understanding, magic and conventional wisdom and servile and loony notions, as reflected in Egypt's *sebayt* wisdom literature. And it is certain, and not just probable, that this Egyptian secret system was largely valorized and amplified by many succeeding esoteric groups and sects which sought to attribute great antiquity and even some kind of an original and permanent nature to their views.

Rightly or wrongly — we'll never know — Egypt's system of secret knowledge, as it became famous and respected in the ancient Greco-Roman world and then in medieval Europe, was above all linked to the god Thoth. Isis was *weret hekau*, "great of magic," Amun, whose "name is hidden," who "created what exists" and who was all-knowing, was said to be a magician and a healer and was also called "the Lord of the silent" (but this title could also be a reference to his role as Lord of the living dead); but without question, the greatest accumulation of references in Egyptian texts and art to a guardian of a system of knowledge not available to everybody concern Thoth. A reasonably good case can be made for Thoth's, or rather his priests', doctrines implying both organized secret teachings and a type of meditation.

In Egypt's Osiris/Seth/Isis/Horus founding myth, Thoth played a key role as a magician and after betraying Osiris in the versions of the myth in the Pyramid Texts (c. 2375–2125 BC), he became an honest broker in all the succeeding versions. He was the scribe of Re and the god of the scribes, the god of writing, wisdom and the moon, "the Dragoman [Interpreter] of the Two Lands," the "measurer" of time and human life. But many texts also explicitly refer to Thoth and secrets. The deified architect Amenhotep, son of Hapu (c. 1430–1350 BC), claimed: "I saw the Tools [the hieroglyphs] of Thoth; I was well schooled in their secrets..." The inscription on the statue of Horemheb, from c. 1336 BC, now in the New York Metropolitan Museum, states: "Who [Thoth] knows the secrets, Who records their expression..." The Ramesside *Instruction of Amennemope* wisdom text (from about 1000 BC, but whose content probably dates to the 20th Dynasty, c. 1186–1069 BC) asks: "Where is a god as great as Thoth, Who invented these things and made them."

We find the key Egyptian notion of the "silent" and the "heated" in *The Instruction of Amennemope*: "The truly silent, who keeps apart" and the "heated man" who "is like a tree growing indoors." Amennemope prides himself on being a "truly silent" man, that is, a man striving to be an ideal man and indeed of all the Egyptian wisdom literature, his *Instruction*, despite the usual advice concerning correct social behavior, comes closest to what can be called a spiritual quest. *The Prayer To Thoth* in the Sallier I Papyrus (c. 1220 BC) explicitly deals with silence and its fruits which are hidden from the "heated": "Come rescue me the silent; O Thoth, your well that is sweet, To a man who thirsts in the desert! It is sealed to him who finds words, It is open to the silent...To the heated man you are [hidden]."[176]

Of course, there is a danger of reading too much into these texts, a danger of extravagantly ascribing esoteric significance to "the silent man" and "the heated man." These terms are frequent throughout Egyptian literature and often are merely notions of superior common sense or superior morality — the type of conventional wisdom that is a hallmark of the *sebayt*, the Instruction or Wisdom Texts. Adolf Erman (1854–1937) adopted such an attitude; he postulated that "the meaning" of "the silent man" was "not doubtful" and meant that "man must wait in silence for help from his god" and that "the silent man" constituted a practitioner of a "superior morality." But Erman also recognized that "This wonderful wisdom does not seem to have been within the reach of all learned men..."[177]

We have here the ingredients of the usual mysteries surrounding esotericism — what appears to be commonplace can also have deep meaning. There is indeed a danger of failing to acknowledge that some of these texts about "the silent man" may be describing people who could be practitioners of "quiet" meditation, people who have renounced being "heated" in favor of esoteric self-control. The Egyptian texts concerning Thoth do not directly deal with meditation techniques, but they can be interpreted to describe practitioners of meditation and the results of meditation. This situation leads to a possibility that Egypt may have invented what can be called "quiet" meditation. It cannot be easily dismissed that, even if there does not seem to be any reference in the Egyptian texts to the key esoteric techniques of higher consciousness, self-awareness and concentration (which, in esoteric terms as understood today, should accompany "silence"), the description in some texts is not just moral, but very close to the result obtained by "quiet" meditation.

The esoteric principle of "quiet" meditation which seeks to silence the incessant, random flow of ordinary thoughts, emotions and physical sensations so that other states of being can appear is one which was practiced, and is still practiced, notably by the Hindu Yoga and the Zen Buddhist Schools, as well as in many modern Western esoteric groups. Fundamentally, it is the altered state obtained through quietness — in contradistinction to the altered state of being produced by various forms of frenzy from song, dance, chanting, intoxication and modifications in breathing which probably went back deep into prehistory. It is impossible to separate a hypothetical Egyptian influence from many locally developed forms of meditation throughout the world, but if the *Instruction of*

---

176. Redford, Donald B., *Akhenaten, The Heretic King*, p. 47, quoting A. Varille and Erman, Adolf, *Life in Ancient Egypt*, p. 347, Lichtheim, Miriam, *Ancient Egyptian Literature, Volume II*, pp. 102, 156-157, 151, 150, 149 and 114.

177. Erman, Adolf, *La Religion des Egyptiens*, p. 171 and *Life in Ancient Egypt*, p. 347.

Amennemope and the Sallier I Papyrus can be interpreted as describing practitioners of "quiet" meditation and its results, then they seem to be the first known references to this type of meditation.

The explicit Egyptian Thoth doctrines defining "the silent man" and its results can be dated with certitude, but the notion of "not sleeping," which is linked in esoteric practice to "silence" and "quietness" could go back at least to about the Sumerian King Gilgamesh, who may have ruled in Uruk, around 2660 BC. The later tales and legends about Gilgamesh, mostly written after 2000 BC, in *The Epic of Gilgamesh*, seem to be the first known references to another state of being obtained by not "sleeping." This term could be an esoteric reference to ordinary existence in which the higher, or soul, functions are asleep and to staying "awake," the other state of being in which the higher functions have been activated. Whether or not the Egyptian texts are referring to practitioners of "quiet" meditation must remain as open a question as whether or not *The Epic of Gilgamesh* expounds an esoteric doctrine.

Between the First and Third centuries AD, both Thoth and Isis were believed to be the original Egyptian teachers of the widespread Greco-Roman magic and mystery cults. *Hermes*, the Greek messenger of the gods, as *Hermes Trismegistus* ("three times great"), identified with Thoth, in the vast body of Greek occult writing, the *Corpus Hermetica*, became the imaginary Egyptian founder of Greco-Roman esotericism.

A loony legend arose that Thoth's secret esoteric knowledge, in the so-called *Book of Thoth*, on 42 papyri, had been hidden in hollow pillars in the Heliopolis Temple and then transmitted to Greek priests! A quest for a hidden *Book of Thoth* is indeed mentioned in some Egyptian texts, notably in the Ptolemaic Period (332–32 BC) Setne Khamwas and Nanferkaptah Papyrus (now in the Cairo Museum). However, rather than esoteric wisdom, the description of the *Book of Thoth* in the Setne Tale is concerned with typical Egyptian magic like charming the sky and the earth, interpreting the language of animals and assuming former earthly forms in the afterlife. Its thrust is the hackneyed search for a book which makes the owner an unsurpassable magician.[178] Needless to add, no *Book of Thoth* containing secret wisdom has ever been found. Moreover, the Egyptian content in Greek Hermetic literature is clearly only one of several elements and any real connection to Thoth, or rather his priests, and to Egypt seem to be small, nonexistent, or faked.

Hermetica literature indicates a mixture of Greek occultism, scientific notions, philosophy, and especially Platonism, Neoplatonism, Gnosticism and fragments of Egyptian religion and traditional lore, notably so-called Thoth

---

178. Lichtheim, Miriam, *Ancient Egyptian Literature, Volume III*, pp. 127-138.

"secret knowledge" texts. The central *Hermetica* concept that god, the cosmos and man are of the same nature, are a single body, and that man is a microcosm of god were deeply opposed to Egyptian beliefs. *Hermetica's* postulation that man is a mortal god and god is an immortal man would have astounded the ancient Egyptians! *Hermetica's* division of the universe into categories, the division of individuals according to spiritual rank and dualism of the good/evil, material/ spiritual, mind/body and light/darkness types seem to owe more to the heretical Christian Gnosticism of the 2nd century AD and to Zoroastrianism than to Egyptian thinking. This remains so even if Gnosticism was particularly strong in Egypt and even if in addition to early Christianity, Judaism and Zoroastrianism, Gnosticism also had roots in an interpretation of some Egyptian beliefs. However, the essential point here is that Egyptian dualism postulated necessary opposing forces resolved after a daily magical struggle in a positive result of *maat* universal harmony. *Maat* was the permanent victor in Egyptian dualism and it was a victory of primeval order and not a victory of spiritual nature; it had nothing to do with a conflict between the material and the spiritual, between the body and the souls. The asceticism which was demanded in *Hermetica* was utterly foreign to Egyptian concepts of joy in the body and to the souls as material parts of the body. On the other hand, the Egyptian systems of immortality, magic and the organization of its priest caste seem to have played roles in the *Hermetica* writings. Perhaps, but really only perhaps, *Hermetica's* description of the first god, the god of light, can be linked to Atum, Re, Shu and Aten.

Hermetica mixed all these elements with sharp, convoluted analysis and a considerable dose of Greek hocus-pocus, plus blatant lies concerning its origins in Egypt. Moreover, the most famous book linked to Hermes/Thoth, *The Emerald Tablets*, may not have been actually composed before the tenth century AD. In 1614, the French Hellenist and Calvinist theologian, Isaac Casaubon (1559–1614), decisively demonstrated that the *Corpus Hermetica* could not possibly have originated in Egypt, had been entirely composed by Greeks in Late Antiquity and was incompatible with Christianity. But the British scholar Ralph Cudworth (1617–1688) astutely minimized Casaubon's conclusions and the loonies and even the less loony, including the Freemasons, continued to favor imaginary links to Egyptian secret wisdom. Ambiguously, the Freemasons continued to propagate the idea of these links while simultaneously playing a key role in Enlightenment rationalism and the virtually atheistic (or at least, deistic) French Revolution.

Cudworth also strongly defended the idea that the hieroglyphs conveyed deep and secret concepts rather than words and sounds. This idea was contained in the *Corpus Hermetica*, but was popularized among European philosophers and scholars by the discovery in the 15th century of the works of Horapollon (fl.5th century AD), a Greek Egyptian who affirmed that the Egyptian hieroglyphs were in fact secret wisdom expressed in symbolic form rather than the ideograms and phonetic signs of language. Horapollon came to this conclusion despite the fact that he was incapable of reading hieroglyphs. Many of the inevitably hieroglyphically illiterate European philosophers and scholars, led by Cudworth, amplified Horapollon's views into doctrines of Egyptian mysteries linked to *Hermetica*.

As discussed in Chapter 10, Cudworth and other Renaissance philosophers of religion, some of whom were linked to Freemasonry, claimed that Egypt was the repository of secret wisdom, and notably secret monotheism which had been directly transmitted to Moses. They also imagined that Egypt was the first source of all human knowledge, civilization and religion (*prisca scientia* and *prisca theologia*). They usually wrapped their package in forms of deism, pantheism and rationalism which they also imagined existed in ancient Egyptian religion. Moreover, they were unaware of the pre-Egyptian religions and societal organizations of Sumer, Anatolia and Cro-Magnon Europe.

Concurrently to this movement, the Jewish *Kabala* had come to the forefront of European occultism and was merged with Greek *Hermetica* and what was thought to be Egyptian *heka* magic. This hybrid was seen by some, including both philosophers and scientists, as a weapon for piercing the secrets of the universe and existence.

Still another key point of contact between imaginary Egyptian esotericism, *Hermetica* and European Renaissance admiration for Egypt was constituted by the French priest Jean Terasson (1670–1750). He ambiguously said that his *Life of Sethos* was fictional, but nevertheless based on a 2nd century AD Greek author's writings who no doubt was familiar with ancient secret Egyptian texts. Terasson painted a picture of vast and secret Egyptian wisdom and science in the 13th century BC, dispensed in temples and pyramids and later directly transmitted to Pythagoras, Thales and Solon. Terasson had extensive influence on the Freemasons and on many scientists, writers and musicians (including Mozart, whose *Magic Flute* was a revamped version of the Osiris tale) and was instrumental in spreading the *Hermetica* idea of secret and ancient Egyptian wisdom.

Freemasons linked their own "secret knowledge" to Thoth/Hermes and the pyramid builders, in addition to a Hiram Abif as the architect of Solomon's Temple, somebody who supposedly used the principles of esoteric architecture. Right from the their founding in the 17th century, and under the influence of *Hermetica*, the Freemasons claimed links to what they believed was ancient Egyptian wisdom and esotericism and even claimed that Freemasonry and its initiation rituals had existed in ancient Egyptian times. The role of the Freemasons in establishing an imaginary vision of ancient Egypt was immense and, even today, Freemasons are a vector for Egypto-*Hermetica* hocus-pocus.

In the final analysis, the origin of Greek *Hermetica* had much less to do with Egyptian teachings than it had with a vast confusion between science, religion and occultism during the first centuries of our era, when science had fallen into disrepute but was still needed to link together loony theories about the operation of the universe, hope and immortality. However, the imaginary Egyptian pillar of this type of esotericism had been firmly anchored in the Renaissance and would continue to play a major role in the development of both esotericism and, paradoxically, science.

Perhaps the ultimate irony in all this was that in Greece, while Hermes was the messenger of the gods, he was also notorious for leading people astray and protecting thieves.

THE HOCUS-POCUS VIEW OF EGYPT AND THE SCIENTIFIC REVOLUTION IN EUROPE

Perhaps the most curious and paradoxical influence of imaginary Egyptian secret teachings and magic was on the Scientific Revolution, beginning in the 16th century, via "Egypto"-Greek *Hermetica*. Some of the finest minds of the Scientific Revolution, including Nicholas Copernicus (1473–1543), Tycho Brahe (1546–1601), Giordano Bruno (1548?–1600), Johannes Kepler (1571–1630) and above all, Isaac Newton (1643–1747), were deeply influenced by what they believed was Egyptian esoteric wisdom with scientific implications. Many other key actors of the Scientific Revolution in Europe, the people who objectively ousted religion from the center of the stage in favor of rationalism and science, were witting and unwitting adepts of various forms of the occult, including astrology, alchemy and mystical immortality beliefs, as supposedly inherited from Egypt and filtered by Greece.

A largely imaginary role of Egyptian esoteric, scientific wisdom came to be seen as a powerful and indubitable reality. In retrospect, it seems that this view was generated by a mixture of romanticism, lack of information, ignorance and surprisingly poor judgment on the part of scientists with such great minds. It is amazing that such a great number of intelligent people, in addition to the fools and the ignorant, could proclaim such views. Certainly, the lack of reliable information about Egypt, the fashion of hermeticism and the false but generalized belief that Egypt was the source of the philosophy and knowledge of Greece and the West were excuses, albeit insufficient.

However, perhaps the motives which played the major roles were an overwhelming irrational desire to maintain the roles of the divine and magic in physical matter and to conciliate so-called ancient and modern science. As we have seen, it was Marsile Ficin (1433–1499), the translator of *Hermetica*, who was the precursor of this movement which sought to combine magic (notably alchemy and astrology), theology, science, philosophy and metaphysics. This movement had a strong influence on Copernicus, Kepler, Bruno, Newton and other many other scientists, even if it did not impress Galileo (1564–1642), who cautiously attempted to situate his work within the limits of formal science, mathematics and philosophy, and Descartes (1596–1650), who may have yielded to Church repression by putting God into his system like a cherry on a cake.

Perhaps the best illustration of this strange concoction of motives was the attribution of an Egyptian role to one of the central discoveries of the Scientific Revolution — the heliocentric thesis that the earth was not the center of the universe as Judeo-Christianity proclaimed, but one planet among many rotating around the sun. Copernicus, Kepler, Bruno and Newton all claimed either to have been influenced by a so-called Egyptian heliocentricism or to support the view that ancient Egypt had similar astronomic views to what science had discovered.

Obviously, the sun was central in the Egyptian system, both as a physical reality and as a god (which in the Egyptian mind was the same thing). Therefore, the main Egyptian god always tended to be a solar god and the creator and sustainer of life — Horus, Atum, Re, Amun-Re, Aten — or if a god rose to preeminence, he was *solarized* in some way as a *ba* aspect, a soul, of Re — Osiris, Montu, Khnum. However, there is strictly no resemblance between the role of the sun in ancient Egyptian cosmogony and in scientific heliocentrism. As we have seen in Chapter 4, Egyptian cosmogony viewed the sky as a watery place, held in position by four pillars, divided into four parts, with two halves, north and south, and filled with the *Ikhemu Seku*, "The Imperishable Stars" — the stars which never seemed to move and were therefore eternal — and the *Ikhemu-Weredu*, "The Stars Which Never Rest" — the stars which were always in motion. The sun (Re) and stars, as gods and goddesses, traveled across the *akhet*, the horizon, from east to west in a solar boat during the 12 daylight hours. The sun, Re, set in the form of the tired, old god Atum. Re then switched to his night solar boat, became the night sun Osiris, lord of the *Duat* underworld, traversed the *Duat* in 12 hours and defeated the huge serpent Apophis who every day tried to prevent the sun from rising.

Is it necessary to repeat that all this had very little to do with scientific, causal, mechanistic heliocentricism in which the earth and all the planets revolve around the center of the system, the sun, due to principles of gravity? Is it necessary to emphasize that, despite the role played by Greek *Hermetica* and Egyptian lore on European science right from Copernicus' time, European heliocentricism was basically born from logical observation, mathematics and astronomy and not Egyptian religious cosmogony with its moving sun personified by a god?

Copernicus was the first European scientist to attribute some scientific credibility to Egyptian wisdom. Giordano Bruno, in *On the Infinite Universe and Worlds* and other works, went much further and became one of the foremost early believers in "the superiority of Egyptian truths," the divinity of the sun and the modern relevance of Egyptian magic and esotericism. Bruno was the major figure of what he himself called the "Egyptian Counter Reformation" and that was what directly led to his execution for heresy. It was this same man who in many ways was a forerunner of modern science, free inquiry and verifiable knowledge. Bruno did much to destroy Christian Scholastic ideas of mingled faith and reason, irrational, religious concepts of the universe and the role of Catholicism and the Catholic priest in society. From its narrow point of view at the time, it was almost understandable that the Roman Catholic Church burned him at the stake in 1600 for heresy.

Bruno's imaginary views about ancient Egypt remain a constant source of amazement. Bruno, and other scientist/occultists like Paracelsus (1493–1541), John Dee (1527–1608) and Robert Fludd (1574–1637), believed the *Hermetica* teaching that god and man were of the same nature and that man was a microcosm of god, apparently never doubting that these concepts were incompatible with so-called ancient and original Egyptian religious wisdom. Especially for Bruno, this meant that man as god on earth was the key actor in the search for knowledge and fulfillment and was not subject to priestly authority and the usual Christian notions that man is powerless and blemished. It is clear that these ideas played central roles in favoring free, scientific inquiry and the development of human independence and atheism, but it was just as clear that that they were magical thinking, born of the Hellenistic confusion between science and religion. Indeed, taken as a whole, the heart of Bruno's system was an imaginary Egyptian-type magical, ritualistic vision, seen through the prism of the irrational *Corpus Hermeticum* and its supposed Egyptian wisdom and real goal of immortality.

The case of Isaac Newton (1643-1747) was even more astounding. Publicly, he hypocritically professed an orthodox, and even aggressive, Protestant religion, but in fact he had a private religion which discounted some of the major Christian principles like the Trinity and was deeply influenced by alchemy and *Hermetica* and its supposed links to Egyptian secret wisdom.

In *Chronology of Ancient Kingdoms Amended, The Origins of Religion* and many other works, Newton proclaimed that Egypt had possessed *prisca scientia* and *prisca theologica*, secret religious and scientific principles, which were God-given first knowledge. He claimed that the ancient religion of Egypt was the true religion before it became corrupted by the idolatry of star and planet worship and reverence for Osiris, Isis, Horus and Amun. He believed that the Egyptians concealed mysteries behind religious rites and hieroglyphic symbols that ordinary people could not understand. He believed that the pyramids were divinely inspired. He believed that there had been some kind of perfect, just, moral, uncorrupt, loving, sexually pure, criminal-free, vegetarian monotheism in Noah's time, that Moses had adopted the Jewish religion from the Egyptians and restored its concealed monotheistic side and that Christianity had been corrupted by pagan metaphysics and idolatry.

However, in the real world and in fact, Newton, with his laws of universal gravity, motion and light, was the genius father of the mechanistic interpretation of the universe, an interpretation which could logically accommodate only a deistic god who had created the universe and then withdrawn from its operation. In fact, Newton's mechanistic view was in utter contradiction not only to Judeo-Christian theology, but also to the very heart of the Egyptian system in which the universe was recreated every day and governed by the gods and their regent, the pharaoh god. In fact, had Newton drawn the obvious philosophical conclusions from his own work, he could not have espoused an imaginary Egyptian religion, alchemy, *Hermetica* or any other religious view; he would have quite simply been an atheist and indeed his scientific views were among those most frequently cited by atheists to prove their beliefs.

But the immense scientific genius Newton never truly recanted the strange esoteric Newton, even if he became somewhat critical of Egypt and its "science" and religious concepts in the final years of his life. In fact, his life was spent more in studying and writing books on theology, alchemy and Egypt/*Hermetica* than on science. Newton was the supreme illustration of the mixture of apologetic rationalism and the occult which marked so many of the actors in the Scientific Revolution. Although it is not proven, somewhere down the line Newton could have also been influenced by the emerging freemasonic views of his time.

Yet despite the links of many European scientists to what they believed was Egyptian religion, esotericism, magic, astrology and alchemy, it is certain that right from the 16th century with Copernicus, and then with Bruno and Newton, these scientists objectively and unwittingly favored the development of a good deal of the opposite of that which they had set out to accomplish. In fact, they provided the credible tools for a rejection of the magical, superstitious approach as so eminently represented by the Egyptian way of thinking. This remained true despite the tortured and sometimes near schizophrenic attempts of some scientists like Bruno and Newton to justify their links to Egyptian magic.

THE WESTERN REJECTION OF THE EGYPTIAN MAGICAL VIEW

The intensive development in philosophy and literature of freethinking in Britain and atheism in France from the 17th century eventually led to the rejection of the Egyptian magical view not only in science, but also in religion. This movement was naturally opposed to all forms of occultism. It culminated in the 18th century Enlightenment and in the war against God of the atheists in 18th and 19th century France.

The "fundamentalists" in this freethinking and atheistic movement, like J.O. de La Mettrie (1709–1751), P.H. d'Holbach (1723–1789) and Claude Helvetius (1715-1771), rejected any form of religion and occultism, which they saw as being fundamentally opposed to the Enlightenment humanist ideals of progress, science, rationalism, secularism and education. Holbach believed that religion was an illness which had originated in Egypt. But even the "moderates" — like David Hume (1711-1776), John Locke (1632–1704) and Voltaire (d. 1778) — usually rejected the dominant, traditional Judeo-Christian theological concepts and their political extensions as well as *Hermetica*, the *Kabala* and Egyptian esoteric symbolism, leaving only forms of deism, atheistic pantheism, so-called natural religion, naturally shared without revelation by all peoples in all times, and hesitations concerning the existence of God and his role.

Beyond this first layer of rejection, what was also being rejected was the "pagan" magical religious view as exemplified by Egypt and supposedly transmitted through Greek *Hermetica* and the mixed bag of so-called Egyptian *prisca theologia* and secret concepts as expressed by Ficin, Bruno, Spencer, Cudworth, Warburton and others. Voltaire rejected Christian clericalism and superstition and Judaism, but he also rejected as childish the Egyptian myth that the Egyptians had been governed by the gods and as liars the philosophers who claimed knowledge about ancient Egypt, since the ancient Egyptian language was lost. This swing of the pendulum gradually led to an exaggerated minimization of Egypt's and Israel's roles in history and an exaggerated amplification of Greece's role.

The cumulative result of all these views sparked the philosophical, sociological, anthropological, archaeological and psychoanalytical reevaluation of religion in the 20th century and the brutal intolerance of the communist movement against religion. The process of secularization and humanism begun by the European scientists and philosophers, and despite their connection to Egyptian hocus-pocus, was completed. In the case of Egypt, this process was perhaps best exemplified by the rise of a new breed of rationalist Egyptologists like Adolf Erman (1854–1937). What was completed was nothing less than rendering religion a matter of doubt at best and silliness at worst. Religion, the system which the Egyptians more than any other ancient people had established as the center of life, was for most people no longer at the center of their lives.

As unapparent and even far fetched as it might seem at first glance, the long and difficult battle waged since sixth century BC Greece was a battle to rid mankind of the type of religious and magical thinking in which Egypt played the major role (both real and imaginary) in propagating. However, the battle against magical religion was never a simple affair and both uneasiness, and even anxiety, about this battle and nostalgia for Egyptian "wisdom" still remain strong. This is perhaps best illustrated by the vague and desperate concept of a super-intelligence, of a non-personal god who "does not play dice with the world" of a pantheist, but *de facto* atheistic Einstein (1879–1955) — and by many 20th century Egyptologists like Henri Frankfort 1897–1954), Erik Hornung (b. 1933) and Siegfried Morenz (1914–1970) who, in one way or another, seemingly suggested that ancient Egyptian religious values were coherent and perhaps still relevant.

THE IMAGINARY EGYPTO-AFROCENTRIC LINK

In recent years, the Afrocentric movement has become one of the imaginary views of Egypt which has drawn the most attention. The acerbic Afrocentric debate began in France in the late 1950s and has continued mainly in the United States from the early 1980s. Despite some positive contributions, the American Afrocentrist movement largely denatures the Egyptian religion and distorts its authentic role in the history of religion. It is basically one more distortion in the long list of Egyptomania phenomena which contact with Egypt seems to have the innate capacity of producing.

The term Afrocentric was first used by the American writer and Africology professor Molefi Kete Asante (b. 1942) to denote a system which postulates the world and its history from an African viewpoint. The roots of Afrocentrism go back to the 19th century among some African-American thinkers and writers.

There is no doubt that the wing of Afrocentrists led by Molefi Kete Asante has been useful in denouncing the racist attitude of some historians and scholars, but there is also no doubt that its insistence on the total "African-ness" and blackness of Egypt is more based on proclamations and distortions than on proofs. Some other Afrocentrists glorify the Egyptian religion into a kind of lucid, near-monotheistic, non-zoolatric and harmonious philosophical religion; others claim that it was neither polytheism nor monotheism, but monolatry, the worship of the divine power in its thousands of names, and hint that it is still valid today — all things it was not and is not. Other Afrocentrists seem more involved with reacting to the terrible persecutions suffered by the Africans over more than a thousand years by a political attempt to create a new and comfortable myth of black identity rather than with the core of ancient Egyptian realities.

Two of the main theses of Afrocentrism are that ancient Egypt was ethnically black African and that Egypt had overwhelming across-the-board influence on Greece. These views were largely re-launched by the American historian Martin Bernal (b. 1937) *in Black Athena* in 1988.

The foremost modern proponent of Afrocentrism (even before this term was used), beginning in the late 1950s, was the Senegalese historian Cheikh Anta Diop (1923–1986). Diop, notably in *Nations Negres et Culture*, (published in 1956 and partially translated as *The African Origin of Civilization*), affirmed that ancient Egypt was black and that West Africans, Egyptians and Ethiopians (Sudanese Nubians) were of the same black racial type. For Diop, not only was "Ancient Egypt...a Negro civilization," but the attempts to "whiten" it "are nothing more than a convenient invention to deprive Blacks of the moral advantage of Egyptian civilization..." and "a falsification of history."

Diop asserted that Ethiopia (today's Sudan) and Egypt were at the origin of the quasi-totality of African religion and society. He also claimed that "The Greeks merely continued and developed, sometimes partially, what the Egyptians had invented."[179]

The central parts of these theses are very seriously flawed, but some of their affirmations in less exaggerated form are credible and certainly contribute to altering many standard views about Egypt's role in history. Despite outrageous exaggerations, both Diop and Bernal draw much needed attention to Egypt's probably important and frequently ignored contribution to Crete and the Greek world. Diop's work draws much needed attention to the black and especially Nubian components and aspects of Egypt and Egypt's religious influence in Africa. Bernal correctly points out that 18th and 19th century Europe, and especially Germany, were engaged in a vast plan to diminish the importance of Egypt and glorify the importance of Greece. All this frequently has been underestimated, but it is an incredibly sweeping evaluation to stress "the invention of antique Greece" in the 19th century, as Bernal does. Overall, Bernal's and Anta Diop's main theses do not stand up to critical examination.

The distressing aspect of Afrocentrist argumentation is its totalizing logic. It is certain that there were some black African origins in the Egyptians; it is entirely another matter to proclaim it as a black African country. It is a credible

---

179. Diop, Cheikh Anta, *The African Origin Of Civilization, Myth Or Reality*, pp. xiv, 9, 43 and 230.

option to assume some African influences on Egypt and a partially common heritage; it quite another matter to proclaim that Egypt was culturally, technologically and religiously African. It is correct to point to Egypt's close relationship with Nubia; it is another matter to downplay Egypt's constant affirmation of its separateness from Nubia and its tough colonial domination in this relationship.

It is extraordinarily misleading to postulate that black Nubian cultural influence on Egypt was central, as Diop did. It is even more extraordinary to assume, as he did, that relations between the Egyptians and the Nubians were harmonious within "the same race" and based on "original kinship" and "alliance."[180] Egyptian influence on Nubia was evidently immensely greater than vice-versa. Above all, the relationship between Egyptians and Nubians never seems to have been harmonious — and not only that, but the Nubians were almost consistently considered enemies and inferior people. At several points in their history, notably during Nubian rule of Egypt (c. 747–656 BC), the Nubians ardently desired to be Egyptian, but the Egyptians hardly ever respected this desire. It is beyond doubt that the Egyptians consistently affirmed that they were a different and superior people and race from all their neighbors, including the Nubians and the Bantus. It is beyond doubt that the Egyptians were consistently preoccupied with maintaining separateness between themselves and all others. However, it is important to note that the Egyptians did not single out the Nubians in what today we would call racism; for the Egyptians, all foreigners, Nubian, Libyan, Bantu or Asian, were "wretched" and "miserable." The ancient Egyptians were across-the-board racists!

In Diop's case, matters are aggravated by a very aggressive attitude, a seemingly faulty knowledge about Egypt and a dose of racism, even if he warns against racism. He attributed an "idealistic shell" to ancient Egypt compared to "the spirit of rapine and conquest" of "the peoples of the north." The interpretation he made of Egyptian religion and especially Osirisian concepts and "moral values" and the existence of a monotheistic "Omnipotent Being" simply do not correspond to Egyptian texts themselves. Almost all modern Egyptologists would dispute that Egyptian texts refer to Osiris and Isis as "Negroes," or that "the priestess of Amon could not be other than a Meroitic Sudanese."[181]

There is a huge misuse of art and a lapse in logical construction on the part of Diop, Bernal and others who claim that the Egyptians not only depicted their gods, but also themselves, as black in art.

It is simply incorrect to declare, as Diop did, that "the Egyptians always painted their gods black as coal."[182] It is a misunderstanding of the Egyptian

---

180. *Ibid.*, pp. 168-169 and 146.
181. *Ibid.*, pp. 230-231, 89 and 147.

color code in art to isolate one of the colors — black — sometimes used to depict Osiris and Anubis (and other gods associated with death, resurrection and the afterlife and also to signify the fertility of the black soil), from Osiris' other colors, like white flesh symbolizing mummy wrappings and green symbolizing his resurrected state. This statement also simply ignores the other colors for the gods and goddesses — blue, generally the color of the solar gods and above all, gold, the color which never faded, the color of immortality.

As discussed in Chapter 3, Egyptian art depicted Egyptians on the one hand and Nubians and other blacks on the other hand with distinctively different ethnic characteristics and depicted this abundantly and often aggressively. The Egyptians accurately, arrogantly and aggressively made national and ethnic distinctions from a very early date in their art and literature.

A comparison of Egyptian and African sculpture and painting (including both those Nubian works of art which were a part of the Egyptian stylistic school and those which were not directly influenced by it) does not indicate ethnic similitude or blackness, as Diop claimed; it indisputably indicates the contrary — a differentiation between Egyptians, Nubians and Bantu — throughout Egyptian history.

As we have seen in Chapter 3, there is an extraordinary abundance of Egyptian works of art which clearly depicted sharply contrasted reddish-brown Egyptians and black Nubians, especially in battle and prisoner scenes, and hundreds of scenes depicting several separate ethnic groups, including Nubians and Bantus. As Cyril Aldred has noted, the Nubians themselves, in their art, when they ruled Egypt between c. 747–656 BC, took into account Kushite Negroid facial characteristics — "broad round face, thick lips, horizontal eyebrows and folds of flesh at the corners of eyes and nose."[183]

Moreover, the aesthetic and conceptual thrust of Egyptian art points to an accentuation and refinement of West Asian, and especially Sumerian, art and then to a unique, independent development, rather than to a family-type relationship with African art or as an expression of "oneness" with "Black culture"[184] as Diop asserted. Even the Predynastic figurines from the Fifth and Fourth millennium BC found in Egypt clearly have more in common with the figurines of Mesopotamia and Libya and show only a vague resemblance with later African art.

The Egyptian artistic desire to idealize, while representing, illustrating and imitating, right from its take off around 3000 BC, contrasts sharply with the

---

182. *Ibid.*, p. 75.

183. Aldred, Cyril, *Egyptian Art*, p. 216.

184. Diop, Cheikh Anta, *The African Origin of Civilization, Myth or Reality*, p. 140.

extraordinarily frank, hyperbolically stylized symbolism and usually non-naturalistic *parti pris* of African art. This African tendency can be noted right from the earliest African art discovered, the Nok sculptures of Nigeria, dated from around -500 BC. Mutual influences, or Egyptian influence on African art (and especially the shared tendency to symbolically summarize human characteristics rather than depicting them according to exact physical reality), should not be misconstrued to constitute the deep substance, the deep feeling, of either art.

Egyptian and African art began from different contexts and said different things in a different way. If a single term has to be used to define Egyptian art, it is idealized representation. If a single term has to be used to define African art, it is hyperbole, it is deliberate exaggeration to achieve deep effects. Egyptian art is idealized realism. African art is expressionism. It seems astounding to confuse the easily recognizable style of Egyptian art with the equally easily recognizable style of African art.

Herodotus (c. 484–420 BC), in *Histories*, did in no way either "always specify that a Negro race was involved...whenever [he] mentioned the Egyptian people"[185] or clearly describe the Egyptians as a black people, as Diop, Bernal and Asante affirm. In fact, while Herodotus described the racial categories of several other peoples, he never directly addressed the question of the racial category of the Egyptians and whenever he addressed this question indirectly, he seems to have taken for granted that they were Mediterranean-type dark-skinned whites. He made clear ethnic and national distinctions between *Aigyptios* (Egyptians) and the peoples whom the Greeks referred to as *Aithiops* ("Ethiopians"), derived from *aithô*, "scorched," "burnt," "fiery looking," "black." The term *Aithiops* became the standard Greek designation for the black peoples whom they designated as "scorched faces." Of course, the region named Ethiopia in our late 19th century derived from *Aithiops* and the Latin *Aethiopia*, and, of course, it does not refer to Nubia which was in today's southern Egypt and part of today's Sudan.

Herodotus made a single reference to the physical similarity of the Egyptians and a dark-skinned people — the people of Colchis (in today's Georgia, where the people are Caucasoid and include some dark-skinned people). Herodotus traveled to Colchis where the Greek mythological hero Jason had gone in quest of the Golden Fleece. He said: "For it is plain to see that the Colchians are Egyptians...I myself guessed it, partly because they are dark-skinned and woolly-haired though that indeed counts for nothing, since other peoples are too."[186] (Dark-skinned is the usual translation of the original Greek *melanchroes* and is

---

185. *Ibid.*, p. 71.
186. Herodotus, *Books I-II*, 2.104.1-2.

used by A.D. Godley, while black-skinned is used by George Rawlinson. *Oulot-riches* is usually translated as wooly-haired or curly-haired.)

It can be assumed that had Herodotus wanted to designate the Colchians as blacks (and by extension, designate the Egyptians as blacks), he would have named the Colchians by the standard Greek terms *aithô* and *Aithiops*, "scorched faces," "Ethiopians." This is precisely what he did on several other occasions when he wanted to indicate that a people — whether an African or an Asian — was of the black race, or what he thought was the black race. But not only did not he name the Colchians as *Aithiops*, "Ethiopians," in the same sentence he once again distinguished between Egyptians and Ethiopians.

In Herodotus' erroneous terminology, there were *western Ethiopians* (the Nubians and other Africans, but also "the ones from Libya [who] have the wooliest hair of all men" and "Ethiopians from the east [Asia] [who] are straight-haired" (apparently the Baluchis of today's southern Pakistan and Iran). He did not, as Diop claimed, use "the same ethnic adjective"... "for Padaean Indians" and "for Egyptians and Ethiopians." The direct comparison Herodotus made was to "Indôn," who are all black-skinned (*melaina*), like the Ethiopians (*Aithiopsi*).[187] And of course, for Herodotus, Egyptians were always described as *Aigyptios*.

Herodotus' fantasies and inaccuracies are legendary, but by any standards he reached unprecedented heights of silliness, fantasy and unintentional humor in his description of the Indians. He declared that the "semen" of the Indians, "which they ejaculate into the women, is not white like other men's, but black like their skin, and resembles in this respect that of the Ethiopians."[188] Needless to say, one can be sure that Herodotus, who was so passionately interested in Egypt, and apparently in the characteristics of semen, would have informed us if the Egyptians also had black semen. This incredible tale is one more indirect proof that for Herodotus, the Egyptians were not blacks.

Concerning Herodotus' direct perception of the Nubians (the *Aithiops*) and so-called other "Ethiopians," matters are quite clear — they were blacks. Concerning his perception of the Egyptians, it is clear that he saw them as fundamentally different from the "Ethiopians" and the best bet is that he saw them as dark-skinned whites. In fact, for all ancient Greek writers, the best bet remains that they took for granted that the Egyptians were a dark-skinned Mediterranean people and the "Ethiopians" a Negroid people.

Herodotus, despite his confused and frequently contradictory descriptions of peoples' characteristics, was clearly not a believer in any kind of ethnic superi-

---

187. Herodotus, *Book VII*, 7.70.1-2, Diop, Cheikh Anta, *The African Origin of Civilization, Myth or Reality*, p. 244 and Herodotus, *Book III*, 3.101.1.

188. Herodotus, *Book III*, 3.101.1-2.

ority; there does not seem to be any anything racist in the ethnic and national distinctions he made. Herodotus declared: "The Ethiopians...are said to be the tallest and handsomest of all men."[189]

However, Herodotus' tolerant view did not become the norm in ancient Greece. The Greeks considered themselves to be "the master race"; it was their physical appearance which was supposedly ideal and they consequently showed a clear disdain for peoples darker skinned than themselves and *a fortiori* for blacks.

For ancient Greek writers, the Nubians were *Aithiops*, "Ethiopians," as were the black African peoples. This designation excluded the Egyptians. The very use of two standard terms — *Aigyptios* and *Aithiops* — and their etymological meanings already indicated an essential difference in the Greek perception. Many Greek and Roman writers professed great curiosity and solid admiration for Egyptians and contempt for "Ethiopians." There were, however, several instances in which Greek writers lumped the Egyptians together with the Ethiopians. For some Greeks, like Aristotle in the fourth century BC, the Egyptians were dark or "scorched" or black enough to be considered disparagingly. The Greeks also did not take into account black phenotypes; notably, they did not clearly distinguish between Bantu and Kushitic types, as the Egyptians themselves usually did.

The Egyptian term the "Black Land," *Kemet*, for the country of Egypt, *remet-en-Kemet* for the people of Egypt and *medet-remet-en-Kemet* for the Egyptian language did not imply ethnic origins; it did not designate Egypt as the home of a black people, as Diop, Asante and others have claimed. The best bet is that the origin of *Kemet* was agricultural, in reference to the fertile black soil of the Nile Valley in contradistinction to the "Red Land," *Deshret*, the arid desert land not flooded by the Nile. The most usual, and sacred, name for Egypt after 3000 BC was *Ta-Wy*, the Two Lands.

Nowhere did Diop or Bernal plausibly answer the obvious question in order to seriously evaluate their thesis that the ancient Egyptians were black — when did the Egyptians evolve into a non-black people? In fact, Diop even denied that the Egyptians are basically a white, or non-black, people today. He claimed that "The color of the Egyptians has become lighter down through the years, like that of West Indian Negroes, but the Egyptians have never stopped being Negroes....[yet] in most cases, the color [of modern Egyptians] does not differ from that of other Black Africans."[190]

---

189. Herodotus, *Book III*, 3.20.1.
190. Diop, Cheikh Anta, *The African Origin of Civilization, Myth or Reality*, pp. 249 and 50.

Certainly, the Egyptians absorbed a significant number of immigrants and conquerors from prehistoric times right to the Late Period conquests from 671 BC of Assyrians, Persians, Greeks and Romans and then the Arab conquest in 642 AD. Many Egyptologists postulate that, after the 2nd century BC, the marriage of poor Greek immigrants to Egyptian peasants was not rare. There are also estimates that today the Arab ethnic type represents about seven per cent of the Egyptian makeup.

Diop and Bernal claim that the Predynastic culture of Upper Egypt was incontestably African. However, as related in Chapter 3, available but uncertain, scanty, evidence tends to indicate a fusion of indigenous people, Hamitic North Africans, and especially Libyans, Asian, Eastern Mediterranean peoples and Kushitic Nubians culminating in the basic physical Mediterranean type of the Egyptians in the period after 3500 BC and tends to indicate that this type has not changed significantly right into the present. The Egyptian type therefore included a significant black contribution, but was considerably distant from the Bantus.

The bottom line is that it seems doubtful that there were ever enough so-called "white" immigrants to change the Egyptian type into the Mediterranean type that it is today, and that after 3500 BC, and certainly after 3000 BC, the ancient Egyptians were probably neither any darker nor any lighter than they are today. However, for Diop " 'Mediterranean'...is a euphemism for 'Negroid' when used by anthropologists. In any case, it means 'non-white.'"[191]

It is sometimes exceedingly difficult to untangle the true, the possible and the false in Diop's work and it is not even certain that he believed such distinctions were priorities — his principal goal of forging a positive African identity originating in Egypt seems to have taken precedence over all the rest. Diop was not just a historian, but a politician actively seeking to establish a Pan-African unity and identity within an anti-colonialist ideology, which was obviously a legitimate goal when he was writing *Nations Nègres et Culture*. The overlap between history and modern political goals concerning both the supposed blackness of the Egyptian people and the supposed Egyptian origin of Greek society and religion were manifest on many occasions in Diop's works and statements.

Overall, Bernal employs a more reasonable and less aggressive tone than Diop, but he goes out on a limb almost as much. I also get an uneasy feeling that, deep down, Bernal does not believe everything he wrote in *Black Athena*. Bernal's professed reasons for titling his book *Black Athena* smack of sensationalism, something he himself seems to obliquely admit. In recent years, Bernal also

---

191. *Ibid.*, p. 241.

seems to have considerably, but ambiguously, backtracked from the position that the Egyptians were totally black. Bernal plays on words and ambiguously leaves open whether the Egyptians, although not in their majority of the West African type, were of another black type. He seems to open the possibility that the ancient Egyptians were indeed a Mediterranean, or North East African type, and that this type was a black type.

There is also something insidious and dreadfully politically correct when Bernal summarizes his general position this way: "...the label 'Afrocentrist' has been attached to a number of intellectual positions ranging from...to those, among whom I see myself, who merely maintain that Africans and people of African descent have made many significant contributions to world progress and that for the past two centuries, these have been systematically played down by European and North American historians."[192] This view is so obviously true (and even weak, in relation to the achievements of African sculpture) that one wonders if it does not conceal still another ambiguity.

Nobody but the hypocritically politically correct would deny the importance of discussing race or, rather, ethnic origins, as one among many elements of identity. However, the chief defining element of a group is cultural rather than racial or ethnic. We have abundantly seen how, after a period of cultural similitude in an African continuum from East Africa to Libya during the Predynastic Period (mainly before 3500 BC), one of the essential points which characterized Egypt's emerging culture and religion was its distinctiveness, and then how Egypt progressively and predominantly became part of an Egyptian/ West Asian continuum. The characteristic Egypt was culturally Egyptian.

Cheikh Anta Diop and Martin Bernal, among many others, have also championed the view that Egypt was at the origin not only of Greek religion, but also of much of its knowledge, culture and societal values.

Bernal's "Revised Ancient Model" (which replaces what he calls the "Aryan Model"), in *Black Athena*, fiddles with the chronology of ancient history to make it fit his theories and he does this using speculation far more than solid evidence or even reasonable probability. Despite its two huge volumes, totaling more than 1300 pages, Bernal's view of Greek evolution, derived mainly from Egyptian sources, is distressingly thin; he seems intent on establishing some kind of grand design that does not square with plausibility. Bernal postulates a massive or at least very substantial colonization and cultural-religious domination of Crete and Greece by the mainly Semitic invaders of Egypt, the Hyksos, carrying Egyptian values, in the 18th and 17th centuries BC, possibly around 1730 BC. "My

---

192. Bernal, Martin, at www.africanhistory.com/bernal, p.1, review of Mary Lefkowitz, *Not Out of Africa: How Afrocentrism Became an Excuse to Teach Myth as History*.

belief," he says, "is that the Aryan Model should be replaced by what I call the Revised Ancient Model. This model accepts, on the one hand, that Egyptians and Phoenicians settled in and had a massive influence on ancient Greece." For Bernal, "Greek language and culture...first took shape" from Egyptian/Hyksos influence: "Thus in many ways, what is known today as 'Mycenaean Material Culture' could be usefully seen as 'Hyksos,' or at least as the 'Hyksos of the non-Cretan Aegean'."

Although Bernal admits that the ancient Greek writers sometimes "had garbled views of Egyptian history,"[193] he nevertheless cites Herodotus as accepting that there was such a massive Egyptian colonization of Greece. It is simply to misconstrue Herodotus to go as far as Bernal does in soliciting his firm support. Herodotus was obviously referring to legends and apparently doing so at least in part erroneously. Moreover, the main thrust of Herodotus' discourse was to describe Egypt and to emphasize the influence of Egyptian religion on Greek religion (as Diop acknowledged) and not the colonization of Greece by Egypt.

It is quite astonishing that somebody as obviously erudite as Bernal should fall into the trap of seemingly taking seriously almost the entire spectrum of hocus-pocus evaluations of Egypt, that is, of an imaginary Egypt, and of failing to cautiously sort out suppositions and facts. Bernal grants credibility to extravagant elucubrations, fantasies and legends in Herodotus, Hecataeus of Abdera, Diodorus Siculus and other ancient writers, as well as to the claims of an authentic Egyptian content or influence on the *Hermetica* and the Freemasons. He accepts Egyptian influences on Copernicus, Bruno and Newton as having made real scientific contributions rather than peripheral effects.

As we have also seen earlier in this chapter, very significant Egyptian influence on Greek religion and mythology is likely, but there just does not seem to be any way of plausibly proving Diop's view of near total assimilation of Egyptian values by the Greeks. Likewise, frequent Egyptian contacts with Crete and Greece are evident, but Bernal's view of Egyptian colonization, massive or otherwise, of Greece can in no way even begin to be substantiated.

Above all, Diop and Bernal do not sufficiently take into account that Egypt's influence on Greece was not only essentially religious, but that Greece's autonomous philosophical, political, artistic and scientific development — its rationalist, materialist revolution — constituted not only an implicit and radical break with the Egyptian view, but a radical break with the entirety of the world at that time.

---

193. Bernal, Martin, *Black Athena: the Afroasiatic Roots of Classical Civilization*, Volume II, pp. 1, 408 and 5.

LOONY AND IMAGINARY EGYPTIAN VIEWS RIGHT INTO OUR TIME

Imaginary and loony views of Egypt persist right into our time, and are more numerous than similar theories concerning any other society with the possible exception of Israel. In addition to being a key reference for esoteric and non-orthodox groups for centuries, Egypt has now also become, like India, the center point of a host of so-called "New Age" beliefs, "new religions," "alternative religions" and sects.

Many loony theories and some imaginary links concerning Egypt have already been mentioned, notably those concerning a connection between Egypt and the "lost continent" of a superior civilization, Atlantis, at least 10,000 years ago; a monotheism in an outer garment of polytheism; and the numerous loony and imaginary links to the Akhenaten period in the mid-14th century BC.

Other loony links and bits of nonsense concerning ancient Egypt range from immense prehistoric Egyptian secret knowledge or a concealed fundamental body of wisdom dating to Egyptian prehistoric times, to the fantasies and mysteries concerning the mathematics, meaning and the dates for the building of the pyramids and of the sphinxes and to a host of claims of origins by esoteric groups and sects, etc.

Perhaps, the so-called mysteries of the pyramids are the looniest of all the loony theories about ancient Egypt. Egyptian primitive magic, served by the great engineering and artistic skill which went into building the pyramids, has been transformed by some into esoteric truth. Not just loonies, but many intelligent people including philosophers and, of course, esoteric teachers, have not only favored the magical afterlife concepts which the pyramids represented for the Egyptians but have added their own magical interpretations which the Egyptians themselves never dreamed of. Their invention of all kinds of functions for the pyramids which were clearly not in the Egyptian mind is a perfect illustration of a key religious tactic — probably practiced from the dawn of religion: the reversal of meaning.

Pyramid mysteries and fantasies include the concept of a direct contact between the pyramids and the gods, the generation of immense powers and health from the pyramids to some humans and the concept that they were places of esoteric meditation and initiation, especially concerning the destiny of man after death. There are theories that the pyramids were built 10,000 years ago, and even 52,000 years ago — that is, before Homo Sapiens Sapiens had emerged! For some, the pyramid is also a scale model of the earth. The crazy notion that the Egyptian and Mesoamerican pyramids — which were temples with flat tops and almost always were not tombs — were both inspired by Atlanteans remains popular. There is also the seemingly imperishable theory that the pyramids still contain immense treasures which remain to be found. The most recent scientific evidence suggests that there are indeed unknown additional chambers in the pyramids, but that they are empty or are filled with sand and were perhaps designed as architectural supports for the great weights on top of them.

Pyramidology, perhaps the looniest fantasy about the pyramids, was invented by John Taylor in 1859. Using a complex system of numerology, Taylor saw the pyramids as an esotericism expressed through numbers and measurements. This was later developed into a system in which the chronology and the meaning of the universe was said to be inscribed in the external and internal measurements of the various elements of the pyramid. Variants of pyramidology continue to flourish, including some which supposedly indicate the dates of the great men of history, before, but also after, the pyramids were built.

Taylor's loony attitude was rivaled by the American "clairvoyant" Edgar Cayce (1877–1945), who in self-induced sleep supposedly answered all mankind's questions. Cayce, while asleep, proclaimed that there had been a coalition between the Atlanteans and the Egyptians, but that the pyramids had been built around 10,500 BC to commemorate Ra-Ta's (now known as Ra) voyage in a balloon from the Kingdom of Araarat (known as Mount Ararat after the deluge) to Egypt...and, of course, the pyramids were not tombs, but places of special service and understanding for initiates.

It is interesting to note that one of the most straightforward, pragmatic descriptions in modern times of the pyramids has been provided by the Director of the Giza Mapping Project, Mark Lehner, in *The Complete Pyramids*, and that Lehner fervently adhered to Cayce's theories before rejecting them as impossible.

It is clear that all of the problems related to the pyramids — engineering, construction techniques and religious — have not been solved, but it is just as clear that most of the loony theories about the pyramids are just that: loony.

Another fantasy, also still prevalent today, is that prehistoric Egypt possessed great techniques, skills and secret knowledge which had been lost or concealed from ordinary people. Available archaeological, anthropological, artistic and literary evidence indicate that this simply cannot be so, even if debate concerning the existence and the extent of an Egyptian esoteric system is justified.

Cheikh Anta Diop believed that Egypt was an advanced society from 8000 BC, that it possessed a vast system of scientific and mathematical knowledge rather than magical beliefs at that time, and that it imposed its prehistoric and historic systems on Africa, Sumer and West Asia. For Diop, Egypt was not only the first civilization, but Mesopotamia was a "belatedly born daughter of Egypt."[194] Diop brushed aside an overwhelming amount of archaeological evidence indicating the impossibility of prehistoric Egyptian influence on Sumer and the plausibility for Sumerian and West Asian influence on prehistoric and proto-dynastic Egypt. He did not even take into account that Egypt was a late starter in the crucial domain of agriculture compared to Mesopotamia, Anatolia and the Levant.

G.I. Gurdjieff (1866?–1949) was also a firm believer in the fantasy of immense achievement in "prehistoric Egypt." He even claimed to possess a so-called "map of pre-sand Egypt" which he said he used as an aid in his search for "an explanation of the Sphinx and of certain other monuments of antiquity."[195] It seems to have mattered little to Gurdjieff that the origins of the Egyptian desert go back three million years ago and that at the beginning of the Upper Pale-olithic Period (30,000 BP), the last pluvial period ended, once again progres-sively drying out the Sahara. Are we to believe that he is referring to this "pre-sand" era as a period of great Egyptian achievement? Can we even believe that the sphinx or the pyramids were built with the primitive flint tools still used in Neolithic Egypt until c. 5800 BC, when we know that copper tools must have been a minimal prerequisite to cut stone? Whatever the problems involved in the accuracy of early Egyptian dates, how can the usually accepted date for the building of the Khephren Sphinx (c. 2558–2532 BC) be thousands of years wrong? As for the "explanation" of the sphinx, Gurdjieff probably confused the mysterious Greek meaning of this statue which strangled passersby who could not solve its riddles and the probable original Egyptian term for this statue *shesep ankh*, "living image." For the Egyptians, the sphinx was a protective *ankh* life force for the pharaoh in his pyramid tomb linked to the power of the lion and the pro-tection of the sun god Re-Atum and later divinized in the New Kingdom (from c. 1550 BC) in the Horemakhet, "Horus in the Horizon," form of Horus.

Gurdjieff's interest in ancient Egypt was considerable and he was a one-man encyclopedia of all the loony theories about Egypt, plus a few more. Like most of the people who manipulated Plato's fourth century BC myth of the island/continent of Atlantis, he reversed the thrust of the original myth and laid the emphasis on the ideal nature of Atlantis rather than on the ideal nature of prehistoric Athens. Gurdjieff believed that some of the Egyptians were the "direct descendants" of the Atlanteans and the wise extra-terrestrial beings, "Akhaldans," from "the chief continent [of the Earth] Atlantis"; that their high priests had inherited esoteric knowledge from the Atlanteans, that the prehis-toric "pyramids and sphinx were the sole, chance surviving remains of those

---

194. Diop, Cheikh Anta, *The African Origin of Civilization, Myth or Reality*, p. 106.

195. Ouspensky, P.D.· *In Search of the Miraculous, Fragments of an Unknown Teaching*, pp. 302-303 and Gurdjieff, G.I., *Meetings with Remarkable Men*, Routledge & Kegan Paul, London, 1963, pp. 99 and 120.

magnificent constructions...erected by...the most great Akhaldans and by the Great Ancestors...of Egypt," that the Egyptians had indeed discovered the secret of the survival of "the planetary body" after death (which also came from Atlantis) through mummification, that at certain times the Egyptian who had amassed the most gouged out "eyes of outcasts" as sacrificial offerings would be elected town chief, etc. [196]

All this is so loony and can be so easily dismissed outright that it might be Gurdjieff, and not Immanuel Velikovsky, Ahmed Osman or the Sabbah brothers, who deserves first prize for the looniest fantasies about Egypt. The disconcerting problem is that, as usual with Gurdjieff, it is difficult to decipher what he really believed, what were metaphorical analogies and what represented some kind of convoluted and obscure system of obstacles which the disciple had to overcome, as outrageous as they might be. The problem is also compounded by the fact that there is much in Gurdjieff's work that clearly represented an attempt at human spiritual development and understanding. Nevertheless, Gurdjieff has been one of the main modern protagonists of wacky theories about Egypt.

Egyptian civilization did, and still does, function as an imaginary hinge or link, not only for the Gurdjieff group but for the Rosicrucians, the Damanhur Sect, the Church of the Eternal Source, the Golden Dawn/Wicca, the Fellowship of Isis, many of the Freemasons and many other groups which claim origins or direct links to ancient Egypt and continue to base a substantial part of their teachings on Egypto-Greek Hermetism. The Rosicrucians continue to claim that Egypt was the source of religion and philosophy. The Mormons continue to link their doctrines to a *Book of Abraham* which their founder Joseph Smith (1805-1844) probably dishonestly claimed he had translated from hieroglyphs. The doomsday Order of the Solar Temple sect seems to believe that some of its members are reincarnations of Egyptian goddesses. Some groups, like the House of Netjer/Kemet Orthodoxy Movement, claim to be a modern continuation of the Egyptian religion as a monolatry rather than polytheism or monotheism, of so-called "Kemetic orthodoxy" and its African origins. And there are even sects which practice old-fashioned hocus-pocus Egyptian *heka* magic.

On the whole, whether we are dealing with obviously loony beliefs concerning Egypt or some of the highly reasoned maverick theories about its religion, esotericism, philosophy and science and their supposed consequences, we are in fact largely dealing with an imaginary Egypt, an Egypt which has been reconstituted. However, this imaginary Egypt has become so powerful that it

---

196. Gurdjieff, G., *All And Everything*, pp. 311, 275, 301-303, 1132-1134, 590, 587-588 and 638-640.

has become some kind of a fact. The German Egyptologist Jan Assmann (b. 1938), has astutely defined this situation as "the history of Europe's remembering Egypt," "mnemohistory...concerned not with the past as such, but only with the past as it is remembered." Assmann's conclusion is simple: in such a process, "Egypt loses its historical reality." And yet, the situation is so complicated that Assmann himself displays indulgence for many maverick Renaissance views and seems to believe that Egypt solved the problem of unity and plurality in religion with a coherent "hidden unity."[197]

---

197. Assmann, Jan, *Moses The Egyptian, The Memory of Egypt in Western Monotheism*, pp. 8, 7, 9 and 206.

CHAPTER 15. THE REDISCOVERY OF EGYPT AS THE TRUNK OF THE TREE

The mix of real, possible, probable, doubtful, imaginary and loony facets of scholarly and popular understanding of Egypt might have continued for countless further centuries. The wheel turned in 1798 when Napoleon — perhaps because he wanted to block Britain's trade routes to India or perhaps because he wanted to imitate the glory of Alexander — embarked with 38,000 soldiers from Toulon, conquered Egypt and briefly occupied it until 1801 when the British defeated his army and occupied Egypt in their turn.

Napoleon did not only take soldiers with him to Egypt; he took 167 scientists, historians, scholars, artists and poets. It was these men who began to uncover the real ancient Egypt, the real *Ta-Wy*, the Two Lands. They rediscovered Egypt's patrimony from the Great Pyramids in Giza, up the Nile to the Karnak temple and up to the Isis Temple at Philae on the First Cataract. And they systematically recorded and made sketches of what they found in the 26-volume *Déscription de l'Egypte*, published between 1809 and 1822. Above all, Lieutenant Pierre Bouchard, an engineer in Napoleon's army, found the Rosetta Stone, upon which the same text was written in hieroglyphics, demotic script and in Greek, in 196 BC. Using the Rosetta Stone, Jean-François Champollion (1790–1832) was able to decipher the ancient Egyptian language, between 1822 and 1832. From then on, the profession of Egyptologist gradually came into being and Egyptologists progressively learned to understand hieroglyphic writing.

The *Déscription de l'Egypte* and Champollion's work opened new roads for a great number of Egyptologists, archaeologists and philologists. This was especially the case for the German Egyptologist Karl Richard Lepsius (1810– 1884), who between 1849 and 1858 produced the 12-volume *Denkmäler aus Ägypten und Äthiopien*, which provided the first exhaustive documentation of Egypt's most important monuments. Even the Egyptians, who had previously been indifferent to their heritage, gradually became concerned by the rediscovery of their ancient society, art, architecture and religion. With the help of the French, notably Auguste Mariette (1821–1881), the ancient Egyptian patrimony was saved from an impending disaster of widespread looting and destruction. Mariette excavated the Sakkara *Serapeum* in 1850 and founded the national Egyptian Museum in Boulaq near Cairo and the Egyptian Antiquities Service, in 1858, which supervised the excavation of temples and tombs buried under the sands and the collection of objects, considerably curbing the looting. Gaston Maspero (1846–1916) succeeded Mariette and continued his work. A great amount of what can be seen today at Egypt's archaeological sites and in the Cairo Museum is due to Mariette's devoted efforts. Although his excavation methods were very unscientific, the world owes much to Mariette, a true, unmercantile lover of ancient Egypt.

In the mid-19th century, the debate on the meaning of Egyptian history and religion, which had been going on since Marsile Ficin's (1433–1499) time, heated up and once again plunged into notions of an original monotheism in ancient Egypt and loony Egyptomania. In the late 19th century and in the 20th century, systematic studies of the huge amount of uncovered art, architecture, inscriptions and papyri by an international "army" of Egyptologists finally and gradually led to a vast re-evaluation and to the restoration of the real, or at least a realer, Egypt. Truly outstanding archaeologists and Egyptologists like Erman, Petrie, Breasted, Wilson, Schäfer, Lauer, Gardiner, Frankfort, W. Stevenson Smith, Aldred, Hornung, Faulkner, Lichtheim, Grimal and many others gave the world a new and myriad focus on ancient Egypt.

Nevertheless, even with the discarding of the imaginary and loony interpretations of ancient Egypt that these Egyptologists made possible, the same central question remained. Was Egypt the trunk of the tree...the trunk of the tree of the history of mankind?

Trying to understand history in such a linear frame of reference is a far cry from embracing all the possibilities, but the answer may be that if we are searching for the earliest period in history when most of the basic concepts, options and illusions of much of mankind, except for eastern Asia, were first experimented or prefigured, then there is only one candidate — Egypt. The extent of Egypt's achievements and its influence and links to the cultures and nations which made our world will probably never be fully known, but plausibly Egypt was, in one way or another, directly, indirectly, through rejection, or in retrospect, the trunk of the tree of religious beliefs, esotericism, hocus-pocus magic and superstitions, architecture and art, intensive agriculture, technology, economy, politics and the civil service and societal structures.

Above all, the trunk of the tree of the history of religion was Egyptian. The seed was in prehistoric Neanderthal burial and afterlife hopes. The roots were in prehistoric Aurignacian, Gravettian and Magdalenian animal-centered mythology and perhaps hunting magic and in the immense release of speculative imagination and fantasy constituted by the invention of figurative art, which may have led directly to religious systems. The sapling was in Sumerian polytheistic organization. The mature trunk which consolidated and fructified all these revolutionary inventions was in polytheistic and monotheising Egypt. The Egyptian trunk of the religious tree perhaps influenced, and certainly prefigured, the Hebrew and Persian monotheistic branches and ethical buds, the bittersweet Christian fruits of fraternity and militant evangelization and the Moslem conclusion of identity, conquest and community. Another tree eventually grew alongside, mixed its roots with the tree of religion and stultified its existence — the tree of atheism, born with the revolution of rationalism, science and philosophy, in Greece.

It may appear astounding that unlike other religions, ancient Egypt has come out of the battle of religion largely unscathed. Perhaps one of the deep reasons for this is the difficulty man has in totally abandoning magical religion. Perhaps Egypt is the only society in the history of mankind which has ever been submitted to such paradoxical treatment — on the one hand, the very core of what it stood for, magical religion, has been almost thoroughly rejected, and on the other hand, admiration for the stupefying immensity of what Egypt accomplished with magical religion still continues to grow exponentially.

There seems to be only one religious concept now in vogue that the optimistic ancient Egyptians never considered — the apocalypse, doomsday.

SELECTED BIBLIOGRAPHY

Wherever possible, the most available editions in non-revised form are listed.

PRIMARY TEXTS

Borghouts, J.F., *Ancient Egyptian Magical Texts*, E.J. Brill, Leiden, 1978.

Breasted, James, Henry, *Ancient Records of Egypt*, Five Volumes: *The First to the Seventeenth Dynasties, The Eighteenth Dynasty, The Nineteenth Dynasty, The Twentieth to the Twenty-Sixth Dynasties* and *Indices*, Histories & Mysteries of Man Ltd., London, 1988. (Re-printed by the University of Illinois, Urbana and Chicago, 2001. First published 1906, 1907).

Breasted, James, Henry, *The Edwin Smith Surgical Papyrus*, Two Volumes, University of Chicago Press, Chicago, 1930.

Budge, E.A. Wallis, *The Egyptian Book Of The Dead*, Dover Publications Inc., Mineola, New York, 1967. (First published 1895).

Faulkner, R.O., *The Ancient Egyptian Book of the Dead*, (Editor Carol Andrews), University of Texas Press, Austin, 1997.

Faulkner, R.O., *The Ancient Egyptian Pyramid Texts*, Oxford University Press, Oxford, 1998.

Faulkner, R.O., *The Ancient Egyptian Coffin Texts*, Three Volumes: *Spells 1-354, Spells 355-787, Spells 788-1185 and Index*, Aris & Philips, Warminister, 1973, 1977, 1978.

Lichtheim, Miriam, *Ancient Egyptian Literature*, Three Volumes: *The Old And Middle Kingdoms, The New Kingdom* and *The Late Period*, University of California Press, Berkeley, 1975, 1976, 1980.

Lalouette, Claire, *Textes Sacrés et Textes Profanes de l'Ancienne Egypte*, Two Volumes: *Des Pharaons et des hommes* and *Mythes, Contes et Poèsie*, Gallimard, Paris, 1987.

Moran, William L., *The Amarna Letters*, Johns Hopkins University Press, Baltimore, 1992.

Pritchard, J.B. (editor), *Ancient Near Eastern Texts relating to the Old Testament*, (Egyptian sections by John A. Wilson), Princeton University Press, Princeton, N.J., 1969.

RELIGION, MYTHOLOGY, SOCIETY

Aldred Cyril, *Akhenaten, King of Egypt*, Thames and Hudson, London, 1991.

Aldred, Cyril, *Akhenaten, Pharaoh of Egypt—a new study*, Abacus, Sphere Books, London, 1972. (First edition 1968).

Andrews, Carol, *Egyptian Mummies*, British Museum Publications, London, 1998.

Andrews, Carol, *Amulets of Ancient Egypt*, University of Texas Press, Austin, 1994.

Assmann, Jan, *Moses The Egyptian, The Memory of Egypt in Western Monotheism*, Harvard University Press, Cambridge, Mass., 1999.

Assmann, Jan, *Egyptian Solar Religion in the New Kingdom, Re, Amun and the Crisis Of Polytheism* (translated by Anthony Alcock), Kegan Paul International, London and New York, 1995.

Breasted, James Henry, *Development of Religion and Thought in Ancient Egypt*, 1972, University of Pennsylvania Press, Philadelphia (First published 1912).

Budge, E.A. Wallis, *Osiris & The Egyptian Resurrection*, Two Volumes, Dover Publications Inc., New York, 1973. (First published 1911).

Dunand, Françoise and Lichtenberg, Roger, *Mummies, A Voyage Through Eternity* (translated by Ruth Sharman), Harry N. Abrams, New York and Thames and Hudson, London, 1994.

Dunand, Françoise and Lichtenberg, Roger, *Les Momies et la Mort en Egypte*, Errance, Paris, 1988.

Erman, Adolf, *Die ägyptische Religion*, 1904 (translated as *A Handbook of Egyptian Religion* by A.S. Griffith in 1907 and in the fuller and revised 1934 *Die Religion der Ägypter* edition as *La Religion Des Egyptiens* in 1952 by Henri Wild, Payot, Paris).

Erman, Adolf, *Life In Ancient Egypt*, translated by H.M.Tirard, Dover, New York, 1971. (Original German edition 1886).

Frankfort, Henri, *Ancient Egyptian Religion, An Interpretation*, Dover Publications Inc., Mineola, New York, 2000. (First published 1948).

Freud, Sigmund, *The Standard Edition of the Complete Psychological Works of Sigmund Freud* (translated by James Strachey in collaboration with Anna Freud), Volume XXIII, *Moses And Monotheism*, The Hogarth Press and the Institute of Psycho-analysis, London, 1991. Also *Moses And Monotheism* (Katherine Jones, Editor), Random House, New York, 1987. (First Published 1939).

Hornung, Erik, *Conceptions of God in Ancient Egypt: The One and the Many* (translated by John Baines), Cornell University Press, Ithaca, N.Y., 1982. (Original German edition, 1971).

Hornung, Erik, *Idea Into Image: Essays On Ancient Egyptian Thought* (translated by Elizabeth Bredeck), Timken, New York, 1992.

Kemp, Barry J., *Ancient Egypt, Anatomy of a Civilization*, Routledge, London, 2000.

Morenz, Siegfried, *Egyptian Religion* (translated by Ann E. Keep), Cornell University Press, Ithaca, N.Y., 1992.

Plutarch, *Moralia*, Volume V (with *Isis and Osiris*), (translated by Frank Cole Babbitt), Loeb Classical Library, Harvard University Press, Cambridge, Mass., 1936. Reprinted 1999.

Redford, Donald B., *Akhenaten, The Heretic King*, Princeton University Press, Princeton, N.J., 1984.

Sauneron, Serge, *The Priests of Ancient Egypt* (translated by David Lorton), Cornell University Press, Ithaca, N.Y., 2000.

Wilson, John A., *The Burden Of Egypt, An Interpretation of Ancient Egyptian Culture*, The University of Chicago Press, Chicago and London, 1965. (Re-published as *The Culture of Egypt*.)

Wilson, John A., *Egypt* (pp. 31-122), in *The Intellectual Adventure of Ancient Man* (also by Henri and H.A Frankfort, Thorkild Jacobsen and William A. Irwin), The University of Chicago Press, Chicago, 1977.

ART AND ARCHITECTURE

Aldred, Cyril, *Egyptian Art*, Thames And Hudson Ltd., London, 1996.

Andreu, Guillemette, Rutschowscaya, Marie-Hélène and Ziegler, Christiane, *Ancient Egypt at the* Louvre (translated by Lisa Davidson), Hachette Littératures, Paris, 1997.

Edwards, Iorweth E.S., *The Pyramids of Egypt*, Penguin, Harmondsworth, U.K., 1972.

Groenewegen-Frankfort, H.A., *Arrest And Movement, Space and Time in the Representational Art of the Ancient Near East (Book One. Egyptian Art*, pages 15–141), Harvard University Press, Cambridge, Mass., 1987. (First published 1951).

Lehner, Mark, *The Complete Pyramids*, Thames and Hudson, London, 1997.

Malek, Jaromir, *Egyptian Art*, Phaidon Press, London, 1999.

Michalowski, Kazimierz, *The Art of Ancient Egypt*, Harry N. Abrams, New York, 1968, Thames and Hudson, London, 1969.

Petrie, W.M.F., *Tell el Amarna*, Methuen & Co., London, 1894.

Robbins, Gay, *The Art of Ancient Egypt*, Harvard University Press, Cambridge, Mass., British Museum Press, 1997.

Schäfer, Heinrich, *Principles of Egyptian Art* (Emma Brunner-Traut, Editor, translated and edited by John Baines), Griffith Institute, Oxford, 1986 (Original German edition, 1919).

Smith, W., Stevenson, *The Art and Architecture of Ancient Egypt*, Penguin, London, 1965. Revised edition by William Kelly Simpson, Yale University Press, 1999.

Tiradritti, Francesco, Al-Misri, Mathat, de Luca, Araldo and Mubarak, Suzanne, *Egyptian Treasures from the Egyptian Museum in Cairo*, Harry N. Abrams, New York, 1999.

Wilkinson, Richard H., *Reading Egyptian Art, A Hieroglyphic Guide To Ancient Egyptian Painting And Sculpture*, Thames and Hudson, London, 1994.

Wilkinson, Richard H., *The Complete Temples of Ancient Egypt*, Thames and Hudson, London, 2000.

HISTORY

Aldred, Cyril, *The Egyptians*, Thames and Hudson, London, 1984.

Bernal, Martin, *Black Athena. The Afroasiatic Roots of Classical Civilization*, Volume I, *The Fabrication of Ancient Greece, 1785—1985*, Volume II, *The Archaeological and Documentary Evidence*, Rutgers University Press, New Brunswick, N.J., U.S.A., 1988 and 1991.

Diodorus, Siculus, *The Antiquities of Egypt*: a translation of *Book I* of the *Library of History* by Edwin Murphy, Transaction Publishers, New Brunswick, N.J., U.S.A., 1990.

Diop, Cheikh Anta, *The African Origin Of Civilization, Myth Or Reality* (edited and translated by Mercer Cook), Lawrence Hill Books, Chicago, 1974.

Breasted, James Henry, *A History Of Egypt, From The Earliest Times To The Persian Conquest*, Bantam Classic Edition, New York 1964. (Also: Simon Publications, 2001,Two Volumes). (First edition, 1905).

Gardiner, Alan, *Egypt of the Pharaohs*, Oxford University Press, Oxford, 1961.

Grimal, Nicholas, *A History of Ancient Egypt* (translated by Ian Shaw), Blackwell Publishers Ltd, Oxford, 1994.

Herodotus, *The Persian Wars, Books I-II* (translated by A.D. Godley), Loeb Classical Library, Harvard University Press, Cambridge, Mass., 1986.

Josephus, Flavius, *The Works of Josephus*, William Whiston, translator, (including *The Antiquities of the Jews* and *Against Apion*), Hendrickson Publishers, Peabody, Mass., U.S.A., 1988.

Redford, Donald B., *Egypt, Canaan and Israel in Ancient Times*, Princeton University Press, Princeton, N.J., 1992.

Shaw, Ian (Editor), *The Oxford History of Ancient Egypt*, Oxford University Press, 2000.

Strabo, *The Geography of Strabo, Vol. 8, Book 17* (translated by Horace Leonard Jones), Loeb Classical Library, Harvard University Press, Cambridge, U.S.A. and London, 1932, revised 1935. Reprinted 1967.

DICTIONARIES, ENCYCLOPEDIAS, GRAMMARS AND HISTORICAL ATLASES

Baines, John and Malek, Jaromir, *Atlas of Ancient Egypt*, LDF, Cairo, 1995 and Graham Speake (ed.), New York, Andromeda, Oxford, 1980. Revised and reprinted as the *Cultural Atlas of Ancient Egypt*, Checkmark Books, New York, 2000.

Bunson, Margaret, *A Dictionary of Ancient Egypt*, Oxford University Press, Oxford, 1995.

Davies, W.V., *Egyptian Hieroglyphs*, British Museum Publications, London, 1987.

Gardiner, Alan, *Egyptian Grammar*, 3rd ed., Oxford University Press, Oxford, 1982.

Hagen, Rose Marie and Rainer, *Egypt, People, Gods, Pharaohs* (translated by Penelope Hesleden), Bennedikt Taschen Verlag, Koln, Germany.

Hornung, Erik, *La Grande Histoire de l'Egyptologie*, (traduit par Michelle Lecoeur), Editions du Rocher, Paris, 1998) (Revised German edition, *Einführung in die Ägyptologie*, 1993).

Manley, Bill, *The Penguin Historical Atlas of Ancient Egypt*, Penguin, London, New York, 1996.

Posener, Georges, with the assistance of Sauneron, Serge and Yoyotte, Jean, *Dictionary of Egyptian Civilization*, Tudor Publishing Co., New York, Methuen, London, 1962.

Quirke, S. and Spencer, J., *The British Museum Book of Ancient Egypt*, Thames And Hudson, London, 1992.

Rice, Michael, *Who's Who in Ancient Egypt*, Routledge, London, 2001.

Shaw, Ian and Nicholson, Paul, *The Dictionary Of Ancient Egypt*, London, British Museum Press, New York, Harry N. Abrams, Inc., 1995.

Vernus, Pascal and Yoyotte, Jean, *Dictionnaire des Pharaons*, Editions Noêsis, Paris, 1996.

SELECTED INTERNET SITES

TRANSLATIONS OF EGYPTIAN TEXTS

www.fordham.edu/halsall//ancient/asbook04.html

www-01.uchicago.edu/01/DEPT/RA/ABZU_REGINDX_EGYPT_PHILOL.HTML

www.enteract.com

www.geocities.com/Athens/Pantheon/5061/submenu.html

TRANSLATIONS OF WRITINGS IN GREEK RELATED TO EGYPT

www.perseus.tufts.edu/

ART, ARCHITECTURE AND ARCHAEOLOGY ONLINE

www.britishmuseum.ac.uk/egyptian/ea/gallery.html

www.metmuseum.org/collections/department.asp?dep=10

www.members.tripod.com/-ib205/VK.html

www.tourism.egnet/AttractionsDetail.asp?code=6 and egnet.net/culture/images/

www.louvre.fr/louvrea.htm

www-01.uchicago.edu/01/01/MUS/HIGH/01_MUSEUM_EGYPT.html

www.brooklynart.org/collection/ancient.html

www.eawc.evansville.edu/pictures/egpages.htm

www.smb.spk-berlin.de/amp/s.html

www.2rom.on.ca/egypt/case

www.ancientneareast.net/egypt.htm

www.friesian.com/tombs.htm

www.kv5.com/html/index_new.htm/

www.pbs.org/wgbh/nova/pyramid/

DATABASES, SEARCHES, GENERAL, HISTORY, RELIGION, SOCIETY

www.thebritishmuseum.ac.uk/compass/
www.ashmol.ox.ac.uk/Griffith.html
http://argos.evansville.edu
www.oi.uchicago.edu/0I/defaut.html
www.newton.cam.ac.uk/egypt/index.html
www.cur-archamps.fr/2terres
www.guardians.net/egypt/htm
www.ancientegypt.co.uk/menu.html
www.aelives.com/ae/htm
www.touregypt.net/Antiq.htm
www.touregypt.net/ehistory.htm
www.members.aol.com/egyptart/battle.html
www.si.umich.edu/CHICO/mummy/kings.html
www.egyptologyonline.com
www.crystalinks.com/egyptgods2.htm/

BIBLIOGRAPHIES

www.us.edu/dept/LAS/religion/rel394/KMTbibliog.htm
www.cofc.edu/-piccione/hist370biblio.html
www.thebritishmuseum.ac.uk/egyptian/ea/further/reading.html
www.brown.edu/Departments/Egyptology/biblio.html
http://guardians.net/egypt/bazaar/books/index.html
www.servtech.com/-greenman/pageMythEgyptian.html

Glossary/Index

A

Abu Simbel (an awe-inspiring temple), 81, 85, 220, 239, 243

Abydos (Abdu) (Predynastic and Early Dynastic religious and political center), 8, 14–15, 17–19, 22, 46, 69–70, 118, 195, 200, 208, 220, 243, 281, 298, 302, 304

Administration (first centralized state), 153, 163, 201–202, 232

Admonitions of Ipuwer (pessimism, a spiritual crisis, in the First Intermediate Period — or a plea for order?), 55–56, 58, 204, 290

Afrocentrism (a seriously flawed theory about a black Egypt), 97, 315–323

Ahmose (the pharaoh who drove out the hated Hyksos), 80, 119, 207–208, 274

Aigyptos (Greek name for Egypt), 242, 255

Akhenaten (invented first monotheism; unusual physical appearance: genetic malformation or portrayed according to a divinity-establishing code?), 20, 31, 67, 74, 81, 84, 86, 91, 97, 99–101, 105–106, 109, 112–113, 115, 117, 119–156, 158–173, 178, 188–192, 200, 205–208, 211–212, 215, 220, 243, 305, 325

Aldred, Cyril (Egyptologist who composed a neutral compilation of known facts and questions about Akhenaten), 31–32, 124, 132, 134, 137, 232–233, 318, 332

Alexandria (Raqote) (non-participation of most Egyptians in its life; role in rise of early Christianity; elaborates and anticipates modern Western outlook), 184, 187, 239, 242, 244, 247, 249–250, 274, 277–278, 280, 282, 287, 304

Amarna Letters (valuable for understanding situation of Egypt's colonies in West Asia), 69, 97, 117, 119–122, 126–132, 134–135, 142–153, 155, 163, 165–167, 169, 173, 200–201, 205, 213

Amenemhat I (first pharaoh to take an Amun chief god name), 78, 118

Amenhotep III (the unequalled splendor of his court; Akhenaten's father), 83, 118–120, 125–126, 130, 135, 141, 144, 150–151, 155, 164, 168, 172, 180, 196, 209, 212–213, 220

Amulets (meket, key role in life and afterlife), 113, 125, 128, 141, 176, 227, 230, 243, 270, 271, 293

Am-mut (most feared composite monster, supposedly eats evil dead), 38, 138

Amun-Re (apotheosis of syncretic chief god theology), 67–70, 78–87, 100–101, 105, 113, 115, 117, 119, 121–122, 124–129, 139–140, 143, 150–151, 154–158, 162, 172, 178, 192, 199, 215, 218–219, 223–224, 229, 243, 260, 272, 311

Animals

    first Egyptian gods and goddesses, See gods, 32, 74, 228, 231, 243

    widespread sacrifice and hunting of, 45, 145, 152, 228, 231, 272, 333

Printed in the United States
15515LVS00001B/116